*PRACTICAL GUIDE
TO STRUCTURED SYSTEM
DEVELOPMENT
AND MAINTENANCE*

Selected titles from the YOURDON PRESS COMPUTING SERIES
Ed Yourdon, *Advisor*

PRACTICAL GUIDE
TO STRUCTURED SYSTEM
DEVELOPMENT
AND MAINTENANCE

Roger Fournier

YOURDON PRESS
Prentice Hall Building
Englewood Cliffs, New Jersey   07632

11-13-91

Library of Congress Cataloging-in-Publication Data

FOURNIER, ROGER
   Practical guide to structured system development and maintenance
  Roger Fournier,
     p. cm.
   Includes bibliographical references and index.
   ISBN 0-13-679671-0: $39.75
    1. Software engineering. 2. Electronic data processing—
Structured techniques. I. Title.
QA76.758.F68 1991
006.1—dc20

90-20816
CIP

Editorial/production supervision
  and interior design: *Kathryn Gollin Marshak*
Cover design: *Ben Santora*
Manufacturing buyers: *Kelly Behr and Susan Brunke*

 © 1991 by Prentice-Hall, Inc.
A Division of Simon & Schuster
Englewood Cliffs, New Jersey 07632

The publisher offers discounts on this book when ordered
in bulk quantities. For more information, write:
     Special Sales; Prentice-Hall, Inc.
     College Technical and Reference Division
     Englewood Cliffs, NJ 07632

Printed in the United States of America

10 9 8 7 6 5 4 3 2 1

ISBN 0-13-679671-0

Prentice-Hall International (UK) Limited, *London*
Prentice-Hall of Australia Pty. Limited, *Sydney*
Prentice-Hall Canada Inc., *Toronto*
Prentice-Hall Hispanoamericana, S.A., *Mexico*
Prentice-Hall of India Private Limited, *New Delhi*
Prentice-Hall of Japan, Inc., *Tokyo*
Simon & Schuster Asia Pte. Ltd., *Singapore*
Editora Prentice-Hall do Brasil, Ltda., *Rio de Janeiro*

TO: Darlene, Karen, Alex, Rose-Aimée, and Noëlla

Contents

I present the first part of this preface in an unusual question-and-answer format; the second part provides synopses of each chapter. I sincerely hope that both sections will give you enough information to decide whether or not this book is for you.

QUESTIONS AND ANSWERS

- Does this book address the entire system development life cycle approach?

Yes. This book describes the set of technical activities that must be conducted to develop progressively and ultimately maintain a large software system. However, rather than concentrating on the "how to," it primarily focuses on the "what to do." Furthermore, most of the project management activities traditionally associated with a software engineering methodology are excluded from the book in order to keep it at a reasonable size.

- We already have a prescribed methodology for systems development. Why should I buy this book?

Does the methodology currently used in your software shop integrate logical data modeling with logical process modeling? Does it cover prototyping, the acquisition of commercial software packages, the use of powerful CASE tools, the JAD-like techniques, the software cost-of-quality concepts, the development center concept, the software maintenance life cycle, and so forth? If not, you should consider this book for its value-added information. Even though you do not plan to revolutionize your shop by throwing away your existing methodology and replacing it with the one prescribed here, you might still want to use this book as an excellent source of ideas. After all, if you get one good suggestion out of it, then it will be worth the expense.

- Do I need to know the structured development techniques to understand this book?

It is preferable but not essential. It is true that this book assumes the reader already knows the basic tenets of structured analysis and design. However, excellent references are provided that address in detail the "how to." In addition, many of the technical tasks described in the text are not related specifically to the structured development techniques. They universally apply to all methodologies.

- The book seems to be packed with many activities. Do I need to do all of them to develop a system successfully?

Yes and no. Very large projects will probably require that you proceed through each development phase with discipline and rigor. As the size of the project decreases, some development phases might be combined and some activities might even prove to be unnecessary. There are several types of systems, all with different needs. Not adapting the methodology to the type of system being developed is probably the best way to fail.

- Who is the intended audience?

Anyone who is interested in developing a quality system: DP managers, strategic system planners, consultants, project leaders, programmers, designers, analysts, user representatives, and on and on.

- Can end users employ this book (or part of it) to develop their own software applications?

Yes, for a medium-sized to large system. However, there are already some very good books that specifically address quite well the development of small to medium-sized microcomputer-based software systems.[1]

- In a nutshell, what can this book be used for?

This book can be used for myriad purposes, including

- A textbook for acquainting students or practitioners with the basic concepts of software engineering development and maintenance

---

[1]One example is *Business Applications with Microcomputers: A Guide Book for Building Your Own System,* written by J. M. Follman (Prentice Hall, 1989).

- A simple cookbook for system development and maintenance practitioners
- A baseline for developing software engineering standards in an MIS organization
- A system development and maintenance reference manual
- An idea book
- A handbook for developing detailed project estimates and work breakdown structures of the technical tasks required for developing a large software system
- A solid foundation for introducing CASE technology in your environment

ORGANIZATION OF THIS BOOK

The book has three broad sections. The first section includes Chaps. 1 through 7. Except for the introductory chapter, each carefully describes in a stepwise manner the specific technical tasks that are necessary for gradually engineering a quality software system and maintaining it in operation. The second section comprises Chaps. 8 through 14. Each provides an overview of some important concepts, methods, or automated tools that reinforce and support the software engineering life cycle described in the first section. The third section contains appendixes with additional information describing in more detail methods or various checklists that can be used to select commercial packages, CASE tools, and so forth.

Following is a brief overview of each chapter and appendix.

Part I Methodology (Chaps. 1–7)

Chapter 1: Introduction.   This chapter examines the special format that is used in Chaps. 2 to 7 for presenting the individual software engineering tasks prescribed by the methodology, along with their input and output deliverables. Additional items also covered in this chapter include the fundamental concept of modeling a system, the need for conducting formal and informal reviews, the use of automated tools, and some basic considerations on how to tailor the proposed software engineering methodology to suit the needs of a specific project.

Chapter 2: Survey Phase.   This chapter describes the technical tasks that specifically address the consolidation of the initial user requirements for a new system and the definition of the project business objectives, priorities, constraints, scope, alternative implementation solutions, and preliminary cost-benefit analysis. Special emphasis is given on gaining adequate support from all the users of the new software system throughout the entire duration of the project. The feasibility of prototyping for the project is also examined.

Chapter 3: Preliminary Analysis Phase.   This chapter describes the technical tasks that should be conducted to analyze the current system and to eventually derive all the high-level functional and operational requirements for the new software system. Furthermore, some optional tasks for covering the selection of an application package versus the traditional in-house development are also presented. It should be pointed out that at this stage of the development process, careful attention has been given not to include detailed technical tasks that normally should be performed only once a final system implementation solution has been retained by the development team and the users.

Chapter 4: Detailed Analysis Phase.   In this chapter the functional properties of the system are carefully exploded at their lowest level of detail and the conceptual data model that was developed during the previous phase is normalized up to the third, fourth, or fifth normal form. Prototyping is used to help users refine their system input/output requirements. The system data conversion, testing, and training strategies are equally defined during this phase, in conjunction with the users. Lastly, the detailed hardware, software, and networking specifications for the new software application are derived from the general system requirements that were identified during the previous phase.

Chapter 5: Design Phase.   In this chapter the various automated components of the system are finally designed into sets of program, file, and database structures according to suggested structured design techniques. Sound test cases are also developed at different levels.

Chapter 6: Implementation Phase.   The coding, testing, and other related system implementation activities are described in this chapter. The system is finally delivered to the users in its real-life production environment.

Chapter 7: Maintenance Phase.   This chapter covers the technical activities that are required to maintain the structured system properly once in production. The software engineering process prescribed in this book emphasizes the importance of performing the maintenance tasks in a systematic manner to retard the degradation of the software applications and ensure their maintainability over time.

Part II Supporting Techniques (Chaps. 8–14)

Chapter 8: Structured Testing.   This chapter presents the generic structured testing strategies and techniques that can be used by system developers to assess the quality and level of operability of the system. The information provided in this chapter is fully supportive of the various testing tasks that are described across the different system development phases prescribed in this methodology.

Chapter 9: Structured Walkthrough.   This chapter describes the set of procedures that should be followed when using a formal review technique called structured walkthrough. It also discusses the impacts this structured approach can have on a software project and provides a set of suggested form samples.

Chapter 10: Prototyping.   This chapter examines the various prototyping techniques that can be advantageously used to complement the traditional structured development life cycle. It discusses the various stages during which prototyping should be considered in the system development process. It also presents the advantages and disadvantages of prototyping as a complementary method of system development. Finally, the generic categories of prototyping tools available to the practitioner are covered.

Chapter 11: Development Center.   In this chapter, the development center function is thoroughly examined, demonstrating how this concept can be used for improving the productivity of the MIS organization while enhancing the quality of the software engineering process itself. Various suggestions are made on how to establish a development center function successfully in an MIS organization.

Chapter 12: CASE Technology.   The advent of powerful CASE tools holds tremendous productivity gains for the MIS organization. This chapter specifically covers the various types of CASE toolsets and integrated workbenches that are available in the marketplace. It also discusses some of the fallacies that too often surround the CASE technology. Finally, a practical approach is suggested for a smooth introduction of CASE technology into the MIS organization.

Chapter 13: Software Quality.   The purpose of this chapter is twofold. The first section explores the concept of software quality and discusses what might constitute the desirable quality attributes of a software system. The second section introduces the cost-of-quality concept and suggests a generic program aimed at improving the quality of the software development and maintenance life cycle.

Chapter 14: Installing a Methodology.   This chapter suggests some guidelines on how to install some specific components of the methodology, or the entire methodology itself, within an organization. It also discusses how to address the critical success factors and potential pitfalls while performing this delicate operation.

Part III Appendix (Appendixes A– C)

Appendix A: Package Evaluation Checklist.   This appendix provides, in a question/answer format, a comprehensive list of selection criteria that can be used when acquiring commercial application packages.

Appendix B: Questionnaire for Selecting CASE Tools.   This appendix presents a list of questions and answers that can be used to assist an organization in formulating a comprehensive set of selection criteria for the acquisition of CASE tools.

Appendix C: JAD-Like Techniques.   This appendix describes a group dynamics method that can be used to accelerate some of the development stages of the software engineering process by having the users and a few representatives of the MIS organization actively participate in defining the requirements for a new system.

Acknowledgments

I would like to acknowledge the contributions of several individuals who offered support during the creation of this book.

- Thanks to the team of reviewers assembled by Prentice Hall. They provided several valuable comments and suggestions for improving the content of sections of this book.

- Thanks to Ed Yourdon, who initially provided insightful comments and ideas and who also believed in the author's ability to produce this book.

- Thanks to the cast of professionals at Prentice Hall who directly or indirectly contributed to the production of this book, especially Paul Becker (acquisitions editor), Noreen Regina (editorial assistant), Kathryn Gollin Marshak (production editor), Mary Louise Byrd (copy editor), Nancy Krueger of Precision Graphics (illustrator), and Laura Dalbey (proofreader).

- Thanks to all the people with whom I have had the privilege to work through my many years in data processing. Thanks especially to my former mentor and friend at Bell Canada, David W. Goldsmith, who patiently supported the author during the long process of writing this book. Dave also provided, on a personal basis, much needed feedback on various sections of the manuscript.

- Lastly, very special thanks to my wife, Darlene, who graciously agreed to type the entire manuscript and whose dedicated support encouraged me to complete this book.

Roger Fournier

*PRACTICAL GUIDE
TO STRUCTURED SYSTEM
DEVELOPMENT
AND MAINTENANCE*

PART I
Methodology

1

Introduction

1.1 THE NEED FOR A ROBUST SOFTWARE ENGINEERING METHODOLOGY

The primary motivation behind this book has been the numerous software practitioners and managers around the world who strongly believe that a disciplined but yet flexible approach to software engineering can only lead to the delivery of quality software systems. To this end, the software engineering methodology advocated in these pages integrates the traditional structured development techniques (i.e., structured analysis, design, coding, and testing) with the various software engineering concepts that have emerged during the last decade, such as data modeling, commercial application packages, prototyping, JAD-like development techniques, and the like.

Rather than concentrating on the detailed "how to," this comprehensive tutorial on software engineering addresses the "what to do." It recognizes the fact that a methodology should reflect an organization's environment and corporate culture and should be augmented by the diversified experiences and various technical backgrounds of the personnel in place. Consequently, this technical guide to software engineering advocates that software practitioners make their own choices and recommends customization of software engineering to meet the specific needs of an organization.

The prescribed methodology reflects a strong focus on technical deliverables. It is no exaggeration to say that a concise description of the technical deliverables is just as important as the detailed description of the tasks that are executed for producing them. Hence, no development phase should be considered complete until all its resulting technical deliverables have been properly documented and officially reviewed for accuracy and completeness. Ideally, the documentation of a software application should be done as the system is gradually developed, and not when it has been put into production.

The proposed methodology has been organized into six phases—survey, preliminary analysis, detailed analysis, design, implementation, and maintenance—to maximize the overall productivity of the people working on a large software project. First, the functional requirements of the system are defined at a high level, along with the more implicit software quality and operational requirements, such as maintainability, response time, and reliability. Then all the requirements are progressively refined in a step-by-step manner throughout the system development cycle, with increasing details being added in each particular phase. Such a top-down approach minimizes the risks of divergence from the original user's requirements and possibly of costly retrofits of the deliverables at later stages of the development cycle.

By its own nature, such an approach might, in particular instances, entail some redundancy throughout the various phases of the development life cycle. However, this controlled redundancy strengthens the essential concepts of the methodology and reduces the need for the development team constantly to refer back to previous sections of this book.

1.2 PRESENTATION FORMAT OF THE TECHNICAL TASKS

All the technical tasks covering the system development and maintenance life cycle discussed in this book share a common presentation format, as shown in Fig. 1.1. Each technical task is characterized by

1. A unique task identification number that has the following structure: XX-YY, where XX is a two-letter acronym that identifies the specific development phase during which the task is conducted and YY is a one- or two-digit number uniquely assigned to each distinct task.[1] Table 1.1 lists each two-letter acronym that corresponds to a specific system life cycle phase. For example, the identification number SU-3 indicates that this task is performed during the survey phase and is uniquely identified within that phase by the number 3.

2. A descriptive name of the task.

3. A brief statement describing the objectives of the task.

4. A list identifying the technical deliverables that are required as input data to execute the task.

[1]The technical deliverables are also uniquely identified with the same organization schema.

Task number:	
Task name:	
Objective:	
Input(s):	
Output(s):	
Task description:	

Figure 1.1   Description of a technical task

5. A list identifying the technical deliverables that are produced as a result of performing the task.

6. A brief description of the detailed steps involved in performing the task itself.

At the end of each task, some practical tips and guidelines are given to help software developers to perform successfully the detailed steps of each task. In several instances, some potential pitfalls or alternative ways of performing the task are also cited.

At the beginning of Chaps. 2 to 7, a basic task network diagram illustrates the relationships among the phase tasks. To enhance the clarity of the data flow diagrams, the input deliverables that are necessary to perform each individual task and the output deliverables produced by the task are not shown.

TABLE 1.1   AN ACRONYM FOR EACH SYSTEM LIFE CYCLE PHASE

Mnemonic	Life Cycle Phase
SU	Survey
PA	Preliminary analysis
DA	Detailed analysis
DE	Design
IM	Implementation
MT	Maintenance

Finally, it is important to point out that the execution of the technical tasks is done in a progressive and iterative fashion. Even though the tasks seem to be set out in a natural sequence, they are not necessarily performed in sequence, but more likely done in parallel.

1.3 MODELING A SYSTEM

The construction of a model of a relatively large or highly complex system is a sound approach in an attempt to manage its size and complexity. It is useful to break the system down into its major components, from the most general to the most detailed level. The resulting architectural blueprint identifies the desirable functional characteristics that the system should possess to meet the user's needs. The model then becomes a very useful tool not only to visualize the proposed system but also to validate and confirm the developer's understanding of the user's requirements. This is a relatively inexpensive process, if we consider that the modeling is done long before the new system is actually constructed. The principle behind software modeling is based on a simple observation: It is far easier, and cheaper, to modify the functions of a system when they are still being modeled on a drawing board (or prototyped) than when the real system itself is in production.

When the system model is created, up to three major perspectives can be captured, as shown in Fig. 1.2. One perspective describes the functions of the system and the major interactions that exist among them. This model is *process oriented* because the emphasis is primarily on modeling the functions of the system. Thus, using the data flow diagram technique, the process model depicts the data flows, data stores, external entities, and processes of the application system. Another perspective describes the system data and their relationships. Using entity-relationship diagrams, it captures the inherent properties of data and the underlying business policies that characterize the relationships among the data entities. This model is *data oriented* because the emphasis is primarily on modeling the structure of the data itself. The third perspective is the *real-time* model. It deals with the modeling of complex real-time system activities such as the synchronization of various system processes that operate in multiple modes or states, showing how the system reacts and responds to various stimuli from the external environment.

Note that even though each of these three models emphasizes a specific dimension of the same system, they also complement one another very well. They have in reality strong interdependencies, and they should be developed in a way that ensures consistency among them. Figure 1.3 shows how the major process-oriented model components are developed in parallel with the major data-oriented model components throughout the various stages of the system development life cycle.

Although the real-time components of a system are not shown in Fig. 1.3, they are embedded in the process-oriented model. To use an analogy, the process and data models are like the two parallel tracks of a railway. One model helps to under-

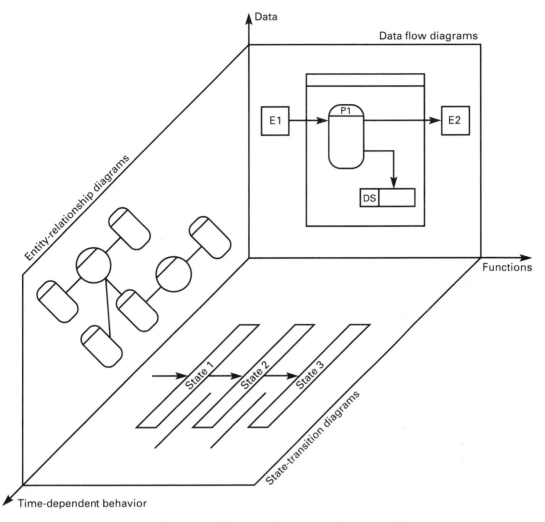

Figure 1.2 The three dimensions of system modeling

stand and validate the other. On the one hand, the functions of the system are analyzed along with the data that are required to perform them. However, the emphasis is not on the data structures themselves but rather on the system functions. On the other hand, the emphasis with data modeling is mostly on identifying the data entities that are manipulated by the system and the relationships that exist among them. This effort cannot be done without addressing a portion of the functional aspects of the system, since data on their own have very little intrinsic value. In reality, the business policies that are associated with the data entities often dictate the types of relationships that exist among them.

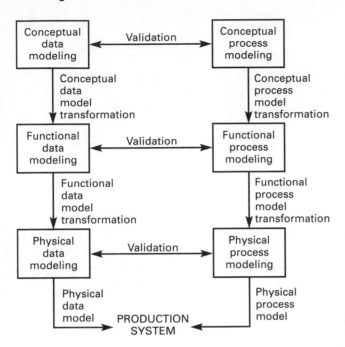

Figure 1.3 Data- and process-oriented models

1.4 MODELING SYSTEM PROCESSES

The diagram in Fig. 1.4 illustrates the different process-oriented models that are progressively developed throughout the various phases (survey, preliminary, and detailed analysis) of the system development life cycle.

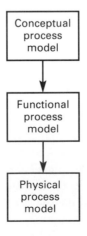

Figure 1.4 The three process-oriented models

The *conceptual process model* is a logical representation of the functions that must be performed by the system, as well as the data flowing between the functions. This model represents the essence of the system, from a functional perspective. The *functional process model* is derived from the conceptual process model. However, the functional process model not only shows the natural interrelationships among the functions of the system but also takes into consideration some physical characteristics of the system. Such characteristics include the administrative and geographic structures of the user organization and the automated solutions that were retained by the development team to implement the system. The *physical process model* is, in turn, derived from the functional process model. It is mainly composed of modules that will be coded into a set of physical instructions ultimately to be executed by a computer. The structure of this model not only depends on the automation choices that were retained during the construction of the functional process model but is also heavily constrained by the performance limitations imposed by the hardware/software/networking technology used to implement the system.

At this point, more detailed description of the different components of the conceptual and functional process models is in order. But before we do this, it is worth noting once again that both models are pictorially developed with the use of the data flow diagram technique.[2]

The conceptual process model is composed of four different types of data flow diagrams, as shown in Fig. 1.5. The first type of data flow diagram that is constructed during the analysis cycle is called the *system context diagram*. It situates

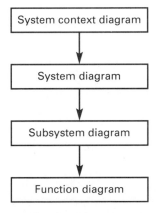

Figure 1.5   Conceptual process model

---

[2]This book uses the Gane and Sarson data flow diagram notation [Gane and Sarson, 1979]. Another popular notation is the Yourdon/DeMarco diagramming notation [DeMarco, 1977]. A major distinction between these symbologies centers around the process symbol. Gane and Sarson use a "bubtangle" (i.e., a rectangle with rounded corners), whereas Yourdon and DeMarco use a circle to illustrate a process.

the system within its proper organizational context. Basically, the interactions that exist between the system and the external entities that communicate with it are depicted in this diagram. The second type of data flow diagram, the *system diagram,* depicts the subordinate subsystems that make up the system and the flow of information that is exchanged.

The *subsystem diagram* is the third type of data flow diagram. There is one subsystem diagram for each subsystem process in the upper-level system diagram. Each subsystem data flow diagram depicts the functions of a particular subsystem, as well as the relationships among them. The fourth type is called the *function diagram.* There is one function diagram per function process identified in a subsystem diagram. The function diagram depicts the set of work unit processes that compose a function.

Regardless of their content, these four data flow diagrams are gradually built during the survey and preliminary analysis phases. Figure 1.6 shows the timing sequence in which the creation of these diagrams is performed.

One last type of data flow diagram developed during the analysis cycle is the *work unit diagram.* This diagram is created during the detailed analysis phase and constitutes a component of the functional process model. There is one work unit diagram per work unit process shown in a function diagram. The work unit diagram depicts all the elementary operations that are performed within a work unit process.

The operation is, in turn, defined as being the smallest entity resulting from the partitioning of the system into its lower-level data flow diagram components. The operation component cannot be further decomposed into other subunits. The description of the logic performed by the operation is done with structured specification methods, such as structured English, decision tables, decision trees, or state-transition diagrams for real-time systems.

Figure 1.7 illustrates the hierarchical properties of the process-oriented components of a software system, regardless of when they are created.

Although the conceptual and functional process models display five levels of detail when they are combined, it is important to realize that this number is somewhat arbitrary. For a typical business system, it is likely that the development team

Conceptual Process Component	Time Dimension
System context diagram	Created during the Survey phase
System diagram	Created during the Preliminary Analysis phase
Subsystem diagrams	Created during the Preliminary Analysis phase
Function diagrams	Created during the Preliminary Analysis phase Finalized during the Detailed Analysis phase

Figure 1.6   Creation of the conceptual process model components versus the time dimension

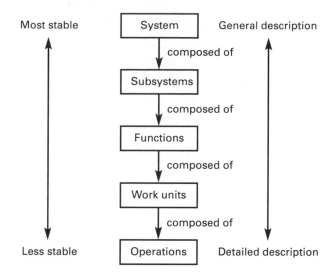

Figure 1.7 The hierarchical structure of the process-oriented system components

will not need more than five levels of partitioning for breaking the system down into its most elementary constituent parts. However, there might be some particular situations where less than five levels of partitioning will be sufficient. For instance, for a relatively simple system, it is quite possible that there will be no need to partition the system into several subsystems. Instead, the system may be broken down into a set of functions. After all, why partition a system into subsystems if it has only two major functions? On the other hand, if the development team is building a large software system similar to the Star War system, they will probably need far more than five levels of top-down partitioning. We might be talking, at the upper level of the partitioning scale, about a "super system" that would comprise nothing less than a set of systems—and who knows, perhaps we would still need a "mega-super system" too. Furthermore, at the lower end of the partitioning scale, we might need to break down the operations into more detailed suboperations.

Even though every system will not fit neatly into a process model of five levels of data flow diagrams, it is quite probable that such a model will meet the requirements of most of today's business systems. If not, the model can be customized to cope with the complexities of larger systems. Above all, what is important is not to assume by default that all systems must invariably be modeled with a fixed number of top-down functional decomposition levels.

1.5 FORMAL AND INFORMAL REVIEWS

The software engineering methodology proposed in this book strongly advocates the consistent utilization of both formal and informal reviews throughout the entire software engineering process. The development of a technical deliverable should always be terminated with a formal review of its contents, using a special review technique called structured walkthrough.[3] On the other hand, the methodology also encourages conducting informal reviews among the members of the development team and with the users or with other software engineering support groups, wherever necessary. The time spent in formal and informal reviews is a very good long-term investment into software quality, if it is done in a proper manner.

1.6 AUTOMATED TOOLS

The use of various automated tools throughout the development and maintenance life cycle phases is strongly recommended. Computer-assisted software engineering (CASE) tools, assuming they are properly integrated in the methodology, will enhance the quality of the technical deliverables.[4] Moreover, as the organization gradually gains more and more experience with these tools, significant productivity gains will result from this sustained effort.

1.7 TAILORING THE METHODOLOGY TO UNIQUE PROJECT NEEDS

There is no one single methodology that can adequately satisfy all the types of projects that can be conducted in an organization. Hence, the methodology proposed in this book may need to be tailored to accommodate the distinct needs of a particular organization. Unfortunately, there is also no secret recipe for successfully customizing a methodology to meet the needs of a specific project.[5] The members of the development team should always use their own experience and technical knowledge for this purpose. Still, two major factors should be carefully examined by the development team when adapting the methodology to the specific needs of their project: the size and complexity of the proposed system.

In the case of a small and relatively simple software project, two or more development phases can be combined to more adequately fit the project's needs and eliminate unnecessary overhead. In particular instances, some of the technical tasks that are prescribed for a specific development phase can simply be omitted or reorganized in a different sequence, whether within the boundaries of that phase or across several phases of the system life cycle. To this end, it is fair to admit that all the technical tasks prescribed here do not always bear the same weight for each

---

[3]For more information on the structured walkthrough, refer to Chap. 9.

[4]For more information on the CASE technology in general, refer to Chap. 12.

[5]Nevertheless, the next generation of experts systems will, it is hoped, assist the inexperienced or even experienced software practitioners who must perform this delicate operation. An automated (and intelligent) methodology driver will successfully guide practitioners through the proper selection and organization of the specific software engineering tasks that are necessary for satisfying the unique requirements of a software project. For instance, the project team would consult the methodology driver for properly customizing the methodology, taking into account several factors such as the potential use of prototyping, the size of the project, the possible selection of application packages, the type of hardware platform that would be used to run the system in production, and the existence of real-time functions embedded in the system.

project. However, it is imperative to point out that tailoring the methodology might not only imply eliminating or modifying the technical development tasks proposed in this book. It might also entail the addition of new tasks that become necessary to satisfy the needs of the project at hand. For a large and fairly complex project, it might be imperative to proceed through all the proposed development phases, conducting the technical tasks one at a time in an orderly sequence and with all the rigor that such a large project requires.

Lastly, the development team might be faced with several constraints, such as limited time and limited staff resources to develop the system or severe budgetary restrictions. In such situations, it is strongly recommended to downsize the number of functions to be embedded in the new system rather than attempt to cut corners in the development methodology.

1.8 REFERENCES

COLLETTI, RENÉ, ARNOLD ROCHFELD, and HUBERT TARDIEU. 1984. *La Méthode Merise: Principes et Outils.* Paris: Les Editions d'organisation.

DeMARCO, T. 1977. *Structured Analysis.* New York: Yourdon Press.

GANE, C. and T. SARSON. 1979. *Structured System Analysis Tools and Techniques.* New York: Improved System Technologies.

2

Survey Phase

2.1 PURPOSE

The primary objective of the survey phase is to decide whether or not a project should be initiated to develop and implement a software system requested by the users. Even at this early stage, the results of this initial study will determine if there are sufficient anticipated benefits to justify continuing the project into the next development phase.

A detailed view of the survey phase requirements would address the following:

- The current problems to be eliminated from the user environment and the exploitation of current and future business opportunities
- The definition of the system mission and the translation of user business needs into a clear set of project business objectives
- The setting of delimiters for the area of study for the project
- The identification of possible project constraints and risks
- The initial search for potential system implementation solutions
- The elaboration of a preliminary cost-benefit analysis

Remember, though, that small projects could easily get by with only a few pages to document the system mission and to project business objectives, constraints, and risks.

Table 2.1 summarizes the major technical tasks that are normally conducted during the survey phase and the anticipated technical deliverables. Figure 2.1 illustrates at a high level the relationships that exist among the individual tasks of the survey phase.

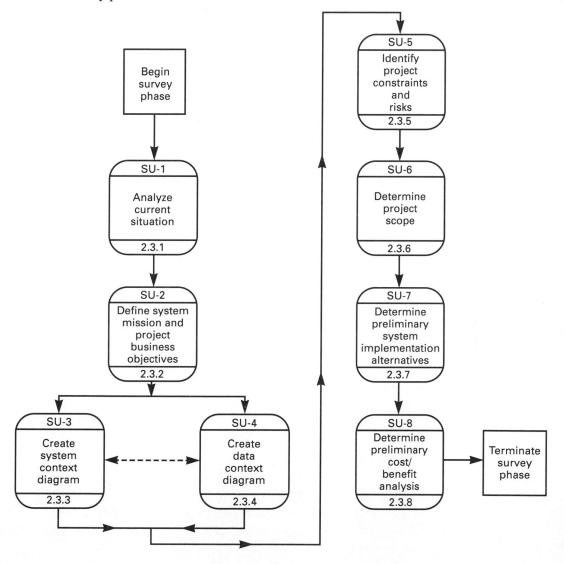

Figure 2.1   Survey phase task network

TABLE 2.1 SURVEY PHASE TECHNICAL TASKS AND DELIVERABLES

Technical Tasks	*Technical Deliverables*
1. Analyze current situation	1. Current problems/opportunities/user's needs
2. Define system mission and project business objectives	2. System mission & project business objectives
3. Create system context diagram	3. System context diagram
4. Create data context diagram	4. Data context diagram
5. Identify project constraints and risks	5. Project constraints & risks
6. Determine project scope	6. Project boundary
7. Determine preliminary system implementation alternatives	7. Preliminary system implementation alternatives
8. Develop preliminary cost/benefit analysis	8. Preliminary cost-benefit analysis

2.2 SURVEY PHASE INITIATION

During recent years, the system development prioritization process has gradually evolved and matured for many companies. In the past, many standalone systems were developed by the MIS (management information system) organization. Today, strong emphasis is placed on the smooth integration of new systems into the existing business environment. For this reason, the selection process to determine which systems will be developed has become more stringent. The findings of the survey phase play an important role in determining whether or not a project will proceed to the next development phase.

Depending on the level of maturity the organization has achieved in planning its systems requirements, the survey phase can be initiated in two different ways:

1. *Starting with a strategic system plan.* This plan outlines the portfolio of corporate systems that must be developed to support the business goals of the enterprise. The plan is based on a corporatewide business strategy, and the information systems are implemented according to a predetermined sequence over a given period of time.[1]

2. *Upon receipt of a request for service from an authorized user representative.* Typically, the business problems and opportunities are identified at the operational level. This situation leads users to issue a request to the MIS organization to develop a system. However, this system may or may not be in line with the strategic system plan.

In the first context, justification for the project should be easily accomplished, as the implementation of the system has already been planned at a corporate level. Thus, it will likely support the strategic long-range plan of the organization. Furthermore, the total effort required to conduct the survey phase tasks should normally take far less time than with a traditional survey phase. This is primarily due to the fact that the high-level technical deliverables that were developed during the strategic planning effort can be used to finalize quickly some of the survey phase technical deliverables, such as the system and data context diagrams, the system mission, and so forth.

In the second context, the project proposal must be elaborated with enough detail to indicate clearly that the proposed system does in fact support the overall strategic business objectives of the organization. Additionally, members of the development team must carefully examine the potential impact the system can have on its direct users and also on the organization at large. Although this is true for all systems, it is especially important for large projects, as the investment for developing a large and complex system is proportionally far greater than for a smaller system.

---

[1]For a detailed coverage of the strategic system planning topic, see the references at the end of this chapter.

2.3 DESCRIPTION OF THE TECHNICAL TASKS

2.3.1 Analyze Current Situation

Task number:	SU-1
Task name:	Analyze current situation
Objective:	To identify users' business needs
Input(s):	Request for service
Output(s):	SU-1 Current problems/opportunities/users' needs

Task description:

- Scrutinize the users' initial request for application development. Ensure that the information provided in the request is complete and accurate. If not, contact the originator of the request to clarify the ambiguities.
- Based on a brief investigation of the service request for a system, identify all the business departments and related systems that will likely be affected by the proposed project request.
- For each prospective user department involved, identify the names of the user representatives to contact during the project. Confirm their participation and get an agreement on their anticipated roles, responsibilities, and availability.
- Conduct various interviews and meetings with the individuals who represent each affected user department.
- Describe the problems that are currently being experienced.
- Describe the new opportunities that are triggering the need for a new system.
- Document all the information gathered during the interviews and meetings with the users.
- Verify the facts gathered and confirm your findings with the interviewees and their respective managers.
- If some problems or opportunities appear in conflict with one another, document the related issues and submit them to the user's management for guidance and resolution.
- Assign a priority to each problem/opportunity that was identified during the preliminary fact gathering processes.
- Review the list of stated problems/opportunities and summarize the current situation. Derive a consolidated statement that highlights all user needs.[2]
- Walk through the identified problems/opportunities/users' needs to ensure they truly reflect the current situation and that all affected business groups have been approached.

[2]If some of the users' needs are basic information retrieval requirements that can be easily satisfied by extracting data from existing files/databases, and if there is an information center function in place in the organization, initiate a request to the information center group. Notify the request's originator accordingly.

The primary objective of this activity (SU-1, Analyze current situation) is to meet with the prime user groups who will likely be affected by the proposed project and derive the business justification for the new system. Obviously, the users would not request a new system if the current environment were considered adequate in the first place. Therefore, it is important, even during the preliminary information gathering sessions, to document all the user views that can lead to possible system improvement alternatives, the current system deficiencies, and business opportunities that are not yet fully exploited.

It is sometimes possible, even at this early stage, to deny the request for service if valid requirements that would substantiate the need for developing a new system are nonexistent. Sometimes there might also be situations where the business problems at hand cannot be resolved by the implementation of a computerized system. Typically, they are the results of organizational deficiencies in the environment that can be resolved more adequately simply by restructuring the operations of the business department(s) involved.

Problem definition is not always a straightforward process. Invariably, it necessitates a thorough understanding of the current situation, which should carefully be examined in its proper context. Figure 2.2 presents some of the fact gathering techniques that the analyst can use to comprehend the current situation. The following discussion is not intended to be exhaustive in terms of describing these techniques. Rather, the aim here is to highlight some important points the analyst should consider when using these techniques.

Interviews.   Depending on the number of affected departments, user needs can be found through a series of interviews. The first step in the interviewing process consists of identifying the most relevant users, who should then be interviewed by the analyst. One simple way of doing this is to obtain from the users an organizational chart of all the business units that will likely participate in the project. It is imperative that such charts are accurate and up to date. The key individuals who

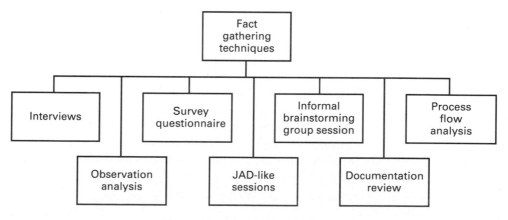

Figure 2.2   Fact gathering techniques

should be interviewed in each particular user area are then identified, usually by following the established line of authority, starting from the head of the department downward.

The analyst should obtain the assistance of the department managers to identify the various people who should be interviewed and how to obtain their cooperation. The interviews can then be scheduled in advance. It is sometimes hard to know, right at the beginning, who exactly will provide the most critical and valuable information about the current situation. For this reason, the analyst might, during the fact gathering process, add new persons to the list of candidate interviewees as their potential contributions to the project become more apparent.

Before meeting with a user representative, the analyst should carefully prepare the interview. Although it is not the intention of this book to discuss in any detail specific interviewing techniques, the basic guidelines provided here should prove useful. For more details on interviewing, consult Yourdon [1989].

Before.
- Schedule the interview ahead of time. Avoid just dropping in without an appointment. Unplanned interviews can turn out to be quite disruptive for the users.
- Identify the current position and responsibilities of the interviewees before the meeting.
- Set up the interview at a time that is convenient for the user. Wherever possible, choose a quiet area which eliminates potential disruptions.
- Gather as much pertinent information as you can on the functions that are performed in the interviewee's area, including the appropriate form and report samples.
- Since the major objective of the interview is to gather information, and since the interviewee values his or her time, it might be appropriate to prepare an outline of the interview and give an advance copy to the interviewee.

During.
- Present yourself, inform the interviewee of the purpose of the interview, and explain the objectives you hope to achieve with this interview.
- If you take notes, explain what you are doing and why you are doing so. Various tools other than the traditional pencil and paper outfit can be used to record the discussion, such as a tape recorder or a video camera. However, the analyst should keep in mind that these devices can make the user reluctant or unwilling to discuss openly issues he or she feels are politically oriented.
- As a rule of thumb, do not take more than two hours for conducting the interview. If necessary, schedule several interviews with the same person to cover completely the related subject of interest.
- If you plan to do so, ask for permission to talk to the interviewee's staff later on.

- Explain that all the information gathered during the interview will be submitted for his or her approval before being officially published.
- Toward the end of the interview, summarize the major points that were discussed to confirm your understanding of what has been said.
- Terminate the interview on a positive note, thanking the interviewee for her or his contribution.

While conducting interviews, the analyst should be careful about three particular situations:

1. The user usually concentrates on the symptoms of the problems rather than on the real causes of the problems.
2. The user expresses his or her needs in terms of predetermined computer solutions without understanding the real nature of the problems. In many instances, the user may not be familiar with the facilities that a computerized system can or cannot provide to ease the current situation. Therefore, the user can make false assumptions on computerized solutions, such as thinking that an automated system will magically solve all problems, no matter what they are.
3. During the course of an interview, the analyst suddenly realizes that there might be some disparities between the official version of how the existing system manual and automated procedures should operate and what really happens at the operational level. If this is the case, the analyst should use tact and diplomacy when reporting these discrepancies to management. Personnel at the operational level may be reluctant to admit that the operations do not always conform to the working patterns officially endorsed by management.

When these situations are encountered, the analyst should acknowledge these inconsistencies while still trying to discover the real causes of the problems. For this reason, the analyst should be highly skilled in the techniques of interviewing. Different users will have different viewpoints that will likely influence their own perceptions of the current situation.

After.
- Document all relevant points that were gathered during the interview.
- Send the documentation to the interviewee for final approval.
- If further clarification is needed, contact the interviewee to set up another meeting.
- Issue the results to the users and their managers.

Survey Questionnaire.   The survey questionnaire is frequently used to gather information. This particular fact gathering tool is very convenient when a large number of users must be canvassed, as is often the case in large organizations, where several user groups can be in several locations throughout the country. In these situations it would be impractical for an analyst to interview all the people in all the sites. Later on, once all the information gathered with the questionnaire is analyzed, specific follow-up interviews can be conducted with selected users, whose potential contributions become more apparent.

The use of a survey questionnaire has some drawbacks. One serious disadvantage is that communication with users is seriously restricted; there is no real face-to-face exchange of information. For this reason, the decision to use a survey questionnaire should be carefully weighed against its shortcomings. Typically, the preparation of a well-written questionnaire requires a considerable amount of time. Further, the questions must be structured in a way that will be meaningful to the people who will fill them out. Ideally, they must be formulated without anticipating the way the users will respond.

Several formats can be used to construct the questionnaire; multiple-choice, checklist, and fill-in-the-blank questions are some examples. In any case, the questionnaire should be developed in a manner that minimizes the time it will take to fill it out. It might be advantageous to allow the respondent to make a choice by checking off or circling the answer. This will also facilitate the compilation of the results from a large number of questionnaires.

The following discussion outlines the steps to follow when using survey questionnaires.

Prepare the Questionnaire.

- Identify the type of information you want to gather, such as problems experienced or opportunities to exploit.
- Once your requirements are defined, choose an appropriate format for the questionnaire. Construct the questions in a simple, clear, and concise manner.
- If you include questions that require a narrative answer, make sure you provide sufficient space for the reply.
- The questions addressing a specific topic should be grouped together under a special heading.
- Ideally, the questionnaire should be accompanied by a covering letter written by a senior executive to emphasize the importance of this survey to the organization.

Identify Respondents.

- The questionnaire can be customized by adding the name, job title, and address of each respondent.
- A log, which identifies all the people who will receive the questionnaire, must be developed. It will be used to monitor the status of the questionnaires that have been distributed.

Distribute the Questionnaire.

- Distribute the questionnaire, along with detailed instructions on how to fill it out. Clearly indicate a time limit for returning the questionnaire.

Analyze Respondents' Answers.
- Analyze and consolidate the information provided in the returned questionnaires.
- Document the major findings.
- Send a copy of the major findings to each respondent as a courtesy for having taken the time to participate in the survey.

Document review.   Document review is one of the most popular ways to gather information about the current situation. Internal procedures manuals, existing system documentation, forms and documents used to perform departmental business tasks, reports produced by the current system—all are important sources of information that describe the user environment. (It is worth mentioning that document review can be performed before, during, and after other fact gathering techniques.)

The multiplicity of documents flowing through the environment often justifies the need to start building an inventory of what currently exists in terms of forms, reports, and other, similar documents. This list will become a useful reference point for planning and organizing interviews and observations. Furthermore, it will become very handy during the next phase, when more detailed information on the existing environment will be required. The process of gathering information on the existing system is discussed in more detail in Chap. 3.

Observation analysis.   Observation analysis is a very effective fact gathering technique. It can be used for several purposes, such as processing and confirming the results of an interview, identifying the documents that should be collected for further analysis, clarifying what is being done in the current environment and how it is done, and similar tasks. The technique is relatively simple. For a given period of time, the analyst observes users on-site as they perform their daily activities. Although the analyst can observe without directly intervening in the process, most of the time he or she will interact with the persons being observed. The analyst frequently will ask questions in order to understand how an operation is done. To the limit possible, the analyst should perform a user's activities in order to gain a better understanding of how users operate in their own environment.

Observation analysis presupposes that proper management approval has been secured with the users in the first place. It is also very important to explain to the people who will be observed what you will do and why. This precautionary measure will help to prevent situations where those under observation feel like if they are under police surveillance. The steps following identify the major activities that should be performed before, during, and after an observation study.

Before.
- Identify the user areas to be observed.
- Obtain the proper management approval to carry out the observations.

- Obtain the names and titles of the key people who will be involved in the observation study.
- Explain the purpose of the study.
  During.
- Familiarize yourself with the workplace being observed.
- Note the current organizational groupings.
- Observe the current manual and automated facilities in use.
- Collect samples of the documents and written procedures that are used for each specific process being observed.
- Amass statistical information of job duties: frequency of occurrence, volume estimates, time duration for each person being observed, and the like.
- While interacting with the users, always try to remain objective and do not comment on their mode of operation in a nonconstructive way.
- Observe not only the normal business operations but also the exceptions.
- Once the observations are completed, thank the people for their support.
  After.
- Document the findings resulting from the observations made.
- Consolidate the results.
- Review the consolidated results with the observees and/or their managers.

In particular instances, observation analysis has some drawbacks. For one, the overall process can be quite time consuming. In other cases, analysts might also be mislead in their observations. Nonetheless, this technique is widely accepted by many people in the data processing field and can often be used to complement the findings obtained with the use of other techniques.

Process flow analysis.   Sometimes, user problems have nothing to do with the software system in place. More often than not, these non-system-related problems can be directly connected to the way the business processes themselves are performed in the user's environment. Typically, the symptoms leading to workflow problems of this nature are associated with complaints about unnecessary interactions, time lost by inability to proceed, too many errors occurring in the workplace, and quite often, an impression that a lot of work is duplicated among various departments for no apparent reason. Ordinarily, this happens when the user's work is partitioned into many processes that are performed by so many business departments that nobody can figure out the complete view of the situation. Process flow analysis can be used to analyze the current situation in such a context.

Process flow analysis is a problem identification technique that has its roots in industrial engineering. It has been successfully used for several decades in various engineering disciplines to study the general flow of processes that cross several business, shop floor or engineering departments in the organization.

The technique uses a simple graphical language that depicts the flow of processes that are performed by different departments on a wall flowchart. Before we describe the symbols that can be used to construct a process flowchart, let's define first the terms process and analysis in the context of the process flow analysis technique. A *process* is a series of operations that are conducted in a department and produce some outputs. *Analysis* means studying a process to divide it into simpler elements and see if they can be enhanced.

Figure 2.3 illustrates the nine basic symbols that are needed to draw a process flowchart. The following is a description of each symbol.

Operation:	A large circle represents a particular operation that is manually performed within a specific process. As a result of this operation, something is created or modified. Examples: Fill out a request for purchase, reproduce a document, prepare a report.
Movement:	An arrow is used to represent the physical movement of an item. Examples: Walk to a filing cabinet, walk to a storage area, deliver a report to a user.
Delay:	An octagon is used to identify a temporary delay in the work process. Examples: Wait for an authorization, wait for a reply, delay the publication of a report until month-end.
File:	A triangle is used to represent the act of storing a document. Examples: Dispose of a document, file or classify a document, record information on microfiche.
Verification:	A square is used when an appraisal task is performed. It represents the task of verifying something. Examples:

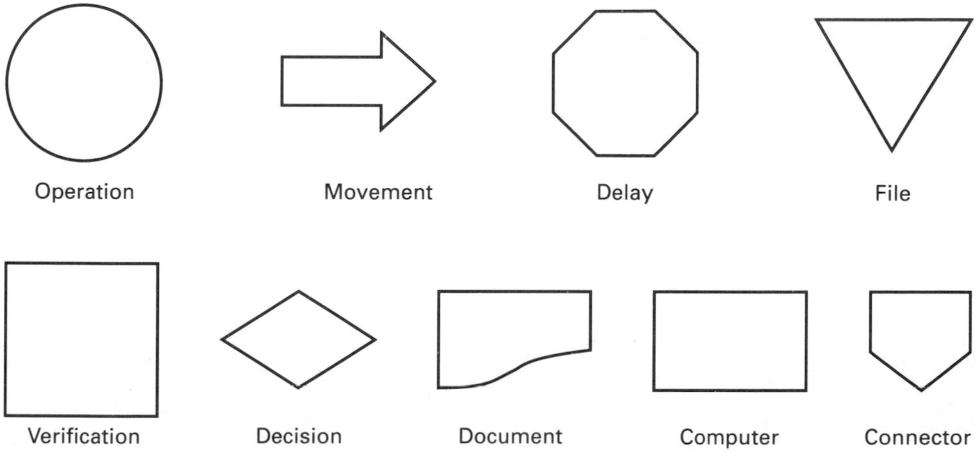

Operation	Movement	Delay	File

Verification	Decision	Document	Computer	Connector

Figure 2.3   Process flow analysis symbols

Verify for completeness, authorize document, verify for conformance to requirements.

Decision: A diamond-shaped form means a decision must be taken. Subsequently, the process workflow is divided in at least two paths. Examples: Reach a yes/no conclusion, reach a conditional settlement.

Document: A document symbol denotes an output that is produced when executing an operation or an input. Examples: A sales report, a customer invoice.

Computer: A rectangle represents a software system or an automated process. Examples: Program computes sales history, program validates a customer credit line.

Connector: A page connector is used to join different components of the process workflow. The page connector is used whenever the addition of workflows would clutter the diagram.

Figure 2.4 illustrates, schematically, a typical process flowchart once it is completed.

The various user departments involved in the process workflow are identified on the left-hand side of the diagram and are separated by horizontal lines. Quite often, the people who participate in the study use a special process flow analysis toolkit that includes all the materials required to easily create a giant diagram on a wall. The participants can then visualize all at once the complete picture. Once

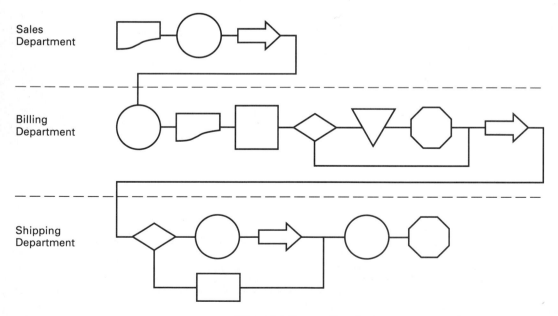

Figure 2.4 Process flowchart

completed, the process flowchart is carefully examined by the participants. Each particular operation is scrutinized to determine if it is really required in the overall process, and if yes, how it can be improved. The flow of operations and documents is traced throughout the different departments that are involved in the work process. In this technique, the sequence of operations performed by the users across several organizational units can sometimes be simplified and improved. Delays or bottlenecks can be eliminated or reduced by resequencing some operations. In some instances, the results of a process flow analysis study can clearly indicate some disparities between the official organizational structure and the actual structure that indeed might exist at a lower operational level.

This technique has always sounded very attractive to users because it is relatively simple to use and quite easy to understand. However, it is very important to select the right people to attend a process flow analysis workshop. The study team should be composed of at least one representative from each department who has its "share" of the process being analyzed. He or she should always be the one who is the most knowledgeable about the process being described.

Informal brainstorming group session.   A particular approach that is often useful to gather information quickly on the current situation is dynamic group sessions. The identification of several problems or opportunities can be performed via the use of the brainstorming technique. The most knowledgeable user representatives, who are involved in the project, simply attend a group discussion lead by a mediator. This person can be nominated by the users themselves, if necessary. During the session all the work-related problems and opportunities that might exist in the environment are identified and reviewed by the group participants.

The principle behind the brainstorming concept is not new; several heads are better than one. Furthermore, one person's identification of a problem might trigger further suggestions from the other attendees. Some user representatives may have difficulty formulating their problems in a way that naturally leads to an analytical statement of the current situation. When this is the case, the brainstorming technique can turn out to be very useful because the other user participants and the mediator can provide assistance to those having difficulty in formulating a concise and logical statement of the problem or opportunity at hand. In other words, the collective knowledge and experience of the team participants is used to identify the problems and possibly generate creative solutions to resolve them permanently.[3]

---

[3]Brainstorming is based on a fundamental principle: The human brain carries on its thinking activities in two basic modes of operation, analytical and logical. The right side of the brain operates using the mechanisms that are typically associated with creativity, intuition, inventiveness, and sensitivity. The left side of the brain has a tendency to operate in an analytical mode. When we think with the left side of the brain, we examine things in a logical, intellectual, deductive, and systematic manner. It was realized through various experiments, that when most human beings think, they normally use either side of their brain, but not both at the same time. If someone wants to be creative, he or she should try to put to sleep the left side of the brain. If a person wants to be analytical, he or she must use the left side of the brain and turn off the right side. If the person does not make a conscious effort to control one side of the brain versus the other, the creative and analytical sides will then struggle with each other.

We now discuss the basic steps in the conduct of a brainstorming session.

Select Participants.   The participants should be carefully selected. They should be invited because of the direct contributions they can provide during the session. The presence of knowledgeable people from different groups will ensure a good representation. If the group turns out to be a mixture of high-ranking and lower-ranking personnel, everyone must understand that during the session they all operate at the same level.

Explain the Technique and the Rules to Follow.   The session leader explains the basic concepts behind brainstorming and the rules that must be followed during the session. It goes without saying that the session leader should be an impartial individual.

Produce a Quantity of Ideas.   The first step is simple. The participants generate as many ideas as they can on the topic being brainstormed—the identification of problems in the work environment, the causes of a problem, new opportunities that are waiting to be exploited, different suggestions to solve a problem, and so forth. Ideally, only one topic should be selected for a brainstorming session.

The participants are invited, one at a time, to come up with a single idea. If someone has trouble, he or she simply passes and waits for the next round. Thus, everyone is invited to contribute, one at a time and in a clockwise manner.

The group session leader controls the session to ensure everyone's participation and that the rules are followed. Participation is very important, but above all, the most critical rule to keep in mind is to forbid any form of criticism whatsoever. People must put aside their analytical skills. The ideas submitted should not be evaluated at all at this early stage. Consequently, the overall process must be fast-paced to increase the number of proposed ideas. This will ensure that people do not "switch" their mind to the analytical mode of thinking. It is like a windmill that turns rapidly to generate as many ideas as possible, as quickly as possible.

Write Down the Ideas.   The ideas are recorded by the session leader on a chalkboard as soon as they are mentioned. They should be visible to the entire audience. In several instances, an idea already suggested by a participant will likely encourage the other participants to come up with several variations centered around the same theme. In a brainstorming session, such an approach is perfectly admissable. Once again, no judgment is made about the propositions. There are no good or bad ideas; there are only ideas that are candidly submitted by the participants. The first part of the brainstorming session should be pleasant and people uninhibited. They should let their imagination flow.

Analyze the Ideas.   Before analyzing the ideas, the group should pause for a few minutes. Ideally, they should wait for another meeting to discuss the merits of the suggested ideas. Once the analysis review has started, the people "activate" the analytical side of their brain. The ideas are reviewed one at a time, and those considered valuable by the group are retained for further analysis.

JAD-like sessions.   In some instances, group brainstorming techniques have been refined to evolve into very structured approaches where the mediator is a highly skilled and well-trained professional. The session leader is often backed up by several other people who are entirely devoted to support the overall process. The most popular of these techniques, originally developed by IBM, is called the joint application design process (JAD). Other, similar techniques have been developed around the initial JAD concepts. All of them have something in common: They all make use of dynamic group discussions involving users and systems people.

The use of JAD-like techniques can often result in a faster definition of user requirements, when compared to the more traditional fact gathering techniques (such as serial interviewing). The same technique can also be customized to gather information that focuses on the data requirements of the application.[4]

Prioritizing the problems/opportunities.   Some of the specific problems that might be experienced or opportunities that might trigger the need for a new computer system include

- A new or revised corporate policy
- Contractual obligations
- Government regulations
- Major technology breakthrough
- Increased company revenues
- Enhancements to existing services
- The support of new services or business functions
- Reduction of operating costs
- Competitive market edge
- New interfaces
- Existing system deficiencies, such as
  - Obsolete technology
  - Excessive maintenance costs
  - Throughput limitations
  - Information reliability/integrity/accuracy problems

The problems and/or opportunities described by the users should be prioritized by order of importance. This ranking is necessary to differentiate between those issues that are very important and those that, although nice to address, are not essential to the project at hand. One possible way of categorizing them would be as follows:

- *Essential:* Requirements without which the user could not properly operate in the business environment.

[4]For more information on the JAD-like techniques, see Appendix C.

- *Adaptable:* Requirements that, if need be, can be partly modified to allow alternative modes of operation.
- *Nice to have:* Requirements that the user is willing to document but that can be excluded from the system list of requirements, if they prove to be too costly to satisfy.

Furthermore, the problems and opportunities should be traceable back to the departments that originally identified them.

Although this should not be seen as a rigid rule, the first three to five most important problems/opportunities should be documented in detail and the other stated problems and/or opportunities can be documented with less detail, at least at this early stage. As a rule of thumb, 80 percent of the total development effort should be directed toward solving the 20 percent that represent the most important needs expressed by the users. Practical experience has proven that the remaining development effort (i.e., 20 percent) should be spent on solving the remaining requirements that are not considered essential.

In sum, there can be a wide range and variety of problems/opportunities that exist in the current user environment. Not only is it important to rank them by order of importance, but it might also be useful to consider them in terms of the following categories:

1. Problems/opportunities for which the involved business departments have full control over, as well as full authority to solve them permanently.
2. Problems/opportunities for which the involved business units have no direct control. Despite this restriction, though, they can still exercise some influence on the decision-making process that could lead to a permanent solution of the current problems.
3. Problems/opportunities for which the involved business departments have no direct control over whatsoever. Furthermore, they have no influence at all on solutions that would permanently solve the problems.

Documentation.   All the documentation resulting from the project fact gathering tasks should be written using the user's terminology. All business terms should be clearly comprehensible, and the use of acronyms should be avoided wherever possible. A glossary of terms can be included at the end of the survey phase document, if necessary. Furthermore, all the intermediary documents that have led to a consolidated statement of user needs should be made available on request.

User participation.   It is mandatory to obtain active participation from the users during this phase. This is, without the shadow of a doubt, a very critical success factor. For instance, the business needs and objectives of the project cannot be properly developed without the users' firm commitment to assist in the initial process of defining them. This is the only way to ensure that the requested system will be precisely aligned with the business goals of their departments and of the entire enterprise. Hence, users must actively participate and articulate their own needs. In fact, this statement remains true for all the deliverables that are produced during the survey phase, from the initial definition of user needs up to the preparation of the preliminary cost-benefit analysis. This emphasis on user involvement should be seen as conducive to the success of the project. The system that will be developed will be as effective in supporting the users' functional areas as the users will be in participating in the development of the system's requirements, especially during the crucial stages of the analysis process. Graph A in Fig. 2.5 illustrates user involvement in a traditional project. Graph B shows the desired level of user participation required to ensure the successful development of a computer system. Furthermore, with the advent of user-oriented development techniques such as prototyping and JAD, more and more systems will be developed successfully by a team of users and analysts who work closely together during the entire project.

In sum, the most successful projects are often those which are placed under the formal responsibility of the users. Although the system might be developed by

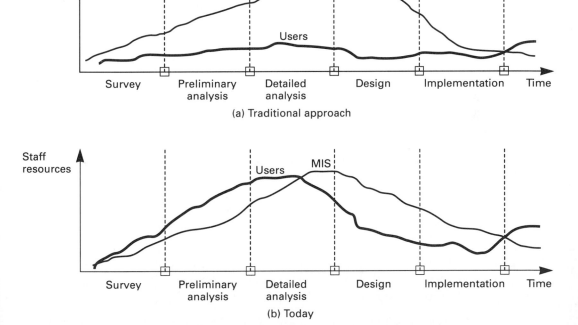

Figure 2.5   User participation in system development

software professionals, the ultimate responsibility of the project lies in the hands of knowledgeable and capable user representatives who are officially held accountable for the new system.

User training.   It is important to familiarize the users who will directly participate in the project with the requirement definition techniques that will be used. This will help bridge the communication gap that might exist between the users and the developers. There are courses designed specifically to help remove the cloud of mystery surrounding the development of a software system. In general, these courses describe the system development process in simple terms that are easy to understand from a user point of view. During these seminars, the specialized (and often esoteric) software concepts and vocabulary used by software developers are also explained, along with a brief description of the various graphical tools and techniques that are applied during the data and process modeling tasks. When we consider the amount of money that will be poured into the development of a large software system, not to mention the fact that such a system will likely last between 10 and 15 years, a one- to five-day course for users is a small price to pay for attempting to deliver a high-quality system that aims at truly meeting user needs.

2.3.2 Define System Mission and Project Business Objectives

Task number:	SU-2
Task name:	Define system mission and project business objectives
Objective:	To identify the system mission and state the major business objectives of the project
Input(s):	Request for service SU-1 Current problems/opportunities/users' needs
Output(s):	SU-2 System mission and project business objectives

Task description:
- Define the mission of the proposed system.
- Document the business objectives that must be achieved with the installation of this system.
- Prioritize these objectives by order of importance and degree of emergency.
- For each listed objective, identify the specific business department associated with it.
- Walk through the tentative system mission and the project business objectives to ensure that they are complete and are expressed as much as possible in quantifiable terms.

System mission.   The primary role of the system mission is to clarify the true *raison d'être* of the system. Whereas life cycle methodology is used to develop the system correctly the first time, the system mission addresses an essential question: Are we building the right system? This may sound like a trivial exercise, but it is not always easy to arrive at a consensus on the exact reason for a system's existence. It is important to develop a clear understanding of the role that the system will play in light of the environment it will support.

Once the mission is clearly defined and agreed to by all involved parties, the team can then produce a development strategy that aims at accomplishing that mission. The system mission statement should be formulated in the context of the enterprise by answering the following questions:

Why should this system exist?

Which business needs does it support?

Where does this system fit into the overall corporate picture?

Project business objectives.   Given the formulation of the current situation and of the system mission, the business objectives of the project must also be defined in conjunction with the users. The business objectives serve as the basic framework for elaborating the justification of the system solution. As mentioned, the system must be directed toward helping the organization fulfill its mission and meet its business goals.

The definition of the project business objectives is produced in relation to the problems and/or opportunities that were identified during the analysis of the current situation. Consequently, there should be at least as many business objectives as the number of major problems/opportunities that were identified. It follows that a business objective should be assigned a priority that is more or less equivalent to that assigned to its related problem or opportunity. Business objectives can be stated in either qualitative or quantitative terms. However, to be truly meaningful, a business objective should be clearly stated in a quantifiable and measurable format wherever it is possible to do so. The following guidelines should be observed as closely as possible when formulating business objectives:

Conciseness.   A business objective must be concise, no more than one to three sentences. The objective statement should be directed toward achieving an end result, not the intermediate steps that are required to accomplish this result. In other words, a business objective should not try to identify the work to be done but, rather, the desirable end result. Objectives are targets for achievement.

Measurability.   A business objective must be measurable. This is the best way to ensure that we can ascertain whether or not the objective has been fulfilled once the system has been put in production. Measurable terms that use dollar values, percentages, or time factors must be employed wherever possible, as in these examples:

- To reduce the control inventory costs by 20 percent within the first two years of operation.
- To reduce the control inventory costs by $50,000 within one year.

- To increase our ability to handle customer requests on the status of their orders from 50 to 75 percent within the next year of operation.
- To reduce the elapsed time between receiving a customer order and validating the customer's credit status by 15 percent.

Attainability.   A business objective must be attainable in light of the current organizational context. In some instances, it might be impossible to satisfy a business objective by the means of a new business system simply because there are still some technological or operational constraints in the environment that cannot be resolved by the project at hand. Furthermore, the business objective should be attainable within a reasonable time frame. Thus, a realistic target date must be determined for this to be achieved.

Project business objectives should not be confused with system objectives. Business objectives are primarily used to define the productivity/quality gains that are expected to be achieved once the proposed system is implemented. In most instances, they are directed toward the definition of business goals such as the reduction of operating costs, the increase in efficiency, quality, and responsiveness, the reinforcement of the enterprise's competitive position in the marketplace, or to be in a position to provide better services or facilities. Well-stated and verifiable business objectives will help the organization to determine better the added value that the system will provide to the users' business community at large. Too often, once the system has been implemented, the actual return on investment is not validated against the original figures that were advanced at the beginning of the project. This verification can be done only if the original business objectives of the project are properly formulated, along with a statement of the strategy that will be used to verify them later on.

It is important to understand that the definition of objectives, whether business or system oriented, is in fact an iterative process. Definitions will be modified or refined throughout the various analysis phases of the system development life cycle. Figure 2.6 shows some measurement indicators that can be used to formulate quantitative business objectives.

- Diminution of operating costs
- Throughput capacity (increase or decrease)
- Level of quality
- Degree of responsiveness
- Accuracy level
- Volume capacity
- Degree of customer satisfaction
- Degree of conformance to requirements
- Percentage productivity increase
- Elapsed time reduction
- Period of time
- Reduction of turnaround time

Figure 2.6   Measurement indicators for business objectives

2.3.3 Create System Context Diagram

Task number:	SU-3
Task name:	Create system context diagram
Objective:	To situate the system within the overall business environment
Input(s):	Existing system documentation
	SU-1 Current problems/opportunities/users' needs
	SU-2 System mission and project business objectives
Output(s):	SU-3 System context diagram

Task description:

- Situate the proposed system within the existing business environment, using the data flow diagram technique.
- Document all the graphical elements that are depicted in the system context diagram with supportive narrative descriptions.
- Verify that the proposed system is not redundant with other systems that are already in place somewhere else in the organization or currently in development.
- Identify the high-level functions that should be included in the proposed system.
- Walk through the system context diagram to ensure that all the interfaces to the proposed system are properly identified and that each item depicted on the diagram is well described.

System context diagram.   The system context diagram is the first type of data flow diagram that is constructed during the analysis cycle. The purpose of this high-level data flow diagram is to situate the system in the enterprise's business environment. It is a very useful tool that will help the development team later on to identify and formalize the scope of the project. All the departments that have a stake in the proposed system should, by looking at this diagram, have a better grasp of what could or should be the external boundaries of the system. It is important to mention that, at this early stage, the scope of the project is not yet entirely crystallized. The boundaries may still expand or shrink, at least until the end of the preliminary analysis phase. At that time, more detailed information will be available to the development team, allowing a better understanding of what should and should not be included in the scope of the project.

Construction of the system context diagram should start only when the analyst is familiar with the business area under study.[5] The input or output data flows shown on the diagram can include several items: reports, information sent to or re-

[5] All the constituent components of the conceptual process model (i.e., the system narratives, related data dictionary entries and graphical data flow diagrams) should be developed with the use of an automated analyst workstation. Three examples of such a tool are System Developer from Cadware, Inc., Excelerator from Index Technologies, and The Developer from Asyst Technologies, Inc. For more information on this subject, refer to Chap. 12, on CASE technology.

ceived from other systems, and other similar types of documents. In the case of real-time systems, control flows (i.e., control signals) are also shown on the diagram. The external entities represent the various departments within the organization that are interfacing with the system. These can also be external suppliers, vendors, or customers that have direct interactions with the proposed system.

Typically, the system context diagram can be developed in the following manner:

- Depict the boundary of the proposed system with a single process bubble and label it with the name of the system.
- Review the list of user departments, existing systems, and outside organizations that communicate with the system.
- Illustrate the above as external entities. The external entities that supply source data to the system should be identified on the left side of the diagram. The external entities that receive data from the system should be represented on the right side of the diagram. Label each external entity with its appropriate name.
- For each external entity shown on the diagram, depict all the control signals and data flows that are entering into the proposed system and all the control signals and data flows that are leaving it. Label each specific data flow and control signal.

Internal system functions.   Once the external interfaces to the system have been properly identified, the next step is to identify the major functions that are performed inside the system. For each high-level function, the following information should be provided:

- The name of the function.
- A brief narrative description of the function.
- The name of the business unit responsible for the function. If the function is performed across different business units, list all the departments that are involved.

At this stage, the analysts should not be overly concerned about how these functions are actually performed but, rather, should concentrate on identifying these logical functions. The purpose of this exercise is to identify tentatively and isolate the business functions that fall within the boundaries of the proposed system. These functions are then studied in more detail during the preliminary analysis phase. At that time, new functions might be added and others modified or even removed, depending on the final scope of the project.

There are various ways of identifying the system functions during the survey phase. The analysts can decide to identify the business functions on their own simply by interviewing the different user groups one at a time. Some dynamic fact gathering techniques such as the JAD-like or brainstorming approaches can also be successfully utilized for this purpose. Sometimes, depending on the nature of the business areas being described and the size and complexity of the system, it may be advantageous, even during the survey phase, to draft a rough sketch of both the system and subsystem data flow diagrams. These preliminary sketches can help users to visualize the internal functions of the system and the various relationships that might exist among them. However, users should be made aware that this is just a preliminary model and that it can change drastically during the next development phase.

If a corporate strategic system plan does exist, then the system context diagram should be mapped against the appropriate high-level process components of the corporate model. Any discrepancy should be documented, and a notification to update either the corporate or application process model should be initiated.

2.3.4 Create Data Context Diagram

Task number:	SU-4
Task name:	Create data context diagram
Objective:	To identify the major data entities used by the system and the relationships that exist among them
Input(s):	Existing system documentation SU-1 Current problems/opportunities/users' needs SU-2 System mission and project business objectives SU-3 System context diagram
Output(s):	SU-4 Data context diagram

Task description:

- Construct a data context diagram using the entity-relationship technique.
- Document all the elements that are depicted in the data context diagram with supporting narrative descriptions.
- Walk through the data context diagram to ensure that all the major data entities used by the system are shown and well documented.

The data context diagram is to the data-oriented model what the system context diagram is to the process-oriented model. It illustrates the business entities that are handled by the system under study, with the important relationships that exist among them. Like the system context diagram, it is a high-level diagram, and because of this, the attributes of the entities are not shown at this stage. The model is expanded and refined during the preliminary analysis phase. At that time, more details are added, including all the data attributes that are associated with an entity or a relationship.[6]

[6]All the constituent components of the conceptual data model (i.e., the narratives documenting the business policies, data entities, and their relationships, along with the graphical components of the entity-relationship diagram) should be developed with the use of an automated analyst workstation. An example of such a tool is ER-Modeler from Chen & Associates, Inc. For more information on this subject, refer to Chap. 12, on CASE technology.

Typically, the data context diagram can be developed in the following manner:

- Identify the major data entities that are of interest to the business area(s) under study.
- Depict the data entities that are manipulated by the system. Label each entity with a unique name.
- Identify the major relationships that exist among the data entities. Label each relationship with a unique name that well describes the relationship. Document the underlying business policies that dictate the nature of the associations established among the entities.
- Identify and surround with dotted lines the data entities and relationships that in some way are related to the proposed system but that are considered outside the immediate bound of the system's domain of information.

The relationships that exist among the data entities that are directly manipulated and those that are indirectly manipulated by the system can also be shown on the data context diagram. However, the entities that are clearly outside the boundaries of the proposed system are surrounded with dotted lines. A multitude of connections can be established among a given group of entities. In fact, the larger the number of data entities, the larger the number of possible connections among them. In practice, what is important is not to identify all the possible relationships that can be established arbitrarily but rather to identify only those that are of direct interest to the business area being modeled. If a conceptual data model for the enterprise already exists, the data entities shown on the local application model should be mapped against those identified in the corporate model.

It is important to realize that even though we discuss the task of constructing the data context diagram after the task of constructing the system context diagram, both diagrams can be constructed in parallel. In some situations, the data context diagram can be constructed even before the system context diagram.

2.3.5 Identify Project Constraints and Risks

Task number:	SU-5	
Task name:	Identify project constraints and risks	
Objective:	To define the project constraints and risks that can affect the initial search for tentative solutions	
Input(s):	SU-2	System mission and project business objectives
	SU-3	System context diagram
	SU-4	Data context diagram
Output(s):	SU-5	Project constraints and risks

Task description:
- Identify the potential business or technical constraints that might affect the scope and objectives of the project.

- Identify the potential business or technical risks that might affect the scope and objectives of the project.
- Identify the stated project business objectives that may somehow conflict with the identified technical or business constraints and risks. Evaluate the degree of conflict, document the related issues, and present them to the appropriate user managers for resolution.
- Walk through the project constraints and risks to ensure that their potential impact on this project is clearly understood and well described.

The business and technical constraints and risks pertain to those conditions that are considered outside the direct influence or control of the project team members. At the same time, however, they might have a direct impact on the scope of the project, its schedule, and the proposed implementation solution alternatives. Their potential impact on the project must be well understood by the development team. They must be fully described and carefully highlighted so that they will be taken into consideration when it is time to make a go/no-go decision to carry on with the project.[7]

Constraints or risks that might affect the project include the following:

- Corporate practices and directives
- Business risks (new business functions never supported before)
- Budget limitations
- Union regulations
- Schedule considerations
- Political considerations
- Legal considerations
- Environmental considerations
- Operational limitations
- Organizational policies
- Government regulations
- Hardware/software/networking considerations
- Personnel considerations
- Technology limitations
- New technology never trialed before

---

[7]Some CASE tools provide a facility to perform certain forms of risk analysis. They will generate a series of risk profile estimates for a given project in terms of several characteristics, such as its size, its structure, or the type of technology used. One such tool is ESTIMACS, from Computer Associates.

The following discussion provides some typical examples of project constraints and risks that the development team should highlight explicitly, where applicable.

Business Constraint.   It is obvious that a budget restriction of $100,000 for a software project might limit its scope when in reality a budget of $1 million would be necessary to satisfy all user requirements.

Technical Risk.   There might be particular situations where a technical element of risk is involved. If so, it must be clearly identified to management. For example, the use of a brand-new technology, which was never trialed in the industry or in the organization, might drastically increase the degree of technical risks associated with the development of the proposed system. Although the evaluation of technical risk factors is not always a straightforward process, and often can turn out to be somewhat subjective, it ought to be done as accurately as possible. High technical risks will often translate into higher development costs because most of the time there is no in-house expertise on how to use the new technology. For instance, the decision to develop a highly sophisticated distributed system across the country using state-of-the-art technology that is not yet completely proven in the industry will involve a certain element of risk.

Technical constraint.   The fact that the new system must be developed using the data base management system already in place is a good example of a possible technical constraint on the software side. Another example might be the necessity to use the "Cobol Application Code Generator" already in place. A third case in point are the physical limitations of the current hardware equipment being used.

Business risk.   The decision to develop a decentralized system to support an organization that in the past was highly centralized might involve a certain element of business risk. There can be a strong resistance to the decentralization process. Therefore, this situation can result in a destabilization period that can turn out to be quite harmful to the organization in the long run.

2.3.6 Determine Project Scope

Task number:	SU-6
Task name:	Determine project scope
Objective:	To delineate the domain of study that will be associated with the project
Input(s):	SU-1 Current problems/opportunities/users' needs SU-2 System mission and project business objectives SU-3 System context diagram SU-4 Data context diagram SU-5 Project constraints/risks

Output(s):	SU-6 Project boundary

Task description:

- Identify the high-level business functions and data entities that fall within the boundaries of the proposed system. Ensure that they are included in the scope of this project.

- Identify the system interfaces that, although they might in a way be affected by the proposed system, cannot be modified by this project. Document the rationale associated with the incurred limitations and describe how this can possibly affect the project.

- Revise all the technical deliverables developed so far and modify them in light of the proposed project boundary and the stated project constraints and risks, where applicable.

- Walk through the project boundary to ensure that it truly reflects the major business functions to be provided by the system, as well as the data entities that fall under its jurisdiction.

Several projects have failed because the development team did not succeed in obtaining a clear agreement from the users and the information system management as to the scope of the project. In reality, one of the biggest challenges of the survey phase is to define the scope of the system properly. Special attention should be given to include only those areas involved in the business environment of the proposed system. But, if in doubt, it might be preferable to include the functional area in question within the project scope. During the preliminary analysis phase, a more detailed analysis of the situation will determine if this particular area should remain.

In theory, the ideal system does not necessarily have organizational boundaries. On the other hand, a project is the logical process by which the boundaries of the system are arbitrarily restricted to a manageable size in order to ensure its successful implementation. This is one reason why a first draft of the system context diagram should be completed before the project constraints and risks are identified by the development team. Doing so decreases the risk that the development team does not prematurely exclude some user areas from the study that should be investigated.

It is not always easy, at such an early stage, to determine how much of the existing user environment should be included within the scope of the project. Experienced analysts are quite aware that a given problem that was originally identified in one business area of the organization turns out to have its root in some other area. If this is the case, such a situation should be highlighted to the user's management, and a decision should be taken by management to include the area in question, if necessary.

A rule of thumb: Although it is true that the initial definition of the objectives and constraints inherent to the current project might limit the search for potential solutions, it is also understood that these objectives and constraints are subject to revision, based on the findings that will come out of the preliminary analysis phase.

2.3.7 Determine Preliminary System Implementation Alternatives

Task number:	SU-7
Task name:	Determine preliminary system implementation alternatives
Objective:	To outline the preliminary system implementation solutions that are likely to satisfy the users' needs
Input(s):	SU-1 Current problems/opportunities/users' needs SU-2 System mission and project business objectives SU-3 System context diagram SU-4 Data context diagram SU-5 Project constraints/risks SU-6 Project boundary
Output(s):	SU-7 Preliminary system implementation alternatives

Task description:

- Identify and briefly describe the alternative system implementation solutions that can provide a method of solving the existing problems or achieve the existing opportunities (while still meeting the project business objectives).

- Prioritize the proposed system implementation solutions with a brief justification for their ranking. The alternative that is prioritized as the preferred one is labeled as the "recommended" solution for achieving the business objectives and satisfying the users' needs.

- If the proposed solutions are all long term, identify any potential short-term solutions that could ease the existing problems in the interim.

- Investigate the appropriateness and feasibility of constructing a prototype of the system. If applicable, provide a recommendation to this effect as an alternative to the traditional development life cycle.

- Walk through the proposed alternatives to ensure that each can meet the established project business objectives and satisfy the users' needs as closely as possible.

There is often a tendency to adopt a single system implementation solution quickly, usually the first one proposed. In general, this is a major problem because such an approach often results in systems that do not properly address the needs of the users. The best way to remedy this situation is simply to propose more than one implementation solution. This does not mean that each proposed solution invariably must be described down to its lowest level of detail. Rather, it should be a high-level statement outlining the general nature of the proposed solution. Obviously, the project constraints that were outlined in a previous task are useful to delineate the general boundaries of the solution.

It is important to note that although several different scenarios can be proposed, it is quite possible that in some instances retaining the existing system still remains a cost-effective solution. Consequently, the development team should always keep in mind this option when the search for identifying different tentative solutions is initiated.

Management should always be offered a menu of proposed scenarios. However, it is the responsibility of management to choose the approach it feels is the most appropriate, considering the situation that prevails at the time of the study. On the other hand, it is also well known that by nature technicians have a propensity to develop a system with the latest state-of-the-art technology. Depending on the nature of the business, it can sometimes be more advantageous to opt for a quick and dirty solution as opposed to a sophisticated and long-term one. Can the organization afford a Ferrari in the first place? Nevertheless, all the preliminary system implementation alternatives, including the acquisition of commercial packages, will be explored in more detail during the preliminary analysis phase. To conclude, using an impartial approach in this matter is important. The main objective is to come up with "adequate" solutions that will help achieve the stated business objectives and that will also take into consideration the existing constraints and the proposed project scope.

Even at this early stage, it is possible to recommend the construction of a prototype to model the proposed system. Either evolutionary or throwaway prototyping can be used for this purpose. If this is a viable development alternative, then the recommendation to prototype the system should include information about the functions that will be modeled, the estimated duration of the task, the justification for selecting this approach, and the anticipated benefits.[8]

Various system development approaches can be proposed to solve the problems at hand. The most frequent implementation solutions usually considered by the MIS organization fall within one of the four categories described here.

1. *Adapt the existing system.* The existing system is modified to satisfy the new business requirements or to resolve the existing problems.

2. *Acquire a commercial package.* A software package is brought in to solve the existing problems or to address the new business requirements. In many instances, such a solution can be very attractive because it minimizes the development cost that would normally be associated with the traditional in-house development approach. Furthermore, because the system is already developed, it can be delivered to the users far sooner than if it has to be developed from scratch. However, some careful consideration should be given to this option. Ideally, the proposed package should be compatible with the hardware/software/networking environment already supported by the organization. If this is not the case, highlight the major operational characteristics that would be required to support the new package.

3. *Develop a new system (in-house).* A brand-new system is developed from scratch. The existing technical facilities and environment are used to build the sys-

---

[8]For more information on prototyping, see Chap. 10.

tem. The system can be developed with either third- or fourth-generation languages or a combination of both. The development is done with the traditional structured techniques or with the iterative prototyping method.

4. *Acquire a turnkey system.* The system is entirely developed by a third party and is delivered to the users in a production mode of operation.

Each of these approaches has its own advantages and disadvantages. It is important for the development team to present the pros and cons of each scenario in light of the existing business environment and its current context.

Although it might seem somewhat unusual to start looking at system implementation alternatives so early in the project, the developers should remember that these potential solutions should still be analyzed strictly from a high-level standpoint. Nonetheless, it is important for a large project to start investigating at a high level the potential implementation solutions at this early stage. For example, if the acquisition of a package is seriously being considered by the organization, then the development team should already start contacting different vendors at least to obtain as much documentation as possible on the most probable candidates while preparing themselves for the preliminary analysis phase.

Sometimes, such intensive data gathering activities can turn out to be quite time consuming and might involve serious delays if they are not started as soon as possible. Furthermore, experienced analysts will admit that even though the emphasis at the early stages of the development life cycle should always be given to defining user requirements and to building a logical model of the system, it is still impractical not to perform a minimal amount of broad-brush physical system design. To reiterate, the analysts should be careful not to concentrate their efforts on describing a unique implementation solution at this stage. Only at the end of the preliminary analysis phase will a single system solution be retained by the development team. The suggested solution that best satisfies user requirements will in turn be described in detail during the detailed analysis phase.

2.3.8 Develop Preliminary Cost-Benefit Analysis

Task number:	SU-8
Task name:	Develop preliminary cost-benefit analysis
Objective:	To estimate the high-level costs-benefits associated with each system implementation alternative
Input(s):	Existing system documentation SU-6 Project boundary SU-7 Preliminary system implementation alternatives
Output(s):	SU-8 Preliminary cost-benefit analysis

Task description:

Cost Estimates.
- Identify the order of magnitude costs associated with the operation of the existing system, on an annual basis.

- Identify, if feasible at this stage, the order of magnitude operating costs of each proposed alternative system, on an annual basis.
- Identify the estimated order of magnitude development costs associated with each proposed system solution.
- Describe the techniques that were used to derive the cost estimates.

Benefit Estimates.

- Identify the order of magnitude benefit estimates associated with each proposed system solution. Categorize them into two groups: tangible and intangible benefits.
- For each tangible benefit, quantify in dollar value the expected reductions in operating costs or increased revenues. Identify the projected payback period associated with the new system.
- For each intangible benefit, describe the added values associated with the system's implementation and provide the appropriate justifications, where necessary.
- Describe the techniques that were used to derive the benefits.
- Walk through the preliminary cost-benefit analysis document.

Cost-benefit analysis.   Following is a nonexhaustive list of the various types of costs and benefits that might be considered for the project at hand.

Operational Costs (Current and Proposed Systems).   The operational costs can be grouped into the following categories:

COMPUTER COSTS

- Costs associated with a package (i.e., software license)
- Dedicated computer equipment costs
- Data storage costs
- Data communication and distribution costs
- Maintenance costs
- Main computer utilization costs

PERSONNEL COSTS

- Computer operating personnel
- User personnel
- Training costs

SUPPLY COSTS

- Paper
- Forms

MISCELLANEOUS COSTS

- Rental of floor space
- Office furniture

Benefits.   The benefits can be classified into two categories: tangible (i.e., quantitative) and intangible (i.e., qualitative).

TANGIBLE BENEFITS

The quantitative benefits are the ones to which a dollar value can be directly assigned. It includes, among other things

- New sources of revenues
- Increased profits
- Cost avoidance (staff)
- Reduction in maintenance costs
- Components of the new system that are marketable in the industry

INTANGIBLE BENEFITS

The qualitative benefits are those to which it is not always possible to assign a direct, tangible dollar value. It includes, among other things

- Improved service
- More accurate and timely information
- Improved controls
- Greater flexibility
- Competitive edge
- Improved employee morale

For each qualitative benefit, a description of the assumptions used to assign an indirect dollar value should be provided, as well as an evaluation of the probability for its actual realization.

Unfortunately, the cost-benefit analysis is a task that is often rushed, even though it might be one of the most important activities of the entire survey phase, at least from a management perspective. The management decision to invest considerable time and money in the next development phases of the project will be, to a large extent, based on the cost-benefit figures for the new system. Therefore, these items must be carefully identified and quantified wherever possible, even though it can only be done at a very high level at the present time.[9] These preliminary estimates will be carried out in more detail during the next development phases.

To illustrate the importance of this task, let's suppose that the cost-benefit analysis was not properly done during the survey phase. Let's also pretend that the system development estimates that were done at that time turn out, during the preliminary analysis phase, to be significantly higher than what was originally expected. Because the benefits previously identified were vague, the investment deci-

---

[9]Nonetheless, the costs and benefits estimates should always be presented to management as ranges of values (e.g., between $100,000 and $300,000 or $200,000 ± 100%).

sion to go ahead with developing the system might be temporarily postponed until extra benefits are finally found. Thus, such a situation can easily translate into additional work and unexpected delays for the project, not to mention the frustration that might be felt by the development team and the users themselves.

This situation can best be illustrated by a real-life example. A large software system was developed by an organization and was almost ready to be implemented in production. However, as strange as it may seem, the costs required to operate the new system in production were never clearly identified. So when the users asked, at the last minute, how much it would cost to run their system in production, the development team suddenly had to come up with these long-forgotten figures. Unfortunately, it turned out that the operating costs were far too high when they were compared to what the users could actually afford. Despite all their efforts to save the boat, they finally had to give up the project. As a result, the system was put on the shelf, after a development effort costing a very substantial amount of dollars.

User management makes the final go/no-go decision in light of what is presented. On the other hand, systems people must understand that if the project is not economically viable, it might be preferable to cancel it at this early stage rather than having to do so during the later phases of the development cycle. At that time, all the efforts invested in the project would be lost, not to mention the emergence of a potentially serious motivation problem within the ranks of the development staff.

Automated estimating tools.   The project software development costs and time can be generated at this point with the use of automated estimating tools. These easy-to-use facilities are gradually making their way into several organizations that regularly use them to cross-check the manually calculated estimates of the development teams or simply to replace them directly with these computer-generated estimates.[10] In their original versions, the project workhour estimates generated by these CASE tools are produced based on actual figures that were compounded on hundreds of projects coming from several different MIS organizations across the nation. Even though the project development time estimates can be pinpointed fairly accurately with these types of tools, their use can be further improved by gradually customizing them to more accurately reflect the unique environmental characteristics of each specific organization.

Moreover, these estimating tools should be integrated into the methodology prescribed by the organization. ESTIMACS, for example, will produce an estimate of the total workhours required to develop small or large batch, online or real-time systems simply by asking the developers to describe the project using a set of 25 basic questions that cover its major characteristics. Some of these questions address the number of functional organizations involved with the project, the project development team's past experience, the number of high-level functions, the number of files, and the like. It is far more practical (and economical) to gather all the input data required to answer these questions properly while conducting the various

---

[10]Two examples of such tools are ESTIMACS from Computer Associates and SPQR/20 by Software Productivity Research, Inc.

technical tasks suggested in the survey phase. Hence, this development phase would need to be slightly modified to accommodate the collection of such information.

Because of their relative simplicity, these facilities can also be used to simulate several what-if scenarios and finally come up with a series of development estimates that might reflect various hypothetical situations.

2.4 REFERENCES

For the reader who wants more information on strategic system planning, the following books can be consulted.

HEAD, Robert V. 1982. *Strategic Planning for Information Systems.* Wellesley, Mass.: Q.E.D. Information Sciences.

IBM CORPORATION; *Business Systems Planning — Information Planning Guide,* GE20-0527-1, New York.

MARTIN, JAMES. 1990. *Information Engineering, Book II: Planning and Analysis.* Englewood Cliffs, N.J.: Prentice Hall.

MARTIN, JAMES and JOE LEBEN. 1989. *Strategic Information Planning Methodologies,* 2nd ed. Englewood Cliffs, N.J.: Prentice Hall.

For the reader who wants more information on system analysis in general and on the data flow diagram technique, the following books can be consulted.

CONSTANTINE, L., and E. YOURDON. 1978. *Structured Design.* New York: Yourdon Press.

DeMARCO, Tom. 1979. *Structured Analysis and System Specification.* New York: Yourdon Press.

GANE, CHRIS, and TRISH SARSON. 1979. *Structured System Analysis Tools and Techniques.* New York: Improved System Technologies.

HATLEY, D. J., and I. A. PIRBHAI. 1987. *Strategies for Real-Time System Specification.* New York: Dorset House.

MARTIN, James, and CARMA McCLURE. 1985. *Diagramming Techniques for Analysts and Programmers.* Englewood Cliffs, N.J.: Prentice Hall.

PAGE-JONES, M. 1988. *The Practical Guide to Structured Systems Design,* 2nd ed., Englewood Cliffs, N.J.: Prentice Hall.

WARD, P. 1984. *Systems Development without Pain.* New York: Yourdon Press.

WEINBERG, VICTOR. 1977. *Structured Analysis.* New York: Yourdon Press.

YOURDON, E. 1989. *Modern Structured Analysis.* Englewood Cliffs, N.J.: Prentice Hall.

For the reader who wants more information on data modeling in general and the entity-relationship diagramming technique, the following books can be consulted.

CHEN, PETER. 1977. *The Entity-Relationship Approach to Logical Data Base Design.* Wellesley, Mass.: Q.E.D. Information Sciences.

FLAVIN, MATT. 1981. *Fundamental Concepts of Information Modeling.* New York: Yourdon Press.

MARTIN, JAMES, and CARMA MCCLURE. 1985. *Diagramming Techniques for Analysts and Programmers*. Englewood Cliffs, N.J.: Prentice Hall.

MELLOR, S., and S. SHLAER. 1988. *Object-Oriented Systems Analysis: Modeling the World in Data,* Yourdon Press Computing Series. Englewood Cliffs, N.J.: Prentice Hall.

For the reader who wants more information on the subjects of dual brain function and brainstorming, the following books can be consulted:

BUZAN, T. 1976. *Using Both Sides of Your Brain*. New York: E. P. Dutton.

GAUSE, D. C., and G. M. WEINBERG. 1989. *Exploring Requirements: Quality Before Design*. New York: Dorset House Publishing.

3

Preliminary Analysis Phase

3.1 PURPOSE

The purpose of the preliminary analysis phase is to investigate the system implementation solutions that were identified during the survey phase and select the
solution that best meets the users' needs. Nevertheless, for a large and complex system, a variety of tasks must be performed before reaching a final implementation decision.

First, the old system must be analyzed to determine the extent to which it
satisfies user needs, present and future. This brief examination of the fundamental
characteristics of the current system should, in principle, provide a firm foundation
for modeling the new system. Second, the essential functions of the new system are
portrayed in the conceptual process model, whereas the data entities and data
elements manipulated by the system are illustrated in the conceptual data model.
Once the conceptual process and data models have been developed, the major
operational characteristics of the new system are elaborated upon in conjunction
with the users. The characteristics include such things as system performance,
security/integrity/auditability, data storage, and hardware/software/networking
requirements that the system should accommodate. For the moment, these
operational constraints should be specified at a high level. Nevertheless, it is very

important to describe them using a rigorous method, so that they remain easily verifiable throughout the development process. In addition, the development team should ensure that these requirements are traceable to the original user needs and project business objective statements that were developed during the survey phase.

Third, the evaluation process will determine how well each proposed system implementation solution satisfies user needs in the light of the stated functional, data, and operational system requirements. The end result of this assessment will be the selection of one system implementation solution over the others. Following this, a formal development strategy is elaborated upon with the active participation of the users. Lastly, the cost-benefit analysis document that was developed at the end of the survey phase is refined, in accordance with the findings of the present phase.

It is worth noting that two of the proposed tasks—develop request for proposal and review vendor proposal—essentially focus on the selection of a commercial application package. They are optional and can be discarded if the alternative of acquiring a package is rejected by the organization. In the same vein, the task develop current system model is also optional. Its applicability to the project is left to the discretion of the development team.

Finally, the development team might decide to deviate from the traditional software engineering tasks proposed in this chapter and use the evolutionary prototyping method for developing the system. If this is the case, see Chap. 10, on prototyping, which provides all the information necessary to tailor the methodology to suit the needs of such a project.

Table 3.1 summarizes the major technical tasks that are usually conducted during the preliminary analysis phase, along with the anticipated technical deliverables.

Figure 3.1 illustrates, at a high level, the relationships that exist among the individual tasks of the preliminary analysis phase.

3.2 DESCRIPTION OF THE TECHNICAL TASKS

3.2.1 Analyze Current System

Task number:	PA-1
Task name:	Analyze current system
Objective:	To collect, analyze, and consolidate pertinent information on the current system and its environment
Input(s):	Existing system documentation Survey phase technical deliverables (SU-1 to SU-8)
Output(s):	PA-1A Current system documentation PA-1B Problems, opportunities, users' needs (detailed) PA-1C Project business objectives (detailed)

TABLE 3.1 PRELIMINARY ANALYSIS PHASE TECHNICAL TASKS AND DELIVERABLES

Technical Tasks	*Technical Deliverables*
1. Analyze current system	1. Current system documentation
2. Develop current physical system model (optional)	2. Current physical system model (optional)
3. Create conceptual process model	3. Conceptual process model
4. Create conceptual data model	4. Conceptual data model
5. Consolidate conceptual process and data models	5. Conceptual process and data models (consolidated)
6. Identify preliminary manual/automated system boundaries	6. Preliminary manual/automated system boundaries
7. Identify preliminary system performance requirements	7. Preliminary system performance requirements
8. Identify preliminary system control requirements	8. Preliminary system control requirements
9. Identify preliminary data storage requirements	9. Preliminary data storage requirements
10. Identify preliminary hardware/software/networking requirements	10. Preliminary hardware/software/networking requirements
11. Develop request for proposal (optional)	11. Request for proposal
12. Evaluate vendor proposals (optional)	12. Package evaluation
13. Select most suitable system solution	13. Selected system solution
14. Recommend system development strategy	14. Preliminary system development strategy
15. Refine cost-benefit analysis	15. Cost-benefit analysis (refined)

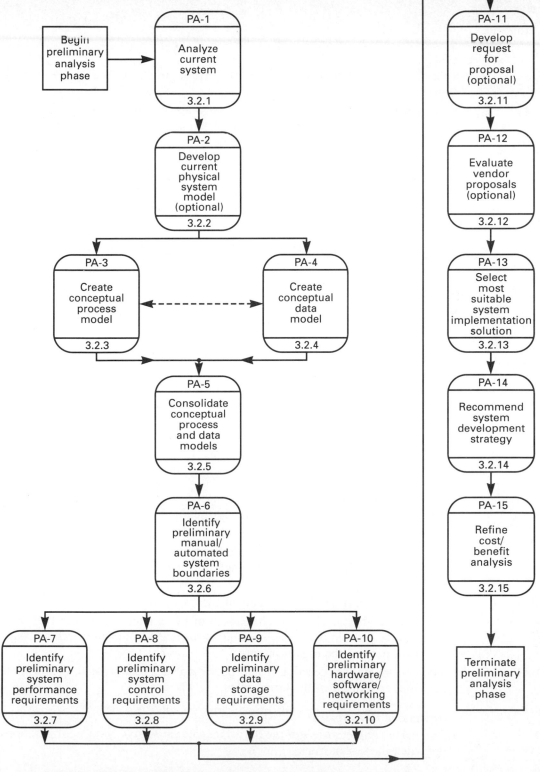

Figure 3.1 Preliminary analysis phase task network

Task description:
- Review the technical deliverables that were produced during the survey phase.
- Review all the documentation that has been assembled to date on the current system. If necessary, complete the information gathering process by collecting all the pertinent documentation describing the detailed operations of the present system.
- Create, if necessary, an inventory of all the detailed documents gathered on the present system.
- Analyze the current system information and consolidate the problems, opportunities, and users' needs that were documented during the survey phase.
- Discuss with the users the major strengths and weaknesses of the current system. If appropriate, identify the essential characteristics of the current system that the users would like to retain in the new system.
- Walk through the current system documentation to ensure it accurately reflects the existing environment and validate the consolidated problems, opportunities, and users' needs.

Gathering existing system documentation.   The first task of the preliminary analysis phase is to assess how well the existing system serves the users in their actual business environment. The analyst's main objective here is to develop a good understanding of the major functional characteristics of the system, whether these turn out to be good or bad, no matter how they are actually perceived by the users.

Some of the documentation items that might be gathered at this stage include the following:

Users' Manual Environment.
- The existing diagrams that portray the hierarchical structure of the users' organization.
- The set of various input/output documents that are used to perform the manual activities of the system. These might include different types of forms, reports, or departmental procedures.
- The description of the present manual files.
- The documents that describe the nature of the manual interfaces that exist between the current users' environment and the environment of other groups within or outside the organization.
- The documents that describe the corporate policies that regulate the business activities conducted in the users' areas.

Automated Environment.
- The major characteristics of the hardware/software/networking configurations on which the system runs.

- The system batch programs, along with samples of the reports produced, as well as the identification of their recipients.
- The system online transactions, along with sample layouts of their related screens.
- The real-time operations of the system.
- The system files and database structures, along with samples of their record or segment layouts.
- The description of the system interfaces.
- The source documents that are used to feed the computerized system, along with a sample for each document.
- A copy of user system manuals.
- The system documentation that describes the major components of the present system (i.e., system narratives, program documentation, system operations manuals, system flowcharts, production run streams).

Advantages versus disadvantages of documenting and analyzing the existing system.   Some pitfalls must be avoided during the documentation and analysis process. One of the first challenges is in deciding how far the development team should go in gathering, documenting, and analyzing facts about the current system. One might rightfully ask: "What are the major reasons that would justify the need to analyze the current system? To what extent should it be done? At which level of detail should this be done? What could be the possible drawbacks?"

Advantages.   The need for the development team to understand how the current system operates, at least at a high level, is indeed very fundamental. The following discussion outlines why this is so.

Chances are that the new system will likely replace an existing system. If this is the case, there might be some apparently very simple but yet very useful facilities that over the years have been gradually grafted onto the old system to improve its efficiency or usefulness. The users, while attempting to identify the problems, might simply neglect to point out to the analysts what they really like about the old system. They assume that these useful features will automatically be transposed onto the new system. This is not always the case.

Hence, the old system characteristics that the users would like to retain should be recorded at the time the current system is analyzed. That way, these requests will not be lost through the maze of the analysis process. However, these conceptual design issues should not be acted upon until the end of the detailed analysis phase or until the beginning of the design phase is reached.

More often than not, at least 70 percent of the functional characteristics already embedded in the old system can be directly transposed into the new system. The remaining 30 percent represents the new functions that might be required to respond better to the ever-changing needs of the users' business environment. The analysts can use this point to convince the users that after all, the essence of the new system is far from being entirely new. Therefore, it might be quite useful to document and analyze the current system because the resulting information will more often than not significantly affect the functional requirements for the new system. Furthermore, the degree to which the new system will rely on information concerning the old system should indicate the level of detail at which this study should be done.

Sometimes it is advantageous to document the current system with the users as it exists today, using their own terminology. In reviewing the documentation, the users might be reminded of problems or opportunities they forgot to mention during the preliminary investigation. Furthermore, because they are generally quite comfortable with the current environment, the users can easily agree with or deny the accuracy of the operations that are portrayed in the documentation of the present system. In addition, while the development team members acquaint themselves with the existing system and its supportive environment, a close "rapport" is progressively established between them and the users. This closeness can very favorably contribute to increased confidence of the users in the development team's ability to construct a quality system.

Although most users are quite familiar with their immediate environment, it is more than likely that very few of them will have a complete picture of the entire system. This is especially true when the system is very large and interfaces with several user departments across the organization. In such cases, the documentation or the modeling of the current system can certainly provide some valuable information to the system development team but also to the users themselves. They might gain some new insights about their own environment and this might trigger new ways of looking at the common problems that exist among the different user departments or new opportunities that should be more fully exploited.

Disadvantages.   One of the major problems associated with documenting and analyzing the existing system occurs when the development team spends too much time on this process, for the wrong reasons. Sometimes the development team will religiously and meticulously develop a very sophisticated, detailed analysis of the current system. In the process, they might even lose sight of the fact that the current system can have several unnecessarily complex or outdated procedures. In reality, many of the current system practices will be discarded if they are technology dependent. It is also possible that from a purely functional point of view, some of the current procedures did not even make sense in the first place.

If the team is not careful about these issues and conducts an in-depth review of the current system, there is a strong probability that the users will become very impatient and start questioning the need for such a detailed exercise.

Another problem might arise when the users (or even some of the analysts) accept the existing physical characteristics of the system as a fact of life. They accept these as if they were an intrinsic part of the system, without even questioning the current ways of doing things. The need for a new system should provide the users with new opportunities of doing business in their environments. It should enlarge their horizons. Consequently, it is very important to examine the efficiency of the current organization and constantly question the intrinsic value of the existing practices and procedures.

Figure 3.2 provides some insights on the reasoning behind the facts.

Facts	The Rationale Behind the Facts
What is done?	Why is it done?
Where is it done?	Why is it done there?
When is it done?	Why is it done then?
Who does it?	Why is it done by these people?
How is it done?	Why is it done like this?

Figure 3.2   The rationale behind the facts

3.2.2 Develop Current Physical System Model (Optional)

Task number:	PA-2
Task name:	Develop current physical system model (optional)
Objective:	To develop a physical model of the current system
Input(s):	PA-1 Current system documentation
Output(s):	PA-2 Current physical system model (optional)

Task description:
- Develop a formal physical model of the current system's manual and automated processes using the physical data flow diagram technique.
- Describe textually all the physical elements shown on the physical data flow diagrams.
- Walk through the physical model of the current system to ensure it is complete and accurate.

The formal modeling of the current system is sometimes a very politically dangerous process. Several analysts have heard through the grapevine about project teams that have spent more than a year documenting in great detail a current system that was about to be completely replaced. Some projects have even been cancelled by the users, out of exasperation because work on the new system itself was delayed too long. For this reason, many experts believe that modeling the current system in its entirety and at a detailed level might not be an advisable thing to do. Some of them even strongly recommend not modeling the current system whenever it is possible to do so.

In spite of this, the team might still decide to create a physical model, especially if nobody seems to understand the way it works in the current environment. As a rule of thumb, though, the team should be careful not to model the system at a lower level of detail than the level of the function processes. More often than not, the system work units and operations processes should not be included within the scope of the modeling study. However, under some exceptional circumstances, it might be necessary to model at a very detailed level one or two specific functions of the system that turn out to be very important or far more complex than the others. In such cases, it might even be necessary to describe the internal logic of the operations with structured specification techniques like structured English, decision tables, and decision trees.

The model of the current physical system should be progressively developed using the same leveling approach that is used to model the conceptual process model. First, a system context diagram is developed that identifies the general flow of information that is exchanged between the system and the external entities it communicates with. Second, the system is broken down into its subordinate subsystems. Finally, each particular subsystem process is exploded into its function data flow diagrams.

The processes shown on the physical data flow diagram model represent the "physical" functions that are performed by the old system. The manual functions are done by individuals or departments. The automated functions describe the set of batch programs, online transactions, and real-time processes that are executed by the system. The data stores represent the computerized files and databases of the system. However, they can also represent filing cabinets, decks of cards, file folders, or Rolodex files for the manual portion of the system. Lastly, the physical data flows depict the exchange of data that occurs among the various physical processes. They represent such physical items as forms, reports, ad hoc requests, verbal directives, files sent to or received from other systems or departments, and the like.

3.2.3 Create Conceptual Process Model

Task number:	PA-3	
Task name:	Create conceptual process model	
Objective:	To develop a logical model of the proposed system functions	
Input(s):	SU-3	System context diagram
	PA-1	Current system documentation
	PA-2	Current system model (optional)
Output(s):	PA-3	Conceptual process model

Task description:

- Review the old conceptual process model of the system, if there is any.
- Based on the information gathered so far on the existing system and its environment, revise the system context diagram that was constructed during the survey phase for its accuracy and completeness.
- Break down the proposed system into its subordinate components, leveling each logical data flow diagram in a top-down manner as follows: system diagram, subsystem diagrams, and function diagrams.
- Map the conceptual process model of the application under development to the appropriate components of the corporate process model. Resolve any in-

consistencies that surface between the application related and corporate process models.

- Provide a textual description of all the graphical elements shown on the conceptual process model (i.e., the context, system, subsystem, and function data flow diagrams).
- Walk through the conceptual process model to ensure that it completely and accurately represents the set of essential functions that must be performed by the proposed system and that it adequately covers all the users' functional needs.

During the preliminary analysis phase, the conceptual process model is gradually broken down into its subordinate logical components, using the top-down technique. The following section describes how this task is done.[1]

Construction of the system diagram.

- Outside the perimeter of the diagram boundary, depict the external entities that interface with the proposed system. These entities should be identical to those that were identified in the system context diagram.
- Inside the perimeter of the diagram boundary, draw the high-level processes that depict how the system is broken down into its subordinate subsystems and describe the relationships that exist among them.
- Draw the high-level logical data stores that contain data used by the subsystems. Label each of them. The names of the data stores should be identical to the names of the business entities that are depicted in the conceptual data model.
- Draw the data flows that connect the subsystem processes, the external entities, and the data stores. Identify each data flow with a name that truly represents the data being carried.

The major criterion that is normally used to break down the proposed system into its subsystem components is based on the identification of a set of functions that can naturally and logically be clustered within a larger set. However, the grouping of functions under a single subsystem must be done in a logical manner. It should be performed in a way that deemphasizes the desired physical implementation characteristics of the system, the organizational structure in place, or any political considerations.

If many processes access the same data entities, then it might make sense, if they truly have strong functional affinities, to group them together. The number

---

[1]An alternative approach is event partitioning. This technique is not a strict top-down approach but rather a middle-out approach. It might be particularly useful when the analysts have difficulties in leveling the functions of the system in a top-down manner. For an in-depth discussion of event modeling, refer to Yourdon [1989], Frantzen and McEvoy [1988], Mellor and Ward [1985], or McMenamin and Palmer [1984].

of data entities handled by a subsystem should always be kept to a minimum, whenever possible. The smallest number of data entities that need to be accessed by a subsystem can be used as an indication of the intrinsic complexity associated with this particular subsystem. Furthermore, if the system is relatively small, it can obviously be directly partitioned into a set of functions.

Lastly, it should be noted that if a data store is accessed by only one subsystem, it should be removed from the system diagram and shown on the appropriate subsystem diagram.

Construction of the subsystem diagram.

- Outside the perimeter of the diagram boundary, depict the external entities that interface with the subsystem. These entities should be identical to those identified in the system diagram. At this level, the external entities can be split into subordinate entities as long as they retain their vertical relationship with their parents.
- Inside the diagram boundary, draw the processes that depict how the subsystem is broken down into a set of business functions. Label each function process with its appropriate name.
- Draw the data stores that are accessed by these logical functions. Label each of them. The data stores can be split into subordinate data stores, where applicable.
- Draw the data flows that connect the function processes, the external entities, and the logical data stores. Identify each data flow with a unique name that is representative of the data being carried.

It should be pointed out that if the system being modeled includes some real-time characteristics, then the traditional data flow diagrams can be augmented with control processes and control flows.[2]

Construction of the function diagram.

- Outside the perimeter of the diagram boundary, depict the detailed external entities that directly interface with the function. These entities should be identical to those identified in the subsystem diagram. Once again, these external entities can be broken down into subordinate entities.
- Inside the diagram boundary, draw the processes that depict how the function is partitioned into a set of work units. Label each work unit process symbol with its appropriate name.
- Draw the data stores that are used by these work units and label each of them.
- Draw the data flows that connect the work unit processes, the external entities, and the data stores involved. Identify each data flow with a representative name.

[2]For more information on how to model real-time systems, refer to Mellor and Ward [1985] or Hatley and Pirbhai [1987].

The following section provides a set of guidelines to help the practitioner break down a function into a set of logical work units.

- The functions should not be too big or too small. If a function contains work units that are not functionally related, split that function into two distinct functions. Other factors that should be taken into consideration include the overall complexity of the procedural logic performed within the function and the number of data entities manipulated by the function.
- As a rule of thumb, the purpose of a work unit can often be summarized by one simple sentence. This sentence explains what is done inside the function versus how it is done—for instance, produce an employee status report, establish a customer credit line, or process a customer order.
- Each work unit must be independent of another. A work unit must not overlap the work performed by others.
- A work unit should have a clear information boundary. It must be performed within the context of a specific domain of information.
- A work unit is oriented toward producing a tangible result. Its raison d'être is to produce this result. If the work unit is ill-defined, it will be difficult to identify its objective in a single sentence. It may yield an unclear result or a combination of different results.
- Usually, error-handling, validation, and editing routines are not shown on the conceptual process model diagrams. These lower-level processes are generally described when the functional process model is developed, during the detailed analysis phase.

Consistency checking.   Once completed, the conceptual process model should be carefully scrutinized by the analysts to detect various inconsistencies that might have been introduced inadvertently in the data flow diagrams.[3] Such inconsistencies include the following:

- Data flow diagram symbols that have no name
- Different processes that have the same name
- Data flows that are shown on the high-level data flow diagrams but are not represented in lower-level diagrams
- Dangling data flow lines
- Processes or external entities with no incoming or outgoing data flows
- Control processes with no incoming or outgoing control flows
- Data flow diagram symbols with no corresponding textual descriptions in the data dictionary

[3]With the help of computer-aided software engineering (CASE) tools, straightforward consistency and validation checking rules (naming conventions, balancing, proper symbol usage, and much more) can be done automatically as the diagrams are created by the analysts. Refer to Chap. 12 for more information on CASE technology.

- Data elements coming into data stores but never leaving, or data stores with no names

The names of the data stores shown in the conceptual process model should reflect the names of the major data entities in the conceptual data model. If the conceptual data model is developed before the conceptual process model, the data entities in the entity-relationship diagrams can be used as a guide to identify the names of the data stores that will be shown in the data flow diagrams.

Deemphasizing the physical characteristics of the system.   It is important while constructing the conceptual process model to deemphasize as much as possible the implementation-related characteristics of the proposed system. The ultimate goal is to reduce the system to the set of fundamental functions that transform the application data from the input format to the output format. When the analysts discover that some physical or political aspects of the system have surfaced in the conceptual process model, they should systematically suppress or replace them with their logical counterparts.[4]

Instead of trying to describe the logical characteristics of a system, we will take the opposite approach and list what is meant by the physical aspects of a system.

1. *References to staff or computerized programs.* The processes shown in the conceptual process model should strictly represent the logical functions of the system. Therefore, the names of these processes should not reference specific individuals, departments, or batch or online programs that currently do the work prescribed in these processes.

2. *References to physical media.* References to physical media, such as magnetic tapes, disks, databases, manual or electronic folders, filing cabinets, screens, and manual files, should not be shown in the logical process model.

3. *Timing/sequencing/scheduling events.* Timing, sequencing, and scheduling considerations should not be shown in the logical process model. Processes that uniquely sequence data records in a given order or combine different data files together should not be depicted at this stage. For instance, the classic sort and merge processes should be eliminated from the diagrams. When the new system is designed, the sorting or merging issues will have to be addressed by the system designers. At such a time, maybe the new files will be structured in a way that will eliminate the sort/merge needs that prevailed in the old system.

---

[4]A word of caution about the logical versus physical gospel is in order when the team builds the conceptual process model: While it is true that the team should be very careful not to let important physical characteristics surface in the model, the team should also be careful to use common sense during this process and not start a holy war against everything that is not purely logical. Sometimes it may be difficult to recognize the physical or political characteristics embedded in a system. The team members remain the final judges of what makes sense and what doesn't. Remember, the only place where you will probably see a purely logical model of a system is in academic textbooks.

4. *Conversion/reformatting.* The processes that convert files from one internal representation to another should not be shown in the model—for example, the conversion of a PC file to a mainframe file (i.e., from ASCII to EBCDIC code). The same rule applies to processes that reformat information from one specific medium to another—for example, a hard-copy report that is converted to a microfiche report.

5. *Control processes.* In principle, the control processes used to sequence the order in which other business processes are performed should not be shown in the logical process model.

6. *Time-delay files.* Files that temporarily accumulate data over a given period of time and are used later on to update more permanent files should not be shown in the logical process model (e.g., a temporary batch transaction file that is created during the day and used to update a database during the night).

7. *Physical transfer of data.* The sole mission of certain processes is to transmit data from one area to another. In a manual system, it might be a clerk who transports different documents between departments. In an automated system, it can be a file that is physically transmitted directly from one computer to another. Processes that control the transmission of data should not be shown in the logical model of the system.

8. *Hardware/software considerations.* Processes that are related to specific software or hardware equipment should not be shown in the conceptual process model, since they are technology dependent.

9. *Political considerations.* Elements that seem to be politically oriented should not be shown in the model. An example is two identical processes that turn out to be performed in two different departments when in fact the only thing that distinguishes them is the name that each department has assigned to each of them.

10. *Coincidental packaging of elements together.* Because of purely physical considerations, some elements of the old system might have been arbitrarily preassembled together. For instance, several physical data flows could have been combined because it was easier and cheaper to transmit them electronically en masse due to constraints that were imposed by the technology of that time. From a logical point of view, these data flow elements should be distinct because, logically speaking, they have nothing in common.

3.2.4 Create Conceptual Data Model

Task number:	PA-4
Task name:	Create conceptual data model
Objective:	To develop a logical data model depicting the relationships that exist among the business entities manipulated by the system

Input(s):	SU-4	Data context diagram
	PA-1	Current system documentation
	PA-2	Current system model (optional)
	PA-3	Conceptual process model
Output(s):	PA-4	Conceptual data model

Task description:

- Review the old conceptual data model, if any.

- Finalize the construction of the conceptual data model, using the entity-relationship modeling technique.

- Resolve the data anomalies that might be detected during the development of the conceptual data model.

- Document each graphical item shown in the entity-relationship diagram with a corresponding textual description.

- Map the conceptual data model of the application under development to the appropriate components of the corporate data model. Verify that the entities, data elements, and relationships in the conceptual data model are consistent with those represented in the corporate data model. Resolve any inconsistencies that surface between the application-related and corporate data models.

- Walk through the conceptual data model and its components to ensure that it accurately reflects the data used by the system and that it is complete.

Construction of the conceptual data model.   The creation of the conceptual data model was initiated during the survey phase, with the construction of the data context diagram. During the preliminary analysis phase, the conceptual data model is gradually refined and expanded to describe the data elements that more precisely characterize the entities and the relationships used by the system. This task is performed as follows:

- Review the data entities and relationships that were depicted in the survey phase data context diagram.

- Refine this diagram to show the new business entities or relationships that were discovered while documenting/modeling the current system and/or developing the conceptual process model.

- Identify all the detailed data elements that characterize each specific entity or relationship illustrated in the diagram.

- Identify each key data element that uniquely identifies a specific occurrence of each distinct entity. Provide a clear definition of each data element attributed to an entity or a relationship and determine if it is a basic or derived data element.

- Document the underlying business policies that govern the connecting of various entities via a specific relationship.

Consistency checking.   Once completed, the model should be carefully scrutinized by the analysts in an attempt to detect various types of inconsistencies, such as the following:[5]

- Duplicate entity and data element names
- Invalid attribution of data elements to an entity
- Entities with no data elements
- Data elements with no entities

Entity supertype/subtype.   During the construction of the detailed entity-relationship diagrams, it might become necessary for the development team to depict at a more detailed level different object types that relate to the same entity. For instance, depending on the nature of the application at hand, as well as the unique context in which each organization operates, it may be relevant for an analyst who works in a banking environment to differentiate clearly the various categories of accounts a customer can have. For example, these could include a personal account, an institutional account, or a retail account. Whereas the entity "account" could be reasonably well described with the use of general terms while the data context diagram is being created, it might be necessary to describe it in a more precise manner when the components of the conceptual data model are further broken down during this phase. The entity account should thus be identified with several but yet distinct subclassifications. It is also understood that, through each successive iteration that the conceptual data model is subjected to, new or old entities or relationships may equally be added or suppressed.

Single/multiple-occurrence value.   When assigning data elements to the entities or relationships shown in the model, the analyst may find it appropriate to declare each data element as having either a single- or multiple-occurrence value. For instance, in Fig. 3.3, the entity "employee" is characterized by six data elements. The data element "employee-number" has a single-occurrence value. This means that for each specific occurrence of the entity "employee," there is one and only one occurrence of the data element "employee-number." At the opposite end, the data element "employee-children" is declared as having a multiple-occurrence value. That is, an employee can have zero, one, or many children.

The process of identifying each data element as having a single- or multiple-occurrence value is not mandatory when the conceptual data model is developed. It does not add much value to the information conveyed by the entity-relationship

---

[5]Most data modeling CASE tools will automatically check all the components of the entity-relationship diagrams for consistency and adherence to the data modeling rules and standards that are prescribed by the organization.

```
   ╭─────────────────────────╮
   │       EMPLOYEE          │
   ├─────────────────────────┤
   │ EMP-NUMBER (S)          │
   │ EMP-NAME (S)            │
   │ EMP-STATUS (S)          │
   │ EMP-BIRTH-DATE (S)      │
   │ EMP-CHILDREN (M)        │
   │ EMP-SKILLS (M)          │
   ╰─────────────────────────╯
```

Figure 3.3 Single or multiple value occurrences of the EMPLOYEE attributes

diagram. However, the single- or multiple-occurrence value assigned to the data elements will greatly assist the data analyst when, during the detailed analysis phase, the data portrayed in the entity-relationship model will be normalized.

Simplicity and readability.   Even though an entity can exist by itself, without its data elements, the true role it plays in the context of the system becomes far more visible once the entity is connected to another entity via a relationship and after all its related data elements have been properly identified by the data analyst. Hence, a clear representation in the model of the entities, relationships, and attributes is very important. Furthermore, an appropriate choice of names for each of the components of the conceptual data model will definitely improve its readability and level of understandability.

Synonyms and homonyms.   During the building of the conceptual data model, attribution of data elements to the various data entities of the system may expose new categories of problems, such as those associated with the detection of synonyms and homonyms. Synonyms occur when two different names are used to identify the same entity or the same attribute. Example: Customer-invoice and customer-bill are synonyms if both have the same definition in the context of a given system (e.g., a list of the goods sold to the customer along with a description of the corresponding charges and terms). Homonyms occur when the same name is used to identify two entities or attributes that, in reality, have different meanings in different contexts. Example: An "assembly" in one department is used to identify a specific part of an engine, whereas another department uses the word "assembly" to identify the complete engine itself, with all its constituent parts.

When inconsistencies of this nature are detected in the data model, they should be clarified with the users as soon as possible. Ideally, a consensus should be reached among the users as to which terminology should prevail. In practice, though, this task may prove to be quite difficult, especially if a strong data administration function has not yet been established in the user organization itself. This is especially true when the myriad business documents that are being processed in several user areas utilize slightly different terminologies. It might not be too practical to change all the existing documentation or create new forms to reflect a consistent terminology across the entire organization, especially for those areas that fall outside the scope of the present system.[6] As a compromise, though, discrepancies of this nature should at least be recorded in the corporate data dictionary and aliases could be created to reflect the current situation. Eventually, the synonyms and homonyms should then be gradually phased out with the eventual redevelopment of the systems already in place.

Derivable data elements.   As noted earlier, when analysts develop the entity-relationship diagram, they must always strive to keep the model as simple as possible. For this reason, there is a school of thought on data modeling that recommends not showing the data elements that can be derived from other data elements on the model. For example, after discussion with the users, the data analyst realizes that a data element called "total-amount" must be attributed to the entity "invoice." Since the calculation of "total-amount" can be derived from other data elements, it must be decided if the derivable data element should be kept in the model. The important issue here is not really to decide whether or not the data element should be kept in the model but, rather, to ensure if it is ever removed that such an action is properly recorded somewhere.

In the user's mind, he or she has definitely identified a requirement for a data item called "total-amount." Such a simple requirement should not be lost in the myriad activities that are part of the development of a large and complex system. In the heat of the action, all the derivable data elements might suddenly be removed from the model without any formal notification. If the analysts do not keep track of these "hidden" requirements, chances are that when the design stage is finally reached, some of these requirements may fall through the cracks and be lost. In reality, the decision to store permanently or derive data elements is generally based on machine performance considerations. These decisions are normally taken at the design stage. However, always ensure that requirements hidden behind derivable data elements are not lost, if it is ever decided to remove them from the model.

3.2.5 Consolidate Conceptual Process and Data Models

Task number:	PA-5
Task name:	Consolidate conceptual process and data models
Objective:	To verify and ensure data consistency across the conceptual process and data models

---

[6]Not to mention the prohibitive costs that can be involved in changing all the different data element names used in the system programs, databases, display screens, and reports. However, the advent of powerful CASE reengineering tools might help to automate the resolution of these types of problems. For example, data restructuring tools can be used to scan automatically the program's source code and detect potential data anomalies, such as synonyms, homonyms, and other data-naming problems of this nature. Once these inconsistencies are properly resolved with minimum human intervention, the same tools can then be used to modify automatically the program's source code with the consistent data element names.

Input(s):	PA-3	Conceptual process model
	PA-4	Conceptual data model
Output(s):	PA-3	Conceptual process model (consolidated)
	PA-4	Conceptual data model (consolidated)

Task description:

- Verify that there are no inconsistencies between the conceptual process model (along with its real-time characteristics, when appropriate) and the conceptual data model.

- Verify that the conceptual data model can satisfy all the data requirements identified in the data flows and data stores depicted in the conceptual process model.

- Assess the level of stability of the conceptual data and process models, in the context of the users' environment, present and future. This is done primarily based on the likelihood of introducing new functions or data requirements into the environment within a reasonable time frame. When required, adjust the models to support the future business and information requirements that are anticipated by the users and document the reasons justifying this approach.

- Walk through, if necessary, the consolidated conceptual process and data models.

Cross-models consistency considerations. Both the conceptual data and process modeling techniques have their respective set of guidelines to monitor better the construction of quality models. With these guidelines, each model can be scrutinized in a standalone fashion by the analysts and the users for consistency and validation checking purposes. It is almost certain that some inconsistencies can also be detected among the various components of the conceptual data and process models. For this reason, it is very important to consolidate the conceptual data and process models to ensure that they are truly consistent with one another:

- Each data store depicted in the data flow diagrams should correspond to an entity type shown in the entity-relationship diagrams.

- A data element shown in a data store does not appear in the list of data elements attributed to the corresponding entity.[7]

- The names of the data stores do not match the names of the entities.

---

[7]Obviously, the expert rules that are used by the CASE tool to cross-check and validate the common components of the two models must be consistent with the methodology in use. For instance, if derivable data items are allowed in the data flow diagrams, but are not permitted in the entity-relationship diagrams, then the CASE tool should be intelligent enough to handle such a situation.

- The names of the data elements of an entity do not match the names of the data elements used by the data flow processes.
- The entries in the data dictionary that are used to describe the common components of both models (e.g., attributes/data elements, entities/data stores) must not be duplicated.

The intermodel validation rules we have just described strongly suggest that there exist several affinities between both models. Thus, if the conceptual data and process models of a large system are developed by different groups of people, these people should work very closely together to avoid unnecessary inconsistencies when their respective models are constructed. The consolidation process should not be a last-minute effort but, rather, an ongoing activity that starts at the very beginning of the project.

Stability considerations.   The primary purpose of modeling the system is ultimately to create programs and databases that not only meet user requirements but also remain as stable as possible over time. In today's dynamic business world, it is unthinkable that the user environment will remain static over the years. Therefore, the system should be constructed in such a way as to allow future expansion while ensuring minimal disruptions in the business environment it supports.

When the two models are completed, the users and the systems people should meet to brainstorm and together determine the likelihood of introducing new requirements in the near future that would significantly affect the architecture of the new system.[8] The objective is to anticipate certain categories of changes—for example

- Will the organization move into a new line of business?
- Will a new function be required in the near future? If so, how would it affect the current system model?
- Would it be possible that an attribute of an entity would soon become an entity by itself?
- Is it possible that new data elements might be attributed to an entity?
- What about the possibility of introducing new entities?
- Will a new relationship be established soon between two or more entities?
- Could some of the fundamental business policies of the organization be changed in the years to come because of anticipated events such as new legislation?

To conclude, anticipating foreseeable changes in the business environment might prevent costly system changes in the future, if they are properly reflected in the architecture of the new system.

---

[8]Expressed in terms of new functions or information needs and covering a reasonable time frame, such as a one- to five-year period.

3.2.6 Identify Preliminary Manual/Automated System Boundaries

Task number:	PA-6
Task name:	Identify preliminary manual/automated system boundaries
Objective:	To delineate the system components that should be manual versus those that should be automated
Input(s):	PA-1B Problems/opportunities/users' needs (detailed) PA-1C Project business objectives (detailed) PA-3 Conceptual process model PA-4 Conceptual data model
Output(s):	PA-5 Preliminary manual/automated system boundaries

Task description:

- For each proposed manual/automated boundary scenario, perform the following activities:
  - Identify on the conceptual process model the functions/work units that are suitable candidates for computerization.
  - Identify in the conceptual data model the data entities that are suitable candidates for computerization.
  - Evaluate the advantages and disadvantages of each proposed automation scenario by judging its ability to satisfy the users' requirements. Document the findings.
- Recommend the preferred scenario of automation, outlining the reasons for its selection over the other alternatives.
- Perform the following subtasks for the automated portions of the system:
  - Identify the functions/work units that will likely be performed in either a batch, online, or real-time processing mode.
  - Identify the data entities of the conceptual data model that will likely be implemented with the use of database or nondatabase technologies.
- Describe the general operational characteristics that are recommended for implementing the various automated portions of the system, such as the following:
  - Centralized, decentralized, or distributed processing of the functions and data.
  - Implementation of some portions of the automated system or the entire automated system on micro, mini, and/or mainframe processors.
- Walk through the preliminary manual/automated system boundaries.

Automating the functions.   The primary objective of this task is to determine which system functions should be automated and which ones should be manual, if any. Some of the guidelines that can be used to determine what functions are suitable for computerization include

- The complexity of the tasks required to execute the function
- The level of repetitiveness involved in executing the internal operations of the function
- The frequency of execution of the function
- The type and volume of data required to execute the function
- The degree of human judgment necessary to perform the function successfully
- The stability of the function over time
- Few exception rules for performing the function

In reality, a variety of alternatives might be proposed to the users, each detailing a different way of partitioning the system into a set of manual/automated functions. Without a doubt, each proposed scenario can lead to different cost-benefit figures. Thus, it is important to highlight to the users the major advantages and disadvantages of each approach. Several factors, such as the project constraints and risks that were identified during the survey phase, each scenario's own ability to satisfy user requirements, and the current state of technology, must all be considered and properly weighed in the light of the present business context. Obviously, there can be varying degrees of functional automation. For instance, the entire system can be automated. At the opposite end, the system functions can be entirely manual, although such a solution is very unlikely. Between these two extremes a multitude of variations can be outlined, depending on the particular needs of the organization.

Automating the data.   The conceptual data model might need to be broken down into several manual/automated portions. However, the "physicalization" of the conceptual data model should only be done at a high level at this stage. Hence, some of the data portrayed in the conceptual data model may be stored manually while other data may be computerized.

If necessary, the automated components of the data model might be broken down further into DBMS and/or non-DBMS data groups. Several factors can be analyzed to determine which approach best satisfies the application needs: A DBMS approach, a non-DBMS approach, or a combination of both approaches. For example, a DBMS approach might better suit the needs of an application when

- Ad hoc access to data will be used frequently by the users.
- Several user groups will access the same files for different purposes.
- Concurrent accesses of the data for read/update purposes will be required by the application.
- Specific security/integrity/auditability/privacy requirements must be enforced at the file, record, or field level.
- A high volume of data must be processed in either a batch or online mode of operation with a lot of volatility.

- Complex data structures must be supported by the application.
- Complex data retrieval requirements must be supported by the application.
- Critical response time requirements must be satisfied by the system.
- The data structures of the application must remain flexible over time.
- The data must be accessed via different entry points.

Figure 3.4 illustrates in a very schematic manner an automation boundary alternative for the various functions and data components of a hypothetical system.

The system has been broken down into different groups of real-time, online, batch, and manual processes. (The manual processes of the system are shown because they should be considered an integral part of the system.) Optimizing the automated portions of the system while neglecting the effectiveness of the manual procedures will only result in a system that fulfills a portion of its obligations. The mechanized data stores can be shared among the online, batch, and real-time por-

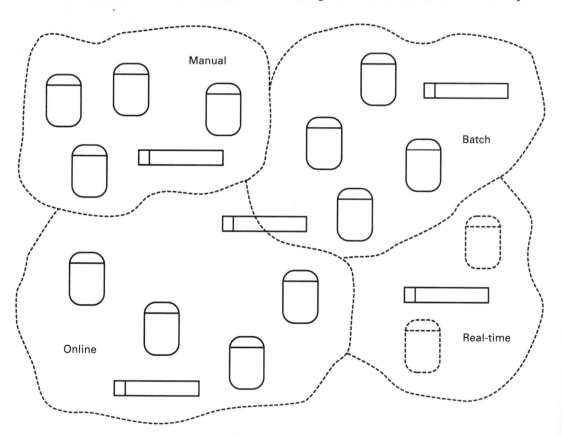

Figure 3.4 Automation boundary for a system

tions of the system, depending on the technology chosen to implement the system. If the technology used imposes constraints in this area, then it might be necessary to duplicate some databases or files. Although not shown in the figure, the high-level automated processes and data components that qualify for distributed processing could also be included in the diagram by surrounding them with dotted lines.

Processor configuration alternatives. The different types of processor configurations that are explored by the development team should not include detailed considerations of a physical nature. Nevertheless, several basic questions might need to be considered at this stage:

- Will the automated portion of the system be implemented entirely within a mainframe computer environment?
- Is the option of using minis or micros a feasible and desirable approach?
- Can certain portions of the system be completely developed and implemented with microcomputers by the users themselves?
- Could the automated components of the system be implemented within a mixed processor configuration (i.e., some functions of the system will be automated on a mainframe computer while others will be implemented on microcomputers)?

Potential impact on the organization. The various scenarios that are proposed for a new human/machine boundary should be judged not only on their technical merits but also on their potential impact on the organization. It is important to realize that the choice of the right system configuration (manual versus automated, centralized versus decentralized versus distributed) might have some serious repercussions on the way the organization does its business. Thus, a scenario must be viewed in the context of the overall enterprise, and the different options should be carefully explained to the users. Among other things, the automated decisions that will be made here will likely affect the users' current practices, the organizational structure of the department(s) involved, the present staffing situation, and some external organizations and possibly the company's customers or suppliers. Let's discuss each of these items in turn.

Current Business Practices. The new system can seriously affect the existing users' practices in many ways. For example, some business policies and procedures might become obsolete with the implementation of the new system. On the other hand, several new business policies and procedures might be required, not only to support the new system better but also to promote dynamically the introduction of more productive management techniques in the workplace. The users' physical environment itself might need to be rearranged to optimize the recommended human-machine interfaces and be able to accept new types of equipment and management techniques.

Organizational Structure. The organizational structure in place today might not be entirely compatible with the new organization patterns that might be introduced with the new system. New roles, responsibilities, and positions might be introduced while existing ones might become obsolete or need to be modified in a minor way. Issues like these should be carefully addressed by management because they involve the human dimension. The benefits that are expected from these changes must be thoughtfully explained to the affected personnel.

Staffing. With the introduction of the new system, the qualifications of the personnel in place might no longer be adequate. Therefore, it might be necessary to allow the staff to develop new skills to work effectively and efficiently in the new automated environment. In some instances, the company might even consider the need for a new training role within the organization.

External Organizations/Customers/Suppliers. Sometimes the new system might directly affect people outside the organization, such as customers, suppliers, or other organizations the company deals with. For example, if the organization introduces an automated order entry system whereby customers can directly order goods without having to deal with an employee, it is likely that some studies should be conducted to analyze the relative impact the new system might have on the targeted customer market prior to its implementation.

In conclusion, the selection of the most appropriate manual/automated system boundary should be made not solely based on localized productivities issues but also by evaluating the total impact the new system will have on current organizational structure and its staff members. This is necessary in order to assess how the new system can best be integrated into the current environment and how well it can coexist with other existing systems of the corporation.

3.2.7 Identify Preliminary System Performance Requirements

Task number:	PA-7
Task name:	Identify preliminary system performance requirements
Objective:	To identify the requirements that should be used to evaluate the performance of the system once in production
Input(s):	PA-3 Conceptual process model PA-4 Conceptual data model PA-5 Preliminary manual/automated system boundaries
Output(s):	PA-6 Preliminary system performance requirements

Task description:

- Identify the high-level requirements that will be used to measure the performance of the system in terms of the following:

  AUTOMATED COMPONENTS
  – Average response time expected for the online or real-time portions of the system

- Average job execution and job turnaround time expected for the batch processes of the system in general
- Overall system availability
- General system throughput capacity (e.g., total volume of online or batch transactions processed per unit of time)

MANUAL COMPONENTS

- Anticipated number of transactions processed per department per unit of time
- Estimated number of individuals needed to perform the manual processes in each user department
- Daily, monthly, or yearly average processing capabilities for each department
- Walk through the preliminary system performance requirements.

Given that the general functional characteristics of the system have been defined, we must now determine the high-level operational criteria that will be used to measure the overall performance of the system in its production environment. Initially, the system performance requirements should be defined at the level of the system as a whole rather than at the level of each specific function. The important point here is to understand the magnitude of the performance requirements for the system at large. The specific performance requirements of the most critical functions of the system will be covered in more detail, during the detailed analysis phase.

The system performance criteria should normally be expressed in terms of general response time requirements, general report turnaround requirements, general system availability requirements, and general throughput capacity requirements.

Today, several large corporations will often translate the system performance requirements into service-level agreements at implementation time. Through a formal, signed contract between the users and the MIS organization, the response time, system availability, system throughput, and report turnaround requirements are rigorously outlined. Various service-level requirements are then guaranteed for a given period of time and under certain conditions. As the development of the system progresses through the various system development life cycle phases, the quantification of the system performance requirements is gradually refined in conjunction with the users.

General response time requirements.   Typically, the response time requirements are directly associated with the online portion of the system. The response time of a transaction can be defined as the speed at which the system responds to a user's input request. It is normally measured as the delay between the moment the user presses a key on the terminal to initiate a transaction and the time it takes for the system to send back a reply on the display screen.

Usually the system response time requirements are stated in general terms, such as "95 percent of all online transactions should have an average response time between 3 and 12 seconds." Obviously, the minimum/maximum response time values will vary, depending on the type of application being implemented. Each particular situation should be discussed with the users, who must understand that there might be trade-offs between system efficiency and other software quality factors, such as reliability, security, and flexibility, among others. In general, the faster the response time, the higher the price of the system.

The definition of the general system response time requirements provides another side benefit to the analysts. Even at this early stage, the system response time requirements can already indicate that the online processes will likely need to be broken down into smaller chunks if a faster response time is requested by the users. Several factors, such as the complexity of the processes, the number of input/output data flows that are involved, and the number of data stores accessed, will lead the analysts to pay closer attention to the functions of the system that should be highly responsive.

We do not suggest that this must be done immediately. However, we contend that the analysts should educate the users on such issues in order to manage better their expectations and to ensure that their response time requirements remain realistic and achievable. The analysts should never leave the users with the impression that they will always be able to meet all their performance requirements. Rather, they should let the users know that, if for whatever reason they cannot meet these requirements, they will explain why and try to provide alternatives.

General report turnaround requirements.   The report turnaround requirements are primarily associated with the batch portion of the system. The report turnaround time is defined as the delay between the time the users submit a request for a report and the time they receive the desired report. Although the detailed requirements for reports are not yet clearly defined, it is important for the analysts to understand the general expectations of the users on this matter. In most cases, the users will accept the delivery of a standard report one day after they request it. In some cases, however, the users will need the report as soon as possible after the request. In a situation like this, such a requirement can clearly indicate the need for installing a local printer at the user site.

Depending on the geographic locations of the users, the report turnaround requirements can become very important for some systems. These requirements can outline special needs in terms of system hardware or networking facilities. It is one thing to send a report to a user who is located on the second floor of the building when the computer room is on the first floor of the very same building. It is another thing to provide the same report to a user who is 1,000 miles away. A similar type of problem might arise when the report must be distributed almost simultaneously to 20 different user locations in 20 different states and provinces (even if the report is transmitted electronically or by satellite).

General system availability requirements.   The determination of the system's availability requirements should always be carefully discussed with the users. The major reason why these requirements need careful attention is because the cost of keeping a system up and running normally tends to increase exponentially as its level of availability reaches the 95 to 100 percent range. Thus, the users and their respective managements must understand the system cost and availability trade-offs that must be taken into account during such a decision process. For example, a second computer might be required for a banking application where the system availability becomes a crucial requirement. If the main computer fails, the control of the operation will automatically switch over to a backup computer in a very short time (less than a minute). Obviously, the costs of such a complex fallback procedure should be clearly justified by the users.

The users should also determine what might be the functional dependencies with other systems. For example, if the system shares data with another application, it might be necessary to keep the application databases online far longer than what the users would have normally expected to satisfy their own operations. The level of functional dependency that will be achieved between the system and other systems might directly affect the system availability requirements.

General throughput capacity requirements.   The system throughput capacity is defined as the system capability to handle a given number of batch, online, or real-time transactions per unit of time. If the analyst develops a relatively simple system that has only two or three online transactions to process per day, then the overall system throughput capacity requirements are obviously not a crucial issue. However, if the system is expected to process 1,000 online transactions per minute, then the system throughput requirements suddenly become extremely important. They might affect not only the conceptual design of the system but also the type of hardware/software/networking equipment required to adequately support such an application.

Finally, the users should also describe the peak periods during which the system must be highly responsive to the environment it supports.

3.2.8 Identify Preliminary System Control Requirements

Task number:	PA-8
Task name:	Identify preliminary system control requirements
Objective:	To define the span and types of controls that must be integrated into the system
Input(s):	PA-3 Conceptual process model PA-4 Conceptual data model PA-5 Preliminary manual/automated system boundaries
Output(s):	PA-7 Preliminary system control requirements

Task description:

- Identify the general system control requirements in terms of
  - Security
  - Integrity

- Auditability
- Major disaster recovery situations
- Document the generalized system control requirements and describe, where applicable, the extent to which these requirements should be commonly applied across the entire system or to a specific subsystem.
- Walk through the preliminary system control requirements.

The control requirements of the system are surveyed at a high level during the preliminary analysis phase. Nonetheless, it is important to start investigating the system security, auditability, integrity, and major disaster requirements even at this early stage because they might affect the functional architecture of the system.

General security requirements.   At this point, the security requirements of the application should be analyzed in the light of their applicability to the entire system rather than at the level of a specific function. In the first place, the analysts should determine if there is a need to protect the system and to what extent. Is the information handled by the system highly sensitive? Would the absence of security controls increase the probability of a loss of profits, loss of a competitive edge, or the disclosure of valuable information to competitors? Does the company have legal or contractual obligations that must be fulfilled and that can be translated into specific security requirements?

In an attempt to overcome these potential problems, several organizations have developed their own security guidelines in which the company's data are classified into different categories of information, each having a specific level of sensitivity directly proportional to its importance. The different levels of sensitivity are often defined by such terms as nonconfidential, confidential, restricted, secret, top-secret, and so forth. Thus, the information that is vital to the proper functioning of the organization should be treated by the system in accordance with the established security guidelines.

Typically, the security requirements are either physical or procedural. They generally cover three different aspects of the system: hazards, protection of computer equipment, and control of accesses to the system itself via the use of terminals or various communication lines.

Hazards.   Hazards are related to unexpected events. Fire, sabotage, riot, vandalism, and power failure are examples.

Protection of Computer Equipment.   The protection of computer equipment is normally handled with physical techniques, such as controlling physical access to the computer areas, installing computer equipment in remote locations, and having emergency auxiliary power units to circumvent power failures.

Control of Access to the System.   In most cases the types of security requirements that the analysts will normally deal with are those related to the prevention of unauthorized user access to the system. Several different techniques can be utilized to minimize such risks. For example, access to the terminals can be physically controlled simply by isolating the terminals in a restricted area. The authorization to use an online system via a terminal can also be granted to selected people with the use of various passwords, at the level of the system or even at the level of specific functions. (Today, several software security packages will automatically provide similar access controls.)

Also, the users can have limited access capabilities when they use the system. For instance, some user might only be allowed to browse through information, whereas others can also update or delete the information they have access to.

At first glance, identification of the security requirements may seem to be a relatively straightforward process. Nevertheless, the analysts should never underestimate them. In one specific instance, a large corporation had installed its most sophisticated mainframe computer equipment in the basement of a building. The security measures that were put in place to control physical access to this remote location were quite impressive. State-of-the-art technology was used. Nothing was neglected in terms of security features. There were security guards, magnetic cards to open doors, closed-circuit TV monitors—the works. Unfortunately, a very simple point was overlooked by everyone—it was probably much too obvious—the possibility of water damage. What had to happen did happen. One day, a severe thunderstorm hit the region and in a matter of an hour, the entire basement was flooded, seriously damaging the equipment.

General integrity requirements.   Integrity requirements are primarily identified through the validity and correctness of the information that is fed or manipulated by the system and consequently its capacity to detect and handle events that can lead to the processing of incorrect or invalid data.

Integrity requirements can normally be defined by specifying the degree of data correctness and accuracy required by the system when it manipulates data. Another requirement can be the identification of the level of tolerance the system should have when detecting errors. Should the system reject the data in error and continue processing valid data? What should be the system error-checking and error-handling mechanisms? Which data entities are the most important in terms of integrity? Are there any specific data elements that would require a high degree of data integrity while other data elements simply do not need such a high level of integrity?

General auditability requirements.   The auditability requirements should not only be defined with the users but also in conjunction with the auditing staff, if necessary. Frequently, especially for financial systems, legal constraints that oblige the users to keep track of specific information for auditing purposes are required. The auditing requirements might even identify the need for the users to archive specific data elements for a determined period of time. In some cases, the system must also be able to provide an audit trail of all the transactions it processed during the day.

General disaster recovery requirements.   If the system is essential to the proper functioning of the organization, then a plan of action should be put in place to include it in its corporate MIS disaster prevention and recovery plan. If such a plan does not exist in the organization, then the development team, with the users, should investigate the feasibility of developing one internally or dealing with a third party to provide proper support in this area. The users should define the maximum tolerable system outage they can cope with, without seriously impacting their business operations. What is the maximum mean time between failures that can be tolerated for this system? What should be the expected mean time to repair the system? Selective system outage alternatives can also be explored with the users for disaster prevention and recovery. While the unavailability of online transactions can cause some difficulties to the users, their environment could still remain partly operational if the batch system transactions are still working properly. Would such an approach be an acceptable scenario?

3.2.9 Identify Preliminary Data Storage Requirements

Task number:	PA-9	
Task name:	Identify preliminary data storage requirements	
Objective:	To obtain the preliminary figures for data storage requirements	
Input(s):	PA-3	Conceptual process model
	PA-4	Conceptual data model
	PA-5	Preliminary manual/automated system boundaries
	PA-6	Preliminary system performance requirements
	PA-7	Preliminary system control requirements
Output(s):	PA-8	Preliminary data storage requirements

Task description:
- Identify the preliminary data storage requirements of the system. Include the initial size of the files and/or databases that will be created or updated by the system. Also include the projected storage estimates for their initial growth rate, covering a two- to five-year horizon.
- Identify the expected data retention requirements for each file and/or subject database.
- Document the preliminary data storage requirements of the system, along with the techniques used to derive the space estimates.
- Walk through the preliminary data storage requirements of the system.

The identification of the system data storage requirements cannot be done in detail at this point because the files and databases of the application are not yet designed. Nevertheless, it is important to estimate the approximate size of the databases and files that will be required to store the data produced and manipulated by the system. For a large application that manipulates thousands or millions of records, this information can become vital to the success of the project. Sometimes it might also take a substantial lead time (between 2 and 12 months) for an organization to order, receive, and install new hardware equipment, such as disk drives, tape drives, and the like. As a matter of fact, if the new system requires substantial main memory capacity, it might become necessary to upgrade the memory of the central computer or even to order a brand-new one.

One of the simplest ways to estimate the order of magnitude volume of data requirements is to gather some statistical information about the conceptual data model. The analyst estimates the average number of occurrences that each entity shown in the data model can have, along with their data attributes.[9] With this information, the approximate number of characters that will be required to store the information provided by each entity can be calculated. The total amount of space required to store all the entities on computerized files can then be calculated. While doing this, the analyst should also take into consideration the data retention requirements of the system, which might directly affect these calculations. For example, the users might want to keep some specific information on computerized files for a five-year period and other information only for one year or less.

3.2.10 Identify Preliminary Hardware/Software/Networking Requirements

Task number:	PA-10
Task name:	Identify preliminary hardware/software/networking requirements
Objective:	To define the generalized hardware/software/networking requirements that are necessary to configure the system properly
Input(s):	PA-3 Conceptual process model PA-4 Conceptual data model PA-5 Preliminary manual/automated system boundaries PA-6 Preliminary system performance requirements PA-7 Preliminary system control requirements PA-8 Preliminary data storage requirements
Output(s):	PA-9 Preliminary hardware/software/networking requirements

Task description:
- Identify the new classes of hardware that will be required to support the new system.
- Identify the new classes of software that will be required to support the mechanized functions and data of the new system.

[9]The variations in the number of occurrences are particularly important. For this reason, it might be wise to ask for the minimum, average, and maximum numbers of occurrences that an entity can have. This information will prove to be extremely valuable when designing the physical databases of the system.

- Identify the geographic locations where the new system will be used. Describe in general terms how the functions and data will be processed and/or distributed at each location. Describe the new data communication facilities that will be required to support the operations of the proposed system.
- Consolidate the hardware/software/networking requirements to ensure that they are compatible among themselves and with the existing hardware/software/networking facilities of the organization.
- Walk through the preliminary hardware/software/networking requirements.

Identifying these requirements might not be necessary if the proposed system can be implemented using the hardware/software/networking facilities currently in place. If, on the contrary, it is determined that the new system will require some new types of hardware/software/networking facilities, it automatically becomes necessary to define the general nature of these requirements. Sometimes this can be difficult because the information the development team has gathered so far about the previous system requirements might still be incomplete. Nevertheless, it is important to understand the magnitude of these new requirements and the impact they can have on the current environment.

Total resource load estimates. The first step consists in analyzing the statistical information that was gathered so far on the estimated number of transactions that must be processed by the system, the estimated volume of data to be remembered by the system, and how often the functions of the system will be performed per unit of time. If the new system will replace an existing system, some of these statistics can be obtained directly from the users or from the systems people who support the present application. Projections might have to be made for the functions of the new system that were not supported by the old system.

If the development team determines that the existing computerized environment can absorb the anticipated resource load, then it might not be necessary to continue this task. On the other hand, if it becomes evident that the existing environment cannot absorb the extra workload, then the development team should contact the different groups of professionals who are responsible for supporting the overall computerized environment and inform them about the current situation as soon as possible in the software engineering life cycle.

New software/hardware facilities. If the proposed system needs new classes of hardware/software items, these should be identified as accurately and as soon as possible. For example, the new system might necessitate the acquisition of a new software facility, such as a database management system, which is not supported in the existing environment, a new report generator tool, or even a new operating system. Some additional types of hardware equipment might equally be required like new terminals or new printers. There might be a need for some special hardware equipment that should be entirely dedicated to supporting the new application.

It is very important to ensure that the new hardware and software facilities being considered are indeed compatible with each other and most preferably with the existing environment, too.

Networking facilities.   The geographic locations where the new system will be installed must be identified by the development team. The information gathered at this point will be used later on to design the communication network of the system. It will also be very useful to determine the type of computer equipment that should be installed in the central or remote sites, in the case where a decentralized or distributed structure is selected to implement the system.

Each distinct site where potential users might utilize the system must be properly described. In principle, the information provided should include the geographic location (country, state or province, city, building, floor), the different categories of users involved, the type of computer equipment in place, the environmental conditions of the site, and the functions and data that will be processed at each site. At this stage, this information should be sufficient to provide a general indication of the types of communication requirements that might be needed for adequate support of the system. During the next development phases, these requirements will be progressively refined to identify more precisely the types of communication links that will be required to link each physical site properly.

3.2.11 Develop Request for Proposal (Optional)

Task number:	PA-11	
Task name:	Develop request for proposal (optional)	
Objective:	To develop a request soliciting vendors to submit a package proposal that satisfies users' needs	
Input(s):	SU-7	Preliminary system implementation alternatives
	PA-3	Conceptual process model
	PA-4	Conceptual data model
	PA-5	Preliminary manual/automated system boundaries
	PA-6	Preliminary system performance requirements
	PA-7	Preliminary system control requirements
	PA-8	Preliminary data storage requirements
	PA-9	Preliminary hardware/software/networking requirements
Output(s):	PA-10	Request for proposal

Task description:
- Review the preliminary system implementation alternatives that were produced during the survey phase.
- If acquiring a commercial application package is still being considered as a viable alternative to in-house development, perform the following activities:

    – Review and refine the original list of candidate vendors.

    – Develop a request for proposal (RFP) that describes the users' needs for a new computerized system.

- Walk through the request for proposal.
- Release the RFP to selected vendors.

The organization might find that a package solution is a viable and economical alternative to a custom system. However, the users, and even systems people, should not opt for the package solution for the wrong reasons:

- The users do not want to spend the time necessary to describe their business problems and needs properly.
- The users or systems people feel there is no need to discuss the functionality of their present system because it eventually will be replaced.
- The users are uncertain about what they want. Therefore, the package approach will dictate, by default, their business requirements.
- The users do not want to spend time in a detailed analysis of the functionality offered by the candidate packages. The first package examined is selected without any further research.
- The users hope that a package will magically resolve their current operational problems.

The final decision to acquire a package should always be postponed until the users' real needs are properly identified and well understood by the development team. The system requirements resulting from this preliminary study are essential for effective evaluation of the ability of the candidate packages to solve the current problems. The wrong software package applied to the wrong business problems will likely create more harm than good and even might aggravate the current situation.

Furthermore, the resulting list of system requirements will become handy when determining the areas where the package might need some additional customization. Very seldom do packages match completely all the stated requirements, in all designated areas. Consequently, they might need some minor to major modifications. However, if too many significant changes become necessary to meet the users' needs, the cost of these modifications might quickly wipe out the benefits of acquiring the package.

The acquisition of a commercial application package might definitely offer some potential advantages but also some potential disadvantages as well. Figure 3.5 summarizes some of these.

If, after weighing the pros and cons of acquiring a package, the option of buying a commercial application package is still viable, the development team should perform three major activities: (1) revise the list of potential vendors that was developed during the survey phase, (2) develop and issue a request for proposal to prospective vendors, and (3) develop a standard list of selection criteria that will be used to judge the merits of each candidate package.

Advantages	Disadvantages
Reduction of the application backlog	Package is inadequate in the support of the users' needs and requires substantial modifications
Cost-effectiveness (acquisition costs lower than development costs)	Vendor goes out of business
The in-house development experts can concentrate their efforts on developing internal systems	Vendor does not adequately support the package
Faster delivery of the system to the users	Package does not integrate well into the environment and is not parameterized
Maintenance costs shared by several organizations	MIS perceives the acquisition of a package as a lost opportunity to acquire new development skills
Pretested system if in existence since several years and used by several organizations	Vendor does not evolve the package over time

Figure 3.5 Advantages and disadvantages of acquiring a commercial application package

Revise the list of potential vendors.   The process of identifying potential candidates that might have a package solution that can satisfy the users' needs began during the survey phase. At that time, a brief list of candidate vendors was probably developed, assuming that the acquisition of a package was considered by the development team and the users as a viable alternative to a custom system. This list should now be reviewed to ensure that it is reasonably complete and is representative of the types of packages that are available in the marketplace. If not, the team should do some research to identify additional candidate packages. Several sources can be used to locate these candidates. They include

- Directories specializing in software packages, such as *Auerbach Applications Software* and *International Computer Programs* (*ICP*) publications
- Various computer and trade magazines—*Computerworld*, *Datamation*, *IBM PC*, *IEEE Software Engineering*, for example
- Hardware vendors that normally supply a list of software programs and packages that run on their processors
- Professional user groups that might provide software directories for their members, such as SHARE

While the detailed list of candidate vendors is being compiled, the development team can study the functional capabilities of the various vendors' packages and a preliminary screening can be done to eliminate quickly those products that clearly do not meet the mandatory requirements of the system. For example, packages that cannot run on the existing computer configurations should be discarded, unless the organization is willing to acquire a new type of computer or software facilities.

Develop a request for proposal.   Since the acquisition of a software package is a very critical operation, it is necessary to adopt a disciplined approach before, during, and after the selection process. A request for proposal is an official document submitted to prospective vendors that might have a package solution that can potentially satisfy the stated users' needs. The RFP should contain all the information a prospective vendor will need from the requestor to submit a proposal that will hopefully satisfy user needs.

One of the major advantages that an RFP approach offers versus a less stringent method of selecting a software package is the attention the users will give to this process. The users have no other alternative than to identify and describe their needs in a careful manner. The simple fact that the RFP is sent to outside companies will probably be sufficient to motivate them to prepare a high-quality document. The more precise and complete the RFP, the higher the chances for the enterprise to acquire a software package that best meets user requirements.

The RFP provides an additional side benefit that should not be overlooked. In principle, the vendors should respond to the proposal in the standard reply format outlined in the RFP. With such an approach, it is far more difficult for a vendor to hide potential weaknesses inherent in its product while at the same time overemphasizing its strongest points. The vendor has no alternative other than to demonstrate clearly that its package can adequately satisfy the functional and operational requirements identified in the RFP.

The RFP should be structured in a standard format that is easy to understand. Figure 3.6 shows a suggested RFP table of contents. It should be adapted to suit the particular needs of the organization.

Covering Letter.   A covering letter should always accompany the RFP to describe the purpose and the objectives of the RFP, the time limit the vendor has to reply (normally between 30 to 60 days, depending on the size of the RFP), and the name of the person who should be contacted to obtain additional information or support, if required. It should also include, if necessary, a statement explaining the confidential nature of the information provided in the RFP.

Title Page.   The title page indicates the title of the RFP. It should be descriptive about the kind of system wanted by the users.

Table of Contents.   The table of contents provides the vendor with all the information necessary to locate quickly any specific section within the document.

Structure of the RFP.   This section of the RFP should contain a brief description on how the RFP is organized.

Situation of the System.   This section should provide a brief description of the company and its background. Also, the proposed system should be situated in its current organizational context, along with a brief statement describing the intended objectives for acquiring a software package.

System Requirements Description.   This section constitutes the heart of the RFP. It contains all the major system requirements that should be satisfied by the package. These can be divided into the following three categories:

1. Functional and data requirements. The first category depicts the functions that the package must support, prioritized by order of importance. It also describes the data requirements of the system.

                            Request for Proposal (RFP)
1. Covering Letter
2. Title Page
3. Table of Contents
4. Structure of the RFP
5. Situation of the System
6. System Requirements Description
    6.1   Category 1: Functional and Data Requirements
    6.2   Category 2: Operational Requirements
    6.3   Category 3: Miscellaneous Requirements
7. RFP Reply Format and Evaluation Criteria
8. Appendix

Figure 3.6   RFP table of contents

2. Operational requirements.   The second category outlines the major operational characteristics of the system, such as the performance, security, integrity, auditability, data storage, and hardware/software/networking requirements. The constraints that might be imposed on the system solution should also be clearly covered in this section. For example, the software package must be compatible with the database management system in place. It must run on a certain type of computer configuration, or it must be compatible with a particular networking facility.

3. Miscellaneous requirements. The third category covers any additional requirements that are not necessarily functional or operational. However, they are still important and should be satisfied by the candidate package vendors. The extent to which the packages can satisfy these requirements might likely influence the selection of a particular package over another, especially when they are more or less functionally equivalent. These requirements might include several items, such as

- Interfaces with other systems
- The quality of the package documentation
- Vendor service and support considerations
- The ergonomical characteristics offered by the package, such as flexibility, maintainability, and ease of use
- Extra features, such as support of more than one language or foreign currency
- Naming conventions

RFP Reply Format and Evaluation Criteria.   This part of the RFP describes the desired reply format vendors should follow when preparing their quotations. Ideally, it should also explain how the vendor's proposal will be evaluated by the organization and which selection criteria will be used during the final selection process.

Appendix.   This section should contain any additional information—data flow diagrams, entity-relationship diagrams and the like—that might enhance the comprehension of the request for proposal.

Develop a standard list of selection criteria.   It is important to let the vendors know the relative value the organization assigns to each specific requirement listed in the RFP. In the first place, the package must satisfy the mandatory functional requirements that have been identified by the development team. The importance the organization assigns to the system operational and miscellaneous requirements must also be clearly spelled out. The list of evaluation criteria will probably vary from one project to another based on user needs. The package evaluation checklist provided in Appendix A should be useful in identifying the desirable criteria that should be retained for the final selection process.

Once the development team has decided which selection criteria will be used to evaluate uniformly all the vendor proposals, the next step is to assign a value to each criterion. The next section describes a simple technique that can be used to assign weight factors to the individual criteria.

3.2.12 Evaluate Vendor Proposals (Optional)

Task number:	PA-12
Task name:	Evaluate vendor proposals (optional)
Objective:	To review the vendor responses to the request for proposal and select the most appropriate candidate package
Input(s):	PA-10 Request for proposal
Output(s):	PA-11 Package evaluation

Task description:

- Conduct a detailed examination of the proposals submitted by the vendors.
- Determine how closely each package meets the requirements, evaluating at the same time their strengths and limitations.
- Consolidate the findings and select, based on the overall ratings assigned to each package, the candidate that best satisfies the users' requirements. Document the findings.
- Walk through the major findings from the package evaluation process.

Weighing the selection criteria.   In the previous task, the development team determined the major selection criteria to be used to evaluate all the candidate packages. The next step consists of assigning a weighting factor to each specific requirement, based on the relative importance the organization assigns to each. The higher the weight, the more crucial the system requirement. Typically, most requirements fall into one of the following classifications.

Essential: If the vendor does not already offer this essential characteristic or cannot provide it without extensively modifying its package, then the vendor should be excluded from the selection process.

Important: In principle, such a requirement should be satisfied by the package with an accuracy level between 75 and 100 percent. A weighting value between 5 and 10 points should be assigned to this category.

Nice to have: A package that does not have a nice-to-have feature might not adversely affect the function of the system. A weighting value of 1 to 3 points should be assigned to this category.

The assignment of weighting factors to the selection criteria is not always straightforward. Sometimes it can be difficult to decide on the relative value of a selection criterion. Because of this, the evaluation team must be very careful not to assign high values to minor selection criteria. If this happens, then the sum of the weights of these minor criteria might neutralize the weight of an important requirement.

In some situations, the number of selection criteria for a large and complex software is so large that it becomes impractical to assign a weighting factor to each of them. When this situation occurs, the selection criteria should be clustered into different groups and each group assigned a weighting factor. For example, the evaluation team might decide to use some high-level selection criteria categories such as functional considerations (functions to be supported), ergonomical considerations (ease of use, quality of documentation), operational considerations (performance, volume throughput, storage capacity), structural considerations (modularity, maintainability, expandability), and so on.

Rating the selection criteria.   Once the system requirements are properly weighted, the next step is the creation of a rating scale. The rating scale is used to determine to which extent the package satisfies the system requirements. A high rating means that the package satisfies a particular requirement very closely; a low rating is just the opposite. A standard rating scale might have the following characteristics:

- Satisfies the system requirement perfectly (4 points)
- Satisfies the system requirement except for a few minor items (3 points)
- Satisfies the system requirement in general, although some important characteristics might be missing (2 points)
- Does not satisfy several important aspects of the requirement (1 point)
- Does not satisfy the requirement at all (0 points)

Figure 3.7 shows an example of a selection criteria table that can be used to evaluate a package. Each rating value assigned to a requirement is multiplied by the weight assigned to the requirement. The sum of the resulting values will determine the final score allotted to the package for meeting or not meeting the requirements. All the packages are evaluated the same way. Figure 3.8 illustrates a slightly different approach, where the detailed selection criteria are grouped into different categories.

Final evaluation process.   Once the vendor proposals have been received, the final evaluation process can begin. Specific weights and ratings should be established for each requirement if not already done. The packages are then examined to determine how well they meet the stated requirements. Finally, each package is assigned a total score. This score represents the total number of points a particular vendor package has amassed during the evaluation process.

The selection team should not be overly concerned, for now, with the cost of the packages. It is true that cost is a critical factor in the evaluation process, however, the team should concentrate now on evaluating the ability of each package to meet the selection criteria. If there is a large variation between the cost of two packages that more or less offer the same level of functionality, then the cost factor might become key in determining the final choices.

Selection Criteria	Weight Factor	Proposal 1		Proposal 2		Proposal 3	
		R	WR	R	WR	R	WR
Function *a*							
Function *b*							
Function *c*							
...							
Function *x*							
Maintainability							
Ease of use							
...							
Total score	100%						

Legend: R = rating; WR = weighted rating (weight factor × rating).

Figure 3.7   Package selection criteria table

The level of rigor and depth applied to the package preselection and evaluation processes should be proportional to the importance of the package for satisfying the needs of the organization as well as its price. Common sense dictates that
a $5,000 package might not need the same level of attention and detail that a
$500,000 package would require. Furthermore, if the request for proposal forces the
vendors to spend too much time answering an overly complex questionnaire or arbi-

Selection Criteria	Weight Factor	Proposal 1		Proposal 2		Proposal 3	
		R	WR	R	WR	R	WR
Functional requirements Function 1 ... Function *x*							
Contractual requirements ...							
Ergonomy requirements ...							
Technical considerations ...							
Total score	100%						

Legend: R = rating; WR = weighted rating (weight factor × rating).

Figure 3.8   Package selection criteria by global categories

trarily constrain them to follow unrealistic procedures, they might simply decide to withdraw. This can be true especially for small software vendors that cannot always afford the extra overhead associated with an exhaustive RFP process. Yet their software package can still be a very good product that potentially could very well serve the needs of the application.

Wherever possible, the detailed evaluation process should be performed at two different levels and by two different categories of people. The functional level is user oriented; the technical level is systems oriented. On one hand, the users should carefully examine the functional features of the package. They must assess not only how well the package supports their desired business functions but also such less tangible factors as ease of use, flexibility, reliability, and the quality of vendor support. On the other hand, the systems people should concentrate their efforts on evaluating the technical characteristics of the package. How well designed is it? Does it use a modularized architecture? Is it easily modifiable or maintainable? What about the quality of its system documentation? Is the database structure easily modifiable? What type of database management system is used? This dual evaluation prevents situations where the users select a package that functionally speaking meets all their criteria but technically speaking is clearly unacceptable, or vice versa.

Before or during the evaluation process, members of the evaluation team might consider different options to familiarize themselves with the candidate packages.

1. Vendors can be invited to make a presentation on their packages. These working sessions can be very useful to establish a direct contact between the organization and the vendor and at the same time to determine the most important characteristics provided by the package, from the vendor's point of view. However, the purpose of the presentation as well as its objectives should be clearly conveyed to the vendor before the session. For example, if the evaluation team plans to ask questions not only on the type of functions provided by the package but also detailed questions of a technical nature, then the vendor should be made aware of this, for this means that in addition to a marketing representative, a technical representative should also be present.

2. Organizations that already use the package can be visited. This is probably the best way to examine the package in a real-life environment.

3. Some vendors might propose to install their package in your environment for a predetermined trial period.

At the end of the evaluation process, the number of candidates should be narrowed down to two or three vendors. A more in-depth examination of the packages can then be conducted, if necessary.[10] Toward the end of the evaluation process, the cost factor is finally addressed in more detail. Cost estimates should be devel-

---

[10]For that purpose, the package evaluation checklist provided in Appendix A provides additional insights as to what important points should be covered when selecting an application package.

oped for the most likely candidates. Besides the price of the package itself, other costs should also be evaluated. They include, among other things

- Costs of modifications that are required to satisfy the essential user requirements
- Costs of additional hardware/software/networking configurations that might be required to support the new package
- Training costs
- Conversion costs
- Maintenance costs
- Documentation costs
- Operating costs
- User support costs

3.2.13 Select Most Suitable System Implementation Solution

Task number:	PA-13
Task name:	Select most suitable system implementation solution
Objective:	To select the most appropriate system solution that satisfies users' needs
Input(s):	SU-7 Preliminary system implementation alternatives PA-5 Preliminary manual/automated system boundaries PA-11 Package evaluation
Output(s):	PA-12 Selected system implementation solution

Task description:

- Review the alternative system implementation solutions that are being considered, including the acquisition of a commercial application package, if appropriate.
- Evaluate the extent to which each particular system implementation solution suits the users' needs, describing its major characteristics and its related advantages or disadvantages.
- Compare the proposed implementation solutions, emphasizing their respective advantages and disadvantages, with the other implementation alternatives.
- Select one system implementation solution that will be further described during the detailed analysis phase.
- Describe, if necessary, the approach that was used to compare and evaluate the alternatives.
- Walk through the rationale behind the selection of a single system implementation solution over the other scenarios.

Through the identification of different manual/automated system boundaries scenarios, the users, with the assistance of the development team, by now should have settled on a preferred functional solution (i.e., what functions of the system should be mechanized by this project). The next step consists in selecting a unique system implementation solution, since the cost of conducting the detailed analysis phase with more than one system implementation alternative would be far too prohibitive.

First, the proposed technical alternatives should be evaluated independently of one another, based on their advantages and disadvantages. Once this is done, they should then be compared together. Some of the criteria that should be taken into consideration during the evaluation process are the ability of each system solution to satisfy the project business objectives, the ability of each system solution to resolve user problems, the economics of each system solution,[11] an assessment of the business and technical risks of each system solution, and the existence of possible resource and schedule constraints on the project. In addition, the impact that each proposed system solution might have on the current organizational structure is very important. The human aspect of the final decision-making process should not be neglected by the development team, especially if major organizational changes might take place with the introduction of the new system.

Various implementation options can be considered by the organization. For example, it is still possible for the organization to maintain the status quo and decide not to develop a new system, at least for the time being. On the other hand, if the expected benefits warrant the continuation of the project and if a package solution is considered, the decision to buy a software package or to develop a new system in-house may need to be further discussed, assuming that there is at least one package that seems able to satisfy the essential user requirements.

The make-or-buy decision involves many factors that quite often will vary from one organization to another. These factors will not carry the same weight for all organizations because business needs often differ considerably from one organization to another. For instance, one organization simply might not be able to afford to wait three years before starting to use a new system that would be developed in-house. On the other hand, another organization might decide to develop the system in-house to ensure a closer fit with its existing environment. Nevertheless, the development team should always base its decision on the assumption that the organization will likely be married to the new system for at least 5 to 15 years (if it is a reasonably large system that has several interfaces with other systems).

3.2.14 Recommend System Development Strategy

Task number:	PA-14
Task name:	Recommend system development strategy
Objective:	To define the most appropriate approach to develop the system

[11]Factors such as the development, operating, and maintenance cost-effectiveness of each proposed alternatives should be carefully examined by the team.

Input(s):	PA-3	Conceptual process model
	PA-4	Conceptual data model
	PA-5	Preliminary manual/automated system boundaries
	PA-12	Selected system solution
Output(s):	PA-13	Preliminary system development strategy

Task description:

- Review the users' needs, the project business objectives, and all the system requirements deliverables that have been developed so far for this project. Based on the priorities set by the organization, identify the feasibility and appropriateness of gradually developing and implementing the proposed system one piece at a time.
- Describe the rationale for implementing the system using a multiple release approach. Describe the potential impact that such an approach can have on the different interfaces that exist with the current system, as well as on the different user departments that might be affected by this strategy.
- Formalize and document the recommended system development strategy.
- Walk through the preliminary system development strategy.

Basically, there are two fundamental approaches to developing and implementing a system. One approach consists of constructing and implementing the entire system all at once. With the second approach, the system is developed and implemented one segment at a time. Each segment is identified as a *release*.

Developing a large system by release offers several advantages:

- It reduces the complexity inherent in the development of a large and complex system.
- It minimizes the risk of developing a huge, monolithic system only to find out too late that it does not meet the users' true requirements.
- It provides the users with the functions they most urgently need before the whole system actually gets implemented.
- It simplifies the distribution of labor and optimizes the utilization of the available resources.

On the other hand, the release concept might add some overhead to the development process because of the extra effort that might be required from the development team to ensure that the different releases of the system remain consistent and synchronized with one another.

Several factors should be considered for grouping the system functions and data into various releases, including

- The affinities that might exist between the various functions and data entities of the system (i.e., various functions using the same data)
- The dependencies that might exist among the numerous functions of the system

- The necessity for the users to implement some particular functions sooner than others to resolve an urgent problem
- The clear distinction between the manual versus automated functions of the system
- The availability of sufficient staff resources to develop the entire system at once
- The type of possibly different computer configurations that might be used to operate various functions of the same system in the production environment (i.e., workstations, minis, and/or mainframes)
- The distribution of functions and data across several geographically dispersed locations
- The size and complexity of the system functions and data
- The physical partitioning of the automated functions into batch, online, or real-time processes
- The benefits that might be expected with the earlier implementation of a particular function of the system

A final criterion that should be taken into consideration is the timing factor. As a yardstick, ideally a release should not take more than 12 to 18 months to develop, test, and implement its functions.

The next step consists of deciding when and how each development release should be implemented. Figure 3.9 shows the relationship between the release concept and the various phases of the system development life cycle.

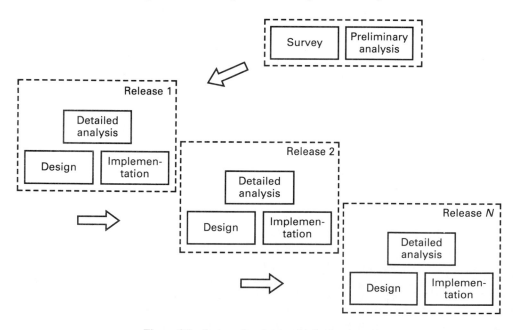

Figure 3.9   System development release concept

Given that the technical deliverables of the preliminary analysis phase have been produced from the viewpoint of the whole system, the system can then be partitioned into several development releases. Subsequently, the different releases of the system can be developed either in parallel, if sufficient staff personnel are available, or in sequence with or without overlapping. Nevertheless, from there on each particular release is gradually implemented through the execution of the next three development phases: detaiied analysis, design, and implementation.[12]

Furthermore, the installation of the various system releases can be done in different ways when several user sites are affected by the project. Some of the possible installation scenarios follow:

- A particular release is installed in each user site simultaneously.
- A particular release is installed in only one user site initially. Once the major problems are ironed out, the release is then implemented at the other user sites.
- All the releases of the system are first developed and implemented at a unique user site. Then the whole system is implemented at each other user site.

If the development-by-release concept is retained for the project at hand, it might be necessary to develop some additional interfaces for the system. This task might be required to allow the implementation of a release of the new system while supporting at the same time the operations of some portions of the old system. For example, it might be necessary to develop some temporary conversion programs that reformat some of the new transactions processed by the new system release into a format compatible with the old system.

The interfaces with other systems should also be very carefully considered while the system development-by-release strategy is being constructed. For instance, should all the interfaces be established at once or at different points in time? Lastly, while developing the release strategy, particular attention should be given to the hardware/software/networking requirements that were identified during this phase. For example, it might be necessary to acquire some hardware equipment ahead of time to support a specific release of the system. In fact, the development team should cross-reference all existing system requirements against each specific release to ensure that they will be properly addressed.

3.2.15 Refine Cost-Benefit Analysis

Task number:	PA-15
Task name:	Refine cost-benefit analysis
Objective:	To refine the cost-benefit analysis that was developed during the survey phase

[12]This strategy presupposes that the development team and the users are reasonably confident that the architecture of the system (i.e., data and functional processes) is relatively well defined and stabilized at this stage. Therefore, the dependencies and interfaces that might exist between each release are reasonably well described and well understood by all parties.

Input(s):	SU-8	Preliminary cost-benefit analysis
	PA-12	Selected system implementation solution
	PA-13	Preliminary system development strategy
Output(s):	PA-14	Cost-benefit analysis (refined)

Task description:
- Refine the estimated costs of operating and maintaining the current system.
- Refine the estimated costs of developing and implementing the new system, based on the recommended system implementation solution and system development strategy.
- Refine the estimated costs of operating the new system in production.
- Refine the tangible and intangible benefits that are anticipated with the installation of the new system.
- If necessary, describe the technique that was used to derive the refined cost-benefit figures.
- Walk through the cost-benefit analysis deliverable.

A preliminary cost-benefit analysis was initially conducted during the survey phase. At that point, though, the cost-benefit estimates derived were probably very gross estimates. This is understandable, given that the information gathered during the survey phase was incomplete. The objective was to produce order of magnitude figures to provide management with a broad indication of the expected costs and benefits of the project.

One more time, the development team should focus its attention on the cost-benefit analysis, but concentrating this time on the selected system implementation solution. The aim is to determine if the proposed solution will generate enough tangible benefits to outweigh its associated development and operating costs. These estimates should be more precise because the preliminary analysis has proceeded further in determining the nature of the system, its boundaries, and its high-level functional and operating requirements.

However, the cost-benefit figures should still be evaluated in ranges at this point. The estimates for the detailed analysis phase could be precise (e.g., ±15 percent), but the estimate for the remainder of the project cannot yet be developed in a totally accurate manner. The detailed cost estimate should be produced toward the end of the detailed analysis phase, when the conceptual design of the system is completed, along with the detailed definition of the hardware/software/networking requirements and of the system testing and conversion strategies.

If a development-by-release approach is recommended by the development team, then the costs of developing the system should be calculated for each release, examining the functions and data entities that it comprises. The related benefits should also be calculated for each release. Finally, the costs of operating and maintaining the new system once in production should also be estimated.[13]

---

[13]For more information on how to perform a cost-benefit analysis, refer to Yourdon [1989].

3.3 REFERENCES

COAD, P., and E. YOURDON. 1990. *Object-Oriented Analysis*. Yourdon Press Computing Series. Englewood Cliffs, N.J.: Prentice Hall.

COOPER, J. 1989. *Computer and Communications Security,* New York: McGraw-Hill.

DICKINSON, Brian. 1981. *Developing Structured Systems: A Methodology Using Structured Techniques.* New York: Yourdon Press.

FRANTZEN, T., and K. McEvoy. 1988. *A Game Plan for Systems Development.* Yourdon Press Computing Series. Englewood Cliffs, N.J.: Prentice Hall.

HATLEY, D. J., and I. A. PIRBHAI. 1987. *Strategies for Real-Time System Specification.* New York: Dorset House.

MARTIN, JAMES. 1981. *Design and Strategy for Distributed Data Processing.* Englewood Cliffs, N.J.: Prentice Hall.

————. 1983. *Managing the Data-Base Environment.* Englewood Cliffs, N.J.: Prentice Hall.

McMENAMIN, STEPHEN, and JOHN PALMER. 1984. *Essential Systems Analysis.* New York: Yourdon Press.

MELLOR, S. J., and P.T. WARD. 1985. *Structured Development for Real-Time Systems,* Vols. 1–3. New York: Yourdon Press.

MEYER, B., 1988. *Object-Oriented Software Construction.* Hertfordshire, U.K.: Prentice Hall International (U.K.) Ltd.

YOURDON, EDWARD. 1982. *Managing the System Life Cycle.* New York: Yourdon Press.

————. 1989. *Modern Structured Analysis.* Yourdon Press Computing Series. Englewood Cliffs, N.J.: Prentice Hall.

4

Detailed Analysis Phase

4.1 PURPOSE

The prime purpose of the detailed analysis phase is to further describe the system solution that was retained at the end of the preliminary analysis study to satisfy user needs.[1] During this phase, the conceptual process and data models are gradually refined and augmented with the detailed functional and data requirements of the new system. The functions carried out by the system are depicted with lower-level data flow diagrams until they can no longer be decomposed into smaller units without losing their integrity (i.e., the atomic or primitive level). The details of their internal processing logic are subsequently documented using several specification tools, such as structured English, decision trees, decision tables, and state-transition diagrams. The data requirements depicted in the entity-relationship diagrams are normalized to the third normal form. In addition to the modeling process, more details are gradually grafted onto the operational characteristics of the new system. The hardware/software/networking, control, data storage, and performance requirements of the system are carried out to their lowest level of detail.

---

[1]If the development team, in conjunction with the users, opted for developing and implementing the system one piece at a time, using the release concept, then this phase will focus not on the entire system but rather on each individual release of the system.

In preparation for the design phase, the development team must also specify the high-level strategies concerning the best possible ways for testing the system, converting the data from the old to the new format, training the staff, and installing the software application itself. These strategies will serve as a baseline during the design phase on which to develop detailed plans of action that adequately address these important issues.

Table 4.1 summarizes the major technical tasks that are normally conducted during the detailed analysis phase, along with the anticipated technical deliverables. Figure 4.1 pictorially illustrates at a high level the relationships that exist among the individual tasks of the detailed analysis phase.

TABLE 4.1   DETAILED ANALYSIS PHASE TECHNICAL TASKS AND DELIVERABLES

Technical Tasks	*Technical Deliverables*
1. Create functional process model	1. Functional process model
2. Create functional data model	2. Functional data model
3. Develop data conversion strategy	3. System data conversion strategy (preliminary)
4. Develop testing strategy (preliminary)	4. System testing strategy (preliminary)
5. Develop training strategy (preliminary)	5. System training strategy (preliminary)
6. Refine hardware/software/networking requirements	6. Detailed hardware/software/networking requirements
7. Refine system control requirements	7. Detailed system control requirements
8. Refine data storage requirements	8. Detailed data storage requirements
9. Refine system performance requirements	9. Detailed system performance requirements
10. Define environmental site(s) requirements	10. System environmental site(s) requirements
11. Finalize cost-benefit analysis	11. Detailed cost-benefit analysis

4.2 DESCRIPTION OF THE TECHNICAL TASKS

4.2.1 Create Functional Process Model

Task number:	DA-1
Task name:	Create functional process model
Objective:	To describe the internal operations of the automated and manual work units of the system
Input(s):	PA-3 Conceptual process model PA-4 Conceptual data model PA-5 Preliminary manual/automated system boundaries

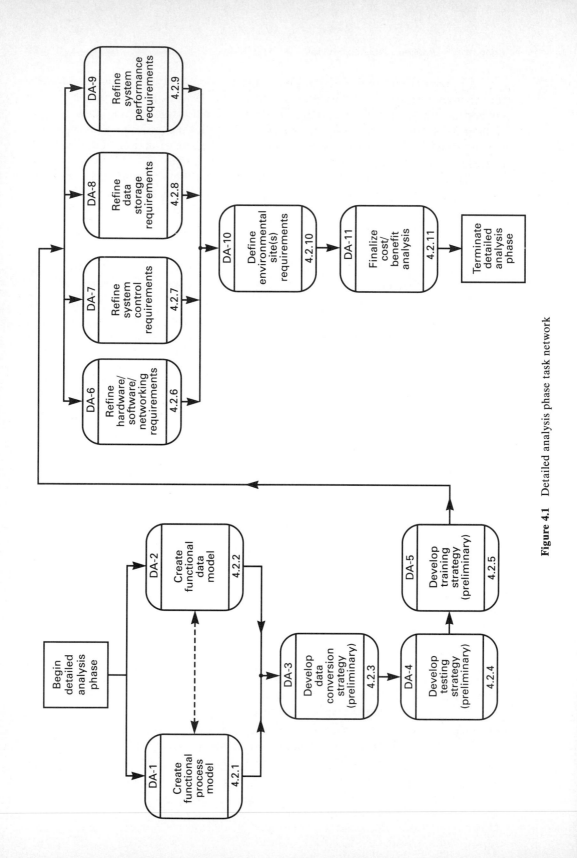

Figure 4.1 Detailed analysis phase task network

Output(s):	DA-1 Functional process model

Task description:

- Review the technical deliverables that were produced during the preliminary analysis phase.
- Precisely identify each work unit shown in a function data flow diagram as being an online, real-time, batch, or manual work unit.
- Construct the work unit data flow diagrams.
- Describe the detailed processing logic that is performed within each operation process with the use of structured specification techniques.
- Provide a textual description of all the graphical elements shown on the work unit data flow diagrams.
- Define the preliminary requirements of the human-machine interfaces:
    - Identify the type of medium (screen display, report, form, etc.) that will be used to support each work unit data flow.
    - Develop prototypes of the layouts of the input/output documents manipulated or created by each work unit process.
- Document the local data access requirements of each automated work unit.
- Walk through the functional process model and its supportive documents.

Finalize the partitioning of the business functions into manual/automated work units.   During the preliminary analysis phase, the conceptual process model was roughly divided into four distinct sets of processes: batch, online, real time, and manual work unit. This partitioning was a first attempt to identify the automation boundaries of the system.

Before developing the detailed components of the functional process model, the automation boundaries of the system should be finalized with the users. While performing this task, the development team should always keep in mind that a work unit process is either entirely manual or entirely automated. One possible way of doing this subtask is simply to indicate in the bottom portion of each process symbol shown on a function data flow diagram if the work unit is manual or automated. If the system is distributed, the physical sites where the automated work units will be executed can also be shown.

Construct the work unit data flow diagrams.   The next step involves developing the work unit data flow diagrams for each manual or automated work unit process identified in a function data flow diagram:

- Depict on a more detailed data flow diagram the basic operation processes that are performed within the work unit.
- Set each operation in relation to the others.
- Identify the data flows that circulate among the operations.
- Describe the data stores accessed by the operations and the external entities that interact with the operations.

Typically, the operations describe some very basic and low-level activities, such as

- Handling of errors or exception cases
- Validation of data elements
- Editing of data elements
- Computation of numerical values
- Access performed on the data stores

Once the work unit data flow diagrams are drawn, the procedural logic performed within each operation is documented with the use of structured specification techniques, such as structured English, decision tables, decision trees, action diagrams, and state-transition diagrams for the real-time processes.

Functional decomposition: reaching the bottom level. How do we know when the bottom level of the functional decomposition process has been reached? Are there guidelines to indicate when the operation depicted in the work unit data flow diagrams can be broken down no further? Unfortunately, there is no secret recipe, but the following suggestions should help:

1. In principle, the operation process should be self-contained and easily described with a single, unambiguous, and highly cohesive process specification.

2. If more than one statement of purpose is necessary to describe the operation, chances are that the analyst might be dealing with two different operations.

3. Typically, when the description of the operation is done with a specification technique such as structured English, it should not take more than one page of narrative to document the internal logic of the operation. However, this is just a rule of thumb. The analyst should not be overly worried if, in some instances, the operation is described with half a page or two pages of written specifications. On the other hand, if the description takes six pages of structured specifications, then the validity of a single operation should be questioned.

4. If the operation accesses more than one or two data stores, chances are that the operation should be split into distinct suboperations.

It is very important to describe procedurally the operations that are performed within the work unit as completely and accurately as possible. Quite often, it is only at this level of detail that several important business policies are uncovered by the development team. Hence, if this level of detail is not reached while documenting the procedural logic associated with each operation process, it is very likely that some very important (yet very subtle) business policy matters will simply be overlooked until the later stages of the development cycle (such as during the design or implementation phase). The resolution of business policy issues at that time might turn out to be very costly, as the design architecture of the system might need substantial revisions.

Define the preliminary requirements of the human-machine interfaces. One of the most important implementation issues in the development of a large-scale system is the specification of the human-machine interface requirements. The design of the layouts of the screens and reports that will be produced by the system are of the utmost importance to its acceptance by the users.

There are several schools of thought on when screens and report layouts should be clearly defined. One particular method suggests that the design of the human-machine interfaces belongs in the design phase. Hence, during the analysis phase, the logical data flow diagrams are strictly developed by uniquely identifying the data elements that are transported by the data flows. No reference whatsoever is made about the type of media that will be used eventually to support the human-machine interface (a form, a screen display, a report) or how the data should be formatted on a screen or a report.

On the other hand, with the emergence of powerful tools that efficiently support it, prototyping has rapidly emerged as an important technique in the arsenal of the system developer to help eliminate ambiguities surrounding the human-machine interface requirements.[2] Even when the prototype is thrown away, prototyping itself remains a very effective way to allow the user hands-on system experience. Prototyping is also effective for defect prevention and removal of external design problems or ambiguities.

As a general rule, it is strongly suggested to prototype all the important human-machine interfaces of the system as early as possible during the development life cycle, once the system has been properly partitioned into its major constituent components. Furthermore, the fact that the detailed functional specifications of the system have already been developed, while creating the work unit data flow diagrams, should eliminate the developers' fears of seeing the prototype become the system without having had the chance to develop a sound logical model first.

The first step in creating a prototype of the human-machine interfaces consists of identifying all data flows that cross the manual/automated boundaries of the system. Once this is done, the data flows are put into a physical format to the extent where the particular medium that will be used to transport the information they contain is clearly specified by the development team, in conjunction with the users. The physical data flows can take the form of a report, a screen, a form, or the like. Finally, the report and screen layouts of the system are interactively developed with the active participation of the users.[3] The users will have strong opinions about the format of their reports and screens, as well as the most effective sequence for presenting the screens.

Once prototyping is completed, it is important to document the results. Hence, the specifications related to each individual screen should include the following information, if applicable:

[2]For more information on prototyping, refer to Chap. 10.

[3]For more information on the design of screens, reports, and forms layout planning, refer to Sec. 5.2.1 in Chap. 5.

Title

Identification number

Description and purpose (2 to 3 lines)

Category (Menu, Help, Action, Display, Single or Multiple Panels)

Predecessor and Successor screens

Validation/editing rules

Layout sample and description of data elements used

Security level

Frequency of use

Response time requirements

To conclude, it is important to emphasize to the users that the layouts of the screens and reports are subject to minor revisions once the design phase is reached. The design of the internal components of the system will be finalized only at that time.

Document the data access requirements of the automated work units.   Analysts should document the data access requirements of each automated work unit. Ideally, these requirements can be modeled in a diagram, as shown in Fig. 4.2.[4]

First, the normalized entities accessed by the work unit operations are identified by examining the functional data model and by analyzing the internal processing logic embedded in the operations. Second, the particular sequence of action is depicted, showing how the normalized records are accessed or updated by the operations. The specific key data elements used to access the records are equally annotated on the diagram. An arrow with a single head symbolizes the access to a single record; a double-head arrow indicates a situation where several records are accessed. Additional information supporting the logic behind the proposed data access sequences can be documented on the left side of the diagram.

Define detailed report requirements specifications.   The development team should be careful when defining the requirements for the planned reports of the system in conjunction with the users. There have been several cases where users have kept only a few pages of some very voluminous reports that were produced on a daily basis. The rest was simply thrown away because the information was not required. The development team should always verify the usefulness of the reports and determine what is actually necessary. At the same time, the team should also pay particular attention to report requirements that look different on the surface but in fact can be satisfied by a single report.

---

[4]The documentation of the data access requirements of each automated work unit can be done at the present time only if the functional data model was constructed before or in parallel with the functional process model.

WORK UNIT   SYSTEM: Accounts Payable (AP)

NUMBER: P1.2.3   TYPE: ☒ Batch   ☐ Online

NAME: Vendor status   ANALYST: _____

DESCRIPTION: _____
_____
_____

DATA ACCESS REQUIREMENT(S):

① Access vendor data base
   directly via vendor - #
   If vendor-type = A
        Access invoice data base
   ② directly via invoice - #
        Access check data base
        via check - #
   Else
        Directly access check
   ③ data base via check - #
        and bypassing the
        invoice data base.

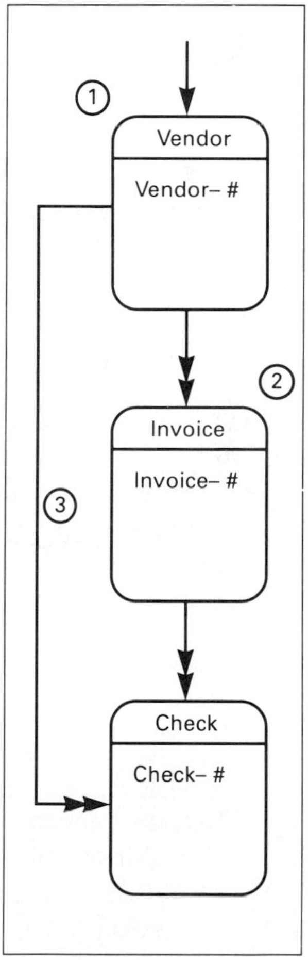

Figure 4.2 Documenting the data access requirements of the work units

Report requirements can be categorized by production frequency. Daily, weekly, biweekly, monthly, quarterly, yearly, on request, and ad hoc are the most common categories.

Lastly, the specifications related to each individual report should include the following information, if applicable:

- Title
- Identification number
- Description and purpose (2 to 3 lines)
- Mechanism used to request the report
- Category (Summary, Detail)
- Layout sample and description of data elements used
- Security level
- Number of pages
- Type of medium (special form, microfiche)
- Selection criteria and sorting sequence
- Frequency of use
- Total number of copies
- Distribution list and number of copies per recipient
- Delivery mechanism
- Retention period
- Audit procedures
- Turnaround requirements

4.2.2 Create Functional Data Model

Task number:	DA-2
Task name:	Create functional data model
Objective:	To normalize the conceptual data model and map the outcome into the logical structure supported by the database management system used for the new system
Input(s):	DA-1 Functional process model PA-4 Conceptual data model PA-5 Preliminary manual/automated system boundaries
Output(s):	DA-2 Functional data model

Task description:
- Derive a normalized data model from the conceptual data model.[5]
- Map the normalized data model into the logical structures supported by the selected database management system (hierarchical, network, or relational).

[5]For detailed information on the normalization process and its terminology, see Date [1986].

- Construct the logical database record/access matrix to ensure that the data access requirements of the work units are adequately supported by the functional data model. Adjust the functional data model and/or the data access requirements of the work units when record updating or retrieval inconsistencies are detected. Document the adjustments made to the functional data model and/or the work units, along with the proper justification.
- Provide a textual description of all the graphical elements shown on the functional data model.
- Walk through the functional data model and its supporting documents.

Normalize conceptual data model.   The construction of the functional data model begins where the creation of the conceptual data model ended. First, the entity-relationship model is further examined for completeness and then gradually put through the formal decomposition process of normalization. It is important to point out that the normalization technique should be done primarily by focusing on the user environment and its related business policies rather than on design-related intricacies. The normalization process is performed as follows:

1. *First normal form.* Identify the primary key of each entity. Remove the repeating data elements (or repeating groups) that are identified in an entity record. Create, if necessary, new record(s) by associating each particular repeating group of data elements with the primary key of the original entity.

2. *Second normal form.* Examine each data element shown in a first normal form record to ensure that it is fully functionally dependent on all the data elements in its primary key. If not, remove the data elements that are only partly dependent on the entire primary key and create new record(s) by associating these data elements with the particular primary key data elements on which they are functionally dependent.

3. *Third normal form.* Examine each non–key data element shown in a second normal form record and indicate if it is functionally dependent on another non–key data element within the same record. If so, remove these data elements and, if necessary, create new records by associating them with the primary key they are dependent on.

4. *Fourth normal form.* Examine the data elements of the records in third normal form and identify if there are two or more multivalued data elements in the same record. If so, create new records by associating each particular multivalued data element with the primary key of the original third normal form record.

Four normal forms have been prescribed in the present "create functional data model" activity. So far, the industry experts have identified five normal forms. Thus, this question might come to mind: Should the data analyst always attempt to normalize the conceptual data model up to the fifth normal form? The primary objective of the normalization process is to reduce certain forms of data redundancy and eliminate updating problems when the database records are manipulated by the system. Hence, the analyst should normalize the model until a minimal level of redundancy is achieved, but no further. As a rule of thumb, once the data model is in third normal form, chances are that this objective will have been met. In fact, a data model in third normal form will usually be in fourth and fifth normal forms. For this reason, and even though this book suggests normalizing the data model up to the fourth normal form, the decision to normalize to the fourth and fifth normal forms is left to the discretion of the analyst.

General considerations on the normalization process.   Given the level of detail and formality at which the conceptual data model was developed, it might be necessary to formalize the description of the data items attributed to an entity. For instance, the normalization technique presumes that all the data elements that are grouped into an entity are properly qualified. Figure 4.3 shows an entity-relationship diagram where the data element "address" is associated, via two different relationships, with the entity "customer."

Usually, relationships are established between the major data entities of the system. However, in the context of the example here, the two relationships "the customer resides at address" and "the customer is billed at address" were so important for the application under study that the analyst decided to model both of them and document the business policies that justified such an approach. Nonetheless, when the entity "customer" is normalized, the data item "address" should be qualified with two distinct names, such as "customer-resident-address" and "customer-billing-address."

The derived data elements were probably kept in the conceptual data model. Ideally, the derived data elements of the system should also be shown in the normalized data model and identified as such. As noted in Chap. 3, the decision to derive their actual value specifically at the time they will be retrieved versus permanently storing them in the physical database is essentially related to a performance consideration. The advantages and disadvantages of keeping the derived data elements in the physical files and databases of the system is weighed at the time the physical data model is developed, during the design phase.

The relationships shown in the conceptual data model might contain certain data elements that are used specifically to characterize them. This situation is illustrated in Fig. 4.4. During the normalization process, the data element "price" will be associated with the concatenated key "vendor #/part #," as shown in Fig. 4.5.

Figure 4.6 shows an example of an entity-relationship diagram with supertype/subtype entities. The supertype entity is characterized by the data elements that commonly apply to all its subtype entities. The converse is not true. Each subtype entity has its own special data elements that do not apply to the other subtypes. During the normalization process, the supertype entity will be defined into a unique table with all its attributed data elements. Each subtype will also be represented in a distinct table, consisting of the individual data elements that are unique to it.

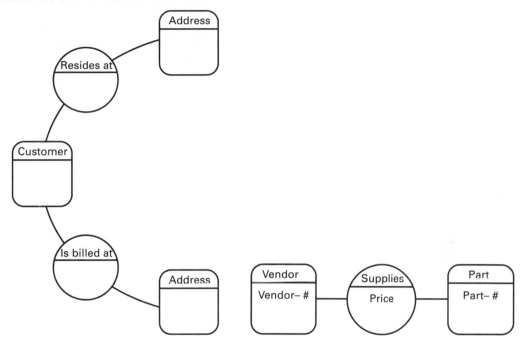

Figure 4.3 Customer-address entity-relationship diagram

Figure 4.4 Vendor-part entity-relationship diagram

Translate normalized model into DBMS logical structure. Once the analysts and the users have successfully completed the normalization process, the resulting normalized data structure should be translated into the logical data structure supported by the application's DBMS. This translation effort constitutes a first attempt at deriving a preliminary draft of the physical data model from the normalized data model. Contrary to the detailed physical data model that will be produced during the design phase, this interim physical data model primarily emphasizes the high-level structural characteristics of the physical model. For this reason, the de-

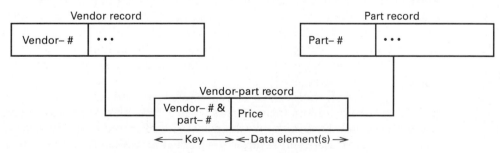

Figure 4.5 Vendor-part relation

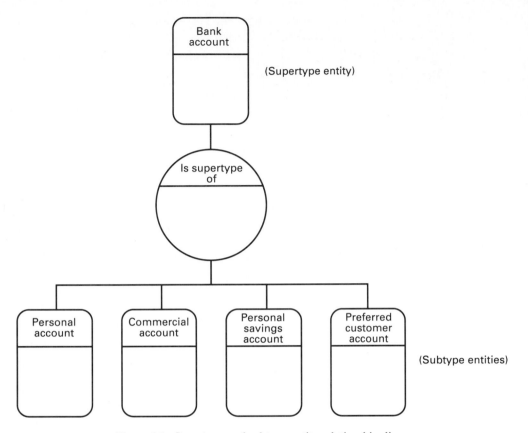

Figure 4.6   Supertype and subtype entity-relationship diagram

tailed physical characteristics of the physical data model, such as the types of pointers and access methods that will be used to construct it, should not be considered now but later on, during the design stage.

If the chosen DBMS supports hierarchical structures, the resulting model will represent a hierarchical data model. If the chosen DBMS supports a relational structure, then the normalized data model should be translated, with minimal effort, into a relational DBMS structure. Although relatively simple, the detailed steps that are necessary to create a structural data model suitable to a given type of physical DBMS are beyond the scope of this book. For more information on the subject, refer to Martin [1983].

Various CASE tools aimed at generating a preliminary mapping of the normalized data model into a logical database structure compatible with a given type of DBMS can be found in the marketplace. However, the resulting structure only constitutes a first draft and invariably will require subsequent refinements during the design phase.

Construct logical database record/access matrix.   During the creation of the functional process model, the detailed processing logic performed by the automated work unit processes was described in detail. Among other things, the work unit access requirements for specific data stores were depicted under the form of local data access view diagrams. These diagrams should now be carefully examined and analyzed by the data analyst to verify that the functional data model can indeed fully satisfy all the user data access requirements, not just the performance criteria. A matrix such as the one in Fig. 4.7 can be constructed to create a consolidated profile of the total system data access requirements.

If a work unit accesses a normalized record, not by its primary key but via a secondary key, then the name of this secondary key should be identified in the table, against the record being accessed. Furthermore, the data analyst should also ensure that all the basic data elements that are required to execute the logic described in the work unit are present in the functional data model.

Parallel development of the functional process and data models. Usually, the functional process and data models should be developed in parallel. This implies that they are constantly cross-validated as thcy arc developed. However, it might by advantageous in some particular instances to create the functional data model before the functional process model. A typical instance is when rapid prototyping is seriously considered for the application to define interactively the batch and online layouts of the application.

Even without prototyping, it might be preferable to develop the functional data model slightly ahead of the functional process model. With such a strategy, the functional data model components can then be used to derive the functional process model and document the local data access requirements of the work units.

File/database housekeeping requirements.   If not already done, the file/ database housekeeping requirements of the system should be identified, along with the planned housekeeping periods (monthly, quarterly, annually). These types of requirements will often translate into additional programs that need to be designed

Automated Work Unit	Processing Mode	Normalized Record A	Normalized Record B	...	Normalized Record N
Work Unit 1	B	X	X (Entry-point 1)		
Work Unit 2	O		X		X
.					
.					
.					
Work Unit X					

LEGEND: (B) Batch (O) Online (R) Real-time

Figure 4.7 Data access matrix

to adequately perform the desired housekeeping functions against the databases at periodic intervals. For example, the records contained in a very large database could be deleted or archived if they are three months old.

Finalize data element documentation.   At this point, all the data elements used by the system should have been clearly described with the users and properly documented:

- Format (alphabetic, numeric, alphanumeric)
- Length (external representation)
- Permissible values or ranges of values
- Validation rules that must be applied against them
- Functional dependencies with other data elements
- Frequency of use/volatility

In preparation for the testing process, the definitions of the data elements can be augmented with a list of representative values that might be used later to create sound test cases that contain valid or invalid data. For instance, let's assume that the data element "customer-account-type" has the following characteristics:

- 1 digit position (numeric)
- 2 possible values (1 = commercial, 2 = personal)

Then the following values could be derived and stored in the corporate data dictionary for creating test cases later on during the design and implementation phases:

VALID VALUES	INVALID VALUES
1, 2	0, 5, A, blank, . . .

4.2.3 Develop Data Conversion Strategy

Task number:	DA-3
Task name:	Develop data conversion strategy (preliminary)
Objective:	To define the preliminary system data conversion requirements, along with the optimal conversion strategy
Input(s):	PA-13 Preliminary system development strategy DA-1 Functional process model DA-2 Functional data model
Output(s):	DA-3 System data conversion strategy (preliminary)

Task description:

- Analyze the high-level data requirements of the new system and identify the primary domains of change that exist between the current and new system data architectures.
- Examine the overall quality and integrity of the data presently stored in the manual and mechanized files and databases of the current system.

- Identify the existing or special software tools and facilities or hardware and networking equipments that will be required to support the data conversion process.
- Derive the optimal strategy to perform the overall data conversion effort, in the context of the current project scope.
- Walk through the preliminary system data conversion strategy.

Once the functional data model is complete, the development team is in a good position to define the initial conversion strategy that will be used to convert the application data from the old to the new system. The magnitude of the data conversion effort is directly related to

- The complexity of the existing and new system data architectures
- The volume of data involved in the conversion process
- The degree of change associated with the application at hand

For some systems, the conversion effort will be relatively straightforward, whereas for others, it will warrant the creation of a dedicated subproject to support adequately the entire conversion process.

Define data conversion requirements.   The first step toward developing the conversion requirements consists in analyzing the scope of the domain of change between the old and new systems. This is done by identifying the following elements:

- The existing application files (manual or automated) that need to be converted, along with a brief description of the records and data elements involved in the process[6]
- The new files (manual or automated) that must be created from scratch, along with a brief description of the data elements that must be loaded into these files
- For each file, the estimated volume of data that needs to be converted to accommodate the new system data requirements
- The major business units of the organization that should be involved in the conversion process

The second step identifies possible constraints that might be imposed on the conversion process:

- Expected target completion dates
- Special handling of highly sensitive data
- Dependencies with other systems and the necessity to construct interfaces with them

---

[6]It might also be very useful to indicate clearly with the users the fields that will not be converted, if there are any.

- Availability of the files for the users (e.g., the current production files must remain available for the users 23 hours a day, 5 days a week)

The third step examines the level of quality of the data currently stored in the existing files. If, for whatever reason, the present data are severely corrupted, it might be necessary to come up with an action plan to clean the existing files before undertaking the conversion itself. Sometimes this might entail extensive effort from the users, especially when a large number of discrepancies are detected in the current files.

The fourth step defines the type of software material, tool packages, and computer equipment that will be necessary to support the conversion. The ultimate responsibility for ensuring the success of the conversion lies with the users, who are accountable for the integrity of the data they use. However, the system developers will play an important role in providing the appropriate software tools (i.e., conversion programs, data validation programs, file comparison facilities) that will be necessary to convert the existing files and databases efficiently and produce the reports needed by the users to validate the results. In some instances, special or additional hardware equipment might be necessary to perform the conversion. For instance, additional terminals might be required for a given period of time to accommodate a massive manual data entry effort aimed at capturing all the data needed by the new system as rapidly as possible.

Elaborate conversion strategy. The conversion strategy is elaborated based on all the information gathered in the previous step. The strategy will be largely influenced by the system development approach that was retained to implement the system. If the system will be gradually implemented release by release, then the dependencies that exist among these various releases and the sequence in which they will be developed will affect the manner in which the conversion process will be performed. In some cases, the creation of temporary bridges between old and new files/databases will be required until all system releases are developed. Nonetheless, the conversion strategy should cover, among other things, the following items:

- The major objectives and scope of the conversion process, along with the major issues to be addressed by the development team and the users
- The roles and responsibilities assigned to each user and systems group involved in the conversion process
- The description of the files and databases that must be converted in association with this particular release of the system; this also includes the new files created by the system
- The type of conversion that will be performed against each affected file or database:
  - Automated to automated
  - Manual to automated

- Automated to manual
- Manual to manual

- The particular sequences in which the files will be converted
- The dependencies that might exist among the files or the different conversion stages
- The type of facilities or reports required by the users to verify the results of the conversion or to analyze the quality of the data contained in the current files
- The fallback procedures that should be in place in case something goes wrong during the conversion process

If multiple geographic locations are involved in the data conversion process, it will also be necessary to determine the sequence and timing in which each particular site will be converted.

If the conversion effort appears to be very complex, it might be appropriate to consider creating a special conversion subsystem of its own and depict the conversion processes (with the help of the data flow diagram technique) in the functional process model. In such an event, the decision to develop the detailed specifications describing the manual and/or automated algorithms that will be used to transform the existing data elements, either at the present time or during the design phase, is left to the discretion of the development team. The screen layouts for manual data entry should be prototyped with the users, where applicable.

4.2.4 Develop Testing Strategy (Preliminary)

Task number:	DA-4	
Task name:	Develop testing strategy (preliminary)	
Objective:	To define the system testing objectives, along with a strategy to meet them	
Input(s):	DA-1	Functional process model
	DA-2	Functional data model
	DA-3	System data conversion strategy (preliminary)
Output(s):	DA-4	System testing strategy (preliminary)

Task description:
- Prepare a preliminary testing strategy for each level of testing planned for the project (i.e., production acceptance, user acceptance, system integration, unit testing).[7]
- Develop, if required, the version test plan for the current release.
- Walk through the preliminary system testing strategy.

---

[7]For more information on the testing cycle in general and its various levels of testing, see Chap. 8.

In this task, the overall system testing strategy is elaborated upon with the active participation of the users. Depending on the development approach that was originally retained to implement the system, the testing strategy can encompass either the entire system itself or specific releases of it.[8] If the system is relatively simple and small, then the testing strategy will be easily developed. On the other hand, if the system is large and complex, more rigorous work will be required to identify the most suitable system testing strategy in the context of the current project.

Elaborate testing strategy. The first step toward elaborating the testing strategy consists of defining the scope of each individual testing stage. Questions as to what will be tested and what will not should be properly addressed with the users. For instance, during user acceptance testing, will the users test only the software product, or will they also test the non-software products, such as the user manuals, the manual procedures of the system, or the user training package? The end result of this activity should be a list identifying the various system components that will be tested during each specific level of testing.

The second step consists of defining the objectives associated with each specific testing stage. The objectives should be stated in direct relation with the major system requirements that have been documented so far by the development team for the given release.

The third step consists of identifying the following items:

- The general-purpose tools and facilities that will be required to test the system
- The type of testing libraries that will be needed to store the various test data files and application programs, along with an estimate of the amount of storage required to accommodate these libraries
- The site(s) where the testing process will be executed
- The estimated amount of machine resources that will be needed to perform the tests

Table 4.2 shows the different types of generic tools that can assist the development team to create, manage, and modify the test environment and its data.

If the required testing tools are already available in the current environment, this step might be superfluous. If they are not available, then a plan should be elaborated on to determine who will develop or acquire them, how they will be used and by whom, and, more importantly, when they will be required during the project. In the same vein, the development team should clearly define the detailed hardware requirements for supporting the testing process. Are special types of

---

[8]If the human-machine interfaces of the system have been successfully prototyped with the users, then the users can start preparing their preliminary test cases to ensure that the system will work as per their initial requirements. Subsequently, these test cases will be refined and augmented during the design phase.

TABLE 4.2 DESCRIPTION OF DIFFERENT CATEGORIES OF
TESTING TOOLS

Tools to ...

Analyze which parts of the program code have been exercised
   by a test.

Help develop the physical file/database test environment.

Maintain the traceability of the test cases against the original
   user requirements.

Generate test cases automatically.

Create and load test data into the test files/databases.

Document the test cases and the expected results.

Extract live test data from existing production files and
   databases.

Validate the program's internal logic (i.e., static code analyzers and code inspectors).

Verify the test input and output results.

Compare the contents of the test files/databases before and
   after a test.

Enforce programming standards.

Store the test data permanently and automatically repeat the
   execution of a particular test scenario with augmented test
   data when required.

Automatically promote the programs from one testing library
   level to another (e.g., unit level to system level).

Interactively test and debug the programs.

Perform automated regression testing.

hardware equipment required, such as dedicated terminals, automated teller machines, graphic plotters, printers, or personal computers?

The fourth step describes the various procedures that govern the execution of
the testing cycle. The extent to which various automated procedures and control
mechanisms need to be put in place to manage the test environment efficiently is
directly proportional to the magnitude of the testing effort. More specifically,
the minimum set of procedures that should be addressed for testing a large system
include

- The change control procedures
- The library control procedures
- The problem reporting procedures
- The error correction procedures
- The tracking procedures necessary to monitor the progress made during the
  testing cycle

This step will be greatly simplified if the organization has already set up an automated testing environment and if standard control procedures already exist in the workplace for that purpose.

Lastly, the responsibilities associated with the various user and system groups other than the development team who will be involved in the testing process should be discussed at this stage. Some experts advocate that the testing activities should be performed by individuals who did not participate in developing the system. This could be the ideal situation, but the particular context in which each organization operates will ultimately determine the best approach there is based on the tools, resources, and time available to the project. Here are some questions that must be answered while performing this activity:

Who will create the test cases and anticipated test results?

Who will actually perform the tests?

Who will verify the test results?

What are the dependencies with other systems or releases?

Who will provide the test data for the system interfaces?

What will be the acceptance criteria for a successful test?

Develop version test plan.   During the preliminary analysis phase, the development team created the system development strategy. If the system was too large or too complex to be developed as a single entity, the development team broke it down into smaller, more manageable units (i.e., releases). During the detailed analysis phase, a similar technique can be used to partition further a specific release of a system into different versions, if needed.[9] The primary reason for this approach is based on the observation that for large and complex systems, the testing process works at its best when an individual system release is broken down into smaller versions. Then the coding and testing activities associated with the various versions of a release overlap in a predetermined sequence. The generic process is best explained with an example, as shown in Fig. 4.8.

First, each program in a version is coded and unit-tested independently of one another. Once fully tested individually, they are then integrated and tested as a whole. From there on, the testing process gradually evolves by progressively combining a new version with the set of versions already tested and finally testing the resulting combination. This incremental testing approach offers numerous advantages:

1. *Easier testing and debugging:* When a new version is integrated with earlier versions that already have been successfully tested together, chances are that any new errors that surface during the testing process will be caused by the new programs that were just added.

_____

[9]A version can be defined as a functionally independent component of a system release that can be tested in a standalone manner.

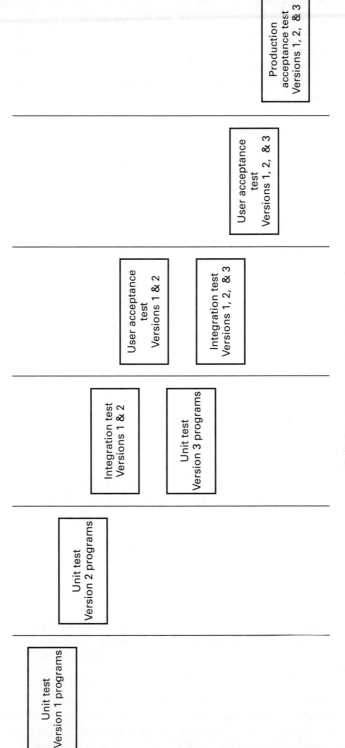

Figure 4.8 Version testing of a release

2. *Earlier testing of the critical system components:* The development team and the users can verify the level of operability and usability before the less complex components of the system are put in place.

3. *Experience gained while verifying the first versions:* The testing process can be easily readjusted at this point if required.

4. *Earlier user involvement.* The use of the staffing resources is optimized since the efforts are more evenly spread over the testing of several versions.

The success of version testing is strongly influenced by the particular strategy that will be used to break the system down into manageable version units. Several techniques are available to combine many programs into a version unit. For instance, all the programs supporting a major subsystem function can be grouped together for testing purposes. Another example might be when all the conversion programs of a system are assembled under a single version. The conversion subsystem can then be tested as the very first version of the system. A third approach might include grouping the various functions of a system that will operate under the same hardware or software configurations. For instance, the versions can be assembled based on the type of processor (mainframe or micro) or database management system that will be utilized to run the system.

As a fourth approach, the programs can be naturally segregated along the lines of batch, online, or real-time functions. Each program is built, tested, and integrated into its proper batch, online, or real-time stream. The batch job stream could be further divided into daily, weekly, monthly, and yearly runs. A fifth approach could include testing the most critical and complex functions of the system first and then integrating them as early as possible to obtain maximum testing time.

While it may appear that these program-grouping techniques are used independently of one another, they can advantageously be combined. Common sense should also prevail when using the integration testing strategy. For example, it may prove costly to reexecute a complete integration test each time a single program is added to a system that will consist of 100 and more programs. A better approach is to test each subsystem independently before integrating it as the system evolves into a fully operational entity.

Figure 4.9 shows how a particular system release was subdivided into several versions.

Pilot testing.   If the same system is to be implemented in different geographic locations, the users should seriously consider conducting a pilot test at one specific location to ensure that the system works properly in an environment as close as possible to a production environment. Once this is done, the system can then be installed at the other locations in either a predetermined sequence or simultaneously.

Parallel testing.   Typically, parallel testing might be considered when the functions provided by the new system do not differ much from those of the old system. For instance, parallel testing can be a valuable aid if the system is converted as

Version Number	Program Identification
1	Conversion PGMS A, B, C, D
2	Online transactions E, F, G
3	Online transactions H, I, J, K
. . .	
N	Batch PGMS X, Y, Z

Figure 4.9 Partitioning of a release into versions

is from one computer environment to another. The results of the test runs of the "new" system are compared against the known results of the existing production system while the two systems are operated in parallel with the same data.

4.2.5 Develop Training Strategy (Preliminary)

Task number:	DA-5
Task name:	Develop training strategy (preliminary)
Objective:	To develop the optimal strategy to satisfy the user/system training requirements
Input(s):	PA-13 Preliminary system development strategy DA-1 Functional process model DA-2 Functional data model DA-3 System data conversion strategy (preliminary) DA-4 System testing strategy (preliminary)
Output(s):	DA-5 System training strategy (preliminary)

Task description:

- Identify the major domains of change between the new and old systems.
- Identify the broad categories of personnel who will be affected by the anticipated changes. Identify also the average number of people who will need training and the geographic areas where they are located.
- For each affected category of personnel, outline the high-level needs for training.
- Develop a preliminary training strategy to address the needs for training the personnel who will be affected by the new system.
- Walk through the preliminary system training strategy.

Effective training is one of the most important issues in the implementation of a system. If it is essential to develop a system that truly satisfies the users' requirements, it is equally critical to ensure that the users are properly trained on how to use their system in an optimal manner. Because of this, a sound and realistic training strategy is required to manage the transition between the old and new system environments successfully.

Obviously, when the current organization does not change drastically, the transition will likely be relatively straightforward. Alternately, a large, complex system that will be used by numerous categories of people and will introduce intensive organizational changes will probably require special attention because of the massive training efforts involved in educating the entire staff.

Even though it might be difficult at the present time to assess completely and precisely the detailed impact the new system would have on the users and their environment, it is very important to evaluate at least the major types of changes that are likely to occur and how these changes will affect each user area. Typically, several types of changes can take place:

Functional Changes.
- Introduction of new business policies
- Introduction of new functions
- Enhancements to existing functions
- Introduction of new control procedures

Organizational Changes.
- Creation of new clerical positions
- Creation of new managerial positions

Technological Changes.
- Introduction of new software facilities
- Introduction of new computer equipment

A brief study of the nature of these changes can sometimes quickly pinpoint specific areas where some kind of basic training will be needed before implementing the system into production. For instance, the creation of new positions might demand that new skills be developed within the task force. The human-machine interfaces specifically designed to accommodate a new online system could represent quite a drastic departure from an old system that was strictly batch oriented. Furthermore, the introduction of new sophisticated hardware equipment to an organization, such as bar code readers and printers, optical character readers, magnetic badge readers, and voice input-output devices, could become a traumatizing experience for personnel if the training is not properly planned and delivered in a timely manner.

The next step is to identify the different categories of personnel who might be affected by the changes introduced with the implementation of the new system. The same system can service a variety of personnel, such as executives, supervisors, office clerks, professionals, and workers on the shop floor. Indeed, each specific category might have different educational and cultural backgrounds and skill sets that would likely influence the type of training that is best suited for them, as well as the type of new skills that must be acquired by personnel in general.

Besides the users, the particular training needs of the information systems personnel, who will be called upon to operate and support the system in production, should not be neglected by the development team.

Finally, a high-level strategy should be developed in an attempt to address all the training needs that have been identified so far. At this point, it is sufficient to highlight the general goals associated with the training process, the magnitude of the planned training effort, the type of training methods recommended, and the hardware/software facilities required to support the entire training effort. During the design phase, the training strategy will be refined at a much more detailed level.

4.2.6 Refine Hardware/Software/Networking Requirements

Task number:	DA-6	
Task name:	Refine hardware/software/networking requirements	
Objective:	To define the detailed hardware/software/networking requirements of the system	
Input(s):	PA-13	Preliminary system development strategy
	PA-9	Preliminary hardware/software/networking requirements
	DA-1	Functional process model
	DA-2	Functional data model
	DA-3	System data conversion strategy (preliminary)
	DA-4	System testing strategy (preliminary)
	DA-5	System training strategy (preliminary)
Output(s):	DA-6	Detailed hardware/software/networking requirements

Task description:

- Analyze the detailed functional and data requirements that are described in the functional process and data models of the system.
- Modify or supplement the hardware/software/networking requirements that were identified during the preliminary analysis phase. Include any additional requirements needed to support the future system conversion, testing, and training processes.
- Consolidate the detailed hardware/software/networking requirements. Ensure they are complete and compatible.
- Describe the physical characteristics of the hardware/software/networking equipment and facilities that are required to support the new system.
- Develop the hardware/software/networking acquisition and installation strategy, if required.
- Walk through the detailed hardware/software/networking requirements.

The preliminary hardware/software/networking requirements of the system are revisited in light of the information that has been gathered so far. The list of major requirements in this area should now be as detailed and as complete as possible. Some of the items that should be covered are

- The identification of the existing hardware/software/networking equipment and facilities that can be used to satisfy the new system requirements
- The identification of the new hardware/software/networking equipment and facilities that must be acquired to develop and operate the new system efficiently in its production environment

Refining the hardware/software/networking requirements will require only a minimal effort if the new system processing and storage requirements can be accommodated by the hardware/software/networking configuration currently in place, without adversely affecting the different software applications that already run in this environment. In such a situation, the present task might simply identify the additional set of terminals and printers that might be required to support the new system. Furthermore, if the organization has already prescribed some basic standards that provide guidance to the developers, when it is necessary to select hardware/software/networking equipment, this process will only be easier to perform and will minimize the risk of acquiring inadequate equipment or facilities.

When defining the detailed hardware/software/networking equipment and facilities, the development team should always view these apparently three distinct entities as one because they often are very strongly interdependent. In fact, one of the most crucial aspects of the decision-making process regarding the acquisition of computer equipment and software facilities is the compatibility factor. For instance, decisions concerning the acquisition of a specific line of hardware equipment from a given manufacturer by default might dictate the selection of some very specific software facilities to maintain an acceptable level of reliability and efficiency for the system at hand.

Even if several software facilities can run on several types of mainframe computers or microcomputers, the same candidate software facility might not necessarily offer the same level of functionality or efficiency when operating in these different computer environments. Lastly, the computer equipment and software facilities that will be purchased for the new system should be fully compatible with the existing automated environment. They should also be compatible with any future computer/software acquisition that might be considered within the next five years.

Hardware/software facilities.   Some of the categories of hardware equipment and software facilities that should be described at this point include[10]

---

[10]The description of the new hardware equipment and software facilities that are needed to operate the software system in production should include the following information: cost of purchase, cost of installation, and cost of operation.

Hardware.

- Mainframe processors
- Microcomputer processors
- Tape drives
- Disk drives
- Graphical plotters
- Printers
- CRT terminals
- Readers (optical, bar code, card)
- Archival storage devices
- Automated teller machines
- Magnetic ink character readers (MICR)

The physical dimension of each new piece of hardware equipment should be specified, along with its major characteristics.

Software.

- Batch monitors
- Software operating system
- Communications network
- Database management system
- General system utilities for backup/recovery, sort/merge, unload/reload, file/ database conversion, and so forth
- Static and interactive testing tools
- Test data generator
- Application code generators
- Application code optimizers
- Programming languages and compilers
- Software security control facilities
- Program debugging tools
- Teleprocessing monitor
- Telecommunication facilities
- Project management tools
- Access method facilities
- Project librarian tools
- Automated tools to support JAD-like interactive sessions
- General-purpose data entry tools
- Ad hoc query and report generator facilities

The desired version of each software component should be clearly spelled out by the development team.

Particular attention should be given to the description of the physical characteristics of the peripheral equipment that will be utilized by the users to interface with the system. In Sec. 4.2.1, on creating the functional process model, the system screens and reports were prototyped by the development team and the users. This effort was accomplished by primarily focusing user attention on the functional and usability characteristics of the system in order to retain as much flexibility as possible while designing these interfaces. It is now time to address some of the issues surrounding the detailed physical characteristics of the human-machine interface equipment.

For CRT terminals, some of the physical characteristics that should be documented are the following:

- Number of units needed per category of users
- Size of the screens
- Desired keyboard features (e.g., a keyboard specifically adapted for specialized functions, multilingual characteristics)
- Need for color screens
- Number of display lines and columns (24 or 30 lines, 80 or 132 columns)
- Basic field editing features (alphabetic/numeric validation, range checking)
- Graphical capabilities
- Screen resolution level (low, medium, or high)
- Formatting capabilities of the terminal

Furthermore, the type of terminals selected can be greatly influenced by where they will be located, such as in an office or on the shop floor. For example, if the working conditions in the manufacturing plants are extreme (heat, cold, dust, vibrations, corrosive atmosphere), select terminals that can withstand such environmental conditions.

Another factor to be considered is the different categories of personnel who will utilize the terminals. For instance, will the terminals be used by people who constantly perform some very specialized functions, or will they be used intermittently by different people who must perform various general-purpose functions? The use of special-purpose terminals can be fairly advantageous when maximum speed and accuracy are required, since they can minimize the need for keying data and therefore errors. On the other hand, multipurpose terminals can increase the flexibility of the users, especially when they frequently change their working methods or are called upon to perform various nonspecialized functions. Nevertheless, it might be advantageous to ensure some consistency across the entire application when selecting terminals or printers.

For printer terminals, some of the information that should be collected includes:

- Desired level of quietness
- Quality of the printing

- Maximum number of characters per line
- Support of special printing characters
- Type of forms that must be supported and the maximum paper width
- Printing speed
- Special printer characteristics desired (microfiche formatting, bar code labeling)
- Maximum number of duplicate copies that can be printed with an impact printer
- Number of printers needed, based on the number of users to service and the estimated print loads (for both local and centralized use)

Network facilities.   The next topic to be covered is the data communication or network environment. A preliminary sketch illustrating the different geographic locations where the computer processors and their peripheral equipment will be installed should be drawn at this stage. At the same time, several questions should be answered:

- Can the current premises satisfy the hardware requirements in terms of floor space, temperature, humidity, and power?
- What changes should be made at the various sites to accommodate the new hardware equipment?
- What will the impact of these changes be on the current environment?

The basic requirements for connecting various pieces of hardware equipment across different sites should also be shown on the chart. But before doing so, the following issues must be finalized:

1. Identify the exact locations where the hardware peripherals (CRTs/printers) and processors (mainframe or micro) will be installed. Will each user have a dedicated workstation, or will all terminals be located in a common area? While most users will interface with the system at predetermined locations, there might be some specific situations where users will require access to the system when they are out of town, such as salespeople or marketing representatives. Will they use portable terminals to communicate with the system? Can the current communication facilities support these special system access needs?

2. Estimate the average number of hours per day and days per week during which each combination of connections must remain in operation.

3. Determine the volume of data exchanged at peak periods, the response speed requirements associated with each major category of transmission, and the maximum number of users connected at peak hours.

4. Identify the level of degradation that could be acceptable to the application in case of overload. Define the network backup requirements in case of failure.

5. Analyze the evolving needs of the application for the foreseeable future while evaluating the different communication network alternatives available (public data networks, public switched networks, meshed networks, local area networks, value-added networks).[11] The costs associated with each option should also be taken into consideration.

The complexity of the network requirements will determine the level of expertise required to develop the optimal network configuration. It is one thing to design a local area network to accommodate two or three microcomputer users located on the same floor. It is something else to design the optimal network strategy necessary to accommodate a complex application that exchanges information across several states, as shown in Fig. 4.10.

Depending on the level of expertise available in the organization, the services of a consulting firm specializing in the design of complex networks might be the most practical approach to derive the best configuration tailored to meet the communication needs of your enterprise. Furthermore, network facilities in general are constantly evolving over time, and only an internal group dedicated on a full-time basis to the design of large networks can cope with the rapid evolution. This should not stop system developers from familiarizing themselves with the basic concepts surrounding this specialized data processing field. Doing so will sensitize them to the importance of gathering the essential application-oriented information that is required as input to the design of quality network structures.

Acquisition and installation strategy.   Once all the detailed hardware/software/networking application requirements have been identified with the users, a plan of action to acquire and install these commodities must be developed. This plan should address the following items:

- The interdependencies that might exist among the related hardware/software/networking components
- The sequence in which they must be acquired and installed for each release
- The roles and responsibilities of each group involved in acquiring and installing these commodities
- The dependencies that exist between the current release and the other releases of the system
- The expected delivery dates of the computer equipment and software facilities and their expected installation dates

Depending on the criticality of the system with regard to the well-being of the organization, it would be preferable in some instances to consider additional alternatives for replacing hardware items in case problems suddenly arise. For example, this preventive approach might be necessary to cover situations when the equipment cannot be delivered by the vendor as per the agreed delivery date or when the equipment clearly does not function as anticipated.

---

[11]For more information on networks and distributed processing, consult Martin [1981].

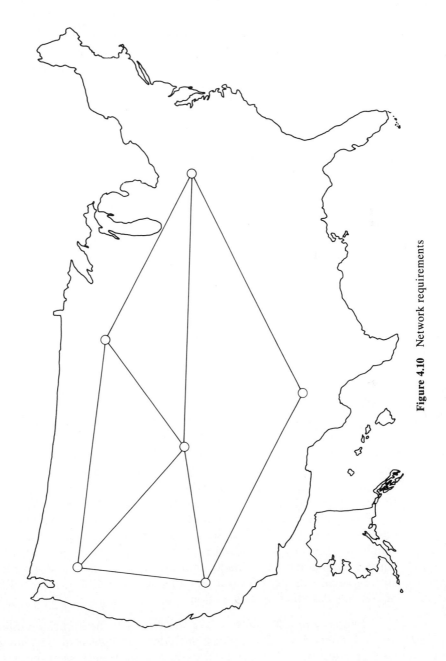

Figure 4.10 Network requirements

4.2.7 Refine System Control Requirements

Task number:	DA-7
Task name:	Refine system control requirements
Objective:	To define the detailed control requirements of the system
Input(s):	PA-7 Preliminary system control requirements
	DA-1 Functional process model
	DA-2 Functional data model
Output(s):	DA-7 Detailed system control requirements

Task description:

- Review the general system control requirements that were identified in the preliminary analysis phase.
- If necessary, modify or supplement the control requirements that apply to the whole system in light of all information gathered concerning the new system.
- Identify the detailed control requirements that are applicable to each function/work unit identified in the functional process model and to each file/database structure shown in the functional data model. Cover the detailed needs in terms of
  - Security
  - Integrity
  - Auditability
  - Backup/recovery
  - Disaster recovery
- Document the findings of this task separating those that apply to the entire system from those that apply to a particular function/work unit or file/database structure.
- Walk through the detailed system control requirements.

In the preliminary analysis phase, the emphasis was primarily on identifying the type of control requirements that generally apply to the whole system. These requirements are now revisited and validated against all the additional information that was gathered during the construction of the functional process and data models. This activity should cover both the automated and manual processes of the system. Furthermore, each set of specific system function/work units and file/database should be carefully scrutinized by the development team to identify the detailed control requirements that might uniquely apply to them and not necessarily to the entire system at large. However, not all systems or all functions will need the types of controls described in this section.

Security requirements.   As noted earlier, the security requirements can be divided into two broad categories: procedural and physical. The *procedural requirements* for security apply primarily to the various functions of the system that potentially can be misused by the staff (i.e., MIS or user personnel). Several security measures can be devised to prevent or at least to minimize these types of threats:

- Proper identification of each user or category of users when accessing the system
- Approval of at least two people for major transactions, such as to make important payments or transfer funds
- Production of an audit trail and regular reports of all transactions made by employees
- Tighter controls when important monetary transactions are executed
- Restriction for use of transactions and access to files on a need to know basis only

Each case must be analyzed in its proper context. In order to truly assess the degree of protection needed for each function/work unit, a statement of the potential consequences of an unauthorized access to sensitive information could be documented. Then the level of security that should be appropriately applied is determined based on the various categories of users who need to access the information.

Different security measures might be applied at the system, subsystem, function, work unit, and even operation levels. The same rule applies to the system files and databases. For instance, access to information might be restricted at the level of the entire database, at the segment, or even at the field level. This is especially true if the users will be able to access the information stored in the files/databases via some powerful ad hoc query facility. The same philosophy should also apply to the manual files of the system.

Special considerations should be given to controlling unauthorized access to classified information that is generated by the system in a hard-copy format, such as program dumps or reports that are printed on paper and stored in filing cabinets. Special equipment might be required to dispose of such sensitive documents in a secured manner, such as a paper shredder. Such equipment should not only be acquired for the production but also for the test environment sites, if these are situated at different locations.

Because several systems or portions of a system are developed and operated with micros, the security measures should also extend to any type of machine-readable document that is stored on a diskette or hard disk and that, in fact, can be easily removed from a central or remote location.

Another potential security threat is hackers, who might try to break into the system. These people are often trying to bypass the existing system security measures to access illegally unauthorized information. This type of threat can be minimized by controlling physical access to the system. For example

- The use of passwords at different levels of the application (i.e., system, function) is also recommended, especially for large-scale multiuser systems, as long as these passwords are frequently changed and not written down on a piece of paper left beside the terminal.

- The utilization of dialup lines into the mainframe computers should be restricted and properly monitored.
- The network configuration could also be scrutinized to evaluate the monitoring of unauthorized attempts to access or tap the communication lines. If sensitive data will be transmitted over the network lines (e.g., via satellite), the use of data encryption can turn out to be a viable alternative to ensure adequate protection of the information. Since more and more companies transmit valuable information to one another using direct computer-to-computer data transmission facilities (e.g., electronic data interchange), data encryption should rapidly gain in popularity.

The *physical requirements* greatly vary from one site to another. Some basic precautions to minimize the potential physical security threats include

- A thorough analysis of the physical sites where the computer equipment will be installed. This is important to detect such potential hazards as flood, fire, riots, or power supply shutdowns. If the risk is high, then the use of smoke, fire, or flood detectors might become obvious, along with special equipment, such as water pumping devices or uninterruptible power supply facilities.
- Electronic surveillance facilities (cameras, videos).
- Restricted access to the computer and the peripheral equipment via security locks, badge readers, security guards.[12]
- Sign-in/sign-out facilities to control physical access to the computer centers.
- Sensitive documentation locked into regular or fireproof filing cabinets.

Integrity requirements.   The integrity requirements are generally related to the correctness of the data manipulated by the system. The ability of the system to automatically detect and even enforce the correction of data errors will greatly enhance its level of integrity. For instance, the functions that are primarily designed to feed the system with basic input data should be carefully analyzed to ensure optimal data correctness. Some of the functions to consider are data entry, data interfacing with other systems, and the transmission processes via network facilities.

Several techniques can be used to improve the level of accuracy of the data entry function. First, the number of keystrokes required to input data should be reduced, wherever feasible. Second, extensive data editing and validation algorithms should be utilized as the data entry function is exercised, whether new data are being input into the system or existing data are being updated. Lastly, the human-machine dialogues should be customized to fit the particular types of functions be-

---

[12]More sophisticated personnel identification technologies such as voice-pattern recognition, fingerprint readers, and even eye iris and retina readers can also be considered, even though they are fairly expensive.

ing designed. A screen that expressly supports an online data entry function should be designed differently than one that would be used for a general-purpose inquiry transaction on a database. Also, the sequence and disposition of the data shown on the screen might be somewhat different for these two functions.

In some instances, the input files coming from other systems should be carefully validated at the time they are received by the new system to ensure that the information provided is indeed accurate and complete. It is easier to detect errors at this early stage than after the interfacing data have been used to update the new files and databases without any formal method of validation. This is particularly appropriate when the input data are coming from an old system that contains few or no validation routines.

The integrity of the databases can be enhanced if their data content is always updated via the facilities provided by the corresponding database management system software. For most types of databases, the database records should always be updated from a single entry point. If the user is authorized only to update record A but not record B and C, then the database management system should have some control mechanisms that enforce such integrity control and do not allow the user to acccss the B and C records. The database management system should adequately support concurrent updating of the same database record by several users.

Finally, the level of accuracy provided by the network facilities should always be evaluated, especially when frequent transmission of high-volume data occurs among the physical sites supporting the new system. What type of error-detection mechanism is used by the network protocol? Are there any specific validation routines?

Auditability requirements.   The audit requirements of the system are expanded, where applicable, to cover the specific needs of internal and external auditing departments. Because the development team's experience is often limited as to what could be the system auditing requirements, the company's internal auditors should be directly involved in this process, at least on a consulting basis. Typically, the types of system controls often required might include

- An audit trail of all the online transactions that update the system files/databases. The facility should identify the originator of the transaction and the input data used, along with the resulting changes.
- A log of all the transactions rejected by the system, as well as the reasons for their rejection and possibly the identification of the originator of the transaction.
- Verification procedures to control the accuracy and completeness of the manual operations of the system.
- A mechanism to verify that the output data produced by the system are properly distributed to the users and other systems.
- A procedure to ensure that the various system transaction files are properly balanced and reconciled at the end of the day.

- Procedures to ensure that standard accounting practices are properly observed.
- Procedures to ensure that aging data are properly archived to meet the legal obligations associated with the preservation of historical information.

Backup/recovery requirements.   The general requirements for the backup and recovery functions of the system should be defined with the users. This entails keeping enough generations of mechanically produced data to be able to resume operations at the point where a system problem occurred in the production environment. The type of medium and amount of space that will be used to back up the application data should also be identified.

Disaster/recovery requirements.   The strategy that should be used to develop the required disaster/recovery plans must be defined if the system is considered critical. The disaster/recovery plan should address both manual and automated functions and procedures. The following are some of the major items that should be covered:[13]

- What elements of the system documentation and user operating manuals must be secured in case of a major disaster? Where will this information be stored?
- Which files, software facilities, databases, and application libraries must be secured?
- What are the alternate processing centers?
- What applications must be restored first and in which order? What are the priorities?
- Who controls the operations environment in case of a major disaster?
- Who is involved in the recovery plan on the system side? On the user side?
- What are the roles and responsibilities of the users? Of the system personnel?
- How quickly can a new site and new equipment be obtained?

Finally, the users should discuss with the development team what they feel is the maximum system outage they can tolerate before their daily operations start to be seriously affected by the current situation.

In a major system failure, fallback procedures should be considered by the development team and the users, especially if the application is considered critical to the well-being of the organization. For instance, are there alternative ways for the users to continue to carry out their business activities while the system is down? Some of the techniques that should be investigated to help the users in such an event include the periodic printing of the entire content of the application files/databases on paper reports or microfiche and the production of daily reports to confirm the status of the major transactions performed against the application files/databases.

[13]For more information on how to develop a major disaster recovery strategy and plan, see Toigo [1989].

4.2.8 Refine Data Storage Requirements

Task number:	DA-8
Task name:	Refine data storage requirements
Objective:	To define the detailed system requirements for data storage

Input(s):	PA-8	Preliminary data storage requirements
	DA-1	Functional process model
	DA-2	Functional data model
	DA-3	System conversion strategy (preliminary)
	DA-4	System testing strategy (preliminary)
	DA-5	System training strategy (preliminary)
	DA-6	Detailed hardware/software/networking strategy
Output(s):	DA-8	Detailed data storage requirements

Task description:

- Revise the data storage estimates that were developed during the preliminary analysis phase, covering the production needs for both database and nondatabase files, including
  - The estimated volume of data to be stored per million bytes
  - The initial file/database growth estimates
  - The data archiving volume estimates
- Analyze the data storage needs of the project during the system development stages.
- Walk through the detailed data storage requirements.

The initial data storage estimates that were developed during the preliminary analysis phase are revised based on the information gathered at this point. Once again, for several projects this task might turn out to be a trivial exercise since the application being developed does not necessarily manipulate voluminous amounts of data. On the other hand, if the application is significantly volume driven, the system sizing effort must be carefully carried out throughout the major stages of the development cycle. As stated earlier, the lead time for ordering such hardware as disk drives and controllers can be fairly significant, and thus the size of the files/databases must be carefully estimated to determine if such hardware must be ordered to support the data volume requirements.

The functional data model consists of normalized records that are regrouped based on their affinities and the type of DBMS structure selected for implementing the new system. Given that all the data requirements relevant to the system have been described at a detailed level, it is now possible to refine the data storage requirements.[14]

---

[14]Note that the physical characteristics of the database records, such as physical pointers, control fields, and indexes required by the DBMS software, can be omitted at this stage. However, the size of the file/database can be augmented by a factor of approximately 5% to 15% to adequately cover such overhead.

The system might also require some additional storage requirements to support the conversion and testing processes or even the training effort. The different files, databases, and libraries that will be used to develop and test the system should be estimated. For some applications, these particular needs can turn out to be quite significant.

Several other factors might directly affect the total data storage requirements of the system. For example, what will be the average time for retaining online information kept in the application files/databases? What are the data archiving needs of the application? How long should data be retained on offline storage facilities? What is the projected annual growth of the application files/databases over a five-year period?

4.2.9 Refine System Performance Requirements

Task number:	DA-9
Task name:	Refine system performance requirements
Objective:	To identify the detailed performance requirements that must be met by the new system
Input(s):	PA-6 Preliminary system performance requirements DA-1 Functional process model DA-2 Functional data model
Output(s):	DA-9 Detailed system performance requirements

Task description:

- Examine the functional process model and identify the detailed manual and automated functions of the system that are related to performance issues.

- Refine the performance requirements associated with the system as a whole or with individual functions, covering the needs for
  - Response time
  - System accessibility
  - System availability/reliability
  - System throughput capacity
  - System flexibility
  - Batch reports turnaround
  - System print loads
  - Expected execution time of the batch processes
  - Data volatility

- Walk through the detailed system performance requirements.

The detailed system performance requirements that are analyzed at this point might greatly affect the design of the architectural characteristics of the system. At the risk of repeating the same leitmotif throughout this book, these requirements might not be too critical for a lightly loaded system. However, for a heavily loaded system, their proper handling becomes essential to the success of the project.

Given that the functional process and data models have been finalized, it is now necessary to examine carefully in detail all the individual system functions and elaborate on the characteristics of their performance criteria. Active user participation is crucial to the success of this task. Users must clearly communicate what their expectations are. The performance requirements, as any requirement, must be stated in a format that can be easily understood by all involved parties, especially the users. Nevertheless, they must also be defined at a level of detail that will facilitate their measurement once the system is fully operational. Finally, they might be further refined during the design phase, once the physical file/database structures are developed and optimized to meet the desired physical performance behavior of the system.

Response time requirements.   At this stage, the online processes of the system can be classified into different transaction categories, based on their expected response time. The broad response time requirements that were gathered during the preliminary analysis phase are refined and ideally stated in a manner similar to that shown below:

> "All online transactions in category 1 must have a response time between 1 and 3 seconds."
>
> "All online transactions in category 2 must have a response time between 4 and 6 seconds."

The response time requirements of each specific online function must be justified by the users because these must remain realistic and achievable. For instance, it might be perfectly justifiable for the users to request a 1- to 3-second response time for a transaction that involves an interactive session at the terminal while they are interacting at the same time with a customer who is inquiring about the status of his or her credit line. On the other hand, would a 5- to 6-second response time be acceptable for a transaction that is not considered critical to the operations of the business unit, that does not require an immediate response to an external or internal customer query, and that is used once in a while during a month?

The definition of response time requirements normally applies to preplanned transactions. If the users utilize a query facility for ad hoc online inquiries, it might become difficult to define precisely what the response times of these unpredictable types of requests will be. In such a situation, the users must be educated in the types of queries they can formulate with these powerful software facilities and the adverse effect that some types of queries might have on the overall performance of the system. If their queries are formulated in a very general manner, then the entire database might be scanned, and the overall system response time can degrade very rapidly. The section on report turnaround requirements covers the end user querying and reporting issue in more detail.

Accessibility requirements.   The accessibility requirements apply to the total number of users the system must support at a given point in time. For example, how many users will simultaneously need direct access to the system? How many users will utilize the system in total? What will be the ratio of users per terminal? This type of requirement will directly affect a variety of other deliverables, such as the proposed network configuration, the number of terminals to connect to the network, and so forth. Projections should also be made to address the next two to five years. This information will be useful to plan the system expansion as the number of users increases over the years.

Availability/reliability requirements.   What is the maximum period of time during which the system must remain fully operational? Is it only during the traditional 9 to 5 time frame? Is it 24 hours a day, all year? How reliable must the system be? Is there a need to duplicate some of the hardware/networking components to increase the level of reliability of the system? In case of a hardware failure, can the critical system operations remain active by rerouting the network traffic or diverting processing to other computer facilities?

Throughput capacity requirements.   What is the average number of transactions that must be handled per unit of time by the manual, batch, online, or real-time functions of the system? What is the expected annual growth in the number of transactions that must be handled by the system? What are the peak loads? Can the current environment handle these peak loads without suffering a serious degradation?[15]

For volume-oriented applications, ideally the computer should be able to process, on average, two days of normal processing work in a single day. This added capacity can turn out to be extremely useful when two or three working days of processing must be recovered following a major system problem. The throughput requirements associated with the manual procedures of the system should also be assessed as accurately as possible at this time. These figures will eventually be used to quantify the number of personnel required to perform these tasks.

Flexibility requirements.   If you ask several users what are the most desirable characteristics that a system must possess, chances are that flexibility would be in the first three positions. In today's competitive business environment, it is a challenge for software professionals to design a system that will remain flexible enough through the years to accommodate with a minimum of effort future business requirements of the organization. On the other hand, it is a definite challenge for the users to eliminate the ambiguity around the flexibility issue and to be more articulate when describing their requirements for a more flexible system. Simply stating that the system must be able to handle any type of change is very nice but

---

[15]While estimating the total system throughput capacity figures, the various user-friendly ad hoc query and reporting software facilities that will be put at the disposal of the users should also be evaluated in terms of estimated resource consumption.

not too helpful for the developers. Although it is impossible to anticipate accurately all types of changes that will likely occur in the business environment during the next five years, it is possible to describe the nature of the most probable changes or at least those that are already planned.

What are the major aspects of a system that will likely be subject to modifications? Some of the areas to explore during brainstorming sessions with the users might include

- Ad hoc queries against the application files/databases
- Modification of existing reports by the users
- Creation of new reports by the users
- Addition of new functions
- Modification of existing functions
- Addition of new data elements to existing records
- Addition of new records to the databases
- Addition of new databases
- Support of new users
- New protocols for telecommunications
- Requests for quick accommodation of new government regulations
- Addition of new computer equipment in different sites, such as terminals and printers
- Users' granting security access to their system to other users
- Uploading/downloading of data from the mainframe to the PC environment and vice versa
- Requirements for merging text and data

The level of flexibility that will be embedded in the system to allow the users to modify its behavior without the direct assistance of the system maintenance team must also be discussed with them. The general parameterized characteristics of the system should be spelled out at this stage, if this was not done previously. For example, various parameters stored in different external tables can be utilized by the users to select the particular set of reports that should be produced on a given day, the various sequences in which the information should be presented, and so forth. Information that is frequently changed should be stored in parameterized tables that can be easily adjusted by the users themselves instead of being hard-coded in the programs. In this way the users can dynamically modify the behavior of their systems with simple transactions.[16] In the past, several programmers were hard-coding these changes into their programs, a technique that invariably led to costly and lengthy recompilation and testing procedures. Tax tables are a good example of the use of parameterized tables.

---

[16]Obviously, some mechanisms will be required to allow the users to update and maintain these sets of parameterized files or databases themselves.

Batch reports turnaround requirements.   At this stage, the various batch reports that the system must produce on a periodic basis (daily, weekly, monthly, quarterly, yearly) should have been completely defined by the development team. The expected turnaround requirements for each of these reports should be finalized now.

There might be cases where the users would like to generate their own online queries or batch reports, but on an ad hoc basis rather than in a predetermined manner. User-friendly query languages or report generators might be very suitable when such a situation prevails. The ad hoc access requirements must be carefully examined by the development team to determine the best approach to satisfy them.

Prior to this, however, several questions must be answered: Can the developers estimate the expected frequency for these types of queries? Will the users formulate queries that only read the databases, or will they also update them? Should the users be allowed to access the production databases directly, or should the requested data be downloaded periodically to other file structures that might be more suitable to provide fast response time to various ad hoc types of queries and report requests?

System print load requirements.   Some applications might print voluminous amounts of data. If this is the case for the project at hand, the total number of print lines that must be processed per day by the system should be estimated by the development team. These figures should cover the total printing needs of the central site(s), as well as the local printing needs of the various user sites. This information will be used to determine the types of printers that should be acquired to support the printing needs of the new system.

Execution time of batch processes.   The job execution time of the major batch processes should be estimated, especially if the application will require running several lengthy jobs that, for whatever reason, cannot be run in parallel. The daily or overnight processing window time that can be made available for running these jobs on the mainframe computer might be limited. Therefore, it can be important to estimate the total elapsed or CPU time required to process these jobs even if it turns out to be a bulk estimate at this stage. This information will be used to determine if all the system batch processing load can indeed fit into the current production window.

Typically, the batch jobs that will run in the production batch window might include file/database utilities (backup, recovery, reorganization, space utilization) and application housekeeping functions (archiving, sorting/merging, download, upload). These estimates will be refined during the design stage if they are considered critical.

Data volatility requirements.   The data volatility requirements are related to the level of activity performed against the files and databases of the system. For instance, how often will new records be added or deleted from the application files/databases, and how many of them? Typically, a high level of database volatility should normally indicate the need to reorganize the database more frequently than what would normally be done for a less frequently updated database.

4.2.10 Define Environmental Site(s) Requirements

Task number:	DA-10	
Task name:	Define environmental site(s) requirements	
Objective:	To determine the user and operating center's environmental requirements	
Input(s):	DA-1	Functional process model
	DA-2	Functional data model
	DA-3	Data conversion plan
	DA-4	System test plan
	DA-9	Detailed system performance requirements
Output(s):	DA-10	System environmental site(s) requirements

Task description:

- Determine the major users' environmental site requirements, covering the potential need for new office equipment and additional floor space to accommodate the acquisition of new personnel or new computer equipment.
- Differentiate between those environmental requirements that can be met with the current facilities and those that cannot.
- If necessary, create a preliminary building/office layout showing the physical arrangements that are necessary for locating the required personnel and related office/computer equipment.
- Repeat the same process for the system operations site(s).
- Walk through the users' or systems operations' environmental site requirements.

In some instances, the environmental requirements of the users' or system operations' sites should be embodied in the system development process, even though many people might argue that this activity has nothing to do with developing a system. Nevertheless, space requirements to accommodate additional personnel or new furniture should not be neglected, especially if the user or systems operation personnel are already overcrowded. Ignoring these issues might only compound the problem.

Besides the important office space issues, a question that often arises is Should the personnel have ergonomically-designed furniture to increase their level of productivity? If some classes of users will operate their terminals all day long, as is often the case for data entry clerks, the answer is yes. Issues such as work posture and lighting conditions should be properly addressed and might require a careful planning effort. The seats and terminal positions should be selected in such a way as to reduce backaches, fatigue, eyestrain, and other similar problems. Adjustable chairs and terminals are often essential for those people who will interact with the system on a continual basis.

If the impact that the new system will have on the current user environment is not negligible, such as putting a specialized workstation on each user's desk, for instance, then a preliminary layout of the workplace should be prepared to optimize the space arrangements of the personnel and the office/computer equipment. Special consideration should also be given to optimize the work flow of documents frequently exchanged among the personnel in the office.

People must feel that the job they do is important for the company and that their contribution is appreciated by management. If they are asked to work in less than adequate working conditions (very crowded space, poor ventilation, inadequate office equipment, poor lighting), their motivation (and productivity) will probably decrease over time. Worse, they might start to believe that management does not care about people and start to react accordingly. To ensure the overall productivity of the business enterprise, several factors are necessary. An adequate office environment that is conducive to generating a pleasant working atmosphere should certainly be one of them.

4.2.11 Finalize Detailed Cost-Benefit Analysis

Task number:	DA-11	
Task name:	Finalize cost-benefit analysis	
Objective:	To finalize the cost-benefit analysis of the system	
Input(s):	PA-14	Cost-benefit analysis (refined)
	DA-1	Functional process model
	DA-2	Functional data model
	DA-3	Data conversion plan
	DA-4	System test plan
	DA-5	System training strategy (preliminary)
	DA-6	Detailed hardware/software/networking requirements
Output(s):	DA-11	Detailed cost-benefit analysis

Task description:
- Finalize the detailed costs of operating and maintaining the current system.
- Finalize the development costs of the new system.
- Finalize the projected operating costs of the new system.
- Finalize the benefits associated with the implementation of the new system.
- Walk through the detailed cost-benefit analysis deliverable.

All the information necessary for accurate estimation of the detailed costs and benefits figures associated with the new system should be available by now. Typically, the level of accuracy of the cost-benefit estimates should be ± 10 percent.

4.3 REFERENCES

DATE, C. J. 1986. *An Introduction to Data Base Systems,* 4th ed. Reading, Mass.: Addison-Wesley.

IEEE, 1983. *IEEE Standard for Software Test Documentation, ANSI/IEEE Std. 829-1983.* New York: The Institute of Electrical and Electronics Engineers, Inc.

MARTIN, J. 1981. *Computer Networks and Distributed Processing.* Englewood Cliffs, N.J.: Prentice Hall.

————. 1983. *Managing the Data Base Environment.* Englewood Cliffs, N.J.: Prentice Hall.

TOIGO, J.W. 1989. *Disaster Recovery Planning: Managing Risk and Catastrophe in Information Systems.* Yourdon Press Series. Englewood Cliffs, N.J.: Prentice Hall.

5

Design Phase

5.1 PURPOSE

The purpose of the design phase is to define the internal architecture of the system. The detailed specifications required to code and test the software programs will be gradually developed in parallel with the design of the physical files and databases of the system.

For a large, complex application, the design issues associated with the performance, usability, and maintainability characteristics of the system are of paramount importance. Consequently, the physical data and process models should be engineered in such a way as to offer as much flexibility as possible while yet taking into account the physical constraints that might be imposed by the technology selected to implement the system. Any deviation from the original requirements in the functional process and data models that might be necessary to accommodate specific system operational criteria should be properly documented and thoroughly discussed with the users. Lastly, the initial strategies that were elaborated upon in the detailed analysis phase concerning the testing, conversion, training, and installation of the system form the baseline for achieving the goals and objectives set in these documents.

TABLE 5.1   DESIGN PHASE TECHNICAL TASKS AND DELIVERABLES

Technical Tasks	*Technical Deliverables*
1. Define architectural system design standards	1. Architectural system design standards
2. Create physical data model	2. Physical data model
3. Create physical process model	3. Physical process model
4. Analyze program file/database access patterns	4. Physical data model (refined)
	Physical process model (refined)
	Physical program file/database access patterns
5. Develop data conversion strategy (detailed)	5. System data conversion strategy (detailed)
6. Develop training strategy (detailed)	6. System training strategy (detailed)
7. Develop testing strategy (detailed)	7. System testing strategy (detailed)
8. Create preliminary system job flowchart	8. Preliminary system job flowchart
9. Define file and database backup/recovery/reorganization strategy	9. File and database backup/recovery/reorganization strategy
10. Produce system manual's tables of contents	10. System manual's tables of contents
11. Finalize physical data storage estimates	11. Physical data storage estimates
12. Finalize system processing load estimates	12. System processing load estimates
13. Finalize hardware/software/networking acquisition and installation strategy	13. Final hardware/software/networking acquisition and installation strategy

Table 5.1 summarizes the major technical tasks that are conducted during the design phase, along with the anticipated technical deliverables. Figure 5.1 pictorially illustrates, at a high level, the relationships that exist among the individual tasks of the design phase.

DESCRIPTION OF THE TECHNICAL TASKS

5.2.1 Define Architectural System Design Standards

Task number:	DE-1
Task name:	Define architectural system design standards
Objective:	To describe the set of architectural standards that will be used to design the system
Input(s):	Existing system development standards
Output(s):	DE-1 Architectural system design standards

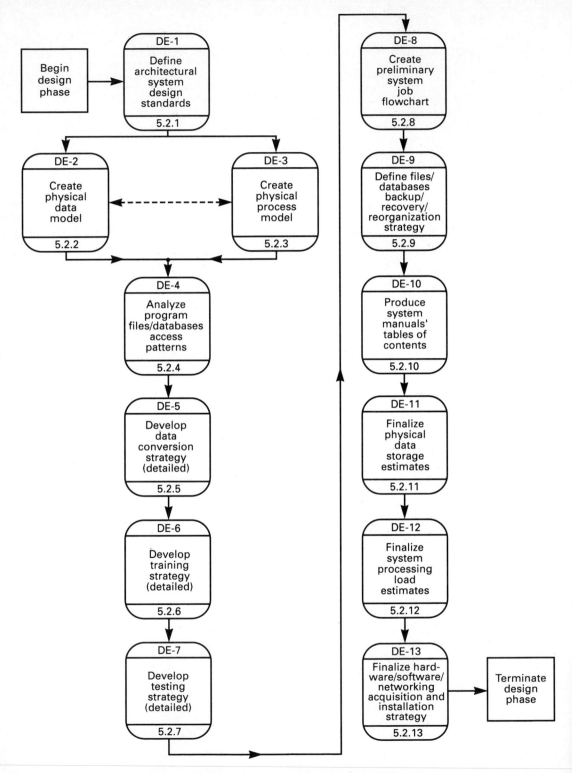

Figure 5.1   Design phase task network

Task description:

- Describe the architectural standards and conventions that will apply to the design and description of the external components of the system, including
  - Report layouts
  - Screen layouts
  - Form layouts
  - Human-machine dialogues
  - Error message formats
- Describe the architectural standards and conventions that will apply to the design and description of the internal components of the system, including
  - Reusable/common processes
  - General security access rules
  - General database access rules
  - Telecommunication protocols
- Walk through the architectural system design standards.

The set of architectural standards and guidelines that will be used to design the external components of the system must be clearly spelled out to all the members of the development team. This task is crucial, especially when several design teams will develop different functions of the same system. Failure to define these standards adequately might result in reduced system usability and maintainability.

Ideally, applying design consistency should not only be the rule for the software application at hand but also for all systems that are developed in the enterprise. For instance, if some basic form of design consistency is observed while developing the human-machine interfaces across various systems, the users will not have to adapt to myriad screen layouts that might radically differ from one software application to another. Moreover, the development team will likely increase the efficiency of the users by reducing the possibility of making errors and probably decrease their frustrations as well when using the system. Lastly, the learning curve associated with these systems will also decrease and the users will quickly become more effective when utilizing them to perform their daily activities.

If such basic guidelines do not exist at the present time, then the development team should decide the kinds of standards to be used to design the screens of the online portion of the system. These rules can cover the recommended generic layouts that apply to the design of menu screens, help screens, tutorial screens, update or inquiry screens, and the location of standard information on these screens. For instance, the standards may state that all dates must be displayed in accordance with the international representation of year, month, and day (i.e., YYYY MM DD) and should appear in the upper right-hand corner of the screen. They can equally cover the standardization of error message formats, color usage for highlighting information on the screen, sound usage, generalized program function keys usage (return to previous screens, screen-to-screen navigation, requesting screen prints, exiting a dialogue, paging forward and backward, scrolling up and down), screen headings, use of windows, mouses, icons, and so forth.[1]

Each organization might have its own standards for formatting screens, reports, or forms. Some of them can be very general and others very specific. One can argue that too many standards might curtail the creative abilities of the software developers. Nevertheless, a minimum set of standards is desirable to ensure that at least some level of consistency is maintained across the various systems of the organization. The staff should not confuse creativity with a lack of discipline. Software design is a creative process but it still requires a standard framework within which to work.

The development team should always keep in mind that the systems developed today are the ones that will be maintained tomorrow. As discussed in Chap. 13, on software quality, it is far more economical to engineer software quality (and maintainability) while designing the internal structure of the system than during the maintenance cycle. Consequently, the standards that will apply to the design of the internal components of the system should also be addressed at this point in the development cycle by the development team. For example, these might state the conventions that will apply to the design of common or reusable processes and to the establishment of general data communication/transmission rules, database access rules, or rules for interfacing with other systems.

5.2.2 Create Physical Data Model

Task number:	DE-2
Task name:	Create physical data model
Objective:	To transform the data components of the functional data model into physical files and database structures
Input(s):	DE-1 Architectural system design standards DA-1 Functional process model DA-2 Functional data model DA-7 Detailed system control requirements
Output(s):	DE-2 Physical data model

Task description:
- Review the file and database requirements that were specified in the functional data model.
- For each specific sequential or random access file requirement, repeat the following design steps:
  - Design the physical structure of the file.
  - Design the physical layout of each record in the file.
  - Specify the physical keys and search arguments used to retrieve data.

---

[1]For detailed information on how to design screen layouts based on sound ergonomic factors, see the references at the end of this chapter.

- Define the access method required.
- Address, if applicable, the system audit, control, security, volume, and performance requirements of the system.
- Document the following deliverables:
  Physical file structure diagram
  Physical record layouts
  Physical data groupings/data elements

- For each specific database requirement, repeat the following design steps:
  - Design the physical database structure, showing the optimal placement of the physical database records.
  - Choose the appropriate access method, based on the application access needs.
  - Choose the types of physical pointers that are needed to optimize navigation within the database structure.
  - Address the database audit, control, security, volume, and performance requirements.
  - Describe the physical database design parameters that might be required to support the randomizer routines, the data compression routines, the data encryption routines, and so on.
  - Document the following deliverables:
    Physical database structure diagram
    Physical database description
    Physical database record layouts
    Physical data groupings/data elements

- Review the physical files (sequential and random) and physical database structures to ensure they are compatible, where applicable.
- Document the rationale for any structural changes required to meet the audit, control, integrity, security, volume, and performance requirements of the system.
- If ad hoc queries and report generation will be satisfied by the users themselves with the use of fourth- and fifth- generation languages, design, if necessary, the additional physical file and database structures required to interface with these powerful tools.
- Walk through the physical data model and its supporting documents.

In essence, the purpose of this task is to augment the logical file and database structures shown in the functional data model with their detailed physical characteristics. Typically, the optimal design of the physical files and databases can be based on several considerations:

- Type of DBMS chosen (hierarchical, network, or relational)
- Need to conform to specific physical design rules that are inherent to the type of DBMS selected

- Efficiency
- Complexity of the data relationships that must be supported
- Size of the application files and databases
- Stated performance requirements, such as system response time and availability
- Volume of transactions processed per unit of time
- Audit, security, and integrity requirements of the system
- Local data access and update requirements that must be satisfied for each functional process
- System recovery and disaster recovery needs
- Volatility of the data stored in the system files/databases
- Requirements for stability, maintainability, and flexibility

Each of these factors or a combination of them will likely influence the structural arrangements of the file and database records. However, for the time being, the initial design effort should focus primarily on quickly deriving a first draft of the structural arrangement of the records. The resulting output will constitute a first-cut physical data model that can ideally be used by the development team to create program specifications.[2]

The creation of the physical data model is iterative in nature. Its internal architecture will be gradually optimized to accommodate the physical performance requirements that must be met by the physical process model. Later, this might entail the physical rearrangement of records, the introduction of controlled data redundancy for achieving better performance, the splitting or merging of data records, the addition of derived data elements, the physical relocation of data elements into different records, or the creation of new relationships among the records or databases for stability purposes or to strengthen the physical database structures to support more adequately some potential ad hoc query patterns.

The following section contains some basic suggestions that can help to design more stable files and databases. For a detailed discussion on physical database design, refer to the technical manuals listed in the references at the end of this chapter.

Sequential files.
- If the file is to contain several types of records, each specific record type in the file should be easily identifiable with a unique key.
- If some fields in the record will be used to sequence the file in a given order, they should be located at the beginning of the record, as much as possible.
- Additional space at the end of the record should be reserved for adding new fields that may be required in the foreseeable future.

---

[2]Sometimes other development options might be retained by the developers (e.g., the physical process model is constructed prior to or in parallel with the physical data model).

- The file should contain header and trailer record types to allow for version control, run dates, transaction counts, statistical balancing information, and so forth.

Databases and random access files.

- The primary keys, secondary keys, and search fields should be properly identified.
- The volatile fields should be grouped together, where possible, and not duplicated in several locations in order to avoid integrity and performance problems.
- Additional space could be reserved at the end of the record to allow for future expansion.
- If a nonkey field is a strong candidate to become a key field in the foreseeable future, it might be wise to create a new record for it now and establish the required relationships with the other records of the database.
- The record keys and the structure of the files should be kept as simple as possible. The simplest structure is often the best option.
- The designer should assess the users' needs for planned versus ad hoc access to data. The nonplanned informational needs should be balanced against the elementary operational needs of the application. If the complex database structure that must be put in place to favor ad hoc processing (extra indexes, pointers, relationships, etc.) creates a burden on the more basic operational data access needs of the application, then the option of creating two sets of physical databases should be seriously considered at that point—one set to meet the stringent fast access performance requirements of the application planned and repetitive processing needs and another set to accommodate the ad hoc processing of the nonplanned management inquiries or what-if scenarios. The database structure developed to satisfy the ad hoc data access requirements could then be installed in either a mainframe or microcomputer environment.

Normalization versus denormalization.   The normalization technique often places the system designers in a situation where eventually they must make some basic trade-offs between the ease of use of maintaining the physical data structures of the system versus the effectiveness of quickly retrieving data in general. A fully normalized data structure tends to be easier to maintain in the long run. However, this might be done at the expense of achieving lower performance when retrieving or updating data from these structures. Consequently, the following points should be carefully weighed when evaluating the possibility of selective denormalization.[3]

- Will denormalization create updating problems when maintaining the data structures later on?

[3]More discussion on database optimization is provided in Sec. 5.2.4.

- Does the full normalization process force the developer to create exhaustive and complex procedural code to maintain referential integrity on the normalized records?
- What type of performance impact does overnormalization have on the most frequently used transactions that update or retrieve data?
- How much space is required for each particular design alternative?

In any case, the reasons why the designer departs from a fully normalized data structure should always be properly documented for future reference.

5.2.3 Create Physical Process Model

Task number:	DE-3	
Task name:	Create physical process model	
Objective:	To transform the various processes of the functional process model into program structure charts	
Input(s):	DE-1	Architectural system design standards
	DA-1	Functional process model
	DA-2	Functional data model
	DA-7	Detailed system control requirements
Output(s):	DE-3	Physical process model

Task description:
- Review the functional process model that was produced during the detailed analysis phase.
- For each batch and online physical work unit identified in the model, repeat the following steps:

  Step 1.
- Derive a first-cut structure chart of the work unit program, using the design strategies supported by the transform and transaction analysis concepts.
- Augment, if required, the initial structure chart with the following details:
  - Add the modules required to read and write data.
  - Add the modules required to validate or edit the input data.
  - Add the modules required to format the output data properly.
  - Add the modules required to handle errors or exception cases.
  - Add the modules required to handle the initialization and termination routines.
  - Add the middle-level modules that might be required to coordinate the work activities of the lower-level modules.

  Step 2.
- Refine the preliminary design of the structure chart by analyzing and optimizing its modular architecture, in light of the following quality design criteria:

- Level of cohesion
- Level of coupling
- Span of control (fan-in/fan-out)
- Module size
- Module complexity
- Inefficient file/database access
- Code redundancy

Step 3.

- Finalize the packaging of the structure chart into a set of physical modules. If required, merge the bottom-level modules of the program into their parent modules, taking into consideration the design criteria that are used for physical packaging, such as
  - Size of the modules
  - Frequency of use of the modules
  - Modules' run time estimates
  - Design restrictions that might be imposed by the selected programming language/compiler/linkage editor facilities
  - Physical constraints that might be imposed by the type of processor that was retained to implement the system
- Document the detailed processing and control logic performed within each module shown on the structure chart, using the structured English, action diagrams, or pseudo-code specification languages.
- Document the physical file/database local data access scenarios of each program.
- Walk through the physical process model and its supporting documents.

The primary objective of this task is to derive the structure charts of the system from the automated work unit data flow diagrams.[4]

Before deriving the final architectural design of the system functions, the development team should review the detailed partitioning of the functional work units into resulting batch, online, real-time, or manual processes one last time and ensure that the original breakdown is still adequate. At the same time, the high-level hardware configuration that was retained to implement the system should be reviewed based on all the information that has been gathered up to this point. As we have seen, the types of processors that can be used to run the system are the mainframe, mini, or micro configuration. In fact, each set of functions/work unit

---

[4]Several program design alternatives other than the structured design technique developed by Constantine and Yourdon can also be favorably considered for different applications. One popular method is that of Jackson [1975], who basically matches the program structure to the file structures it manipulates. Two other widely used approaches are the Warnier [1981] and the Orr [1977] techniques. Both are somewhat different from the Jackson approach but are, nonetheless, other viable "data-oriented" techniques that are very effective for designing programs.

processes that are allocated to a specific type of processor can indeed be viewed at a high level as a physical subsystem of its own and designed accordingly.

Step 1: Derive first-cut structure chart.   Given that the formulation of the system's manual/automated boundaries has been finalized, along with the selection of the most appropriate processor technology to satisfy the users' needs, the method used to convert the detailed automated system processes that are depicted in the work unit data flow diagrams into hierarchical structures consists of two major design strategies: transaction and transform analyses.[5]

A *transaction-centered* system will usually process several types of transactions. Typically, a dispatcher type of process handles the different transaction categories the system manipulates and will frequently be identifiable as such in the data flow diagrams that are used to depict the system. The processing path that must be traversed by a given transaction is determined by its type.

A *transform-centered* system is often characterized by some typical processes that are easily identifiable as input processes, others that transform the input data into output data (i.e., central transform processes), and processes that dispose of the output data. Once the central transform processes are located on the data flow diagrams, the structure chart is then derived by placing the input processes that obtain input data on the left leg of the hierarchical structure, the processes that dispose of the output data on the right leg, and the processes that convert the input data into output data in the middle.

Note that more often than not, a transaction-centered design will frequently process individual transactions via a transform-centered structure.

Once the batch and online work unit data flow processes of the system have been systematically converted into rough-cut structure charts, the next activity consists of augmenting each of them with the lower-level modules that are necessary for validating the inputs, formatting the outputs, processing the errors, and so forth. While performing this activity, it is important to identify the general-purpose modules that can be designed in such a way as to be reusable by several other programs or even other systems.

Step 2: Refine structure charts.   The structure charts are refined to ensure that the number and complexity of interconnections among the modules are kept to an acceptable level. Doing so will increase the overall quality of the design and will positively contribute to the development of more flexible systems that will be easier to maintain. Several design heuristics can be used to develop software systems that are well structured and modularized. Some of the most important and frequently used quality criteria to guide the design process are briefly discussed next.[6]

[5]For more information on transaction and transform analysis design strategies, refer to Page-Jones [1988] and Constantine and Yourdon [1979].

[6]For more information on these topics, refer to Page-Jones [1988] and Constantine and Yourdon [1979].

Module Coupling.   Module coupling can be defined as the number of inter-connections between one module of a program and its other modules. Although there can be several types and degrees of coupling between two modules (data coupling, control coupling, stamp coupling, etc.) the primary goal of this concept is to decrease as much as possible the level of dependence of one module with another. In turn, the possibility of creating a defect in a module while changing another one, as during the maintenance phase, for example, is minimized.

Cohesion.   Cohesion is defined as a measure of the degree to which all the components of a module are effectively required to carry out a single function or process. For instance, the operations of a work unit process are highly cohesive if all are mandatory to carry out that process. Several varieties of cohesion have been identified so far. Some of the most important ones are coincidental, logical, temporal, procedural, communicational, and functional cohesion.

Span of Control.   Span of control is defined as the number of immediate modules that can be directly invoked by another module. In principle, the number of modules that can be called by another module should not be too high or too low. In general, a module should not call more than seven lower-level modules. This is suggested in order to avoid overcomplex program structures, which can prove to be difficult to maintain once the system moves into production. However, one possible exception to this rule of thumb can be the dispatcher module of a transaction-centered system.

Module Size.   There are no absolute rules for limiting the physical size of a module because size can greatly vary from one programming language to another. Nevertheless, if the module is too large, chances are that it will be more difficult to maintain. On the other hand, if the application is implemented with modules that contain only four or five lines of code each, the system overhead will probably increase beyond an acceptable level of performance. An acceptable size for a module, coded with a third-generation language such as Cobol, will usually range between 30 lines and 200 lines of procedural code. However, note that this is far from being a rigid standard. No matter what, the designer should always keep in mind that it is certainly easier to regroup smaller modules into larger units to improve system performance than to break a large program down into smaller units.

Module Complexity.   If the module is very complex, the designer should try to decompose the internal module logic into smaller logical units while at the same time retaining a high degree of cohesion among them. Even though it is difficult to develop universal guidelines that can be utilized to analyze the level of complexity of a module objectively, simplicity of execution and clarity are certainly two strong candidate criteria in such a situation.

Inefficient File/Database Access.   In some cases, the calls made to the files and databases can be optimized to obtain a better response or execution time. One of the best ways to achieve a good response time is to limit the number of calls made by the module to the databases, hence reducing the number of I/Os. In some instances, the database structure itself is not designed for efficiency, but in many cases, the database calls made by the program modules are not always properly sequenced to achieve optimal performance. For both reasons, the database access scenarios performed by the program should be properly documented by the developer. They will then be verified by the database designer at a later stage to assess the effectiveness of the database structures against the different calls made by the system programs.

Code Redundancy.   The modules should be reviewed to detect any duplication of code among them. If this is the case, a decision should be made as to whether the duplicated code should be eliminated by creating a common module. The advantage gained in such a situation is not having to maintain the same piece of code in several places.

Step 3: Package structure chart.   The last step involves packaging the logical modules of the structure charts into physical modules. Several grouping criteria can be used for packaging a design. First, the modules that are executed within a loop should be physically placed with the module that invokes the loop. Second, if a large amount of data is passed between two modules, they should be combined. Third, modules that are frequently activated should be grouped for better performance.

Application code generators and structure charts.   The advent of fourth- and fifth-generation languages, along with the emergence of powerful Cobol application code generators, has led many developers to question the usefulness of creating program structure charts when these tools are used in the MIS organization. To illustrate this point, several Cobol application code generators already provide a generic program structure chart, composed of an input leg, an output leg, and a main processing section. Because some of the logic used to handle an online program differs somewhat from the one used for a batch program, some application code generators even supply two types of program structure charts—one for online and one for batch programs.

Most of the repetitive logic involved in the handling of the input and output legs of a program is automatically taken care of by these online development tools. Yet the creation of a large and complex program usually cannot be completely satisfied by this kind of tool. Even when the developers are fully aware of all the technical facilities provided by these powerful code generators, some additional custom code logic will often have to be added to satisfy the most complex processing requirements of the program. In such a situation, the structure chart might still prove to be a valuable tool to describe at least graphically the extra processing logic that needs to be added by the programmers themselves to perform the most complex functions of the program.

Online help facility.   As noted earlier in this book, the online portion of most software applications includes a comprehensive help facility that provides guidance to the users while interfacing with the system. In fact, several categories of help facilities can be designed for that purpose. For example, online help facilities can provide general orientation information on how to utilize the system, such as describing the transactions available to the users and giving specific examples. Another category would describe error messages in a context-sensitive manner. A third category would describe the valid values or ranges of values that can be entered by a user for specific data items displayed on a screen.

A comprehensive online help facility for a large system calls for a lot of effort from the software developers. If necessary, the help facility can be prototyped with the users, like any regular online function of the system.

5.2.4 Analyze Program File/Database Access Patterns

Task number:	DE-4
Task name:	Analyze program files/databases access patterns
Objective:	To ensure that the physical file/database structures can satisfy the batch/online/real-time data access requirements of the application as stated in the performance requirements
Input(s):	DE-2 Physical data model DE-3 Physical process model
Output(s):	DE-2 Physical data model (refined) DE-3 Physical process model (refined) DE-4 Physical program file/database access patterns

Task description:
- Analyze the file and database access patterns of the most critical and frequently used programs. Ensure that they can be fully satisfied by the physical file/database structures of the system.
- If deemed necessary, perform database prototyping to verify that the database access requirements meet the stated performance objectives.
- Make the necessary adjustments either to the physical database structures or to the program database access requirements to meet the performance criteria of the system. If appropriate, revise the original performance criteria to reflect the physical limitations that might be imposed by the selected DBMS technology or the existing computing environment.
- Document the changes made to the databases and/or the application programs.
- Walk through the consolidated physical program file/database access patterns.

The detailed physical data access requirements of each program should be carefully analyzed to verify that the expected system performance requirements can be satisfied by the newly created physical data structures. The records accessed by each critical program should be analyzed in light of the access pattern favored by the program, the order in which the physical records are retrieved from the databases, the type of access (read or update), and the estimated access frequency.

These access requirements are then matched against the structural architecture of the databases involved in the process.

The findings of this analysis might prompt the database designer to modify the structure of the physical databases to satisfy better the performance requirements of the most critical or most frequently used transactions of the system. On the other hand, the design of the application transactions themselves might also need to be adjusted to meet the stated performance requirements. In some extreme cases, the original performance requirements will have to be revisited and modified accordingly. This is especially true when the performance issue becomes subordinate to database integrity or maintainability issues. An additional trade-off that might also need to be evaluated centers around satisfying the specific data access requirements of a single software application versus those of several applications that are all sharing the same subject physical databases.

Database prototyping.   In some situations, the application performance requirements are so critical to the success of the project that the physical design of the database is evaluated with the assistance of a DBMS modeling tool.[7] Some of the particular situations where it might be appropriate for the development team to consider database prototyping include

- Applications that have highly critical response time requirements
- Applications that are developed with a new type of DBMS software
- Applications that are highly volume oriented and require very large databases
- Applications that must satisfy overly complex processing needs and are characterized by complex data relationships

Typically, the resulting database prototype model is used to

- Optimize the database access paths of the critical online transactions
- Estimate the job turnaround time of the large batch programs
- Evaluate the validity and effectiveness of different physical database design alternatives

Figure 5.2 illustrates the generic process required to prototype a physical database structure for performance evaluation.

The costs involved with database prototyping should be considered and properly weighed against the anticipated benefits. Most of today's database environments are fairly complex compared to those of the past, and they are expensive to develop, maintain, and enhance. Consequently, it might be far more economical to prototype them now and design a stable database environment that can evolve over time rather than having to modify the database environment in a real-life production environment.

---

[7]An example of such a tool is DBPROTOTYPE, which can be used to model the hierarchical database software product marketed by IBM (IMS).

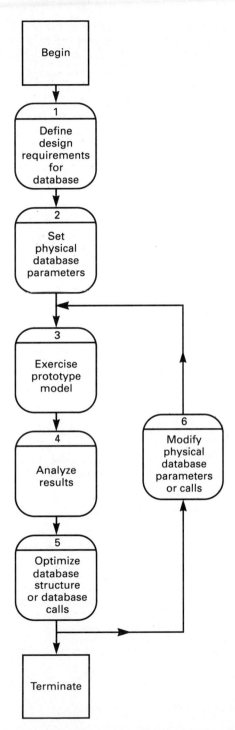

Figure 5.2   Physical database prototyping

Physical record usage matrix.   For a large system, a consolidated record usage matrix can prove to be a valuable tool to depict the relationships between the physical work unit processes of the system and the physical records of the physical data model. Figure 5.3 illustrates such a matrix. This matrix can be progressively constructed in the following manner:

1. Show each physical program of the system in the first column of the matrix and identify all the physical records accessed by each program on the upper rows.
2. Specify the processing mode of each program: batch, online, or real time.
3. Specify the program execution frequency per unit of time—that is, the number of times the program is executed per minute, per hour, per day, per week, per month, or per year.
4. Specify the access mode of each physical record: read, update, create, or delete.
5. Specify the number of records processed by each program per unit of time.

5.2.5 Develop Data Conversion Strategy (Detailed)

Task number:	DE-5
Task name:	Develop data conversion strategy (detailed)
Objective:	To refine the preliminary system data conversion strategy, derive the detailed data conversion requirements of the system, and design the conversion programs
Input(s):	DA-3 System data conversion strategy (preliminary) DE-2 Physical data model DE-3 Physical process model
Output(s):	DE-5 System data conversion strategy (detailed)

Task description:
- Review the preliminary data conversion strategy that was outlined during the detailed analysis phase.
- For each existing manual or mechanized file/database that will require conversion to satisfy the data requirements of the new system, analyze the general

Program Identification	Processing Mode	Execution Frequency	Physical Record Type A			Physical Record Type X	
			Access Mode	Access Volume	...	Access Mode	Access Volume
Program A	Online	10 tx/day	R	5		—	—
Program B	Batch	4 times/month	R	200		C	200

Figure 5.3   Physical record usage matrix

conversion effort in terms of the required input processes, transform processes, and output processes.

- Develop the structure charts of programs that are necessary to perform the detailed conversion processes or to populate the new files/databases of the system.
- Develop the test cases that will be required to verify the conversion programs.
- Describe in detail the type of software tools, utilities, and hardware networking equipment that will be required to perform the conversion process.
- Refine the original estimates concerning the volume of data that must be processed during the entire conversion effort.
- Finalize the detailed data conversion strategy.
- Walk through the detailed system data conversion strategy.

Data conversion specifications.   At this point in the project, the physical data structures of the new system can be accurately compared with those of the old system. This comparison can be performed by viewing any file/database that must be converted as being the major component of the input leg of a "conversion" program while the output leg reflects the data structures required by the new system. In the middle is the main transform process that will read the data elements stored in the old data structures, convert them according to a predetermined algorithm, and store them in the data structures required by the new system. Figure 5.4 schematically illustrates this concept with two relatively simple data structures.

Input Process.   Identify all the data elements that are stored in the old data structures and need modification. Identify those that will simply be transferred directly onto the new system data structures without any further transformation. Finally, identify those that will not be transferred at all.

Transform Process.   For each identified transform process, describe the detailed algorithmic operations that should be performed to convert the input data into the desired output data formats. Depending on the level of complexity involved with the transform process itself, several operations might be necessary:

- Converting data from one internal machine representation to another
- Validating the content of the fields
- Comparing various data elements originating from several files/databases
- Merging different fields that are located in different files/databases
- Establishing relationships or dependencies among different fields currently stored in different files/databases
- Synchronizing several files/databases at the same time
- Expanding or shortening the size of a data element
- Reordering records or data elements in a different sequence
- Modifying the contents of the fields

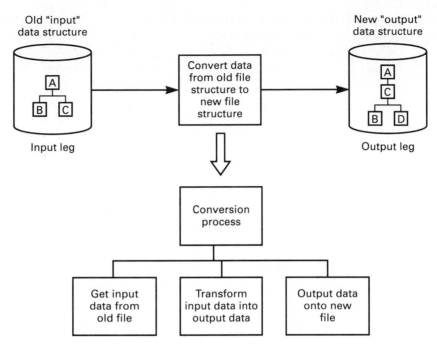

Figure 5.4   Data conversion process

Sometimes the transform process can turn out to be very straightforward, such as reading the fields contained in the old file records, slightly modifying their formats, and then copying them onto the new file. Another example might be to sort fields into a different sequence. A third example is to transfer the current data from one medium to another, as from tape to disk. On the other hand, the transform process can be complex, as having to compare and/or modify myriad data elements that are extracted from several files and databases that are not necessarily synchronized and reside on different types of PCs and mainframes.

Output Process.   For each output process, specify the expected results in terms of each new field's format, internal representation, and content. The approach that will be used to initialize the new fields created from scratch expressly for the new system files/databases should also be documented as completely as possible at this stage. For instance, the detailed specification associated with the creation of new fields could well be read as

New Field A = Old Field A + Old Field B
New Field C = New Field A + Old Field D
New Field D = Must be initialized to spaces
New Field E = Must be initialized to zero
Old Field A = New Field B + Old Field B

Before the conversion effort itself, it is strongly suggested, if this has not yet been done, to verify the level of data integrity of the current files and databases, whether they are manual or mechanized. If the existing files/databases contain too many errors or inconsistencies, extra effort will have to be made to correct these errors. Ignoring these issues will only compound the problem during the implementation phase.

Many people would readily assume that, by default, the data in the manual files of the current system are probably more error prone than those in the mechanized files and databases of the system. Unfortunately, this is not always the case, especially for the old mechanized files/databases that were created many years ago. These are often characterized by a low level of integration. For example, the same field is replicated in several files and used in a slightly different manner by different applications. Sometimes the same logical field will have a different length from one file to another. For example, in one file it might have four characters, and in another file it might have three characters. In situations like these, the users should intervene to decide which field in which application file is the most accurate.

Detailed data conversion strategy.   The broad data conversion strategy that was elaborated upon during the development phase should now be revisited in light of the detailed information that has been accumulated so far concerning the new system. Among other things, the initial strategy should be expanded to cover all the detailed conversion steps that are required to perform the conversion process, along with their sequences and dependencies. In addition, the following conversion subjects should also be clearly defined and finalized with the users and any other MIS groups that might be involved in the conversion effort:

- Scope and objectives of the conversion effort
- Roles and responsibilities of each group implicated in the conversion effort
- Required software tools and hardware/networking equipment
- Estimated duration of the entire conversion process
- Detailed description of the proposed cutover scenario to phase out the old system components (e.g., files, databases, and processes)
- Detailed description of the fallback procedures, if required

In some cases, the user and system personnel will also need to receive some special training to perform the conversion process. If this is the case, the training strategy should reflect such a need.

The complex programs that will be required to perform the conversion of voluminous and complex files/databases should be designed with the help of structured charts. This is required to improve their processing efficiency, even though in principle they should run only once. Usually, the conversion programs should also produce several audit and control reports that flag incorrect records or fields, provide several kinds of statistics on the total number of records processed in the input and output files, and even print a log of all the records that were processed in the old and new files on paper or another medium. The detailed content and format of these reports should be discussed with the users, based on the specific needs of the software application at hand.

If the conversion process is expected to be particularly lengthy and will likely necessitate running several separate conversion programs in a predetermined sequence, then some backup and recovery mechanisms should be set up between each intermediate step to avoid having to restart the entire conversion task from the very beginning when a major system failure occurs in the middle of the process.

In some organizations, where large volumes of data are to be processed, the conversion effort is considered so crucial to the success of the project that the conversion programs are coded and tested before any other type of program during the implementation phase. These tested conversion programs are then used to populate the new application test files and databases with real-life production data samples. This procedure also allows more accurate estimation of the total processing and elapsed time it will take to convert all of the old system data, based on the actual time it took to convert a subset of the production files/databases. In other instances, the online transactions required to manually add data records to the new files/databases are developed first and then used to create test data or directly load production data into the new production files/databases.

Finally, the detailed test cases that will be used to exercise the conversion programs should now be developed, along with their expected results.

5.2.6 Develop Training Strategy (Detailed)

Task number:	DE-6	
Task name:	Develop training strategy (detailed)	
Objective:	To develop the optimal strategy to satisfy the user/system training requirements	
Input(s):	DA-5	System training strategy (preliminary)
	DE-2	Physical data model
	DE-3	Physical process model
	DE-5	System data conversion strategy (detailed)
Output(s):	DE-6	System training strategy (detailed)

Task description:
- Complete the identification of personnel training needs and finalize the description of the detailed training specifications.
- Develop the detailed system training strategy, covering for each targeted audience the following:
  - Scope and objectives of the training program
  - Training methods recommended
  - Identification of who should provide the training
  - Type of physical facilities needed to deliver the training effort
  - Type of office equipment required to support the training process

- New training material that must be developed
- General timing, duration, sequencing, and dependencies of the major training events
- Total number of people to be trained and estimated machine resource consumption that will be utilized to deliver the training
- Type of hardware equipment or software facilities required to support or conduct the training sessions

- Develop, if necessary, the test cases that will be used to verify the training subsystem.
- Walk through the detailed system training strategy.

If, as prescribed in the chapter on the survey phase, the users actively participated in the development of their system, it should be relatively easy at this point to involve them in the creation of the detailed training strategy, especially if some basic form of early prototyping has been used during the project.[8] The reasons for such a positive attitude are obvious. The users probably feel far more comfortable with the new system because they have been gradually exposed to its major features through active participation, especially while developing the required screens and report layouts. Furthermore, their sense of ownership should be greatly enhanced because they have been actively involved in the project from the beginning.

The first step involves reviewing the detailed changes that the new system will introduce to the work environment, refining the list of categories of personnel who will be affected by these changes, and completing the description of all the corresponding training requirements in detail. In addition, the detailed estimates on the total number of people who must be trained per category of user should be verified with each affected business area user representative. Once these prerequisite activities have been completed, the detailed strategy for effectively training all personnel can be finalized with the active participation of the users.

In the development of detailed training strategy for a very sophisticated system, several items should be covered:

Target audience: *Who will be trained?* Every user in all areas, or some selected users who in turn will train other users? How many people per user category must be trained? Should the courses be tailored to suit the specific needs of each category of user (i.e., people on the shop floor, clerks, managers, executives)? What should be the level of training—basic? intermediate? advanced?

Training methods: *Which type of training method is recommended?* The classroom approach with hands-on exercises? The self-study approach? On-the-job coaching? Audiovisuals? Formal presentations? Tutorials? Seminars? Interactive computer-based training? Pilot project? Should some

---

[8]For more information on prototyping, see Chap. 10.

mechanism be put in place to obtain constructive feedback on the effectiveness of the training materials?

Trainers:

Who should deliver the training? The development team? The users themselves? Some internal training department or a specialized external training firm? The vendor that is supplying a commercial package?

Physical facilities/ office equipment:

What type of facilities are required to train the staff? Where will they be trained, in-house or outside? In a general-purpose classroom or in a dedicated training center? On-site, in their own working environment? How many people can attend a single training session? What equipment is required (overhead projector, 35 mm slide projector, video machine, whiteboards, flip charts)?

Training materials and documents:

What type of documents are required to train the staff? Are special forms needed? Will preassignment booklets be utilized? What type of documentation will be provided to the trainee during or after a course— presentation transparencies, classroom notes? Will the new user operating manuals be used during the training sessions?

Timing, duration, sequence, and dependencies:

When will the training sessions be scheduled? What will be the duration of the training sessions? What will be the sequence? Will the staff be trained at one physical location at a time? One region at a time? All at once? Are there any training dependencies among the various releases of the system?

People and resources:

How many people will be needed to conduct the training sessions? How many machine resources will be consumed? Is there a need for a guaranteed system response time while training people?

Hardware/ software/ networking equipment:

Will some special hardware equipment be required to train the staff? Dedicated terminals, printers, plotters, automated teller machines, large-screen computer projection systems, microcomputers? What about the software facilities? Will the new system itself be used to train the staff? Will help screens be provided with the new system? Would a prototype model suffice? Does the software package offered by the vendor include a training subsystem? Can some portions of the training material that already exists for the old system be used with some minor modifications?

As previously discussed, most people realize that quality training and education is worth the expense if one wants to achieve economic productivity. However, it is important for the development team to highlight the benefits that will result from effective training to management. Presenting the detailed costs of training is relatively easy, but it is far more difficult to present the benefits in quantifiable terms. In addition, as the project progresses through the design and implementation phases, the pressure to deliver the system on time and within budget will probably greatly increase. Consequently, it might be very tempting to downgrade the training effort, especially if management was not convinced of the payoffs and if the initial project delivery date has already been delayed, for whatever reason.

In an attempt to overcome these potential shortcomings, the detailed training strategy and the resulting educational cost-benefit figures should be completely covered at this stage of the project and embedded in the project plans for the subsequent phases. Furthermore, if the training plan is presented as a one-time effort, the investment spent in developing a sophisticated user training environment might be hard to sell to management. On the other hand, if the training program is designed to evolve with the system, then its usefulness will be greatly enhanced.

5.2.7 Develop Testing Strategy (Detailed)

Task number:	DE-7
Task name:	Develop testing strategy (detailed)
Objective:	To refine the preliminary testing strategy and generate quality test cases for each specific level of testing necessitated to verify the system adequately
Input(s):	DA-4 System testing strategy (preliminary)
	DE-2 Physical data model
	DE-3 Physical process model
	DE-5 System data conversion strategy (detailed)
	DE-6 System training strategy (detailed)
Output(s):	DE-7 System testing strategy (detailed)

Task description:

- Perform the following activities for each particular level of testing that is planned for the new system (production acceptance, user acceptance, system integration, unit testing):
  - Identify the detailed manual and automated processes of the system that are subject to testing. Identify, if applicable, the sequence in which they must be tested within a release (by version).
  - Analyze in detail the input, main processing logic, and output requirements of each process.
  - Derive from these requirements the test cases that should be exercised in an attempt to identify potential defects in the system.

- Determine the start/completion criteria of each individual testing stage, along with a description of the dependencies among them, if any.
- Refine the initial testing strategy and its associated version test plan.
- Walk through the detailed system strategy and its supportive material.

Given that the manual and automated processes of the system have been analyzed in terms of their respective input, main processing logic, and output components, the test cases are finally developed to attempt to demonstrate that the system *cannot* satisfy its requirements. A successful test case is one that uncovers as many defects or unexpected results as possible. Furthermore, in order to be truly meaningful, a test case scenario must not only specify the input data that will be used to detect defects in the programs or modules but also the expected results. For these reasons, the quality of the system test data can only be as good as the quality of the system design specifications themselves. System design specifications that are clear, precise, and complete will lead to test cases that have similar quality characteristics.

Preparation of test cases.   The following section describes the different types of test cases that can be constructed for each particular level of testing used to verify the system.[9]

Unit Test Cases.   The unit testing process is based on what is called a whitebox testing concept. It verifies the correctness of a program by means of producing test cases that are specifically engineered to uncover errors in the internal structure of the program. Consequently, the unit test cases should verify the following elements of a program:

- Correctness and accuracy of the program's internal logic
- Interfaces among the various modules of the program
- All the procedural statements contained in the program modules

The following categories of test cases may be used to exercise the internal logic of a program as thoroughly as possible:

- Statement coverage tests
- Branch/loop coverage tests
- Value sampling tests
- Boundary value coverage tests
- Program interface tests
- File-handling tests
- Error message tests
- Error-prone tests

[9]For a detailed description of these test cases, see Chap. 8, on structured testing.

Since the programs are not yet coded, the unit test cases are initially developed from the program specifications. Once the programs are coded, during the implementation phase, additional test cases will be developed to satisfy completely some or all of the testing requirements.

System Integration Test Cases.   The system integration testing process is based on a black-box testing concept. It verifies the system by creating test cases that are specifically engineered to demonstrate that the various automated components of the system do not work properly together or do not satisfy the various input/output requirements of the system. Consequently, the system integration test cases should verify the following elements of a system:

- Interfaces between the various programs of the system
- Manual to automated interfaces of the system (screens, reports, etc.)
- External interfaces with other systems

The following categories of test cases may be used to exercise the functional specifications of the system, along with its nonfunctional specifications, as thoroughly as possible:

- System interface
- Control
- Conversion
- Security
- Backup, recovery, and restart
- Screen dialogue
- Volume
- Performance
- Stress
- Usability
- Documentation
- Storage
- Maintainability
- Compatibility

User Acceptance Test Cases.   The user acceptance testing process is similarly based on a black-box concept. However, its primary objective is to verify the total system solution by means of test cases that are specifically constructed to demonstrate that the automated and manual components of the system do not work properly together or do not satisfy the original user business requirements. Consequently, the user acceptance test cases should verify the following elements of a system:

- Manual procedures
- Automated processes with their input/output requirements
- Interfaces with other systems

The following categories of test cases may be used to exercise the external design specifications of the system and its related nonfunctional specifications as thoroughly as possible:[10]

- Functional
- System interface
- Control
- Conversion
- Security
- Backup, recovery, and restart
- Screen dialogue
- Volume
- Performance
- Stress
- Usability
- Documentation
- Storage
- Compatibility

The vast majority of the test cases that will be prepared by the users will focus primarily on the functionality of the system, its screen dialogue scenarios, its reports, and its usability characteristics. To prepare their test cases, the users must utilize the original system requirements and the design specifications that have been developed by the systems analysts and designers.

It is worth pointing out that a side benefit to having the users prepare their own test cases is that they will probably detect some requirements and design errors, inconsistencies, or ambiguities in the system specifications. Thus, chances are that the software specifications will improve through this indirect validation process. Sometimes the users might not be able to create test cases that will adequately challenge the original system requirements and design specifications of the system. Such a situation might clearly indicate to the development team a potentially serious problem: either the software specifications are not detailed enough or the users cannot understand them. In both cases, the problem must be resolved.

Since some of the nonfunctional tests (volume testing, e.g.) might turn out to be both significantly time and resource consuming, they could be executed by the

---

[10]The categories of test cases for user acceptance and for system integration are very similar. However, the system integration test cases are developed by the systems people, whereas the acceptance tests are developed by the users themselves.

system development team, but with the active participation of the users. Furthermore, they can be exercised only to the degree where the test environment in place can adequately support them. In some instances, there might be a number of environmental constraints that will preclude the execution of some types of tests, such as stress testing.

The manual procedures supporting the automated environment should also be tested during the user acceptance testing process to ensure that the total system solution works according to the stated design specifications. Hence, some real end users should be directly involved in the user acceptance process, not just some user representatives.

Production Acceptance Test Cases.   The production acceptance testing process verifies the total system solution by means of test cases that are constructed to demonstrate that the system does not work properly in the production environment. Consequently, the production acceptance test cases should verify, among other things, the following elements of a system:

- System operations documentation
- Performance and data storage requirements for production
- Complete processing cycle in production

The test cases that were applied in the user acceptance process can be augmented with real production data to reflect the real-life production environment.

The production acceptance cycle should provide the end users and systems operations staff with the opportunity to test the system completely using, in a production mode, the following components:

- Job control statements
- Files/databases
- Hardware/software/networking configurations
- Documentation of the system

Regression testing.   Considering the importance that maintenance has in the total system life cycle costs, the development team should make all efforts possible to design a test environment that will be reusable for regression testing.[11] This reusable test environment will be invaluable for testing the major functional enhancements that will be made to the system during its entire lifetime, not to mention the advantages it can provide when significant defect repairs have to be made against it. Hence, a representative subset of the test cases that are developed at the present time should be salvaged for such a purpose. The idea behind regression testing is not to save a voluminous amount of test data but rather to archive a given amount of downsized quality test data that will excrcise most of the logic performed by the system programs.

[11]For more information on regression testing, see Chap. 8.

Detailed testing strategy. Once the test cases are created, the initial testing strategy and its associated integration test plan are finally refined with all the information gathered to date on the project. The following activities are performed for this purpose:

- Describe the detailed hardware/software/networking tools and facilities needed during each specific testing cycle.
- In addition to the manual or automated library control mechanisms that will be put in place to manage the test environment, describe the procedures necessary to monitor the progress made by each group involved in the testing process.
- Describe in detail the roles and responsibilities of each group of users or MIS personnel who will be involved in the support or direct execution of the various system testing activities.
- Describe in detail the files and data storage requirements needed to support the test environment.
- Refine the time and machine resource estimates of each particular level of testing that will be performed against the system.
- Confirm, if required, the different sites where the testing process will be performed.

5.2.8 Create Preliminary System Job Flowchart

Task number:	DE-8
Task name:	Create preliminary system job flowchart
Objective:	To describe the high-level job flow structure of the batch programs
Input(s):	DE-2 Functional data model
	DE-3 Physical process model
Output(s):	DE-8 Preliminary system job flowchart

Task description:
- Identify all the batch programs of the system.
- Group these programs into tentative production job streams.
- Produce a preliminary system flowchart of the batch production job streams.
- Walk through the preliminary system job flowchart.

The batch portion of the system now needs to be further partitioned into several production job streams. A production job stream consists of one or more programs that are executed in a predetermined sequence under the control of the operating system. The execution of each program within a job is done under the control of a job step. Finally, the program running in a particular job step can, in fact, be an application program or a utility program, such as a sort facility or a database backup/recovery facility.

Ideally, there should be one system flowchart for each type of processor con-figuration under which the system is implemented. Each system flowchart structure presents the sequence in which the production job streams should be executed. First, the programs that should be grouped into a job stream should be identified. Second, the jobs are analyzed to determine in which sequence they should be executed. For this reason, the dependencies among the various jobs of the system should be clearly defined. In fact, two scenarios can occur. With the first scenario, there is no dependency among the jobs, and therefore, they can all be executed in parallel. However, in the second scenario, there are some dependencies among the different jobs, consequently, they cannot run in parallel. In such a situation, the jobs that are executed before and after the current job should be clearly identified and properly documented.

Quite often, the production jobs can be categorized into different production cycles—on request, daily, weekly, monthly, or annually. It might be advantageous for a large system to develop one flowchart for each specific production cycle.

It is important to point out that the preliminary system job flowchart will be refined during the implementation phase and serve as a major baseline for the preparation of the production job cycles and their related operating instructions. The flowchart will also come in handy when determining if the proposed job streams will have difficulties running within the processing window allocated to batch jobs in the production environment.

5.2.9 Define File/Database Backup/Recovery/Reorganization Strategy

Task number:	DE-9
Task name:	Define file and database backup/recovery/reorganization strategy
Objective:	To define the utility runs needed to support the system files/databases
Input(s):	DA-7 Detailed system control requirements DA-9 Detailed system performance requirements DE-2 Physical data model DE-3 Physical process model DE-4 Physical program file/database access requirements DE-5 System data conversion strategy (detailed) DE-7 System testing strategy (detailed) DE-8 Preliminary system job flowchart
Output(s):	DE-9 File and database backup/recovery/reorganization strategy

Task description:
- Analyze the system performance, control, and security requirements that specifically apply to the file/database environment.
- Analyze the file/database update patterns of each production job.

- Identify the production jobs that are required to back up, recover, and reorganize the application files/databases.
- Estimate the execution time of each file/database utility job.
- Walk through the file and database backup/recovery/reorganization strategy.

In order to maintain an adequate control over the integrity and availability of the data manipulated by the system, a well-thought out plan must be developed to satisfy the file and database backup, recovery, and reorganization needs of the application. Several factors might affect the plan for *backing up* an application file or database:

- File/database size
- Type of processing performed against the file/database (e.g., read only versus update mode of operation)
- Type of processing mode (batch, online, or real-time)
- User requirements for timely recovery in case of a system failure
- Frequency of updates performed against the file/database (volatility of the data)

As a rule of thumb, online databases are typically backed up right after an initial load, at the end of each day, and after a reorganization. A batch database is normally backed up right after an initial load, at the end of a job that updates it, on a regular basis determined by the frequency and volume of update transactions processed, and after a reorganization.

The database *recovery* runs are executed after an application programming error or a software system failure has damaged the database. The database is reconstructed with the data contained in the last backup that was taken before the problem occurred. All the update transactions that have been processed since then and stored in a log data set are also applied against the database.

Typically, the database *reorganization* utilities are run in two specific instances: to improve the database performance by optimizing the current physical placement of the database records or to restructure the database to satisfy new user requirements.

In the first instance, the frequent and massive additions and deletions of physical records against the databases will cause the data stored in them to be physically disorganized, thus generating extra I/Os when trying to access the data. Hence, the frequency and volume of update transactions (insertions and deletions) processed against the physical database can dictate how often the reorganization utilities should be executed (once a day, once a week, etc.).[12] In the second instance, the original database structure must be redefined to accommodate new

---

[12]Most DBMS software provides some utilities that will monitor the physical arrangements of the database records and highlight the need for a reorganization.

changes for the application, such as adding a new record type or reorganizing the existing relationships among the current records. In such circumstances, the database might need to be reconstructed, using the reorganization utilities.

The database backup/recovery/reorganization plan should comply with the major disaster requirements that might be applicable to the system at hand, if any. For very large databases, the expected running time of the backup, recovery, and reorganization utilities should be estimated as accurately as possible at the present time. This is important, as normally the databases are not available to the users for regular processing while these jobs are running in the production environment. Hence, these jobs might directly affect the stated system availability requirements. The larger the database, the longer it will take to perform the backup, recovery, and reorganization utilities. If necessary, the backup, recovery, and reorganization jobs of a very large database can be prototyped with a minimum, yet representative, amount of data. The resulting figures are then extrapolated to reflect the size of the actual databases in the production environment.

5.2.10 Produce System Manuals' Tables of Contents

Task number:	DE-10	
Task name:	Produce system manuals' tables of contents	
Objective:	To develop a preliminary version or table of contents for each category of system guide that must be developed	
Input(s):	DE-2	Physical data model
	DE-3	Physical process model
	DE-6	System training strategy (detailed)
Output(s):	DE-10	System manuals' tables of contents

Task description:

- Identify the types of system manuals that are required to document the detailed operations of the system.

Nonautomated Procedures User's Guide.
- Identify the intended audience.
- Identify the set of manual procedures that must be performed by each user group.
- Produce a draft table of contents for the manual.
- Specify the format of the manual.
- Describe the medium that will be used to create and maintain the guide.

System Maintenance Guide.
- Develop a draft table of contents.
- Specify the format and type of medium that will be used to create and maintain this guide.

System Operations Guide.
– Develop a draft table of contents.
– Specify the format and type of medium that will be used to create and maintain the system operations guide.

System User's Guide.
– Develop a draft table of contents.
– Specify the format and type of medium that will be used to create and maintain the system user's guide.
• Walk through the table of contents of each system manual.

Four different system guides or manuals can be developed during the implementation phase. The following is a brief description of the purpose of each guide and a typical table of contents, where applicable.

The purpose of the nonautomated procedures user's guide is to describe the manual activities that must be performed by users in their environment. It does not contain the manual procedures that relate to the utilization of the automated system facilities.

The system maintenance guide describes the internal architecture of the system. It is primarily targeted for the systems professionals who will maintain the production system. A typical table of contents for such a guide is illustrated in Table 5.2.

The system operations guide describes the activities that are required to operate the production system. Typically, the intended audience is the systems operations personnel who will run the system in the production environment. A typical table of contents for such a guide is illustrated in Table 5.3.

The system user's guide describes in nontechnical language the various procedures that users must follow to interface with the automated portion of the system and to use its facilities in the most effective manner. It presents the users with an external view of the system. A typical table of contents for such a manual is illustrated in Table 5.4.

Although the general format should remain more or less identical, the actual content of each guide can greatly vary from one system to another. As a simple rule of thumb, though, the larger and more complex the system, the more thorough the documentation should be. The system documentation process may require only a few pages of narrative or it may encompass several manuals. At this point in the development process, a draft table of contents should be created at least for each of the manuals.[13]

In fact, each table of contents can be seen as a high-level prototype of a guide; it presents the high-level sections that will compose the manual. The detailed content of each section will be further described during the implementation phase. One should not forget that the amount of written procedures that must be developed

---

[13]If the organization already has system documentation standards, the effort should be minimal.

TABLE 5.2   TABLE OF CONTENTS FOR SYSTEM MAINTENANCE GUIDE

Section 1	*Introduction*
1.1	The system maintenance manual
1.1.1	Purpose
1.1.2	Organization
1.1.3	Intended audience
1.2	General system description
1.2.1	General online facilities
1.2.2	General batch facilities
1.2.3	General system external interfaces
1.3	General operating environment
1.3.1	Software configuration overview
1.3.2	Hardware configuration overview
1.3.3	Network configuration overview

Section 2	*General Description of Programs*
2.1	Online environment
2.1.1	General description of the online menu(s)
2.1.2	List of online transactions and brief description of each transaction
2.1.3	List of common facilities applicable to online programs
2.1.4	List of standard PF keys
2.1.5	Common copybooks
2.2	Batch environment
2.2.1	List of batch programs with brief description
2.2.2	Flowcharts of batch programs
2.2.3	Batch job streams and dependencies

Section 3	*General Description of Files/Databases*
3.1	Physical layouts of files/databases
3.2	General description of records
3.3	General description of fields

Section 4	*Test Environment*
4.1	Description of files, databases, and test libraries used
4.2	Description of application test facilities and tools

Section 5	*Production Environment*
5.1	Description of files, databases, and production libraries used
5.2	Description of production facilities

Section 6	*Appendixes*
6.1	Updating of the system maintenance manual
6.2	Glossary of terms
6.3	References to other manuals
6.4	History of system change requests

TABLE 5.3: TABLE OF CONTENTS FOR SYSTEM OPERATIONS GUIDE

Section 1	*Introduction*
1.1	The operations manual
1.1.1	Purpose
1.1.2	Organization
1.1.3	Intended audience
1.1.4	General system usage
1.2	Description of the physical environment
1.2.1	General software maintenance procedures
1.2.2	General hardware maintenance procedures
1.2.3	General networking maintenance procedures
1.3	General operating procedures
1.3.1	Daily hardware start-up/shutdown procedures
1.3.2	Daily software start-up/shutdown procedures
1.3.3	Disk and tape library procedures
1.3.4	System failure logging procedures
1.3.5	General backup/recovery procedures
1.3.6	Ordering general supplies
1.4	Job scheduling procedures
1.4.1	System flowchart and production JCL
1.4.2	Program operating instructions
1.4.3	Output distribution procedures
1.5	Miscellaneous
1.5.1	File/database reorganization procedures
1.5.2	Special recovery procedures
1.5.3	User/maintenance programmer call list
1.5.4	References to other manuals
1.5.5	Updating of the operations manual
1.5.6	Glossary of terms

to exercise the proper control over all the manual/automated components of a large system can turn out to be fairly substantial. By developing a preliminary table of contents for each required manual, the development team will be in a better position to assess the scope and complexity of the overall system documentation process.

Ideally, however, the development team should try to go beyond the table of contents. In fact, a preliminary version of each required guide should be developed during the design phase, especially the manual procedures and system user's guides. For instance, the documents resulting from the system prototyping effort, such as the various screens, forms, and report displays, should be inserted directly into the appropriate sections of these two guides. General information describing how to use the various screens, reports, and forms could then be gradually inserted into each respective section of the guide.

TABLE 5.4 TABLE OF CONTENTS FOR SYSTEM USER'S GUIDE

Section 1	*Introduction*

Section 2	*The user manual*
2.1	Purpose
2.2	Organization
2.3	Intended audience

Section 3	*System overview*
3.1	System mission
3.2	Situation of system within the organization
3.3	Functional description

Section 4	*Online facilities*
4.1	Getting started
4.2	Help mode
4.3	Ad hoc queries
4.4	Guide to the online menu
4.5	List of detailed transactions and their usage
4.6	Online data entry instructions

Section 5	*Batch facilities*
5.1	Description of general batch functions
5.2	Daily reports
5.3	Weekly reports
5.4	Monthly reports
5.5	Yearly reports
5.6	Ad hoc reports
5.7	Housekeeping and archiving facilities

Section 6	*Miscellaneous*
6.1	Updating of the user manual
6.2	Glossary of terms
6.3	References to other manuals
6.4	List of error messages and explanations

5.2.11 Finalize Physical Data Storage Estimates

Task number:	DE-11
Task name:	Finalize physical data storage estimates
Objective:	To define with accuracy the physical data storage estimates of the system

Input(s):	DA-8	Detailed data storage requirements
	DE-2	Physical data model
	DE-3	Physical process model
	DE-5	System data conversion strategy (detailed)
	DE-6	System training strategy (detailed)
	DE-7	System testing strategy (detailed)
Output(s):	DE-11	Physical data storage estimates

Task description:

- Refine the estimates concerning the total volume, in millions of bytes, of active data that must be stored in the various production files and databases of the system and their annual projected growth over the next five years.
- Refine the estimates concerning the total volume, in millions of bytes, of inactive data that must be archived per unit of time.
- Estimate the total volume of data that must be stored in backup files to meet the requirements of the file/database backup/recovery/reorganization strategy.
- Refine the estimates concerning the data storage requirements of the test or training environments.
- Walk through all the physical data storage estimates concerning the new production system.

The file and database size estimates that were developed during the detailed analysis phase should now be refined based on the detailed information available and that relate to the physical characteristics of the system. For example, the space overheads associated with the physical data model components should be calculated with more precision, including

- Physical pointer overheads
- Data duplication overheads
- Free space/block size overheads
- Alternate index overheads

Furthermore, these estimates should also cover each additional file or database that will be necessary to hold intermediate results. These can be daily transaction files that will be processed during the night, report files, files used to store statistical information about the system's behavior, and so forth.[14]

The data archiving requirements of the system should be finalized with the users as well, if this was not already done. As discussed in earlier chapters, data archiving might be mandatory for financial types of applications. However, several other types of aging data can also be archived for future references, such as for producing various trend analysis reports.

---

[14]Other types of databases might also be needed to hold the extra security, audit, or control data that are required to support the system.

The type of archival processing that needs to be done by the users will often determine what the most suitable archiving medium should be for the future application. Some of the typical questions that should be answered in this area follow:

- How often does the archived data need to be accessed?
- How rapidly must the archived data be accessed?
- What are the data archival growth rates per year?
- Will the archived records be directly retrieved in using their keys?
- Will the archived data be accessed in a sequential manner?
- Will multiple copies of the archived data be needed at one site? At several sites?

Some of the most widely used archiving media are magnetic tape, disk and diskette, optical disk, microfiche, and paper.

Magnetic tape or disk are very suitable when a significant amount of data must be accessed to produce various trend analysis statistics. However, the cost of this type of storage media might turn out to be expensive, especially if massive amounts of data must be archived. On the other hand, storing data on microfiche can be very effective when single records need to be searched with a specific key in mind. Furthermore, the microfiche medium is relatively inexpensive and can be used to store a significant amount of data at different locations.

The data storage requirements that can be indirectly generated by the backup/recovery files should also be evaluated by the development team. Depending on the frequency of execution of the backups, the volume of data that must be backed up, and the number of generation data sets that might be required to store the backup data, the data storage figures for the backup files can turn out to be significant. The type of physical medium that will be used to store the backup data, such as magnetic disks or tapes, should also be finalized with the user and systems operations personnel.

5.2.12 Finalize System Processing Load Estimates

Task number:	DE-12	
Task name:	Finalize system processing load estimates	
Objective:	To refine the processing load estimates for the batch, online, and real-time portions of the system	
Input(s):	DA-9	Detailed system performance requirements
	DE-2	Physical data model
	DE-3	Physical process model
Output(s):	DE-12	System processing load estimates

Task description:

- Finalize the processing load estimates for each mainframe and microcomputer system configuration:

- Finalize the batch processing load estimates for each batch program and software utility.
  - Finalize the online processing load estimates for each online transaction.
  - Finalize the real-time processing load estimates for each real-time process.
- Refine the performance-related estimates, including
  - Response time of each online transaction
  - Job turnaround/execution time of the batch programs
  - Total mainframe and local print load figures
  - Data communication traffic loads, along with the frequency of data transmissions and anticipated peaks
- Walk through the system processing load estimates.

The total processing load estimates related to each specific processor configuration must be determined as precisely as possible at this stage of the development cycle. This information will be extremely valuable for the systems operations and capacity planning staff to determine if the actual processor configuration can indeed accommodate the extra computer processing load that will be generated by the new system.

The performance-related estimates are also refined based on the information that has been accumulated to date for the online transactions of the system, the batch programs and their related print load figures. The data communications load between each connected point of the network must also be determined with as much precision as possible. This information will then be used to calculate the total communication traffic load that the network facilities must support on a daily basis.

5.2.13 Finalize Hardware/Software/Networking Acquisition and Installation Strategy

Task number:	DE-13
Task name:	Finalize hardware/software/networking acquisition and installation strategy
Objective:	To specify the final hardware/software/networking equipment and facilities that must be put in place to support the new system
Input(s):	DA-6 Detailed hardware/software/networking requirements
	DE-2 Physical data model
	DE-3 Physical process model
	DE-4 Program file/database access patterns
	DE-5 System data conversion strategy (detailed)
	DE-6 System training strategy (detailed)
	DE-7 System testing strategy (detailed)
	DE-11 Physical data storage estimates
	DE-12 System processing load estimates

Output(s):	DE-13	Final hardware/software/networking acquisition and installation strategy

Task description:

- Review and finalize the detailed list of the *existing* hardware/software/networking facilities and equipment that will be required to develop and operate the new system in the production environment.
- Review and finalize the detailed list of the *new* hardware/software/networking facilities and equipment that needs to be acquired and installed to develop and support the new system.
- Order the set of new hardware/software/networking equipment and facilities that are required for the new system.
- Finalize the hardware/software/networking acquisition and installation strategy.
- Walk through the final hardware/software/networking acquisition and installation strategy.

The information related to the hardware/software/networking requirements of the system was gradually developed during the preliminary and detailed analysis phases. At the design stage, this information is reviewed primarily to ensure that no major items have been omitted. This is just a precautionary step inasmuch as the vast majority of these requirements were finalized during the detailed analysis phase. At that time also, the important pieces of equipment should have been ordered. If this is not the case, the procurement orders for any new major or minor hardware equipment or software facility should be placed, based on the acquisition deadlines that were previously established in the last phase.

The specific requirements that were gathered during the detailed analysis phase for the eventual installation of the new system equipment should be reviewed and carefully finalized before the end of this phase. All the information that has been gathered is consolidated to produce the final installation plan. The following section describes the steps required to finalize this plan.

Installation plan.
1. Complete the detailed description of all the major and minor hardware/software/networking items, along with their characteristics.
2. Finalize for each particular site the list of the detailed hardware/software/networking equipment and facilities that must be installed in the test or production environment.
3. For each site, finalize the environmental needs in terms of
   - Power supply
   - Temperature, ventilation, humidity requirements
   - Spacing needs for the equipment
   - Electrical and communication wiring needs

- Physical security requirements
- Auxiliary furniture and system supplies

4. For each site, prepare a detailed floor layout showing the exact location where the hardware components will be installed and how they will be interconnected. Some of the physical items to cover include

- The exact location for the terminals, printers, and other system-interfacing devices of a similar nature
- The exact location for the mainframe computers, disk drives, tape drives, device controllers, and the like
- The exact location for the personal computer workstations and related peripheral equipment
- The exact location for the network-related equipment

5. Define the detailed procedures that will be required to install the hardware/ software/networking components at each specific site. Develop the detailed hardware/software/networking installation test cases that will be used to verify that the newly installed equipment functions properly.

6. Describe in detail the roles and responsibilities of each group involved in the procurement and installation cycle of the hardware/software/networking commodities.

7. Review the interdependencies that might exist among the hardware/software/ networking facilities of the system. Finalize the sequence in which these facilities will be installed at each specific site. Provide a detailed estimate of the time it should take to install them, along with the expected delivery and installation dates.

8. Special care should be given to "subtle" dependencies that might exist. In fact, several types of dependencies might exist, such as

- Hardware-to-hardware dependencies
- Software-to-software dependencies
- Network-to-network dependencies
- Hardware-to-software dependencies

Each specific hardware/software/networking commodity should be carefully examined to determine if some simple yet important dependencies might have been overlooked. For instance, the team might suddenly discover that the acquisition of a brand new commercial application package or a new database management system will require the upgrading of the current operating software environment to the latest release available. Another example might be when an important functional feature offered by a software product turns out to be available only on a very specific type of hardware processor. It might be impossible to cover all the potential cases, but nevertheless, it is still important to detect these sudden surprises as early as possible and assess the impact they will have on the project prior to its implementation.

5.3 REFERENCES

CONSTANTINE, L., and E. YOURDON. 1979. *Structured Design*. Englewood Cliffs, N.J.: Prentice Hall.

GALITZ, W. O., 1988. *Handbook of Screen Format Design,* 3rd ed. Wellesley, Mass.: QED Information Sciences.

HUBBARD, G. U. 1981. *Computer-Assisted Data Base Design*. New York: Van Nostrand Reinhold.

INMON, W. H. 1989. *DB2: Maximizing Performance of Online Production Systems*. Wellesley, Mass.: QED Information Sciences.

JACKSON, M. 1975. *Principles of Program Design*. New York: Academic Press.

MARTIN, J. 1983. *Managing the Database Environment*. Englewood Cliffs, N.J.: Prentice Hall.

ORR, KEN. 1977. *Structured Systems Development*. New York: Yourdon Press.

PAGE-JONES, M. 1988. *The Practical Guide to Structured System Design,* 2nd ed. Yourdon Press Computing Series. Englewood Cliffs, N.J.: Prentice Hall.

WARNIER, JEAN-DOMINIQUE. 1981. *Logical Construction of Systems*. New York: Van Nostrand Reinhold.

6

Implementation Phase

6.1 PURPOSE

The primary purpose of the implementation phase is to deliver a fully operational system to the users. Based on the system design specifications that were produced during the previous phase, the software programs are coded, tested, and gradually integrated into a complete system. The manual and administrative procedures of the system are finalized and also tested in conjunction with the automated portion of the system. The user and system documentation manuals are completed and the staff is properly trained. The data in the old files are loaded into the new file/database structures of the system. The proper hardware/software/networking equipment and facilities are installed at the user sites, and the system and its supporting material are transferred into the production environment. If necessary, the system is fine-tuned during the first month following its installation in production.

Table 6.1 summarizes the major technical tasks that are normally conducted during the implementation phase, along with the anticipated technical deliverables. Figure 6.1 illustrates, at a high level, the relationships that exist among the individual tasks of the implementation phase.

TABLE 6.1   IMPLEMENTATION PHASE TECHNICAL TASKS AND DELIVERABLES

Technical Tasks	*Technical Deliverables*
1. Install hardware/software/networking equipment and facilities in test environment	1. Installed development hardware/software networking equipment and facilities in test environment
2. Create system test environment	2. System test environment
3. Code application programs	3. Coded application programs
4. Conduct unit testing	4. Unit-tested programs and test results
5. Conduct system integration testing	5. System integration–tested programs and test results
6. Prepare draft system manuals package	6. Draft nonautomated procedures user's guide/system maintenance guide/system operations guide/system user's guide
7. Prepare draft system training package	7. Draft system training package
8. Train initial testing user team	8. Trained testing user team completion report
9. Conduct user acceptance testing	9. User acceptance–tested system and test results
10. Finalize system manuals package	10. Final nonautomated procedures user's guide/system maintenance guide/system operations guide/system user's guide
11. Finalize system training package	11. Final system training package
12. Formally train all users/systems personnel	12. Trained staff and final training completion report
13. Conduct production acceptance testing	13. Production acceptance tested system and test results
14. Install hardware/software/networking equipment and facilities at user sites	14. Installed hardware/software/networking equipment and facilities at user sites
15. Perform conversion of existing production files/databases	15. New production files/databases and production data conversion completion report
16. Migrate new system into production and turn it on	16. New operational production system
17. Perform postimplementation optimization	17. Production system (optimized)
18. Develop system maintenance strategy	18. System maintenance strategy

6.2 DESCRIPTION OF THE TECHNICAL TASKS

6.2.1 Install Hardware/Software/Networking Equipment and Facilities in Test Environment

Task number:	IM-1
Task name:	Install hardware/software/networking equipment and facilities in test environment
Objective:	To receive and install the hardware/software/networking equipment and facilities that are required to develop and test the system

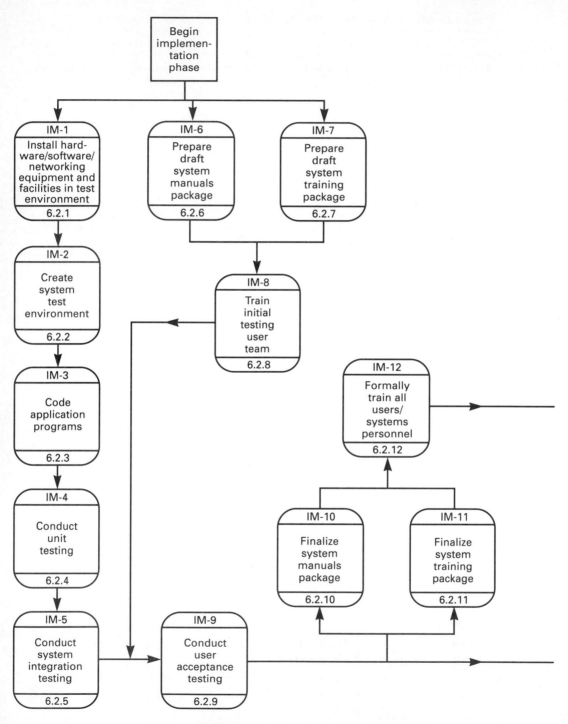

Figure 6.1   Implementation phase task network

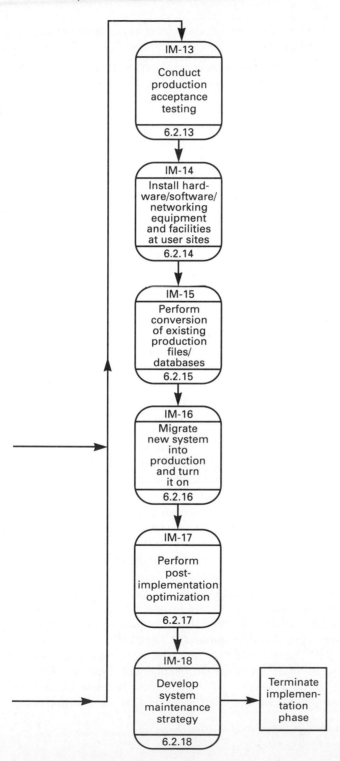

Figure 6.1 Continued

Input(s):	DE-13	Final hardware/software/networking acquisition and installation strategy
Output(s):	IM-1	Installed development hardware/software/networking equipment and facilities in test environment

Task description:

- Ensure that each system development site has been properly prepared to accept the new hardware/software/networking equipment and facilities that will be used to develop and test the system.
- Receive the necessary hardware/software/networking equipment and facilities.
- Install the hardware equipment.
- Install the software facilities.
- Install the networking equipment and facilities.
- Verify the newly installed hardware/software/networking equipment and facilities by exercising the installation test cases.
- Notify the development team of the successful installation of the hardware/software/networking equipment and facilities.

Certain projects might require the installation of some new hardware/software/networking equipment and facilities before you can begin to develop and test the system. This is especially true in cases where special hardware devices are required to test the system, such as badge readers, sophisticated automated teller machines, special-purpose terminals, or real-time manufacturing devices. These types of computer equipment should be directly installed in the system development area to allow proper testing by the development team. On the software side, an example is the acquisition of a new database management system that adequately supports the new application. The functionality of the DBMS software itself should then be fully verified prior to developing and testing the application databases.

For a large project, the reception and installation of different equipment and facilities will likely involve the participation of several groups, such as hardware and software vendors, database experts, and networking experts. The amount of time required to coordinate the delivery and proper installation of all the required material can be fairly significant. In some instances, it might even be necessary to dedicate one person, on a full-time basis, to monitor the progress made in preparing the development sites, receiving and installing the equipment, and testing it.

Moreover, reasonable time allowances should be planned to cover some potentially critical situations like missed delivery dates, unforeseen environmental problems, or defective equipment. Another important aspect is to ensure that the material received has not only been properly installed but also performs well in both standalone and integrated modes of operation. Hence, the test cases that were developed initially to test the functionality of the hardware/software/networking equipment and facilities should now be exercised to verify that the equipment and facilities are effectively working together before they are handed over to the system developers.

6.2.2 Create System Test Environment

Task number:	IM-2
Task name:	Create system test environment
Objective:	To construct the test environment required to support the various system testing cycles
Input(s):	DE-2 Physical data model DE-3 Physical process model DE-7 System testing strategy (detailed) DE-9 Database backup/recovery/reorganization strategy
Output(s):	IM-2 System test environment

Task description:

- Analyze the application testing requirements defined in the detailed system testing strategy deliverable.
- Create the different sets of libraries that are required to support each particular level of testing adequately (i.e., unit, system integration, user acceptance, production acceptance).[1]
- Develop, if necessary, the manual/automated library control procedures required for proper management of each specific test environment.
- Code and test all the database definitions, program control blocks, file data set definitions, and backup/recovery utilities that will be used in the test environment.
- Initialize the test databases and files, if required.
- Populate, where applicable, the application file/database test environments with the appropriate test data or default values.
- Create, if necessary, a test environment guide, describing how to use effectively the various facilities that are provided in the test environment.
- Walk through the system test environment.

A comprehensive centralized test environment should be created to support the overall testing process. However, the four different testing environments required for this purpose do not necessarily need to be created all at once. Instead, they can be constructed at different stages during the implementation phase, more specifically at the time they are needed to execute a particular level of testing, such as unit testing or system integration testing.

The number of testing libraries that must be controlled by the development team of a large project can be fairly significant. See Table 6.2. Because of the large

---

[1]For more information on structured testing, see Chap. 8.

TABLE 6.2 DESCRIPTION OF TYPICAL SYSTEM TEST LIBRARIES

Type	Description
Application Job Control Library	Contains the job control statements used to execute the application jobs
Program Library (Source)	Contains the source code of the application programs
Program Library (Load)	Contains the load modules of the application programs
Database Description Library (Source)	Contains the source code for the test database descriptions
Database Description Library (Load)	Contains the compiled test database description members
Database Utilities Library	Contains the job control statements required to execute database utility jobs, such as backup or recovery
Test Data Library	Contains the various test data sets required to test the programs
Screen Definition Library (Source)	Contains the source code statements used to define the screens of the online portion of the system
Screen Definition (Load)	Contains the compiled code library statements of the screens
Program Specification Block (Source)	Contains the source code used to define each program's internal view of the databases
Program Specification Block (Load)	Contains the compiled versions of the program specification blocks

number of test libraries and related test material that should be created and maintained to support the four levels of testing, it might become imperative for a very large system to assign on a full-time basis a person who's unique role is strictly to manage and keep up to date the system's various test environments.[2]

Depending on the level of sophistication that was used to create and automate the various facilities provided by the test environment, it might be appropriate to develop a thorough test environment guide.[3] Some of the sections covered in such a document are shown in Table 6.3.

6.2.3 Code Application Programs

Task number:	IM-3
Task name:	Code application programs
Objective:	To code the machine-executable instructions of the individual programs and their related job control statements
Input(s):	DE-2 Physical data model
	DE-3 Physical process model

[2]For a detailed description of the project librarian function, see Yourdon [1979] or King [1984].

[3]It is typical in several large organizations to have a centralized database administration group that will develop for the application development team all the jobs that are necessary to create, initialize, modify, save, and restore the test databases that are required to test the application system.

	DE-5	System data conversion strategy (detailed)
	DE-6	System training strategy (detailed)
Output(s):	IM-3	Coded application programs

Task description:

- Analyze the original program structure charts and specifications.
- If not already done, code the screen or report layouts manipulated by the program.
- Develop the program source code in the software language that was retained to develop the application.
- Code the job control statements that are required to compile the program.
- Obtain a clean compilation of the source modules of the program.
- Document each program as per the programming standards prescribed by the organization.
- Walk through each program source code and its documentation.

Several software development tools are at the disposition of the development team to generate application programs at an accelerated pace while preserving the quality of the code as if they had been written by a programmer who knows structured coding techniques. Cobol application generators are one example. These tools are very effective when it is time to code programs using a third-generation language because the code generated by these tools is defect-free.[4] Obviously, fourth- or fifth-generation languages can also be used for developing systems that are not too large and where the performance requirements are not overly stringent.

TABLE 6.3   TEST ENVIRONMENT GUIDE

- Table of contents
- Introduction
  - Purpose of the guide
  - Description of its structure
- Main body
  - Brief description of the test libraries and how to use them
  - Brief description of the hardware/software facilities that are available to create or automatically generate test data, to run the tests, to verify the results, to copy a test database, to restore a test database, to modify the test environment, and so on.
- Appendixes
  - The appendixes contain general-purpose information on the test environment. For example, one section can describe how to utilize the various symbolic parameters that were set up in the cataloged procedures put at the disposal of the testing team for managing the test database environment. These procedures could be used to alter the job control statements of the different database utilities required to create, initialize, copy, load, and restore the test databases.

---

[4]Some of the Cobol application generators available on the market include GAMMA from Tarkenton Software, Inc., PACBASE from CGI Systems, Inc., and TELON from Pansophic Systems, Inc.

Some software facilities will generate the application code directly from design specifications. However, manual programming might still be used in several organizations. If this is the case, and whether or not the system organization has already implemented some of the underlying concepts surrounding software reusability, the development team should investigate the feasibility of copying some of the existing application source code into the new project development libraries. The existing source code could then be adapted to meet the requirements of the new application. In some instances, such an approach might be worth the effort, assuming the existing source code was developed with the use of structured coding techniques and is still in good shape. If this is not possible, then the new project might be a good starting point to try putting in place the software reusability concept. That is, the team should look at the various programs and modules of the application and identify those that, with a little bit of extra effort, can be written in such a way to allow them to become reusable by other applications.

In any case, all written programs should conform to the naming conventions and structured coding standards already established by the organization. Particular attention should be given to the need to define clearly the construction rules by which an online program can communicate with another online program. Also, the need to determine the universal format that will be used across the application to transmit data between two programs must be examined. Another example might be to decide which standards will be used to locate the error messages in application programs (i.e., directly at the location where the errors are detected or ensure that all are located in a common area).

Ideally, programs should be documented while they are being developed. Several comments should be embedded in the programs themselves to explain clearly the major peculiarities of each program and the purpose of each module.

The application programmers should always write the source code keeping in mind the future maintainability of the program. Table 6.4 lists some of the quality guidelines generally prescribed to enhance the future maintainability of the software programs.[5] The program's external view of the application databases should be described in detail at this point. This information will be used by the database administrator to code the database external views that will allow the programmers to test their programs with the databases they manipulate.

The programs that make up the conversion subsystem should also be created at this point in the development cycle. In several instances, these programs will be the first ones to be coded and fully tested. They will then be used to create "live" but downsized test data files that will be utilized during the system integration test-

---

[5]Automated tools can be used to verify the program's level of compliance with the existing programming standards, such as naming conventions. Furthermore, different source code metrics can be used to measure the complexity of the generated source code. Most of these tools are designed to measure the complexity of the source code by analyzing the number of branches, loops, and other structural elements of this nature. Two of the most popular techniques are Halstead's effort equation and McCabe's cyclomatic complexity. For more information on this subject, see Halstead [1977] or McCabe [1976].

TABLE 6.4 QUALITY GUIDELINES TO ENHANCE SOFTWARE PROGRAM MAINTAINABILITY

Adherence to structured coding standards (modularity and simplicity: sequence, iteration, and selection constructs only)

Creation of single-entry and single-exit point constructs

Traceability of the program code to the design specifications

Creation of standard program documentation that explains what the program does but not how it does it

Creation of standard documentation prologues embedded at the beginning of each program's module

Symbolic parameters or shared data used for modules' data connections

---

ing process. This approach allows the development team to verify the soundness of the data conversion strategy early in the implementation phase. Unexpected problems can be addressed quickly, without having to deal with a last-minute crisis situation. Based on actual running figures that were produced during the trial data conversion, the team should also be in a better position to estimate more precisely the conversion time required to change data from their existing to their new formats.

6.2.4 Conduct Unit Testing

Task number:	IM-4
Task name:	Conduct unit testing
Objective:	To attempt to identify defects in the internal logic of the application programs grouped in a version of a release
Input(s):	DE-2 Physical data model DE-3 Physical process model DE-7 System testing strategy (detailed) IM-2 System test environment IM-3 Coded application programs
Output(s):	IM-4 Unit-tested programs and test results

Task description:

- Construct representative test cases to exercise the internal logic of each program.
- Develop the job control statements required to test the program.
- Execute the unit tests against the program's modules.
- Analyze the test results and compare them with expected results.
- If errors are found, determine their cause. If it is a unit construction error (e.g., code defects), correct the error and reexecute the unit tests against the program. If the errors result from incorrect analysis or design specifications, follow the change control procedures that are prescribed for the project.

- If no error is found, promote the tested programs to the system integration test libraries.
- Document the unit test results.

Unit testing is performed against each program to ensure that all modules operate according to their original specifications. The tests are executed independently of other programs, in a standalone manner. In most instances the test data used for unit testing is created by the same individual who developed the program.[6] Normally, the test data are fictitious. However, the unit test cases should not be randomly selected but should be developed to exercise all the procedural statements of the program and its physical modules. The use of a test coverage tool that monitors the execution of the program and measures the level of coverage achieved by exercising a particular set of test cases will definitively speed up and improve the unit testing process.

Function testing should first be performed with valid test data to ensure that the program works well in a normal situation and satisfies the program specifications. Then test data that simulate abnormal situations should be used to verify that the program works as expected under borderline conditions. Lastly, destructive testing should be performed using extreme test cases in an attempt to break the program.

While performing unit testing, the programmers can also apply a certain amount of performance tuning to their programs. However, they should be careful not to spend too much time in this, for two reasons. First, the primary objective of unit testing is to identify defects in the program, not to fine-tune it. Second, a lot of effort might be spent on fine-tuning a standalone program that, in the end, contributes little to the overall performance of the software application. Normally, performance testing is best performed in a truly productive manner during system integration testing and/or post-implementation.

The development team must be aware of an important point. Even though sound unit test cases can be built to exercise full coverage of the program's entire executable source code statements, there is still no guarantee that the program will be totally defect-free. Rather, it only certifies that the internal program logic works with the test cases that have been used to exercise the procedural code. To construct all the test cases that would thoroughly investigate all the possible combinations of paths in a program, which contains several branching and loop statements, is almost impossible. Consider the fact that a program with X branches will have 2^{X+1} possible paths, which are all different ways of executing in a particular se-

---

[6]In some organizations, the overall testing process is handled by an independent group that did not participate in the development of the programs. The proponents of this approach believe that "outsiders" who have not been involved in the creation of the application code will not have "psychological" difficulties in attempting to intentionally "destroy" the programs. Experience has shown that projects that use an independent testing team will likely identify more defects than the development team would normally do, while spending the same amount of effort on such a task. If, for whatever reasons, this approach cannot be used, an acceptable alternative could be to ask programmer X to test the programs written by programmer Y and vice versa.

quence some segments of the source code statements. For instance, if the program has 10 different branching statements, it would mean there are 2,048 different possible execution paths.

It still remains very important, though, to come up with a test completion measure that will indicate to the software tester that the internal logic of the program has been adequately tested and therefore the unit test process for this program can be recognized as complete. Two of the most widely used unit testing completion criteria are

- *Statement coverage*: At the bare minimum, all the program's executable source code statements have been executed at least once.
- *Branch coverage*: Each branching statement of a program is executed at least once for each alternative execution sequence (i.e., path).

Furthermore, the program simply might not include some procedural statements that should be there in the first place. Nevertheless, such errors can be detected later, during system integration or user acceptance testing, for instance.

If the top-down testing technique is used to verify the correctness of the software system, it might be necessary to develop test stubs, dummy program statements or modules that are used to simulate real procedural code not yet in place. If a bottom-up approach is favored, then the simulation of test drivers will be necessary when the time comes to feed some data to the lower-level modules being tested.[7]

Static or desk check testing can still be favorably used by the programmers as a relatively inexpensive starting point to perform unit testing. The test data sample is logically traced through the program logic by the programmer. However, such a technique should never be used alone because it normally has a low level of reliability. Rather, it should always be used in combination with other complementary unit testing techniques.

Performing unit testing uniquely with "live" production data should be done with caution, as there is no guarantee that all the logic paths of the program will be fully exercised during the testing process. Once again, performing quality unit testing is not necessarily a question of volume of data but rather of engineering a representative yet minimal set of test data samples that will uncover as many internal defects as possible.

The unit test data created to uncover program logic defects should be saved in a special project library for the duration of the project in case retests become necessary. For this purpose, a tool that can store the test results and test cases and that can equally provide online editing facilities would be extremely useful to manage and dynamically update the test data. Developing, updating, and maintaining test cases might become a burden, as their number rapidly increases when testing a

---

[7]Several testing and debugging tools on the market support the unit testing process. An example is XPEDITER, a dynamic testing and debugging tool that operates in an IBM mainframe environment and that among other things, can be used to unit-test a portion of a program without the absolute need for a driver or a stub module already coded.

large and complex system. Such a facility would offer better control over the test cases that are traditionally dispersed in each programmer's private library. Furthermore, the test data can be made readily available to everyone who needs it and can also be easily modified or augmented to meet new testing criteria.

6.2.5 Conduct System Integration Testing

Task number:	IM-5
Task name:	Conduct system integration testing
Objective:	To attempt to identify defects when the programs of a new version of a release are integrated with those of existing versions and progressively tested together
Input(s):	DE-2 Physical data model DE-3 Physical process model DE-7 System testing strategy (detailed) IM-2 System test environment IM-4 Unit-tested programs and test results
Output(s):	IM-5 System integration–tested programs and test results

Task description:
- Complete the creation of the system integration test cases.
- Develop the detailed job control statements required to test the batch job streams.
- Execute the system integration tests.
- Analyze the outcome of the tests and compare them against the expected results.
- If errors are found, determine their cause. If required, demote the defective programs to the unit test environment and issue a system change request to resolve the problems encountered during the system integration test process.
- If no errors are found, promote the new version program(s) to the user acceptance test libraries.
- Document the system integration test results.

The primary purpose of the system integration testing process is to demonstrate that the system design requirements are not met and that the unit-tested programs do not interface properly within a single version or with other versions of a release. However, the integration testing cycle should also be concerned with verifying additional system requirements:

- File/database backup and recovery procedures
- Audit, control, and security features applicable to the entire system
- Desired system throughput, capacity, and performance characteristics
- External interfaces with other systems

- Batch job streams and their dependencies
- Permanent and temporary storage needs of the system
- Usability, validity, correctness, and understandability of the reports produced by the system and of the various human-machine dialogues

A critical success factor inherent in integration testing is the establishment of a sound problem-reporting procedure. The problems that are uncovered during this testing process must be properly documented and logged in a central repository. They must then be prioritized and assigned to someone for resolution. They must also be tracked while the programs are being repaired. Once the problems are fixed, the test results must be reviewed again and then approved. The corrected programs are repromoted and integration testing is then performed.

Most of the time, integration testing is done by the project leader or an independent testing team. The "politics" of testing will often start to surface during the system testing integration process. When defects are detected in the software programs, some programmers might react as if they were the victims of an organized witch hunt, especially if the project leader views the testing cycle as a destructive process. Furthermore, the programmers can easily translate having to change and retest their programs as more work.

The best way to avoid such potential problems is to educate the programmers on the concept of destructiveness and how it is applied to software testing. Moreover, the project leader should acknowledge the need for programmers to repair their programs and should reflect this reality by including additional time for this purpose in the test plans.

The second category of people to be concerned with is the system managers. If too many problems are uncovered during system integration testing, the system manager might feel threatened by the destructive process because this probably means some schedule slippage for the project. The manager might be tempted only to document the problems and see that they get resolved with the delivery of the next release. This approach might work fine for minor problems but certainly not for major ones. Another type of problem might arise when the system integration testing process is done at a high level since the testing manager assumes by default that the users are responsible to demonstrate fully that the entire system does comply with their original requirements. This is where it is also important to explain to the management team the rationale behind the destructive philosophy and emphasize that it is far better to resolve these issues now than when the system goes into production. Finally, the same tools that were used during unit testing can also be used for the system integration testing process.

6.2.6 Prepare Draft System Manuals Package

Task number:	IM-6
Task name:	Prepare draft system manuals package

Objective:	To develop a preliminary version of the different types of system manuals that are required to use, operate, and maintain the system in production	
Input(s):	DE-2	Physical data model
	DE-3	Physical process model
	DE-8	Preliminary system job flowchart
	DE-10	System guides' tables of contents
Output(s):	IM-6	Draft nonautomated procedures user's guide/system maintenance guide/system operations guide/system user's guide

Task description:

- Review the preliminary table of contents that was developed during the design phase for each type of system manual. Verify its organization and completeness in light of the information that has been gathered so far on the new system.
- Draft the contents of each individual system manual.
- Walk through the four draft system manuals for clarity and completeness.

The following sections describe the type of information included in the various system manuals. At this stage, these manuals can be developed in a draft format. However, they should contain enough detailed information to support the users and eventually the systems operations staff during the user acceptance and production acceptance testing cycles.

Nonautomated procedures user's guide.   The manual work unit data flow diagrams that were developed while constructing the functional process model should be used as the main source of documentation for producing this guide. Some examples of the manual operations that should be described include the following:

- Receipt of documents
- Filing of documents
- Sorting of documents in a given sequence
- Validation of documents or specific fields on a document
- Manual computation of numerical values
- Logging of documents
- Gathering of information
- Updating of manual files
- Authorization to perform an activity
- Recording of information
- Manual archiving of documents
- Housekeeping of a manual file

- Preparation of documents, forms, or reports
- Physical transportation of documents from one area to another
- Correction of an error
- Searching for information

The minimum information that should be supplied while developing the detailed manual procedures of the system includes

- Statement of purpose
- Who is responsible to perform the procedure
- When the procedure should be performed
- What the input and output documents are
- How the procedure should be performed

System user's guide.   The system user's guide should always be written in a language that is easy to understand from a user's point of view. Technical jargon should be banished. The users do not need to know how the system works internally but, rather, how to interface with its automated component properly and efficiently. In some organizations, the system user's guide is written by a professional technical writer to make sure that the system information is provided in terms that the various categories of user personnel can easily understand. In others, the users develop their own system user's guide to ensure that their perspective always remains predominant. As a last resort, the guide can be developed by the systems personnel.

A quality user's manual will contribute positively to ease the acceptance of the system by its users. Furthermore, if it is well organized and well written, it might significantly reduce the possibility of making costly errors while using the system. At the same time, it should lend itself naturally to assist in the training of new personnel. The design of the user's manual should allow modular development. At the same time, a simple method should be put in place to modify its content easily when changes are required during the useful lifetime of the system.

Although the detailed content of the system user's guide depends to a large extent on the specific needs of each application, in general it should provide the answers to the following basic questions:

Introduction.
- What is the purpose of the manual?
- Who is the intended audience?
- How is it organized?

Overview.
- What are the major automated functions supported by the system?
- What are the different modes of operation?
- Where does the system fit in with the overall organization?

Online Facilities.

- How to log in?
- How to log out?
- How to use the help facility?
- How to navigate from one screen to another?
- How to use the standard program function keys?
- How to fill in data?
- How to deal with error messages?
- How to obtain data?
- What are the standard command types?
- How to use the ad hoc query facility?
- Who to call if there is a problem?

Batch Facilities.

- How to schedule predefined reports?
- How to get reports?
- How to submit ad hoc reports?
- How to prepare input data?

Miscellaneous.

- What are the procedures to update the user's manual?
- How to get a copy of the user's guide?
- What other manuals can be consulted?
- What are the error messages, and how should they be interpreted?

System maintenance guide.   The system maintenance guide describes the high-level functions and facilities that are carried out by the software application, primarily focusing on a technical perspective. It contains general program narratives and describes the important technical characteristics of the system (i.e., its internal architecture). It is primarily aimed at supporting the maintenance team's efforts. However, it does not necessarily describe in detail the program specifications. The detailed information associated with a program (input description, program logic, output description, etc.) could be in a separate guide.

System operations guide.   The operations guide provides a description of the detailed documentation required by the data center personnel to operate the system in production. Typically, the type of information that should be described for each production job within a specific processing cycle (daily, weekly, monthly, yearly) includes the following:

Job Preparation.

- Provide the job control instructions that are necessary to run the job.
- Describe the software facilities that must be active or inactive during the execution of the job stream.

- Describe the files/databases that must be available to run the job.
- Describe the data entry files that must be provided as input to the job.[8]
- Describe the type of special preprinted forms that might be necessary to print the information produced by the system.
- Describe briefly the type of processing performed by each step of the job stream.
- Describe the detailed job scheduling requirements, as well as the potential dependencies with other production jobs.

Job Execution.
- Describe the messages that highlight the correct execution of the job.
- Describe the error messages that should be generated in case of a job application failure or hardware/software failure. Document the actions to be taken with reference to the required restart or recovery procedures.
- Describe the security procedures that are prescribed for creating the input data fed to the system or the output data produced by the system. Describe the security measures that apply to any type of information produced in either hard-copy or electronic formats.
- Describe the restart/recovery procedures that must be submitted in case of hardware/software failure or application job failure.
- Provide the list of user/system personnel to contact in emergency situations.

Job Output Distribution.
- Describe how to distribute outputs produced by the production jobs.

If the system (or a portion of the system) operations are handled by the users themselves, then the following activities should also be performed for each hardware facility installed at the user site(s):

- Describe the procedures required to report equipment/communication malfunctions.
- Describe the procedures required to start up or shut down the hardware equipment and software facilities.
- Describe the regular start-of-day and end-of-day procedures.
- Describe the emergency shutdown procedures.
- Describe the backup, restart, and recovery procedures required to handle application system or hardware/software failures.
- Describe the security procedures that must be observed while operating the system.

---

[8]This is assuming that the data entry function itself has been performed in advance by the users themselves or a specialized data entry group according to the detailed data entry procedures and instructions that were specially developed for that purpose.

6.2.7 Prepare Draft System Training Package

Task number:	IM-7
Task name:	Prepare draft system training package
Objective:	To install the system training tools and develop the training support material

Input(s):		
	DE-2	Physical data model
	DE-3	Physical process model
	DE-8	System training strategy (detailed)
	IM-6	Draft nonautomated procedures user's guide/system maintenance guide/system operations guide/system user's guide

Output(s):	IM-7	Draft system training package

Task description:

- Review the detailed system training strategy in light of all the information that has been produced so far on the new system.
- Develop in draft form the material that is required to train the initial user testing team.
- Install and test the software training tools, if applicable.
- Walk through the draft system training package to verify that it is accurate and meets the stated training objectives.

The training material can be developed in a draft form at this stage. Nevertheless, it should contain enough information to support the initial training of the user team participants who will conduct the user acceptance tests. If vendor-supplied software training tools, in-house application prototypes, or the test system itself will be utilized to support this first training effort, then these facilities should be installed and tested with predetermined test cases to ensure they do work properly in the actual test environment.

6.2.8 Train Initial Testing User Team

Task number:	IM-8
Task name:	Train initial testing user team
Objective:	To train the initial user team that will conduct the user acceptance tests

Input(s):		
	IM-6	Draft nonautomated procedures user's guide/system maintenance guide/system operations guide/system user's guide
	IM-7	Draft system training package

Output(s):	IM-8	Trained testing user team completion report

Task description:
- Train the core user team that will perform the user acceptance tests.
- Produce the initial training completion report.

During the user acceptance testing process, ease-of-use testing becomes as important as error testing because the acceptance tests should determine the ease of use of the system from the user's perspective. However, a prerequisite for ensuring the success of testing ease of use might be to train the user representatives who will be called upon to test the system in advance on how to use it properly. Although they might not be fully developed at this stage, the draft user's manual procedures and user's system guides should be used to this effect, wherever possible. This activity might be required to differentiate ease of use versus ease of learning. At the same time, the effectiveness of the training material is also partly verified prior to train the entire user staff on how to use the system. Obviously, once the usability factor has been evaluated, the testing process will become more destructive.

6.2.9 Conduct User Acceptance Testing

Task number:	IM-9
Task name:	Conduct user acceptance testing
Objective:	To attempt to identify defects in the automated/manual portions of a version of a system release, therefore demonstrating that it does not perform as per the user's requirements
Input(s):	DE-2 Physical data model DE-3 Physical process model DE-7 System testing strategy (detailed) IM-2 System test environment IM-5 System integration tested programs and test results IM-6 Draft nonautomated procedures user's guide/system maintenance guide/system operations guide/system user's guide
Output(s):	IM-9 User acceptance–tested system and test results

Task description:
- Complete the creation of the representative user acceptance test cases.
- Execute the user acceptance tests in accordance with the detailed system testing strategy.
- Analyze the outcome of the tests and compare them with expected results.
- If errors are found, determine their cause. If required, demote the defective programs to the unit test environment. If necessary, issue a system change re-

quest to resolve the problems that were encountered during the user acceptance testing process.

- If no error is found, promote the program(s) to the production acceptance test libraries.
- Document the user acceptance test results.

The user acceptance process can start as soon as a version of a release has successfully completed its integration testing cycle. However, the library control, change control, problem reporting, and problem resolution procedures must be in place prior to starting user acceptance testing. In addition to the system integration testing requirements (see Sec. 6.2.5), the following items should also be verified by the users:

- Manual procedures used to interface with the system
- Detailed conversion strategy and related conversion programs, where applicable

To achieve these objectives, the test cases that were developed by the users are finally executed at this point in an attempt to demonstrate that the system does not fully satisfy all user requirements.

6.2.10 Finalize System Manuals Package

Task number:	IM-10	
Task name:	Finalize system manuals package	
Objective:	To finalize the system manuals package required to use, operate, and support the system in production	
Input(s):	DE-2	Physical data model
	DE-3	Physical process model
	DE-8	Preliminary system job flowchart
	DE-10	System manuals' tables of contents
	IM-6	Draft nonautomated procedures user's guide/system maintenance guide/system operations guide/system user's guide
Output(s):	IM-10	Final nonautomated procedures user's guide/system maintenance guide/system operations guide/system user's guide

Task description:
- Review the draft system manuals package and complete all appropriate sections, where applicable.
- Prepare the detailed distribution list of all the departments and related personnel who will receive the individual system manuals. Identify the total number of copies required for each area.

- Walk through the four system manuals to ensure clarity and completeness and to verify adherence to existing standards.

6.2.11 Finalize System Training Package

Task number:	IM-11
Task name:	Finalize system training package
Objective:	To complete and refine the draft system training package
Input(s):	DE-2 Physical data model
	DE-3 Physical process model
	DE-8 Preliminary system job flowchart
	IM-7 Draft system training package
	IM-8 Trained testing user team completion report
	IM-10 Finalize system manuals package
Output(s):	IM-11 Final system training package

Task description:

- Review and finalize the contents of the system training package in light of all the information gathered so far on the system.
- Evaluate the duration of each particular type of training session and prepare the detailed training schedule, along with the complete list of attendees.
- Confirm, if required, the availability of the various training facilities (classrooms, training equipment, etc.).
- Walk through the final system training package with the users and systems operations/maintenance representatives.

The formal training material should finally be prepared so that the users and system operations and maintenance personnel can be trained on how to use, operate, and support the system in the most effective manner, prior to its implementation in the production environment. The training material could include student handouts, slides, overhead transparencies, and so forth. This material should be designed in a top-down manner, describing the system from the very general down to the very specific. In some instances, it will be necessary to tailor some specific components of the training package to suit the specific needs of the targeted audience.

One of the best ways to verify the effectiveness and technical accuracy of the formal training material for a large system is to conduct a small pilot session during which a few direct users and systems representatives are trained with the developed material. These people will not only receive positive feedback on how well the training objectives have been met, but they will also be in a better position to evaluate subsequent training sessions. A side benefit is that more accurate schedules can eventually be prepared with this new information. It is also important to negotiate directly with the users to determine the most appropriate training schedules that would have the least effect on their daily operation.

6.2.12 Formally Train All Users/Systems Personnel

Task number:	IM-12
Task name:	Formally train all users/systems personnel
Objective:	To formally train all the personnel on how to use the new system
Input(s):	IM-10 Final nonautomated user's procedures guide/system maintenance guide/system operations guide/system user's guide
	IM-11 Final system training package
Output(s):	IM-12 Trained staff and final training completion report

Task description:
- Finalize the detailed training schedule with all affected personnel.
- Train the direct user staff and their various levels of management, if required.
- Train the systems operations staff and management.
- Train the systems maintenance personnel and management, if required.
- Produce the final training completion report.

6.2.13 Conduct Production Acceptance Testing

Task number:	IM-13
Task name:	Conduct production acceptance testing
Objective:	To demonstrate that the automated/manual portions of the system will not function properly in a productionlike environment
Input(s):	DE-2 Physical data model
	DE-3 Physical process model
	DE-7 System testing strategy (detailed)
	IM-2 System test environment
	IM-8 Final nonautomated procedures user's guide/system maintenance guide/system operations guide/system user's guide
	IM-9 User acceptance tested system and test results
Output(s):	IM-7 Production acceptance tested system and test results

Task description:
- Complete the creation of production acceptance test cases.
- Execute the production acceptance tests in accordance with the detailed system testing strategy.
- Analyze the outcome of the tests and compare them with expected results.
- If errors are detected, determine their cause. If required, demote the defective programs to the unit test environment and issue a system change request to

resolve the problems that were detected during the production acceptance testing process.

- If no error is found, promote the program(s) to the production libraries.
- Document the production acceptance test results.

During the production acceptance testing process, the normal communication channels are established among the different user departments and systems operations groups that will participate in this final testing cycle. Together, they will test the entire system and ensure that it does work properly in an environment as close as possible to the real-life production environment. The computer operations personnel perform their daily tasks, using the operating instructions provided by the development team and documented in the system operations guide. The direct users will also perform their daily activities using both the automated and manual portions of the system. The test data used during the production acceptance cycle are usually a mix of "live" production data and special test cases that might be required to test the system's behavior when it fails in the production environment.

Most of the time, the production acceptance process that is applicable to a large system is performed using a pilot location. That is, the system is tested in a productionlike environment, but the impact caused by a system failure resulting from an uncovered, devastating error is purposely restrained to a unique location.

Production acceptance testing might prove to be costly to run in either a pseudo-production environment or a real-life production environment. For this reason, some organizations might decide to bypass this last testing cycle. If this is the case, special attention should be given to all the software application deliverables as a whole to ensure that they accurately reflect the production environment. This is necessary because it is very likely that the test and production environments differ on several points. For instance, the naming conventions can be different and physical devices used to store the production files/databases might differ. Also, the storage requirements of the production files/databases might be significantly bigger than those of the testing files.

It is important to point out that it is not unusual to see a large production system fail simply because the system production parameters were not properly set up when the system was put into the production environment.

6.2.14 Install Hardware/Software/Networking Equipment and Facilities at User Sites

Task number:	IM-14
Task name:	Install hardware/software/networking equipment and facilities at user sites
Objective:	To receive and install at the individual user sites the hardware/software/networking equipment and facilities required to support the new system in production

Input(s):	DE-13	Final hardware/software/networking acquisition and installation strategy

Output(s):	IM-14	Installed hardware/software/networking equipment and facilities at user sites

Task description:

- Verify that each user installation site was properly prepared to accept the new equipment and facilities.
- Receive and install the new hardware/software/networking equipment and facilities.
- Test the equipment and facilities with the installation test cases to ensure that they work properly in a standalone or integrated mode of operation.
- Verify that the various system computer supplies have been received in sufficient quantities in each user area, if required.
- Produce the final hardware/software/networking installation completion report.

6.2.15 Perform Conversion of Existing Production Files/Databases

Task number:	IM-15

Task name:	Perform conversion of existing production files/databases

Objective:	To convert the production files/databases of the old system into the files/databases formats of the new system

Input(s):	DE-2	Physical data model
	DE-3	Physical process model
	DE-5	System data conversion strategy (detailed)

Output(s):	IM-15	New production files/databases and production data conversion completion report

Task description:

- Verify that the manual data of the old system have been properly captured within the new system, if applicable.
- Execute the conversion programs in the sequence proposed in the final conversion strategy and plan.
- Verify that the content of the new production files/databases is complete and accurate.
- If there are discrepancies, identify the causes and apply the appropriate corrective measures.
- If necessary, archive the files and databases of the old system for future reference or audit purposes.
- Produce the production data conversion completion report.

6.2.16 Migrate New System into Production and Turn It On

Task number:	IM-16

Task name:	Migrate new system into production and turn it on

Objective:	To transfer the system development deliverables from the development environment to the production environment
Input(s):	DE-2 Physical data model DE-3 Physical process model
Output(s):	IM-16 New operational production system

Task description:

- Transfer the entire system from the development environment to the production environment.

- Verify that all the system elements were successfully transferred into production libraries.

- Distribute the various system manuals to the official user and systems departments representatives.

- Turn on the production system and verify if its level of operability is adequate.

- Turn over the system to the users.

- When applicable, turn off the old system.

- Complete the production system migration report.

6.2.17 Perform System Postimplementation Optimization

Task number:	IM-17
Task name:	Perform postimplementation optimization
Objective:	To fix minor problems detected after the system was put into production and optimize its operations, where necessary
Input(s):	IM-13 New operational production system
Output(s):	IM-17 Production system (optimized)

Task description:

- Assess the overall performance and level of operability of the entire system from the viewpoint of
  - Response time of the online programs
  - Execution time of the batch programs
  - Execution time of the software utility runs (sort/merge, backup/recovery, etc.)
  - Security facilities
  - Installed computer equipment
  - Computer operating instructions and job control instructions
  - User/system documentation in general
  - System communications network

- Identify the specific areas where the original system requirements have not been fully attained. Determine the causes of the problems and apply the appropriate remedies.

- Complete the system documentation, if this was not already done.
- Complete the production system optimization report.

Despite all the efforts spent trying to meet the performance requirements while designing and even prototyping a new software application, chances are that a large system will still need to be optimized once it has been transferred into its production environment. For example, the fine-tuning of the most important online transactions might become an important issue because the performance of the entire online environment might drastically decrease if these critical transactions do not perform as planned.

The postimplementation optimization process could normally take one to two months for a very large system. At the same time, the documentation of the system should be completed, if necessary, prior to disbanding the development team.

6.2.18 Develop System Maintenance Strategy

Task number:	IM-18
Task name:	Develop system maintenance strategy
Objective:	To prepare the system maintenance strategy necessary to support the new production system
Input(s):	IM-16 New operational production system
Output(s):	IM-18 System maintenance strategy

Task description:
- Develop the system maintenance strategy, taking into consideration
  - Change requests that were officially approved during the development cycle but were purposely deferred until the maintenance phase.
  - Total MIS maintenance personnel resources required to support the various user areas that will be serviced by the new system
  - Future system releases that are already planned
  - Ongoing system training activities
- Walk through the system maintenance strategy.

6.3 REFERENCES

BEAIZER, B. 1984. *Software System Testing and Quality Assurance*. New York: Van Nostrand Reinhold.

HALSTEAD, M. 1977. *Elements of Software Science*. New York: Elsevier.

KING, D. 1984. *Current Practices in Software Development*. New York: Yourdon Press.

McCABE, T. 1976. "A Complexity Measure," *IEEE Transactions on Software Engineering*, SE-2, No. 4, December.

MYERS, G. J. 1979. *The Art of Software Testing*. New York: John Wiley.

YOURDON, E. 1979. *Managing the Structured Techniques*. New York: Yourdon Press.

7

Maintenance Phase

7.1 PURPOSE

Typically, the useful life of a large and complex system spans five to ten years. However, it is not unusual to find such systems that are fifteen or even twenty years old. For this reason, experts in the computer field view the delivery of a system to its users as the beginning of its useful life. From that point on the system will continue to evolve until it is discarded or replaced with another one. Figure 7.1 illustrates this concept of constant evolution.

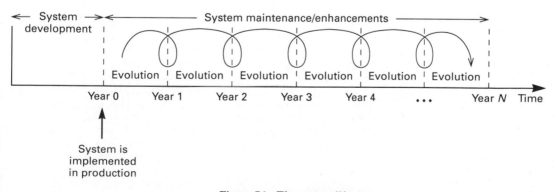

Figure 7.1 The system life span

Based on this simple observation, two major goals can be readily derived from the software engineering process. First, the software engineering development life cycle must constantly emphasize the need to construct software systems that are flexible and adaptable. In other words, such quality factors as usability, flexibility, and maintainability should be built into the system as it is developed, not after the fact. Second, the software engineering maintenance process should be performed in a systematic and structured manner to retard the degradation of the system over time and to ensure its maintainability. Table 7.1 shows the five generic categories of maintenance activities, along with their individual objectives, that exist for a system.

As we can see in the table, the traditional concept of maintenance (a programmer fixing a bug) is not an accurate picture of the entire maintenance process. In fact, various surveys conducted demonstrate that more time is spent enhancing the system to meet changing user needs than on any other type of maintenance ac-

TABLE 7.1   THE GENERAL CATEGORIES OF MAINTENANCE ACTIVITIES

Category	Objective	Examples
Perfective	To enhance the system with the changes requested by the users to meet the evolving needs of the business	Adding new functions Adding new reports Modifying existing reports
Adaptive	To modify the system to accommodate physical changes in the environment itself.	Introducing a new operating system version Adding new peripheral devices Introducing a new compiler version
Corrective	To modify the system with changes necessitated by the detection of defects or ambiguities	Fixing a screen that returns invalid data Correcting a report that displays inaccurate totals Fixing an abend in production caused by an invalid input transaction
Preventive	To modify the system with changes that are necessary for maintaining its effectiveness and reliability	Reorganizing the databases for optimal performance Increasing the size of the production files/databases Regular housekeeping of the network equipment and facilities
Structural	To modify the internal architecture of the system with changes aimed at improving its future maintainability	Improving the existing program documentation Restructuring the code to increase its readability Reengineering the application programs to increase their modularity

tivity. Consequently, the maintenance process suggested in this chapter prescribes a strategy whereby

1. Emergency program fixes are temporarily applied to the system as quickly as possible, where necessary. Subsequently, these fixes should be more formally incorporated into a scheduled system maintenance release. At that time, more sophisticated and permanent corrective measures should be applied to resolve the application software system deficiencies.

2. Wherever feasible, the planned maintenance enhancements should be accumulated over a given period of time and regrouped into one or more system maintenance release(s). A system maintenance release should then be treated like any other system development effort, except on a smaller scale.

This strategy is certainly not a new approach; its effectiveness has been proven many times in the software industry, especially by major vendors. The advantages of applying the release concept to the maintenance process are numerous:

- It emphasizes the need to perform a rigorous analysis and design of the requested user enhancements and allows the proper modification of the supporting system documentation.
- It maximizes the utilization of the maintenance staff because it is usually far more economical to enhance the system with several enhancements at a time as opposed to one.
- It eases the computer operations scheduling process by minimizing the frequency of ad hoc enhancements that are applied to the system in its production environment.
- It allows the users to take more time to verify the major system enhancements that need extensive testing.
- It deemphasizes the arbitrary distinction that exists between the software engineering development and maintenance processes.

Table 7.2 summarizes the major technical tasks that are normally conducted during the maintenance phase, along with the anticipated technical deliverables. Figure 7.2 illustrates, at a high level, the relationships among the individual tasks of the maintenance phase.

7.2 DESCRIPTION OF THE TECHNICAL TASKS

7.2.1 Evaluate System Enhancement Request

Task number:	MT-1
Task name:	Evaluate system enhancement request
Objective:	To analyze the users' requests for modifying the production system, based on evolving business needs

Input(s):	Users' request for system enhancement Production system documentation package Production system programs
Output(s):	MT-1 Proposed system enhancement solution

Task description:

- Acknowledge receipt of the request for system enhancement from the designated user area coordinator and coordinate with other similar requests, where applicable.
- Analyze the users' needs as described in the request for service.
- If necessary, contact the originating user coordinator representative to obtain clarification on the related subject and verify the benefit assessment.
- Identify the other areas of the organization that might be affected by the request.
- Describe briefly the possible solution alternatives, along with their potential impact on the current production system and its supportive environment.
- Provide a preliminary estimate of the total development hours required to satisfy the users' request.
- Return the evaluated request to the user area coordinator for prioritization.

The software maintenance process requires a formal change control mechanism to track and monitor all the maintenance activities related to system enhancements. If the organization does not enforce some form of change control mechanism on the systems being maintained, chances are that the level of maintainability of these systems will quickly deteriorate over time.

TABLE 7.2   MAINTENANCE PHASE TECHNICAL TASKS AND DELIVERABLES

Technical Tasks	*Technical Deliverables*
1. Evaluate system enhancement request	1. Proposed system enhancement solution
2. Evaluate request for correcting production system problem	2. Proposed production system problem solution
3. Apply emergency program fix	3. Implemented emergency program fix
4. Organize enhancement requests into individual system releases	4. Scheduled system maintenance release(s)
5. Analyze system maintenance release requirements	5. Detailed system maintenance release requirements
6. Design system maintenance release	6. System maintenance release design
7. Code and test system maintenance release	7. Tested system maintenance release
8. Implement system maintenance release	8. Production system maintenance release
9. Perform preventive maintenance	9. Production system (optimized)
10. Train staff	10. Updated training material
11. Conduct periodical system appraisal	11. System appraisal report
12. Conduct postimplementation review	12. Postimplementation report

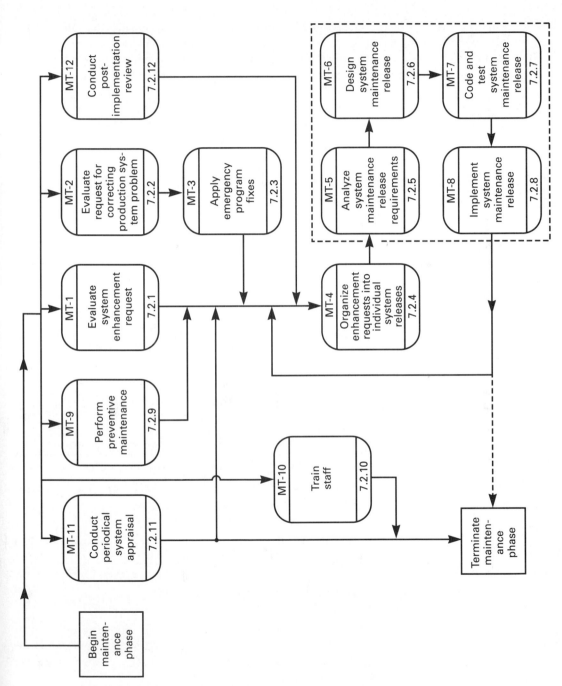

Figure 7.2 Maintenance phase task network

A typical change request form looks like the one illustrated in Fig. 7.3. An important aspect of the change management procedure is to ensure that all users' requests are funneled through a certified user coordinator. Doing so will ensure that the forms are properly filled out by the users. It will also permit proper screening and tracking of valid requests originating from the coordinator's area.

Once the request is received by the MIS organization, it is reviewed for completeness and accuracy. Then, based on the information provided on the form and with additional discussions with the requestor, if required, the request is analyzed in light of a possible solution, which might entail the following:

- Creation of new programs
- Changes to existing programs
- Changes to existing files/databases
- Creation of new files/databases
- Changes to the existing documentation

Finally, an order of magnitude estimate of the time required to satisfy the request is submitted to the user coordinators. They will decide what priority should be assigned to the request.

Along with the estimate, a brief impact analysis should be provided to the users to explain the potential effect the proposed enhancement might have on other functions of the system. This is important because the users might not fully understand the possible repercussions their requests might have on other components of the same system or on other associated systems.

7.2.2 Evaluate Request for Correcting Production System Problem

Task number:	MT-2
Task name:	Evaluate request for correcting production system problem
Objective:	To analyze a system problem occurring in the production environment and propose an adequate solution
Input(s):	Request for correcting system problems Production system documentation package Production system programs
Output(s):	MT-2 Proposed system problem solution

Task description:
- Determine the nature of the problem and its magnitude.
- Analyze the probable causes.
- Identify the solution alternatives to correct the problem (applying either a quick fix to the system, proposing a more permanent solution, or compromising with an interim solution that does not necessarily require changes to the automated components of the system).

CUSTOMER

Date: _____ _____ _____
YY   MM   DD

Page _____ of _____

To: _____
      Name   Department

Requester: _____   Department: _____
Title: _____   Telephone: _____

User coordinator signature: _____

| Type of Request | Priority | Category | Request Number: _____ |

Type of Request
○ Minor enhancement
○ Major enhancement
○ Consulting
○ New development

○ Attachments included

Priority
○ Very urgent
○ As soon as possible
○ To be determined

Category
○ Mandatory
○ Discretionary

Date required: _____ _____ _____
                YY   MM   DD

Description of Request

Expected Benefits

SYSTEMS

Proposed Solution

Approved by: _____
Title: _____
Department: _____
Date: _____ _____ _____
      YY   MM   DD

Estimate of total
development hours:

Status

○ Cancellation   ○ Revision   ○ Completion   (Date completed: _____ _____ _____)
                                                                  YY   MM   DD

Figure 7.3   Change request form

- Determine the urgency for fixing the problem:

  Emergency Program Fix.
  - Proceed with activity MT-3 (apply emergency program fix).

  Permanent System Solution.
  - Forward proposed system solution, with an estimate of the required development hours, to the user area coordinator for prioritization.

  Interim Procedural Solution.
  - Document the interim procedural solution by describing the manual administrative procedures that are necessary to circumvent the documented system problem.
  - Walk through the interim procedural solution with the users.
  - Implement the procedural changes that are suggested in the interim solution and monitor its effectiveness in the production environment.
  - If required, forward a permanent automated system solution (which implies changes to the automated environment) to the user area coordinator for prioritization.

A system problem report is usually initiated by either the end users or the system operations personnel who run the production jobs. Let's consider a scenario where the users have detected a problem. Depending on the urgency of the situation, the solution must be implemented immediately, before the next production run cycle, or it can be delayed until further notice if it has a limited impact on the users' ability to perform their day-to-day job. In the latter case, the users will probably find a way to circumvent the problem temporarily. The request can then be treated like a normal request for system enhancement and prioritized accordingly. For example, the users might report a problem with an element of the documentation that appears to be incorrect or ambiguous. Obviously, these types of requests, even though they are valid, might not entail the same priority as one for fixing a program that produces an invalid customer invoice statement.

The production system problem reported by the system operations personnel results in temporarily stopping the production cycle; the problem must be fixed before the production cycle is resumed. Most of the time, the maintenance analyst supporting the application system is immediately notified of the production problem. The production job statements, error messages, and other output material such as the system dumps are forwarded to the maintenance analyst for quick troubleshooting and problem resolution. These types of problems are usually given top priority because they prevent the production cycle from proceeding.

To conclude, the disposition of the request might be as follows:

- Reject and return to the user coordinator with appropriate explanations (not a system problem).
- Add to the list of other nonemergency requests that will be included in the next scheduled system maintenance release.
- Fix immediately or as soon as possible (task 7.2.3).

Figure 7.4 shows a sample of a typical form used to report a system problem in production.

7.2.3 Apply Emergency Program Fix

Task number:	MT-3
Task name:	Apply emergency program fix
Objective:	To apply an emergency fix on the defective program(s) of the system and quickly resume system operations in the production environment
Input(s):	MT-2 Proposed system problem solution
Output(s):	MT-3 Implemented emergency program fix

Task description:

- Gather the information required to investigate and fix the production problem.
- Analyze the nature of the problem and its impact on the currect production cycle.
- Determine the probable causes of the problem and identify the defective programs that are involved.
- Demote the sources of the defective program(s) into the test environment.
- Determine the minimum level of testing required to promote the program(s) back into the production environment.
- Code and unit-test the changes.
- If necessary, perform system integration and/or user acceptance testing.
- Implement the tested solution into the production environment.
- Communicate to all affected users the completion of the emergency fix.
- Document all the changes made to the system and close the original system problem report request.
- Update the affected system documentation, including the user's manuals, where applicable.

In an emergency situation, the maintenance analyst must respond as quickly as possible to a request for fixing a problem in production. More often than not, the challenge is in identifying the source of the error.[1] Once this is done, it is usually easy to find a solution to the problem. The scope of the problem at hand and its magnitude will determine the types of testing done to verify that the proposed solution does work properly the first time and does not produce an undesirable ripple effect on other components of the system.

---

[1]The maintenance analyst can review the central log of system problems that previously occurred in the production environment for potentially identifying an old problem similar to the current one.

Date: _____ _____ _____
YY   MM   DD

Page _____ of _____

To: _____
       Name   Department

Requester: _____

Department: _____

Title: _____

Telephone: _____

User coordinator signature: _____
                                      (if applicable)

Problem Number: _____

System ID: _____   Program ID: _____   Job ID: _____

Level of Criticality

○ High (production halted)   ○ Medium (local degradation)   ○ Low (substandard performance)

Problem Description

Recovery Steps Taken So Far

Proposed Solution

Status of Problem

○ Open
○ Close

Closed Date: _____ _____ _____
              YY   MM   DD

Figure 7.4 System problem report form

7.2.4 Organize Enhancement Requests into Individual System Releases

Task number:	MT-4
Task name:	Organize enhancement requests into individual system releases
Objective:	To plan, prioritize, and assemble the user requests for system changes into distinct maintenance releases
Input(s):	MT-1 Proposed system enhancement solution MT-2 Proposed system problem solution MT-3 Implemented emergency program fix
Output(s):	MT-4 Scheduled system maintenance release(s)

Task description:

- Review all the user requests for system changes that are still open.
- Determine the priority of each particular request and the possible dependencies with other requests.
- Review the system development hours that were estimated to satisfy the request and compare the development costs versus the user expected benefits.
- Evaluate both the business and technical effects that the requested change and its proposed system solution might have on the current business and system environments.
- If not technically feasible or not cost-justified, reject the request and document the rationale.
- Rank the requests in a priority sequence.
- Assemble the requests into specific system maintenance release(s) and schedule the release(s) accordingly.
- Walk through the proposed system maintenance releases.

Grouping the different user enhancement requests into a distinct system maintenance release can be done based on several factors:[2]

- The magnitude of the requested system enhancements (e.g., estimated number of development hours)
- Their priorities in relation with one another, as perceived by the users
- Their potential impact on the corporate databases manipulated by the system
- Their functional affinities with particular subsystems of the software application
- Their impact on the interfaces with other systems

---

[2]It is understood that the software engineering maintenance process must always provide alternative ways of implementing urgent system changes independently of planned maintenance releases. However, the change requests that are not considered high priority should be integrated into a planned maintenance release.

In some instances, partial releases might be assembled for groups of changes that do not require an extensive development effort. If a system maintenance release is fairly large, it can be broken down into different versions, as is done for the development of a new system.

7.2.5 Analyze System Maintenance Release Requirements

Task number:	MT-5
Task name:	Analyze system maintenance release requirements
Objective:	To analyze and document in detail the requirements associated with a specific system maintenance release
Input(s):	MT-4 Scheduled system maintenance release(s) Production system documentation package Production system
Output(s):	MT-5 Detailed system maintenance release requirements

Task description:

- Review all the requests for system enhancements that have been incorporated into the system maintenance release.

- Interview the users and document the detailed requirements associated with the release.

- Specify the functions of the system that must be modified to satisfy the user requirements or the additional functions that must be integrated in the current system environment. Update the current system data flow diagrams to reflect the functional changes or new additions necessitated by the new release. Develop the detailed functional specifications associated with the new or modified system processes. Wherever feasible, develop a "live" prototype of the screen and report layouts.

- Specify the data changes or additions that must be made to the existing logical file/database structures of the system. Update the current entity-relationship or normalized data models to reflect the new information requirements necessitated by the new release.

- Develop the detailed data specifications associated with the new or modified logical data structures.

- Determine the extent to which the following nonfunctional requirements must be considered for the release at hand:
  - Data conversion
  - Testing
  - Training
  - Hardware/software/networking
  - System control

- Data storage
- Performance

• Document the additional requirements, other than functional, that apply to the new release.

• Walk through the detailed system maintenance release requirements.

The same tools and techniques used to develop a new system should be used to develop and implement major enhancements and adaptations that must be made to an existing system. Hence, the automated tools that are normally used to draw the data flow diagrams, to develop the detailed functional specifications, and to create the logical data structures should also be utilized to model the changes that must be made to the existing system. However, common sense must prevail when defining the system requirements. For instance, it might not be practical to remodel the entire system if the changes only apply to an existing function. Depending on the scope, size, and complexity of the work to be done, the development team should decide the level of detail at which the requirements must be described and documented and how this might affect the existing logical models of the system.

Sometimes the users and development team personnel might be tempted to enhance the system beyond the scope that was originally set for the current maintenance release. There is no doubt that this change of direction might turn out to be advantageous for the organization. However, it is important not to deviate from the original objectives set for the maintenance release at hand. If, despite this warning, the team feels that the unforeseen enhancements are still valuable, these new requirements should always be renegotiated with the proper user management.

7.2.6 Design System Maintenance Release

Task number:	MT-6	
Task name:	Design system maintenance release	
Objective:	To design the programs and physical data structures of the system maintenance release	
Input(s):	MT-5	Detailed system maintenance release requirements
		Production system documentation package
		Production system
Output(s):	MT-6	System maintenance release design

Task description:

• Design the changes that must be made to the existing physical file/database structures or the new file/database structures required for this release.

• Design the changes that must be made to the existing program structure charts or the new program structure charts required by the release.

• Develop the detailed structure chart and database design specifications.

- Specify the detailed activities associated with the release test plan, along with the preparation of sound test cases.
- Update the affected components of the production system documentation package.
- Walk through the system maintenance release design.

7.2.7 Code and Test System Maintenance Release

Task number:	MT-7
Task name:	Code and test system maintenance release
Objective:	To develop and test the programs of the current maintenance release
Input(s):	MT-6 System maintenance release design Production system documentation package System test environment
Output(s):	MT-7 Tested system maintenance release

Task description:

- Code the programs and the job control statements required to compile them.
- Finalize the unit test cases for each program.
- If necessary, create the manual procedures that support the automated processes.
- Unit-test the programs of the release.
- Finalize the system integration test cases.
- Exercise the system integration tests.
- Update the operations support procedures.
- Finalize the user acceptance test cases.
- Perform the user acceptance testing process.
- Update the components of the production system documentation package that are affected by the release.
- Walk through the release test cases and results.

7.2.8 Implement System Maintenance Release

Task number:	MT-8
Task name:	Implement system maintenance release
Objective:	To transfer the system maintenance release into production
Input(s):	MT-7 Tested system maintenance release Production system documentation package
Output(s):	MT-8 Production system maintenance release

Task description:

- Prepare new training materials and train staff, if required.
- Transfer the system maintenance release to the production environment.
- Release the updates made to the production system documentation package to the user and systems personnel.

7.2.9 Perform Preventive Maintenance

Task number:	MT-9
Task name:	Perform preventive maintenance
Objective:	To monitor the system's behavior to ensure it remains efficient and produces accurate results
Input(s):	Production system documentation package Production system
Output(s):	MT-9 Production system (optimized)

Task description:

System Oriented.

- Monitor the system's performance behavior.
- Monitor the growth of the traffic network.
- Monitor the growth of the system's files/databases size.
- Monitor the growth of the total volume of transactions processed per month.
- Monitor the system's overall availability trends.
- Monitor the overall performance of the hardware/software/networking equipment and facilities.
- Monitor the adequacy of the security and disaster recovery procedures.
- If required, make the changes or adjustments necessary to keep the system in its most optimal operating condition.

User Oriented.

- Monitor the distribution and delivery of the system outputs and their usage.
- Monitor the overall efficiency of the system human-machine interfaces, including the effectiveness of the supporting manual processes.
- Monitor the system's ability to produce accurate results.
- Monitor the adequacy of the security and disaster recovery procedures.
- If required, document and report any serious deviation or degradation that might occur in the system.

As discussed in Chap. 13, on software quality, prevention is the most cost-effective technique to prevent failures in the production environment. Most software applications will gradually degrade over time if the necessary technical housekeeping functions are not regularly performed on the computer equipment that supports them. However, several operational failures, such as those related to computer equipment, can often be prevented if the hardware/software/networking infrastructure is properly maintained. Several computer equipment facilities have built-in diagnostic reporting capabilities that can be used to prevent hardware failures and tune the equipment to obtain an optimal performance.

On the software side, several tools can be utilized to monitor and provide statistical information on the overall performance of the system. One example is IBM's System Management Facilities (SMF) package. Another is IBM's DB MONITOR facility, which is used to collect and report information on the performance of batch IMS databases. When such tools are activated in the IBM software environment, statistical information is automatically gathered as the production jobs run. The collected data are analyzed to verify that the system's behavior meets the predetermined performance requirements. The collected information is also used to fine-tune the system, when necessary.

Monitoring the effectiveness of the system should also extend to the manual processes that were developed by the users.

7.2.10 Train Staff

Task number:	MT-10
Task name:	Train staff
Objective:	To train regularly new personnel or retrain existing personnel on effective use or support of the evolving system
Input(s):	Production system documentation package Production system software training materials
Output(s):	MT-10 Updated training materials

Task description:
- Periodically update the system training materials to reflect the important enhancements made to the system.
- Determine if there is a need to train new people who will be called upon to use or support the production system.
- Determine if the existing staff needs refresher courses on how to use certain components of the system.
- Accordingly train the staff, where required.

In principle, a substantial and well-organized training effort was performed at the time the system was implemented. However, as time goes by, training materials should be updated. The materials will be used to train new personnel who are hired or transferred into the various user areas serviced by the system. They can also be used to train new maintenance analysts, system operations staff, and management personnel. In some instances, even the user and system old-timers might need a refresher course on some particular aspects of the system.

The rationale for ongoing training for large, complex systems is justified by the fact that, over the years

- There will be some staff turnover.
- The system will probably have to adapt to new hardware/software/networking configurations.
- The software system will be enhanced as per the users' requests.
- Over time, the staff might forget how to use the system in the most effective manner.

7.2.11 Conduct Periodical System Appraisal

Task number:	MT-11
Task name:	Conduct periodical system appraisal
Objective:	To assess the degree of effectiveness and usability achieved by the system as it ages
Input(s):	Production system documentation package Production system software Accumulated user requests for system enhancements
Output(s):	MT-11 System appraisal report

Task description:
- Evaluate the degree to which the system meets the evolving business needs of the organization:
  - Assess the value and accuracy of the outputs produced by the system.
  - Assess the value and accuracy of the system input processes.
  - Assess the completeness and accuracy of the system documentation.
  - Assess the overall usability of the system.
  - Assess if the system still performs useful functions.
  - Assess the maintainability of the system.
  - Assess the level of operability of the system.
  - Assess the level of reliability of the system.
  - Assess the level of performance achieved by the system.
  - Determine if the number of accumulated enhancement requests indicates that the system should be modified, terminated, or completely replaced.
  - Evaluate the cost-effectiveness of the system in terms of its business objectives versus the number of staff resources consumed in supporting and operating the system.
- Consolidate the findings and submit the appropriate recommendations to management.

A thorough assessment study should be performed periodically to verify if the entire system still satisfies the needs of the users. As a rule, such a study should be conducted every two or three years. The first assessments will probably highlight enhancements that will help to improve the effectiveness and usability of the system. As the years go by, the system will probably be frequently modified to meet new user requirements or to adapt to new hardware/software/networking configurations. Therefore, symptoms of obsolescence might eventually surface, such as increasing maintenance costs and a decreasing business value. This might be especially true if the maintenance process has not been performed in a controlled and rigorous manner.

There are two types of obsolescence: functional and technological. Functional obsolescence arises when the system no longer adequately fulfills its mission or the business environment has evolved so drastically that the original mission no longer holds true in light of the new business functions that must now be supported. Technological obsolescence occurs when the technology that was used to implement the system becomes inefficient, unreliable, and outdated.

Depending on the situation at hand, several strategies can be used to remedy technological or functional obsolescence:[3]

Restoration.   The restoration process entails correcting technical deficiencies while maintaining the status quo on the functions supported by the system. Among other things, it can include

- Restructuring the code and augmenting the system documentation to ease the maintenance process.
- Redesigning the file/database structures for optimization purposes.
- Reengineering existing programs to increase their modularity and cohesion.
- Migrating from a given database structure to another (e.g., hierarchical to relational).
- Reverse-engineering—that is, reverting a program back to its original design specification and then reimplementing it with a new technology that uses a more modern programming language.

Expansion.   The expansion process entails the addition of new functions around or as a front end to the current system while maintaining the status quo on the technical architecture surrounding the system. Among other things, it can include

- Downloading information in a personal computer environment for reporting and graphical purposes.

[3]Numerous automated facilities are available to rejuvenate existing systems. Examples of these reengineering CASE tools include database reengineering tools, such as Bachman Information Systems' Bachman/DA, which, among other things, can be used to migrate IMS database designs into DB2 database designs; Cobol restructurer codes, such as Retrofit from Peat, Marwick, Mitchell & Company or Recoder from Language Technology, Inc.; Cobol code analyzers, such as Via/Insight from Viasoft, Inc., or Navigator/MF from Centura Software; and data name standardizers, such as CSA from Marble Computer, Inc.

- Introducing a fourth-generation tool that interfaces with the older technology that was used to implement the system. The users can then query the older files/databases with the new tool.
- Introducing new functions such as an online data entry facility as a front end to replace or complement the older system batch input facility.

Elimination.   The system is discontinued without a replacement since it achieves a very low business value.

Replacement.   The existing system is replaced by acquiring a commercial package or building a new application in-house.

7.2.12 Conduct Postimplementation Review

Task number:	MT-12
Task name:	Conduct postimplementation review
Objective:	To examine the project in retrospect and determine its effectiveness in satisfying the business needs of the organization
Input(s):	Production system documentation package Production system software Production system performance statistics Original cost-benefit analysis
Output(s):	MT-12 Postimplementation report

Task description:
- Obtain information from the direct users of the system and their management on
  - General level of user satisfaction attained with the system
  - Level of usability achieved by the system and the extent to which it is used by the staff
  - Timeliness, correctness, accuracy, and effectiveness of the information processed by the system and the usability of the human-machine interfaces (screens, reports, forms)
  - Level of performance achieved by the system versus the original specifications
  - Extent to which the system satisfies the cost-benefit figures projected by the users and the reasons for any serious variance
  - Adequacy, timeliness, and effectiveness of the training provided to the personnel
  - Appropriateness, completeness, and accuracy of the user documentation
  - Verification of the internal controls embedded in the system
  - Reliability of the hardware/software/networking equipment and facilities

- – Effectiveness of the disaster prevention and recovery plan
- – Effectiveness of the security procedures to prevent system abuse
- – Need to improve some particular areas of the system or to resolve unexpected problems that have surfaced since its installation
- – Relevance, reliability, and effectiveness of the manual or automated system interfaces that have been established with other systems
- – Timeliness and quality of the support services provided by the system operations and maintenance staff
- – Impact of the system on the users and their environment

- Obtain information from all the users and system professionals who participated in the development of the system on
  - – Appropriateness and effectiveness of the technical activities and standards prescribed in the development methodology and used during the former project
  - – Adequacy and accuracy of the development time estimates developed at the beginning of each development phase of the project
  - – Reasons for deviating from the original schedules, if applicable
  - – Whether the scope of the system was appropriate and the extent to which it was maintained during the entire project
  - – Level of quality achieved while developing the technical deliverables of the project
  - – Effectiveness of the testing process and its various supportive environments
  - – Relevance and usefulness of the automated tools used by the development team and the users
  - – Appropriateness and effectiveness of the project management tools, activities, and standards prescribed by the methodology for controlling and monitoring the development of the system

- Obtain information from the system operations team on
  - – Completeness, technical relevance, and effectiveness of the computer operating procedures used to run the system in production
  - – Appropriateness of the production job scheduling information
  - – Major computer-related problems experienced so far, if any

- Obtain information from the system maintenance team on
  - – Nature and number of requests received for system enhancements
  - – Nature and number of defects encountered while supporting the system
  - – Completeness and correctness of the technical system documentation
  - – Level of maintainability achieved by the system (quality of design, structured coding, etc.)

- Consolidate all the findings of the study in terms of the problems and successes encountered during the development cycle and after the installation of the system in its production environment. Provide, if applicable, recommendations on how to avoid future problems that were experienced during the development of the system. Document the current needs for system changes or enhancements and present the appropriate recommendations to management.

- Walk through the postimplementation report deliverables.

Traditionally, the primary goal of the postimplementation review is to examine the system with the direct users and evaluate its effectiveness in satisfying the stated business objectives. Based on the results of the study, suggested changes might be proposed to enhance the system. However, such a study should also extend to those persons who developed the system as well as those who maintain and operate it in the production environment. This is essential to improve not only the system product but also the software engineering methodology, and to keep it up to date and effective. Hence, the postimplementation study should be integrated into the system life cycle as an integral part of the overall process of developing and maintaining the system.

Formal postimplementation studies are rarely conducted in some organizations for the simple reason that they are considered as an organized witch hunt. The only reason for the study is to identify scapegoats who can be blamed for all the problems encountered during the project. Thus it is imperative that the postimplementation study be conducted in an open and honest atmosphere that is conducive to gaining the cooperation of people rather than scaring them to death. This is why it is so important to inform the affected staff and its management about the real objectives of the study, how it will be conducted, and the anticipated benefits. The entire process should be geared toward gaining experience and learning from the problems encountered during and after the project. This is the only way an organization can learn not to repeat the same mistakes and use the newly acquired knowledge to improve the way future projects will be conducted. At the same time, it is also crucial to highlight those aspects of the projects that turned out to be very positive. These should be used to reinforce and solidify the system development and maintenance methodology.

Sometimes, postimplementation reviews are not conducted simply because the organization does not feel it has the time to do so. In such circumstances, the organization has failed to recognize evaluation reviews as a valuable approach to improve the current system development and project management practices which in fact lead to the delivery of high-quality software systems.

Proper timing of the study is very important. The best time to schedule the study is approximately three to six months after the system is delivered to its users. Any earlier, the users might not have had the opportunity to familiarize themselves with all the functions and facilities of the system. At the end of six months, the system should be relatively stable and most of the major problems should have already been discovered. Furthermore, the users should have had enough time to drop the old habits they developed working with the previous system.

Ideally, the people who conduct the study should be objective and experienced individuals who are well respected in both the user and systems communities. In some organizations, the study is sometimes performed by an independent group in order to preserve objectivity.

7.3 REFERENCES

KUMAR, K. 1990. "Post-Implementation Evaluation of Computer-Based Information Systems: Current Practices," *Communications of the ACM,* 33, No. 2, February.

LIENTZ, B., and B. SWANSON. 1980. *Software Maintenance Management,* Reading, Mass.: Addison-Wesley.

MARTIN, J., and C. MCCLURE. 1983. *Software Maintenance: The Problem and Its Solutions,* Englewood Cliffs, N.J.: Prentice Hall.

PARIKH, G. 1986. *Handbook of Software Maintenance,* New York: John Wiley.

_____, and G. ZVEGINTZOV. 1983. *Software Maintenance.* New York: IEEE Computer Society.

8

Structured Testing

8.1 INTRODUCTION

This chapter describes structured testing concepts and how they should be utilized throughout the system development life cycle prescribed in this book to ensure the engineering of a quality system. The testing process attempts to identify defects in the software system being constructed. The defects can be caused either by deficiencies present in the system specifications or deficiencies inadvertently embedded in the program code itself.

Two generic categories of defects can be defined: errors and ambiguities. Errors are flaws in the application software that will cause the system to fail or to generate invalid results. Hence, it is important to identify as many errors as possible during the testing cycle and eliminate them prior to delivering the system to its customers. To achieve this objective, testing must be seen as a *destructive process* that is executed with the firm intention of uncovering errors.

As discussed in Chap. 13, on software quality, the term *quality* should not be defined only as conformance to requirements but also as overall fitness for use. This is where ambiguities come into play. Ambiguities will not necessarily cause the system to fail, as we just said for system errors. However, they might drastically affect its fitness for use or, to be more precise, its level of usability. To demonstrate this point, Table 8.1 shows some of the ambiguities that might crop up during the development of a large software system.

Thus, the goal of software testing should not simply encompass error detection and correction. It should verify that the system truly satisfies its customers in terms of effectiveness and usability. Also, the system professionals who will be called upon to support the system in production should equally verify its degree of fitness for maintainability during the testing process.

TABLE 8.1   EXAMPLES OF SYSTEM AMBIGUITIES

User Oriented	*System Oriented*
Reports or screens that are awkward to use from a user perspective	Unnecessarily complex computer algorithms
Error messages that are difficult to understand or are incoherent	Poor or inefficient system and program documentation
Help facility that is unclear or incomplete	Massive monolithic programs that are not properly modularized
Inefficient user manual procedures	Unstructured code that is difficult to maintain
Overly complex system user manuals with highly technical terminology	Inefficient interfaces with other systems

8.2 THE FOUR LEVELS OF SOFTWARE TESTING

Testing activities are organized around four separate, functionally distinct levels of testing: unit testing, system integration testing, user acceptance testing, and production acceptance testing. Each specific level focuses on the identification of a distinct class of errors or ambiguities.

Unit testing is typically executed by the programming staff. Its prime objective is to demonstrate that the various modules composing a program do not operate according to their original design specifications and do not interface properly with one another.

System integration testing is performed by either an independent test team or the system development team itself. Its prime objective is to demonstrate that all the components of the system do not function together properly or do not meet the original system design specifications. The manual components of the system can be tested at this point or deferred until user acceptance testing.

User acceptance testing, as indicated by its name, is executed by the user representatives or direct users. Its prime objective is to demonstrate that the system does not meet the original user requirements. The manual components of the system are also tested to demonstrate that the complete system solution does not work properly.

Production acceptance testing is typically executed under the control of the end users and the systems operations staff. The system development team acts primarily as technical consultants during this stage. Its prime objective is to demonstrate that the total system does not function properly in a nearly real-life environment or in an actual real-life production environment.

8.3 CREATION OF THE TESTING STRATEGY

Figure 8.1 shows the specific instances at which the software testing strategy is created and subsequently refined during the system development life cycle, along with the construction of sound test cases and the actual execution of the tests themselves.

The preliminary strategy for testing the system is initially developed during the detailed analysis phase. The major objectives of the overall testing process are defined with the users and should cover the four levels of testing—the unit, system integration, user acceptance, and production acceptance testing cycles—where applicable. Other issues concerning the roles and responsibilities of each group that

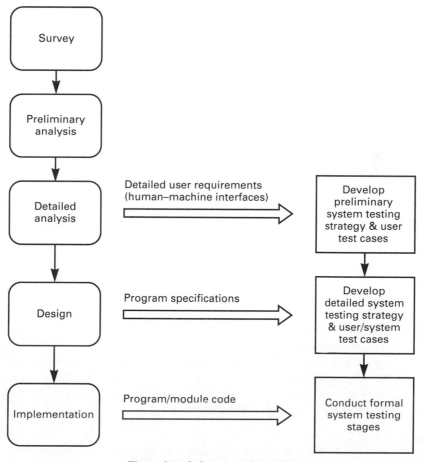

Figure 8.1   Software testing cycle

will be involved in the testing process are also discussed. For instance, the decision to allow the development team to perform the system integration testing process, instead of an independent testing team, is made during this phase. During the design phase, the detailed testing strategy is developed concurrently with the engineering of effective test cases. Finally, the formal testing cycle is officially activated during the implementation phase.

A significant advantage with this approach is the fact that the software testing process is fully integrated into the system development life cycle. Moreover, testing is no longer seen as an activity that occurs only after the programs have been coded. Rather, the preparatory testing activities parallel the detailed analysis activities (high-level testing strategy) and design activities (detailed testing strategy and preparation of test cases). This shift in focus toward the early stages of the software engineering development process also allows the development manager to highlight to management some very important testing issues—the time it would require to test the system properly, the need for using automated testing tools, the overall costs of testing the system, and the availability of adequate computer resources for performing the testing process.

8.4 TEST LIBRARIES AND CONTROL PROCEDURES

The thorough testing of a large software system will necessitate several control procedures that must be put in place before starting the testing process. These procedures are necessary to manage efficiently the entire testing process and its supportive environment. Figure 8.2 shows the generic set of software testing libraries that are required to support the entire testing process throughout its four testing cycles.

Following is a description of the procedures that should be established for better control of the testing process and its supportive environment.

Library control procedures.   Library control procedures are used to transfer programs among any of the four distinct sets of testing libraries. They also clearly identify who should coordinate the transfer of programs among these libraries. Typically, only one person will have the authority to make the transfers. In some organizations, this function is assigned to a project librarian;[1] in others, the project leader fills that role. In any case, access to the programs residing in these test libraries (except the unit test libraries) is normally restricted to one individual. Thus, nobody else can alter these programs while tests are being performed.

When a program has been successfully tested and is promoted to an upper-level testing library, its source code is transferred from one library level to another and then recompiled. This procedure enforces security and control over the contents of the programs being transferred.

---

[1]For more information on the project librarian function, see Yourdon [1979].

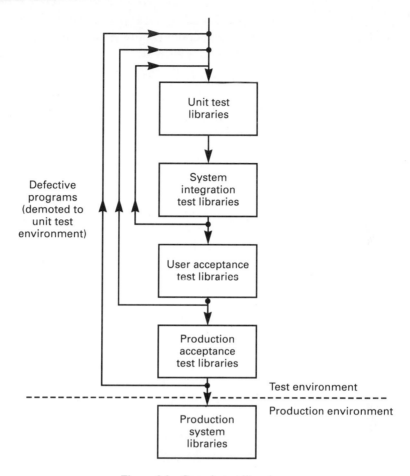

Figure 8.2   Generic test libraries

When defects are found in a program, the program is demoted to the unit testing level. The source code is transferred back from the production acceptance, user acceptance, or system integration test library to the unit test library. The affected program is corrected and once again unit-tested. It is then repromoted and should be retested at all lower levels before it reaches the level where the deficiency was first detected.

Change control procedures.   Change control procedures must be put in place to record, evaluate, control, and track requests for change that can be submitted by the users during the development process. A change request may cause modifications to the system requirements and therefore to its architectural design. These requests should be approved by both a user representative coordinator and a system representative coordinator before performing the work. This control mechanism is required because system changes can have a serious impact on the project cost estimates, the architectural design of the system, and the duration of the test cycle. Hence, it must be properly managed.

Problem reporting procedures.   These procedures are very important, especially when several persons will test different portions of the system at the same time. The problem reporting procedures describe the manual or automated mechanisms that are put in place to document and report all the discrepancies that are uncovered between the actual and expected results of a test execution.

First, the problems or required enhancements must be properly documented and reported to the appropriate system test or user test coordinator. The problem is evaluated and prioritized with a severity code. For instance, if a problem detected by the users (the program does not meet the original user requirements) does not halt the testing process (a "cosmetic" problem on a screen), its severity code could be 1. The user simply logs the problem in a central file, notifies the user coordinator, and continues testing the system. However, if the problem is an important one and consequently has to be resolved prior to resuming testing, then its severity code could be 5. Depending on the nature of the problems, the severity code could range on a scale between 1 and 5. In this way, the testing process is not arbitrarily halted when minor problems that do not affect the operability of the system are detected by the users.

8.5 REGRESSION TESTING

Every maintenance programmer knows by experience that a change to a specific function of a system might inadvertently cause an error somewhere else in the same system. Regression testing is the process of retesting some or all of the functions of an application system to verify that they still work properly once changes have been made to the system.

Typically, a regression test environment is composed of the following items:

- A list of all the test samples currently stored in the regression libraries, along with the expected test results
- Identification for each test sample of the system components it exercises
- A description of the instructions required to use them
- A brief description of the testing objectives of each test sample

Ideally, regression testing libraries should be created during the development process at the time the programs are initially verified with specific test cases. Some representative subsets of the test scripts are then gradually saved in a regression testing library as the testing cycle progresses. Such a library can then be utilized not only during the development cycle (system integration and user acceptance testing, e.g.), but it can also be reused during the maintenance cycle.

The regression testing process can be cumbersome and time consuming when performed manually. However, it can be automated with tools that will execute the necessary test cases in a predetermined sequence. Basically, these tools save the test cases and their expected results in a centralized library. When necessary, the test cases are automatically rerun and the resulting outputs are compared with the expected results. The detected discrepancies are highlighted to the software tester.[2]

It is important to point out that regression testing must be properly managed to avoid proliferation of redundant test cases. When not properly controlled, regression test cases tend to grow very rapidly into very huge files. It then might become difficult to assess which test cases should be run because many of them might be redundant and consequently verify the same segments of code over and over. Furthermore, running all of them at once might prove to be very time consuming and can drastically increase overall test costs.[3]

To remain cost-effective, regression testing should be performed when there is a high probability that the changes made in a specific area of the system will likely affect other areas as well. Hence, it might not be appropriate always to use regression testing each time a small change is made to the system. Wherever possible, the extent of regression testing should be limited to the functions that potentially will be affected by the proposed corrections or enhancements.

In some instances, regression testing should be performed even though the changes occur outside the boundaries of the application system itself. This might be the case when a new release of the current operating system is introduced in the environment. Regression testing can also be very useful when the software system is migrated to a new hardware environment but retains the same functionality as before.

8.6 TEST CASE CATEGORIES

The testing process might be subject to several constraints: limited time and computer resources, a moderate budget, or the like. Consequently, it is very important to develop meaningful and effective test cases that remain cost-effective—that is, test cases that with a minimal amount of input data will thoroughly exercise the entire program logic and uncover as much as possible a high number of defects.

---

[2]Examples of tools supporting the automated regression testing concept are Traps by Travtech and Autotest by Sterling Software.

[3]Some tools can assist the software testers in trying to reduce the number of necessary test cases to a strict minimum. For example, Transfixxer is a tool developed by Marble Software that can be used to decrease the number of test cases required to verify a software system. While running the various test cases, the tool analyzes the code segments that are executed in the program and identifies the test cases that end up being redundant. These can then be deleted without affecting the quality of the regression testing process.

This section lists some of the different types of tests that can be executed to verify the correctness or incorrectness of the software system, along with a brief description of their intended purpose.

1. *Statement coverage test.* To verify that each procedural statement in a program has been exercised at least one time. Automated tools can be used to report several coverage conditions such as the extent to which every procedural statement in a program has been exercised.

2. *Branch coverage test.* To verify that each branching condition of a decision statement has been exercised at least once (e.g., an "if" statement in Cobol).

3. *Loop coverage tests.* To verify the conditions used to initiate and terminate a loop in a program (e.g., a "perform-until" statement in Cobol).

4. *Value sampling tests.* To verify the input conditions of a program by providing test data samples that fall within the range of acceptable values that would be expected in a normal situation. This type of test is used when it is not practical to cover all possible situations because of the overwhelming number of possibilities. These tests are ordinarily utilized to verify that the program can handle normal data.

5. *Boundary value coverage tests.* To verify the input/output conditions of a program by using test cases composed of minimum, maximum, and out-of-boundary values. For instance, if a table has ten entries, the test cases should be prepared with the following values: entries 0, 1, 10, and 12. These tests also apply to output data. For example, assume that an output report displays a percentage value with two digits plus two decimals (25.55%). What would happen if a test was set up to generate a 100% condition?

6. *Program interface tests.* To verify the module-to-module and function-to-function internal interfaces contained in a program. Are the data and control parameters passed properly between the modules of the programs?

7. *File-handling tests.* To verify normal and abnormal file-handling conditions. For instance, an empty file or a file that contains only one record can be expressly created to verify if the program can handle these conditions.

8. *Error message tests.* To exercise the known error conditions that must be handled by the program. The accuracy and completeness of the error messages can also be verified while the program is tested to determine if it can handle invalid transactions.

9. *Error-prone tests.* To test the program using invalid or error-prone test data. For instance, if an input field on a screen must be numeric, what would happen if spaces are entered by mistake?

10. *Volume tests.* To verify that the system cannot handle the volume of data that was specified originally in the user requirements. Volume testing can easily become complex and expensive to execute when large files are involved. Common sense must prevail in such situations.

11. *Performance tests.* To verify that the system does not operate according to the stated response time, throughput rates, and batch job turnaround/execution time requirements. Performance testing can be favorably conducted for those frequently used online transactions that are considered critical to the proper functioning of the system.

12. *Stress tests.* To verify that the system cannot handle unexpected situations. These tests are normally applied to online or real-time systems, where unusually large volumes of data can suddenly cause these systems to crash in catastrophe (the online system abruptly goes down). Stress testing must be used in a discretionary manner because it might be difficult to construct the test scenarios that satisfy all the conditions necessary to cause the system to crash. If the system is properly designed, it should come down in a controlled manner, even in a stressful situation.

13. *Backup, recovery, reorganization and restart tests.* To verify that the application restart, backup, reorganization and recovery procedures will fail when the system abends due to a hardware or software failure.

14. *Usability tests.* To verify that the human-machine interfaces of the system are not easy to understand or use from a person's point of view. The ideal ergonomical characteristics that a system should possess might vary considerably from one user to another. Hence, it might be difficult to come up with precise testing guidelines on this subject. However, if prototyping was used earlier during the project, chances are that the users already provided some constructive feedback on this very important subject.

15. *Documentation tests.* To demonstrate that the user and system documentation material does not adequately describe the workings of the system. These tests can also cover the systems and user training packages.

16. *Security tests.* To demonstrate that the system can be infiltrated by bypassing the security measures and facilities that were designed to prevent such actions.

17. *Manual procedure tests.* To demonstrate that the manual procedures that coexist with the automated portion of the system are defective. Although subjective, these tests are designed to verify the accuracy of the manual procedures of the system, such as data entry procedures, the preparation of source documents, the use of output documents produced by the system, or the assessment of the quality of the forms used.

18. *Storage tests.* To demonstrate that the system is not fully satisfied with the stated data storage requirements. For example, the primary and secondary data storage requirements of the system are not satisfied. Ditto for the temporary work files used by the system.

19. *Compatibility tests.* To demonstrate that the hardware/software/networking configurations that will be ultimately used in the production environment are not entirely compatible when used together.

20. *System interfaces tests.* To demonstrate that the connections established between the system and other systems do not function properly. For example, the data received or sent are corrupted or simply nonexistent.

21. *Control tests.* To demonstrate that the control features embedded in the system do not function properly. For example, the audit trails are not working properly, the log records are not created, the integrity of the data is exposed to corruption, or the system is not reliable.

22. *Conversion tests.* To demonstrate that the manual and automated data conversion procedures do not work properly.

23. *Screen dialogue tests.* To demonstrate that the screen dialogues of the system do not work properly or are incomplete.

24. *Installability tests.* To demonstrate that the system cannot be installed in different geographic locations because of defects identified or created during the installation process.

25. *Functional tests.* To demonstrate that the functions of the system do not work properly as per the users' business needs.

26. *Maintainability tests.* To demonstrate that the system will be difficult to maintain or enhance once in production.

27. *Disaster recovery tests.* To demonstrate that the procedures put in place to overcome an eventual disaster recovery situation do not work.

8.7 REFERENCES

BEIZER, B. 1984. *Software System Testing and Quality Assurance.* New York: Van Nostrand Reinhold.

EVANS, M. W. 1984. *Productive Software Test Management.* New York: John Wiley.

FAGAN, M. E. 1976. "Design and Code Inspection to Reduce Errors in Program Development," *IBM Systems Journal,* 3.

IEEE, 1987. *IEEE Standard for Software Unit Testing, ANSI/IEEE Std. 1008-1987.* New York: The Institute of Electrical and Electronics Engineers, Inc.

MYERS, G. J. 1979. *The Art of Software Testing.* New York: John Wiley.

YOURDON, E. 1979. *Managing the Structured Techniques.* New York: Yourdon Press.

9

Structured Walkthrough

9.1 OVERVIEW

A structured walkthrough is a formal review of project technical deliverables. Its primary objective is to identify defects, ambiguities, weaknesses, or omissions in the product. The walkthrough process begins with a brief description of the material presented by those who created the deliverable. It is then followed by a structured review session where the deliverables are formally subjected to an in-depth examination by the participants according to a preestablished set of criteria.

Structured walkthroughs can affect the overall quality of a software system so drastically that whenever a technical deliverable is completed during the project, it should be subjected to a structured walkthrough to ensure that it conforms to the organization's software quality standards, fits the users' needs, and does indeed meet the original specifications of the system. This review process should be consistently applied to all the deliverables that are produced throughout the software engineering life cycle process. Users' needs, functional requirements, human-machine interfaces, cost-benefit analysis, prototype models, logical data models, design specifications, programs, test specifications, and users manuals are examples of the items that should be scrutinized.

This chapter describes in detail the structured walkthrough and gives some suggestions on how to successfully introduce the method in an organization.

9.2 SELECTION OF WALKTHROUGH PARTICIPANTS

The walkthrough participants should always be carefully selected to ensure a successful review session. In principle, the review process should include, but is not limited to, the following participants:

- The author of the deliverable, who briefly describes the product and answers questions from the other participants
- Coworker(s) with relevant technical expertise
- A representative of each user or system groups directly affected by the deliverable to ensure that it is complete and accurate

The number of people in the walkthrough should be the smallest possible that will still ensure an adequate representation of all users. Under some very unusual circumstances, managers can participate in a walkthrough, when their knowledge of the subject matter will directly contribute to the effectiveness of the review process. When this is the case, they should no longer act as managers but as individuals who operate at the same level as the other participants.

Some of the participants, in addition to being reviewers, might play other roles: The role of the *moderator* is to ensure that the review session is progressing as per schedule and to control the interactions among the participants. This individual should be experienced in conducting effective meetings involving several people and should have good interpersonal skills. The role of the *recorder* is to note the issues raised by the participants.

9.3 WALKTHROUGH ACTIVITIES

The success of the walkthrough is ensured by its careful preparation.

9.3.1 Before the Walkthrough

- The walkthrough participants are usually selected on a voluntary basis, and each is asked to play a specific role: moderator, recorder, or reviewer.
- The official date, time, duration, and location of the walkthrough are confirmed via the structured walkthrough notice form (see Fig. 9.1).
- The walkthrough materials should be distributed to all participants at least two working days before the review session. This is necessary to allow sufficient time for everyone to become familiar with the review material.
- The material is reviewed by all participants prior to the walkthrough. The walkthrough comment form (see Fig. 9.2) is used to note questions, errors and issues to be raised during the review session.

9.3.2 During the Walkthrough

- Before the session is started, the moderator introduces the participants to one another and indicates their assigned roles and responsibilities.

STRUCTURED WALKTHROUGH NOTICE	
Project Name: Phase:	
Scheduled by: Date:	
Expected Duration: Time:	
Location:	
Deliverables Reviewed:	
Participant Names Moderator (M); Recorder (R); Author (A); Reviewer (RE)	Department

Figure 9.1   Structured walkthrough notice form

- The author of the deliverable opens the session and briefly presents the material.
- The reviewers are invited by the moderator to comment on the material. This is done by progressively reviewing the deliverable in an orderly sequence, inviting each participant to present the issues she or he has noted on the walkthrough comment form.
- Issues are raised, discussed, clarified, and documented on the walkthrough action item list form, if appropriate (see Fig. 9.3). No attempt should be made to provide solutions at this point; rather, they will be addressed by the author of the deliverable after the review session.
- At the end of the walkthrough, all issues pending resolution are summarized and given a tentative target resolution date by the author and the other review team members.
- A group decision is finally reached:
  - The material reviewed does not require a subsequent walkthrough, although some minor revisions might be necessary.
  - The material requires substantial revisions and a follow-up walkthrough must be scheduled in the near future.

STRUCTURED WALKTHROUGH COMMENTS		
Deliverable Reviewed:		Page ___ of ___
Reviewer's Name:	Project Name:	Phase:
Page	Comments	

Figure 9.2   Structured walkthrough comment form

9.3.3 After the Walkthrough

- Following the review session, copies of the walkthrough action item list are distributed to all the walkthrough participants and the management and project documentation files.
- The author of the deliverable resolves the issues that were raised by taking the appropriate corrective measures.
- A follow-up walkthrough should be scheduled to review the revised deliverable, if deemed necessary by the walkthrough participants.

9.4 RESPONSIBILITIES

The responsibilities discussed in this section are only general guidelines. Depending on the nature of the project and upon agreement of management, they can be tailored to meet the specific requirements of any project team structure. For instance, the roles of the participants may be combined. This approach is especially recommended when only a few people participate in the walkthroughs. Indeed, in certain cases some roles might not be necessary at all.

STRUCTURED WALKTHROUGH ACTION ITEM LIST			
Project Name:	Phase:		Page __ of __
Start Time:	Stop time:		Date: $\overline{\text{YY}}$ $\overline{\text{MM}}$ $\overline{\text{DD}}$
APPRAISAL OF MATERIAL UNDER REVIEW			
☐ Material Accepted — Some Minor Revisions May Be Required		☐ Material Rejected — Schedule Another Review	
Item — #	Raised by:	Description of Item Raised	Action Item Assigned to:

Figure 9.3   Structured walkthrough action item list form

9.4.1 Author's Responsibilities

- Notify management that a walkthrough is scheduled to review a deliverable.
- In conjunction with the project leader, schedule the date, time, location, and expected duration of the walkthrough.
- Select the participants on a voluntary basis and assign specific roles and responsibilities to everyone. Sometimes the walkthrough team is assembled by the project leader or is based on a consensus reached by the entire development team.
- At least two working days before the walkthrough, provide the participants with a copy of the material to be reviewed.
- At the beginning of the walkthrough, briefly describe the deliverable.
- During the review, answer the questions asked by the participants.
- Distribute the walkthrough action item list after the review session.
- Take the necessary corrective actions to fix the problems that were detected during the review.
- Organize and schedule a follow-up walkthrough, if necessary.

9.4.2 Reviewer's Responsibilities

- Reviewers confirm their attendance. If they are not able to attend, the reviewers may suggest a replacement.
- Review the material before the walkthrough, noting any errors, ambiguities or issues that should be addressed during the session. The walkthrough comment form should be used to this effect.
- Raise and explain the issues at the meeting, in an orderly sequence, closely controlled by the moderator. Lengthy discussions about solutions should be avoided.
- Assist the moderator, if necessary, to obtain a group agreement on the issues to be recorded.

9.4.3 Moderator's Responsibilities

- Assist the author, if necessary, in selecting the review participants.
- Impartially control the walkthrough session to ensure that
  - Discussions are kept to the business subject under review.
  - Issues brought up are valid and pertinent.
  - The meeting is properly paced to ensure that all the material is reviewed according to agreed-upon time limits. If there is not enough time to review all the materials, schedule a second walkthrough.
  - Side conversations are avoided, and everyone actively participates in the review process.
  - A neutral atmosphere is maintained. The issues raised and the discussions that follow are kept at an objective level, ensuring that personalities are kept separate from problems raised during the review.
- Ensure that the participants agree on the issues to be officially recorded on the walkthrough action item list.
- Poll the group for acceptance or rejection of the deliverable:
  - The material is accepted as is. However, some minor revisions may still be required after the review process.
  - The material is not accepted. Another walkthrough must be scheduled.
- Ensure that the minutes of the walkthrough are issued within a specified time.
- Optionally participate as a reviewer if the number of attendees is small.

9.4.4 Recorder's Responsibilities
- Record all the valid issues that are brought up during the review session on the walkthrough action item list.
- Submit a legible version of the walkthrough action item list to the producer of the deliverable at the end of the review session.
- Participate as a reviewer, where applicable.

9.5 PRACTICAL GUIDELINES

The remainder of this chapter presents a few guidelines that can be useful to prevent some particular problems from occurring during a structured walkthrough.

A structured walkthrough should not be confused with the official approval of a deliverable. These are two different processes. During a walkthrough, the author of a deliverable and his or her peers review the material in an attempt to identify potential defects and assess the completeness of the product. Team participation is the keyword and the result can only be an improved product. Trying to obtain an official user sign-off for a deliverable using the structured walkthrough technique might jeopardize its primary purpose.

The introduction of the walkthrough process within an organization might take a long time, depending on the organization's size and level of receptivity. It is important to point out that the transition to using structured walkthroughs is a delicate process that demands a lot of diplomacy and carefulness because it directly involves the human factor. The best way to fail is probably to ask management to issue a new standard rule, such as: "Thou shalt have structured walkthroughs from now on, for all products coming out of our factory." A more realistic approach would be to familiarize a small group of individuals on this approach and then try it in a small pilot project. Then, based on the experience gained, customize the technique to your own organization's needs and do a constant selling job to management. Focus on the benefits of walkthroughs:

- Defects or omissions are caught earlier during the life cycle. Thus the organization saves money, as it is far easier and more economical to correct defects at that time then once the system is in production.[1]
- The communication between the various project team members and other supporting software groups is improved via the exchange of technical information that occurs during the review sessions.
- The process can be used as a learning tool for junior people who are developing their skills in such various disciplines as structured analysis, design, or programming.
- It can help new personnel to familiarize themselves quickly with the project at hand.
- The walkthrough technique allows people with practical experience and technical expertise to review the work done by others and therefore contribute positively to the project. These people can help to enhance the quality of the deliverables without being involved on a full-time basis.
- The motivation of the development team is improved.

[1]As noted in Chap. 13, on software quality, detecting and fixing defects or omissions early in the software engineering life cycle can represent savings up to 100:1 for large software projects. Structured walkthroughs are a typical example of the various appraisal cost-of-quality activities that can be performed during the construction of software systems.

- The overall quality of the technical deliverables can be drastically improved for a project.

The type of deliverable that is walked through will often determine the number and category of participants to select for the review process. For instance, a code walkthrough requires only one or two technicians with a good background in structured programming. On the other hand, the walkthrough of a conceptual data model of a large and complex system might require the participation of many people: data administrators, database administrators, system representatives, and user representatives. The participants will provide comments based on their respective area of specialization and their knowledge of the subject matter.

Some of the different groups of experts that eventually might be called on to participate to a walkthrough process of a large project include

- EDP auditors
- Quality assurance experts
- Systems operations representatives
- Security experts
- Data administration/database experts
- Maintenance representatives
- Telecommunications experts

A factor that is very critical to the success of walkthroughs is to budget sufficient time for conducting walkthroughs during the entire project. The amount of work required to prepare for the walkthrough, review the product prior to the walkthrough, conduct the formal walkthrough itself, prepare and send the minutes to all affected parties, and finally to make the necessary modifications to the product after the walkthrough should not be underestimated. To this effect, the walkthrough sessions should be embedded within the schedule right at the beginning of the project so that they are regarded by everyone as part of the normal workload activities instead of being seen as an overload commitment. Practical experience has demonstrated that as much as up to 10 to 15 percent of total staff resource time might be spent in walkthroughs.[2] Also, when this effort is being planned, the users should also be included in the process so that they can allocate sufficient time in their schedule for active participation.

Management should encourage people to participate in walkthroughs by showing a strong commitment to the process. Management should ensure that its people are adequately trained in the use of this formal review technique and progressively exposed to the process one step at a time. Doing so will ensure that

---

[2]If this sounds high to management, it can be pointed out that the investment should be viewed in light of the full software engineering life cycle, which also includes the maintenance process that will take place during the entire useful lifetime of the software system. From a cost-of-quality perspective, conducting walkthroughs should reduce the cost of non-conformance.

everyone understands the important principles behind walkthroughs (such as the concept of teamwork) and develops a positive attitude toward them. Once again, it is worth emphasizing to everyone that what is reviewed is the deliverable and not the author of the deliverable. Management should also understand that a walkthrough is not the place to evaluate its people.

A few years ago, when the author was trying to introduce walkthroughs in a large organization, one of the senior technicians pointed out that the overall process was negative because the emphasis was mostly on detecting defects. It is as important to highlight the positive points as well as the negative ones. Walkthroughs can then become very educational and constructive for all participants.

One of the major attitude problems that can surface with the walkthrough process is the fear of the authors to present their deliverables to other people, thus exposing themselves to some form of criticism. This situation can be overcome if the emphasis is put on helping people to develop higher quality deliverables with fewer defects rather than to highlight people's weaknesses. Management should instill a constructive attitude toward walkthroughs. Teamwork is everything in this context. If one deliverable fails to deliver what it is supposed to deliver, then in a way the entire development team (and its management) has failed.[3]

Once everybody understands the concept of "egoless" teamwork, the sooner a defect will be detected during the development life cycle and the lower the cost to fix it will be. Only then can the walkthrough process be more easily accepted by the software developers. Ultimately, the deliverables that are produced during the project should be perceived as public documents by everyone. If somebody has something to hide, then maybe this situation in itself might be a valid reason to conduct a walkthrough.

A good comprehension of the corporate culture within the organization should help to determine the degree of conformance and formality that should be applied when introducing the walkthrough process. A very rigid approach, as well as a very informal approach, can compromise the possibilities of success. Above all, the guidelines suggested in this chapter should not be considered as absolute standards.

Many years ago, structured walkthroughs were tentatively introduced in a firm. One project had been selected for this purpose. The team's mission was to migrate an old batch system to a more modern online environment. When the practitioners started to use the walkthrough process, they deliberately decided to exclude their supervisor from the reviews. They were claiming that in a videocourse they had taken, the "instructor" edicted a religious rule clearly stating that under *no circumstances* should a supervisor attend the reviews. Unfortunately, the only individual in the development team who at that time had some practical experience with developing online systems was the supervisor himself. Needless to say, the project turned out to be not as successful as was originally expected by the development team. Once again, good old common sense should prevail over rigid rules.

---

[3]For a detailed coverage of the numerous attitudes and psychological game plans people can play during walkthroughs, see Yourdon [1989].

To ensure the successful use of walkthroughs, the review sessions should always be conducted in a professional and productive manner. The participants should review the material in an open, relaxed, and nonthreatening atmosphere, once again keeping in mind that what is reviewed is not the author of the deliverable but the deliverable itself. Consequently, people should objectively focus their attention on detecting defects or omissions in the product rather than trying to understand how the deliverable was created with the objective of attempting to destroy someone's ego.

A quiet, remote location is desirable for a walkthrough because it should be free of external interference during its entire duration.

As a rule of thumb, structured walkthrough sessions should last between 15 minutes and 2 hours. If it lasts longer, participants might have difficulty concentrating on the deliverable and lose interest. It might also frustrate individuals who have other important activities to perform during the day. Thus, the time limit, although not a rigid rule, should be respected by all participants. Depending on the size and complexity of the deliverable under review, it might be practical to break down a large deliverable into smaller yet cohesive components and review each of them separately.

A very important success factor that should always be considered when conducting walkthroughs is the careful selection of the moderator. The individual selected for that job should be very experienced in group dynamics techniques and be gifted with good interpersonal skills. The moderator should always be someone who is well respected by her or his peers. Many attempts to introduce the walkthrough process have been doomed to failure simply because the moderator was not carefully chosen taking into consideration the demanding interpersonal skills required for that task.

The structured walkthrough process, like any other review technique, works at its best when a minimum set of system development and maintenance standards exist within the organization. Sound standards will provide guidance to the development team members when they develop or inspect their software deliverables. The more widely accepted the standards are across the MIS organization, the more easily the walkthrough process will be for a project. The use of various specialized quality checklists (see Chap. 13) should definitely enhance the ability of the reviewers to detect defects or omissions in the technical deliverables being reviewed for a large system. For example

- The users should review the external specifications of the system (e.g., human-machine interfaces) from an end-user perspective and use a human engineering checklist.
- The software people who will maintain the system once it is in production should review the detailed design and programming specifications from a system maintenance perspective and use a system maintainability and reliability checklist.

Remember, common sense should always prevail, and the team should be very careful not to let the review process degenerate into a destructive war about standards or elements of style.

The CASE technology, through software automation, gradually allows the software developers to concentrate on reviewing the quality contents of the analysis and design phase deliverables rather than spending additional time on verifying the coding deliverables. This is especially true when CASE code generators automatically produce most of the already tested code required to operate the system in production. It is then only necessary to walk through the custom code added by the programmers themselves to accommodate the most complex processing logic of the system. The same process happens for those organizations using CASE tools for the analysis and design phases of a project. The most fastidious error-checking activities can then be done automatically by the CASE tools, such as error balancing of data flow diagrams, and cross-validation among the various components of the process, data, and real-time portions of the system model. The resulting time savings can then be recuperated by the software developers to concentrate on the more important quality dimensions of the software system, such as user friendliness, reliability, and maintainability.

9.6 REFERENCES

FAGAN, M. E. 1976. "Design and Code Inspections to Reduce Errors in Program Development," *IBM Systems Journal,* 15, No. 3.

FREEMAN, D. P. and G. M. WEINBERG. 1982. *Handbook of Walkthroughs, Inspections and Technical Reviews,* Computer Systems Series. Boston: Little, Brown.

YOURDON, E. 1989. *Structured Walkthroughs,* 4th ed., Yourdon Press Computing Series. Englewood Cliffs, N.J.: Prentice Hall.

$$\boxed{\begin{array}{c} \text{——— } 10 \text{ ———} \\[2em] \textit{Prototyping} \end{array}}$$

10.1 INTRODUCTION

In the context of building a "live" model of an application system, prototyping is certainly not a new concept among software professionals. In fact, this option always presented itself as an alternative to the traditional system development approach. However, in the past, prototyping was not considered very practical, as the benefits of building a prototype were offset by the costs of doing so—not to mention the frustrations and long delays that were involved in undertaking such a tedious task with third-generation languages like Cobol and Fortran.[1]

The emergence of new software technologies centered around powerful interactive development tools has suddenly made prototyping far more attractive than ever. Today, it is not uncommon to hear systems developers use new buzzwords, one more exotic than the other: evolutionary prototyping, throwaway prototyping, incremental prototyping development, iterative prototyping development, rapid

---

[1]One possible exception to this situation is prototyping for machine or database performance. The fundamental objective of this highly technical modeling technique is to assess the likelihood of obtaining an acceptable response time from a system when complex algorithms or database design structures are used. Since the inception of computers, this particular technique has been widely used in the software industry. However, because of its technical nature, the users are usually not directly involved in such tasks.

prototyping. Encountering such a proliferation of terms, a novice would be tempted to conclude that prototyping probably means something different to everyone. In fact, these different terms are all used to describe the same underlying concept of building a working model of a system.

The various terms used are not really important, but the concept is. Moreover, several people in the field view prototyping as a panacea for all the problems incurred with the use of the traditional system development methodologies. Others contend that, without a shadow of a doubt, this approach can lead only to a major disaster. Despite these two extremes, the fact remains that prototyping is a very effective technique that can help to develop better systems. Like anything else in this world, prototyping should be considered in its proper context and managed accordingly.

This chapter addresses the following questions:

- What are the most popular prototyping techniques used on the market today?
- When should they be applied?
- Which tools are needed to make prototyping successful?
- What kind of impact might prototyping have on the system development and maintenance life cycle?
- How is prototyping integrated into the current software engineering life cycle?

10.2 REVISITING THE APPLICATION DEVELOPMENT PROCESS

If a quick survey were conducted among systems professionals to find out why so many software systems often fail to meet user requirements, chances are that the absence of a systematic development approach would be one of the major reasons given. But even those using the structured techniques are not totally assured that the system they develop will indeed meet all user needs satisfactorily. The point is not that these techniques are inefficient, far from it. However, there will always be the possibility of a communication gap between the users and the analysts. If the users poorly define their requirements, then the results invariably will translate into system specifications that are erroneous or incomplete. If, in turn, the analysts fail to understand the true needs of the users, the results will still end up being more or less the same.

Quite often, too, the users' perspective and the analysts' perspective are somehow different. Chances are that the analysts will likely concentrate most of their efforts on trying to determine what the system should look like from a conceptual point of view instead of a physical point of view, at least initially. In contrast, the users are often very practical individuals who usually base their thinking on their past working experience and the way the existing system operates today. Sometimes this situation creates a divergence in the thinking of the users and the analysts, simply because they are not talking at the same level. In the worst case, it causes significant clashes.

Another problem might arise because the users are also expected to be able to express their requirements right the first time and in a way that will lead to the translation of these requirements into a clear set of data flow and entity-relationship diagrams. Of course, this is not always the case. Even the most cooperative user may not always be entirely sure about the exact requirements needed. The static process and data models that are developed during the early stages of the development life cycle will most likely capture all the essential elements of the puzzle—there is no ifs, ands, or buts about it—but to contend that this communication vehicle is invariably accurate at a 100 percent level is indeed asking for trouble. The data flow and entity-relationship diagrams created by the analysts are generally well understood by most users, but not necessarily to the extent where all the possible nuances are fully appreciated. Omissions and ambiguities coming from both sides of the fence might still exist. At best, these oversights will turn out to be cosmetic and consequently have a minimum impact on the current system design. If it turns out that they are important, then they could definitively cause some serious problems once the system is put into production.

Let's be optimistic and assume that we are dealing with the best users and analysts in the world. Even though any communication problems are hypothetically avoided, another insidious factor can still come into play. It is the impact that the system will end up having on the users themselves and on the rest of the organization. Once the system is operational, the users, over a reasonably short period of time, will have familiarized themselves with most of the functions supported by the system. In turn, this acquaintance process will likely lead the users to modify some of the perceptions they might have about their own environment. They might even foresee new opportunities. This phenomenon, which is perfectly natural, can occasionally lead to some major revisions on the actual production system.

How does prototyping relate to the potential problems we just mentioned? In many situations, the use of a working prototype helps to elicit and clarify the users' needs. It enhances the effectiveness of the traditional structured system development life cycle, especially during the early stages of the development process. It allows the users to have a "sneak preview" of what their system will actually look like, providing them with the unique opportunity to experiment with it before too much effort is invested in building the real thing.

10.3 PROTOTYPING: A DEFINITION

"Prototyping consists in the construction, in context, of a working model of a system. This model is generally quickly developed, but can either be thrown away once the system requirements are well understood or gradually expanded to evolve eventually into a full-blown operational system." Stated simply, the prototype is nothing more than a "live" model of a system that emphasizes user interfaces. This model is built for experimentation, for gaining valuable information on the users' needs, and for obtaining a positive confirmation of the initial system requirements.

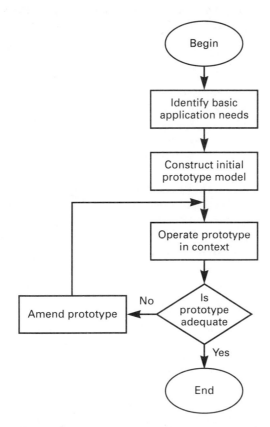

Figure 10.1 A generic view of the prototyping process. Adapted from B. H. Boar, *Application Prototyping: A Requirements Definition Strategy for the 80's* (New York: John Wiley & Sons, ©1984), p. 8.

A generic view of the prototyping process is shown in Fig. 10.1, as proposed initially by Boar [1984].

First, the prototyping cycle is triggered by the identification of user needs that require automated solutions. The prototyper, with the assistance of the users, quickly derives from these needs the preliminary system requirements that will be used to construct a mock-up of the proposed system. No attempt is made at this early stage to formalize the application requirements. Once these preparatory activities are completed, a first-cut working model of the system is developed with the objective of satisfying as much as possible the identified functional requirements. The prototype is then demonstrated and in context to the user community.[2] During the demonstration, user feedback is sought for refinements and additional requirements. Based on the input provided by the users, the prototype is quickly updated to reflect their requests. Then the prototype is run again in the context of the user environment. One more time, the users assess its functionality. The evaluation and

---

[2]In some instances, the users themselves will experiment with the prototype for a given period of time.

revision cycles are repeated as many times as necessary until the users are finally satisfied with the model.

10.4 CATEGORIES OF PROTOTYPES

Several prototyping techniques are used successfully in various manufacturing industries, such as in the automobile industry. Relevant to the data processing industry are *throwaway* and *evolutionary* prototyping.

With the first approach, the prototype is simply considered as a throwaway model. Once the prototype has been created and gone through several iterations to meet the users' requirements, the prototyping process is then terminated. At that time, the system is developed via other means and the mock-up model is kept only for reference purposes for the remainder of the project. To be more precise, all the logic and functionality embedded within the prototype model are subsequently built into a real production system using the traditional system development techniques. This approach is often referred to as throwaway prototyping because the prototype is physically discarded once the real production system is implemented.

In evolutionary prototyping, the prototype is not discarded but is retained and iteratively refined to evolve gradually into a full-blown production system.

10.4.1 Throwaway Prototyping and the System Development Life Cycle

As mentioned, throwaway prototyping may be used for the sole purpose of developing a clear and concise set of system requirements. Once this goal is achieved, the model is discarded and the system is developed in compliance with the regular phases of the traditional structured system development life cycle. With such an approach, prototyping is normally embedded into the early phases of the structured system development methodology (more specifically during the preliminary or detailed analysis phase, but even during the design phase in some instances), as shown in Fig. 10.2

There are at least three specific instances where throwaway prototyping can fit relatively well into the development cycle. During the preliminary analysis phase, several alternative solutions may be suggested to the users by the development team. Each proposed solution can be dynamically modeled as quickly as possible to verify in light of the current situation its usefulness, validity, ease-of-use and technical feasibility.

A slightly different scenario may also be proposed when, at the end of the preliminary analysis phase, a single system implementation solution was retained for further expansion during the detailed analysis phase. A prototype is built during the detailed analysis phase to validate and firm up the detailed system requirements, allowing the users to have some hands-on experience with the live model before moving on to the design phase.

In the last instance, a small prototype can be constructed during the design phase simply to model a large number of screens and show the users how they interact together. In all three cases, the prototype is carefully "cleaned up" and properly

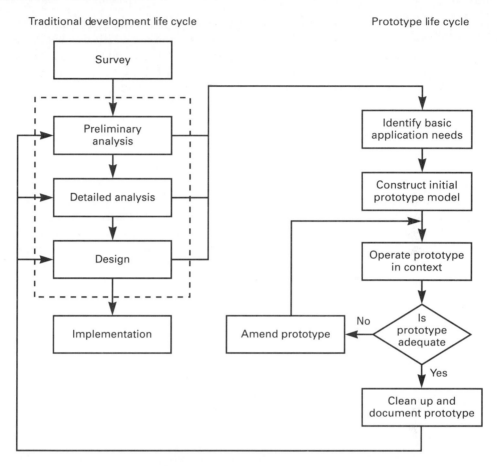

Figure 10.2   Throwaway prototyping

documented once completed. Although documentation will always remain a challenge, it should not be overdone since the prototype itself will serve as a documentation baseline.

To some extent, the throwaway prototyping technique can be classified into three major categories:

1. *Screen painting only.* This is the simplest form of the three throwaway prototyping techniques. Sample panel layouts of screens and reports are developed for information display purposes. In many instances, some basic navigation can also take place between screens.

2. *Screen painting with field editing.* In addition to painting screens and traversal through various hierarchies of online panels, this technique allows for basic editing and validation of the most important fields. Unlike the fully functional model simulation prototype, it offers only a subset of the system functions with limited options.

3. *Fully functional model simulation.* This is the most sophisticated form of the three techniques. The working model elaborated with this approach simulates in detail all the functions of the application but on a much smaller scale than the future production system. Nonetheless, it is a fully functional model, and the degree of realism achieved is very close to the real system.

10.4.2 Throwaway Prototyping: A Case Study

This section illustrates in generic terms a typical case study where a throwaway prototype can be constructed to validate user needs.

Some time ago, a small project was initiated in a company's finance group. During the preliminary analysis phase, a viable solution to solve the users' problems was identified by the MIS department. The proposed system was composed of several online and batch functions. Analysis of the users' needs had identified many inquiry and update functions for the interactive portion of the system, including a data entry facility. It was determined that a combination of detailed and summary reports was also needed on a daily, weekly, and monthly basis. In addition, the users also wanted a facility that would allow them to submit some special requests at any time during the regular working hours directly from their terminal to trigger the printing of batch reports during the night. However, they were not too sure about what exactly was needed to use this added-value facility efficiently.

After several discussions with their system representatives, the users indicated some willingness to participate in the construction of a small prototype. The objective was to clarify some of their needs and at the same time to assess one or two functional design alternatives that were offered to them. The system project manager was more than happy to build a prototype because she had already anticipated problems with some of the inquiry/update screens that, if not taken care of now, would end up with far too many fields to be truly user-friendly. Furthermore, she was fully aware that many of the relationships that existed among the various screens were indeed fairly complex. Because of this, she was convinced that the design of the human-machine dialogues required close attention.

At last, an orientation session was held with all the key user participants with the purpose of managing their expectations in terms of the objectives of the prototyping exercise. During the meeting, a flexible plan of action was finalized, outlining the major tasks to be performed during the prototyping effort, along with the identification of some tentative target dates to cover at least the major milestones.

The prototyping process was finally initiated by an experienced analyst who had spent a day or two observing the users on site to understand how they operated in their environment. Once he familiarized himself with the existing system and the major user requirements, the analyst quickly developed some programs for the data entry function as well as some basic inquiry transactions. At one point he was very tempted to optimize the programs he just wrote, but because it was more important at that time to concentrate on the functional issues rather than on the efficiency issues, he resisted the temptation.

He ran the completed model with the users, who were keen to experiment with the screens and immediately suggested some changes. During this first demonstration, the project manager noticed that no user clerks were present. This surprised her, as one of the functions prototyped during that session was the data entry facility. Knowing that many clerks in the user department would have to spend most of their time using the data entry function, she suggested to the users that another session should be scheduled with some of the clerks. She emphasized the importance of allowing the clerk representatives to evaluate the screen designs as data gathering tools. The users agreed, and they also decided to expand the audience to review another function that could potentially affect another user group.

The analyst quickly revised his prototype and ran another demo with the users. This time, he added some extra logic to link the screens together. The users were pleased with what they saw. This approach enabled them to understand better the relations that existed among the various screens, as well as the conditions that lead them to move from one screen to another. A third iteration was made. This time, additional functions were integrated into the model, including a proposed approach allowing the users to submit their requests for the production of batch reports during the night.

The prototyper had the foresight to save all the previous versions of the prototype. So when one user expressed a desire to go back to an earlier version of the model to reassess the functionality of a particularly complex screen image, it turned out to be relatively easy to retrieve it and to compare the previous version against the new one.

The system project manager knew that many users from different areas were involved in the project. Therefore, she insisted that all the revisions made to the prototype would be passed on by all the user representatives before any drastic changes were made to the prototype. Because timing is also important, she insisted that all major changes be prioritized. This proved to be very useful to help keep the reviews on schedule and concentrate on the important issues.

The prototype experiment was a success. The users were now feeling more comfortable about the proposed system. Interestingly enough, the prototyping process identified the need to add an important function that was overlooked by the users during the preliminary analysis process. The final screens and reports were finally printed and given to the users to be included in their documentation. The system prototyper also kept a copy of all the printed screen images and reports that were integrated with the existing prespecification documentation. The logic used to link the screens together was carefully documented. The fields' editing and validation requirements were also documented. The system was finally developed using the traditional system development life cycle with a third-generation language.

This case study highlights some critical factors that must be properly addressed to ensure that the prototyping project starts on the right track. Note, as in Fig. 10.2, that the decision to prototype or not should be taken only after a survey phase has been conducted. After all, prototyping should not become an excuse to discontinue or bypass a structured methodology that works. Besides, it is very unlikely that a prototype could be successfully developed at such an early stage. A clear statement of the true problems at hand, not the symptoms, must be made and the project scope must be determined along with all the user functional areas affected by the proposed system.

Before more costly activities are undertaken, the completion of a preliminary cost-benefit analysis should also help to determine if a feasible solution does indeed warrant the spending of extra time and money to solve the problem. Likewise, before building an initial version of the prototype, it is preferable to develop an adequate understanding of the current application and its environment. The construction, during the survey phase, of the system and data context diagrams will prove to be extremely useful in highlighting the major functions that should be supported by the system along with the major relationships that exist among the data entities most frequently used by the system. The prototyping technique is not too helpful to break down a large system into a cohesive set of subsystems and functions.

This hybrid process of merging the throwaway prototyping approach with a structured life cycle methodology naturally reinforces both techniques. Prototyping, with its animated definition process, helps to elicit and validate the users' requirements. The structured methodology provides the discipline necessary for the project to rigorously progress along predetermined phases to ensure proper control over the development cycle. The end result can only be a system that will enhance the human-engineered qualities of the system, such as user friendliness and ease of use while preserving the soundness of its flexible design architecture and therefore its future maintainability.

10.4.3 Evolutionary Prototyping and the System Development Life Cycle

The evolutionary prototype model basically has the same characteristics as those of the throwaway prototype. More importantly, though, it is able to evolve into a fully operational system. However, in the context of evolutionary prototyping, it is necessary to perform additional tasks to complete, optimize, and document the system. This approach is normally used when the prototype model closely matches the characteristics of the future operational system. Figure 10.3 illustrates the evolutionary prototyping cycle.

Although the figure shows three major iterations to build the prototype, not all systems will invariably require the three versions, nor will they absolutely need to start at level 1. Depending on the level of complexity of the proposed system, some steps can be favorably combined. For the same reason, more than three iterations might also be necessary in some instances. It is the responsibility of the development team to select and tailor these activities to the needs of a specific project. But it is important to limit the number of iterations and the time allowed for each specific iteration, as otherwise, enthusiastic prototypers and users can easily overprototype the system by continually adding to or modifying its functions. The benefits associated with the prototyping technique are then diminished by endless

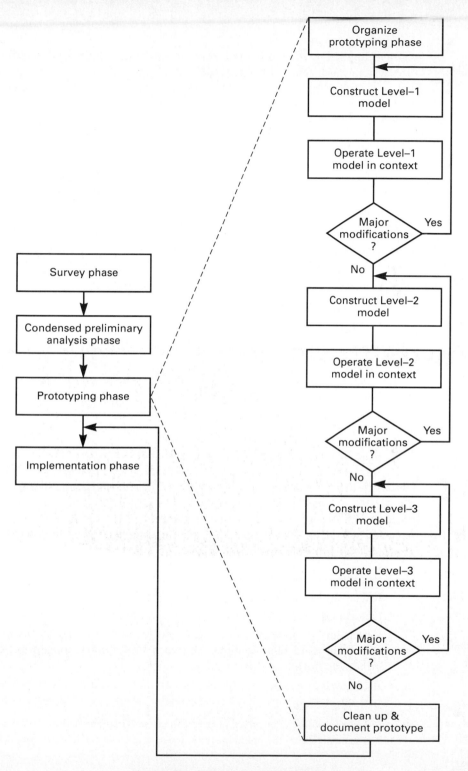

Figure 10.3 Evolutionary prototyping

changes applied to the model, not to mention the possibility of delivering an important system much later than expected.

The following paragraphs describe the development phases that constitute the evolutionary prototyping cycle, or protocycle.

Step 1: Survey phase.   During this phase, the following activities are performed (as they are for any other regular project):[3]

- Analyze the current situation.
- Define the system mission and project business objectives.
- Create a system context diagram.
- Create a data context diagram.
- Identify project risks and constraints.
- Determine the project scope.
- Identify a viable system implementation alternative.
- Develop a cost-benefit analysis case

As discussed in the case of the throwaway prototyping technique, creation of the system context and data context diagrams will greatly facilitate the identification of the major functions and data entities that are intended to be used in the proposed system. It is also important to determine the scope of the project to ensure that it does not get out of control. Once all these activities are successfully completed, a final decision is then made to use or not use evolutionary prototyping for the project.

Step 2: Preliminary analysis phase (condensed).   This phase is nothing more than a condensed version of the preliminary analysis phase.[4] Not all the activities of the preliminary analysis phase need to be performed; likewise, those that are carried out do not necessarily need the level of detail and precision that would normally be expected with a more traditional approach. The condensed preliminary analysis phase should be conducted reasonably quickly. Following is the minimum activities to be carried out:

- Become familiar with the current system.
- Revise and finalize the system functions.
- Determine the basic input/output requirements of each function.
- Revise and finalize the set of data entities that are used by the system, along with their data relationships. Derive a preliminary conceptual data model, preferably normalized if possible.
- If the system has several online functions that are highly interrelated, then a first-cut screen flow diagram should be developed. The goal is to develop a

---

[3]For more details on the survey phase technical activities and deliverables, see Chap. 2.

[4]For more details on the preliminary analysis phase technical activities and deliverables, see Chap. 3.

highly visual menu of the most important online transactions. Initially, the user should be able to access the system by making a selection from the highest-level menu and then progressively work down to the specific function to be performed.

At this early stage, the prototyper should be careful not to spend too much time trying to precisely format the general flow of control information that governs access to the screens. During the actual prototyping phase, experienced users will likely identify some specific needs to bypass directly the primary menus or invoke functions that are at a higher level than where they are currently positioned. At such times, the analyst should then consider the feasibility of combining the menu interfaces with commands that can be used to bypass the suggested menus. Figure 10.4 is an example of a simple online transaction hierarchy chart.

Step 3: Prototyping phase.   At last, the prototyping phase is reached.

Organize prototyping phase.   Before the first working model of the proposed system is built some prerequisite activities must still be performed to manage the expectations of the users. An agreement on the development strategy that will be used to develop and review the prototype versions should be negotiated with the users. One simple way to alleviate false expectations on both sides is to sign a contract agreement. The main items to cover might include the following:

1. The primary objectives of the prototyping exercise must be clearly established. These criteria will be used to assess the level of success on which the completion of the project will be based.

2. The scope of the prototype must be determined. What are the functions that will be prototyped? What are the functions that will not be prototyped? In which sequence should the functions be prototyped? An agreement on the level of detail for each successive iteration, as well as the duration of each iteration, should be identified and agreed upon with the users.

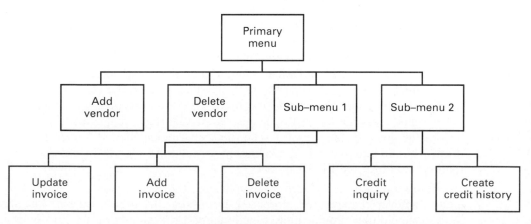

Figure 10.4   Transaction hierarchy chart

3. A strategy describing the most important activities that will be performed during the prototyping phase should be developed. The users' involvement should be explicitly covered in the plan. For that matter, the role and responsibilities of each participant should also be clearly defined. The level of commitment of each participating group is stated, as well as the number of working hours that will be allocated for the duration of the project.

4. A final schedule should be developed highlighting the project's major milestones. However, the schedule should still remain flexible even though tentative target dates are set up for each successive prototyping iteration to be conducted.

A presentation should be scheduled with the users to familiarize them with the major prototyping issues. During the presentation, it should be clearly emphasized that user participation is the most critical success factor for that type of project. Their involvement must never be underestimated. If the users do not have the time to participate, you might as well forget about the whole experiment. If you do not have time to do it right, you certainly don't have time to do it wrong. Among other things, during the project the users are expected to explain their requirements, to resolve ambiguities, to emphasize their preferences, to attend demonstrations, to learn how to operate the working model (where applicable), and to reach a consensus on suggested modifications and prioritize them. All this must be done in a relatively short time because each prototyped version must be developed and demonstrated quickly in order to keep the proper momentum.

Construct Level 1 Model.   The level 1 model constitutes the first real attempt to dynamically model the basic inputs and outputs of the system. The screen layouts that are created during this stage should be displayed with literals. This first-cut mock-up should also allow a basic navigation scheme from one screen to another. First-cut sample report layouts can also be developed that show the major headers, footers, and page and control breaks. Summary reports can also be constructed during this phase.

Operate Level 1 Model in Context.   The preliminary sample report and screen mock-ups are reviewed with the users. This is the beginning of the refinement process. Omissions must be pointed out and ambiguities addressed. All the screens associated with a particular function should preferably be demonstrated at the same time. This technique will elicit the users' feedback for all the requirements related to a particular function. During the review process, the people, particularly the prototypers, must not be on the defensive. At this stage, major modifications may become obvious. If it is the case, then the level 1 model should be sent back to the drawing board and another demonstration session scheduled. Minor changes can be incorporated into the level 2 model.

Construct Level 2 Model.   If applicable, the level 1 model is refined to include whatever changes were proposed during the first demonstration. The screen designs should now provide more functionality. Users should be able to key in data, basic editing and validation of the most important fields should take place, and data should be easily carried over from one screen to another. The human-machine dialogues, along with their human-engineered characteristics, should be evaluated with more rigor. During the process of building the level 1 prototype, most of the data needed to support the business functions became apparent. Nevertheless, it is worth mentioning that the objective at this point is not to build an extensive database structure but, rather, to ensure that all the data necessary to support the fields shown on the screens are available. Hence, the data do not necessarily need to be stored in real physical databases. They can be stored in the programs themselves or somewhere else, as long as it is possible to simulate access to the databases. With such an approach, the development team can more adequately concentrate on the crucial issues, such as the external characteristics of the system affecting the users.

Remember that the developers should primarily focus attention on the functionality of the application. For that reason, internal design issues such as performance, should be dealt with later on. Following these guidelines will allow the prototyping iterations to take place more rapidly, without having to involve too early in the process other specialists.

Operate Level 2 Model in Context.   The added functionality provided by the level 2 prototype should allow the users to operate the system almost as if it were a real-life system. Any missing item should be reported immediately, and the impact of the changes on the model should be well understood by all involved parties. The most obvious error messages should be displayed on the screens when a mistake occurs.

Construct Level 3 Model.   Functionally, this prototype version should be as close as possible to a fully operational production system. Very detailed logic requirements—complex mathematical computations, error detection and correction scenarios, data reformatting facilities, fully automatic field editing and validation algorithms, help screens—should now be integrated into the model.

Operate Level 3 Model in Context.   This is normally the last review with the users, at least for small and simple projects. This final prototype should be extensively operated and tested by the users. Requests for changes should be minor now, if the two previous iterations have been applied in a rigorous manner. The prototype can be fine-tuned but still from a functional perspective.

Clean up and Document the Prototype.   The prototyping phase is now completed. The users and the systems people have come to an agreement on the desired level of functionality provided by the prototype. It is now time to document the prototype. The information gathered at this stage will serve as the documentation basis for the next phase of the evolutionary prototyping cycle, the implementation phase. At a minimum, the documentation should cover the following elements:

- The working model of the application (i.e., the prototype itself and all the screens and reports)
- A list of the system data elements, along with their description

- A description of the logical database structure required to support database access
- A description of the procedural and field editing logic embedded in the programs

Begin the Implementation Phase.   Given that the "external" design charac-teristics of the application have been formalized, much more work is yet to be done to address the less visible "internal" design aspects of the application. The hard-ware/software/networking requirements of the application must be dealt with. Statistics must be collected on the volume of transactions to be processed per unit of time, their frequency and so forth. Performance considerations must also be ad-dressed. If the new system is to be integrated with other systems, the proper inter-faces must be put in place. Security, backup/recovery, and conversion procedures must be finalized. User documentation and production operating instructions must be developed and user training conducted. Audit and controls requirements must be implemented, if required. The final database design structure must be physically implemented, and database sizing requirements must be gathered. The programs that were developed during the prototyping phase must be properly tested, docu-mented, and cleaned up to enforce structured coding rules and guidelines for ease of maintenance. They must conform to the production environment and standard naming conventions in place. Prototyping is not a magical way to bypass all the necessary steps for successful implementation of a system into production.

10.5 CHOOSING THE PROPER PROTOTYPING CANDIDATES

By its very nature, the prototyping approach might sound appealing to the users. Unfortunately, prototyping is not suitable for all types of applications. When should prototyping be used and for which types of projects? Table 10.1 shows some of the criteria for prototyping, as well as some against it. Each particular situation should be carefully analyzed and the pros and cons properly weighed in light of these fac-tors. It is important to assess the viability of the prototyping technique and to ascer-tain if the expected benefits outweigh the potential disadvantages.

10.6 PROTOTYPING TACTICS

The evolutionary and throwaway prototyping techniques can be successfully used in several different situations. More specifically, the evolutionary prototyping tech-nique can be used to develop small online application projects that are entirely managed by the users themselves, with the assistance of fourth-generation lan-guages. In fact, microcomputer users and even mainframe users in many instances can use evolutionary prototyping as an interactive method of system development. More importantly, large systems can benefit from prototyping. A comprehensive

TABLE 10.1   POSITIVE AND NEGATIVE INDICATORS IN REGARD TO PROTOTYPING

Positive Indicators in Favor of Prototyping	*Negative Indicators against Prototyping*
Applications that are highly interactive and that require the design of a significant number of screens	Batch-oriented systems with minimum user interfaces and with complex edit/update functions
Projects where user requirements are unclear and ambiguous	Systems that are algorithmic
Systems that are predictive	Systems for which the requirements are clear and concise
Systems used for marketing demonstrations	Systems where users' active involvement over short period of time cannot be guaranteed
Batch systems aimed at the production of numerous predetermined reports	Systems that are nonpredictive
Applications where the users have never been exposed to online systems	
Data entry application	

system can be broken down into several subsystems. Each subsystem can in turn be iteratively developed with the evolutionary prototyping approach.

Even though you might not want to use the evolutionary approach as is for all your projects, other forms of prototyping can still be very useful, allowing the users to have hands-on experience on selective portions of the system. Some companies even use prototyping as a means of selecting application packages. They quickly build a working model of a system and validate the users' requirements against the candidate packages.

In some instances, such a prototype might even demonstrate the superiority of a system to be developed in-house versus acquiring a commercial package. As discussed previously, throwaway prototyping can also be used simply to help define the functional requirements of the system. Once this is done, the system is then developed using traditional structured development techniques in conjunction with third-generation languages if the application is high volume–oriented or fourth/fifth-generation languages if the application is low volume–oriented. In some situations, portions of the system can be developed using conventional third-generation languages and others using fourth/fifth-generation languages. For instance, the core of the application is developed using Cobol and the batch reports are produced with the assistance of a report-writer facility or a fourth-generation language.

Prototyping can be used for the sole purpose of developing all the major human-machine interfaces, such as screens, report layouts, and even forms during the analysis or design phase. It allows users to experience how these interfaces will look later on. Prototyping can model a very complex function. It can be used in the maintenance world to prototype a minor enhancement requested by the users. For instance, a new online transaction can be quickly prototyped to see how well it fits with the existing system. A new set of functions can be prototyped not only to validate the users' requirements but also to find out the best way to integrate them with the existing application.

In any case, regardless of the strategy used, prototyping without the support of a well-defined development life cycle, suitable project control procedures, and a sound project plan is a risky business that can do more harm than good.

Table 10.2 shows some of the advantages and disadvantages of prototyping a system.

TABLE 10.2 PROTOTYPE ADVANTAGES AND DISADVANTAGES

Advantages	Disadvantages
Well-defined user requirements	Insistence on keeping the prototype
Improved communication	High costs of prototyping
Increased user participation	Prototyping phase running in circles
Faster development	Poor system maintainability

10.7 PROTOTYPING TECHNOLOGY

Third-generation technologies (e.g., Cobol and Fortran used for batch-oriented applications) did not provide the speed or the flexibility necessary for cost-effective and rapid prototyping. During the last decade, exciting technological developments (4GL, application generators) have made application prototyping a reality. But before you decide to introduce prototyping at large within your organization, several important issues about the tools to use and their suitability to the job must be addressed.

One of these issues relates to the target environment in which prototyping will be conducted. Will the prototype be operated on a mainframe, a micro, or a combination of both? What types of models do you intend to develop: throwaway, evolutionary, or perhaps a mixture of both? Who will create the prototype? The users themselves? The systems people? Who will operate it? Answers to such questions will influence your selection criteria for the acquisition of hardware/software/networking facilities that best suits your needs.

Regardless of whether the prototype is developed using a micro or a mainframe, several software facilities are necessary to develop a prototype that is capable of evolving into a fully functional production system. The following discussion describes some of these software and hardware facilities.

10.7.1 Software Requirements

Central repository. The central repository feature should be proficient enough to be able to store all the information pertinent to the system at hand, such as the description of related fields, records, files, panels, reports, and programs. Ideally, the repository should support an integrated software architecture that allows the dynamic control of all the peripheral software facilities that are used to develop the prototype. For instance, modifications to screens and reports layouts should be automatically emulated in the repository. Various cross-reference features should also be available to the prototypers. For example, they should be able to generate various reports, such as a list of the screens, a list of the fields and where-used elements, and the like. The storage of multiple versions of the same prototype model should also be supported by the prototyping tool.

Screen painter/menu generator.   An interactive screen painter facility is mandatory to simulate such various functions as online data entry, update, and retrieval transactions. This versatile facility should be relatively easy to use and allow the rapid development of screens, reports, and even mock-ups of forms, especially if the users will be called on to construct prototypes themselves. It should provide basic interscreen flow capabilities that simulate the navigation paths between the different hierarchies of panels. Full-screen editing capabilities is a much needed feature. Simple to complex field editing options should be provided for such tasks as numeric/alphabetic checking and range value checking. Modifications to existing panels should be allowed with a minimum of effort. For systems running on a personal computer platform, the following features should also be supported: multiple windows, mouse navigation, and scroll bars.

Flexible database management system.   The database facility should be capable of modeling all the data structures and files needed to support the application. It should be flexible enough to support the modifications of the programs and files structures without having to redefine and rewrite the entire application from scratch. Network, object-oriented and relationallike databases are good candidates because they provide the flexibility necessary to construct such prototypes.

Report and form generator.   The nonprocedural report generator feature should be capable of producing easily relatively complex report layouts with multiple control page breaks and page headings. It should also be able to generate printed reports in various formats. Finally, this facility should support the design of forms.

Query language.   The query language facility should support ad hoc inquiries against the application databases. English-like syntax statements should be supported by this tool.

Graphic generator.   A versatile graphic generator capable of creating simple graphics such as pie charts, bar charts, and histograms can be very useful. Some applications often need this facility for statistical and trend analysis purposes, especially in the financial world.

Fourth-generation language or application code generator.   A nonprocedural fourth-generation language considerably facilitates the rapid development of prototypes. It reduces the coding intricacies that are often associated with third-generation languages such as Cobol and Fortran. If the language is interpretive, it will also provide some additional flexibility when modifications to the code are required. The coding statements will not need to undergo an extra compilation step before execution time because the code is dynamically interpreted as it is being executed. This becomes quite handy when the prototype is demonstrated to the users and rapid changes are necessary during the presentation.

Nonetheless, caution must be exercised with fourth-generation languages if the system being prototyped will eventually evolve into a robust production system. Interpretive languages often create a burden on computer resources. For this reason, if the system is a high-volume type of application, the prototype should become the object of volume and stress testing during the development cycle to warrant the proper handling of large volumes of data. A small system would probably not need such precautionary measures.

If the prototype is developed with an application code generator, it is likely that the users will not be able to use the generator themselves because it is generally less user-friendly than fourth-generation languages. However, it can be advantageous to use such tools where response time and large volumes of data are critical issues for the system being modeled and yet evolutionary prototyping is still used.

Security.   The vast majority of applications developed today need some basic security features. The software should be capable of supporting such features at the system level in general and at the transaction or field levels.

Testing facility.   An interactive testing facility can be of great assistance to help debug the errors that are detected in the prototyping code.

Reusability.   The prototyping tool should ideally support the reusability concept. Portions of the prototype model (screens, reports, procedural code) should be easily transferred and integrated into the models of other systems that will be prototyped later on. An index facility should be provided to search existing prototype components with a brief description of their major characteristics.

Text editing/word processing.   This facility helps the prototyper to document the working model as it is built.

In addition to the above mentioned facilities, other important characteristics should also be considered, including:

- Ability to support multiple versions of the prototype
- Performance efficiency
- Portability from micro to mainframe platforms and vice versa
- Ease of use
- Ability to interface with other tools
- Compatibility with existing hardware/software/networking environment
- Backup/recovery from failures

10.7.2 Hardware Requirements

In terms of hardware requirements, the most critical factor is undoubtedly the terminal. To operate the working model in context, the hardware equipment selected for prototyping should closely emulate the terminals that will be put into the hands of the users once the system is moved into production. Table 10.3 lists some of the characteristics that should be considered.

TABLE 10.3   TERMINAL CHARACTERISTICS

32-, 48-, or 80-line full-screen display
80-, 132-, or 160-column displays
Color/monochrome screen
High-resolution graphics
Standard/specialized keyboards
Dedicated keys supporting built-in functions (erase screen, print screen, etc.)
Programmable keys (PF keys) for frequently used functions
Support of special characters, symbols, or icons
Support of multiple languages (French, Spanish, Japanese, etc.)

10.8 INTRODUCING PROTOTYPING INTO THE ORGANIZATION

Prototyping, like any other tool or technique, is not a magical cure for systems people whose second nature is consistently to bypass all standards and derive bad system designs. After all, you would not put a racing car into the hands of a bad driver. The results could be disastrous, not only for the driver but also for the car too. If you intend to introduce prototyping in an environment that already has a history of poor development practices, chances are that prototyping will not provide much benefit, unless the real problems are properly addressed first.

   To be truly effective, the introduction of prototyping within the organization must be carefully planned. Several strategies can be used for this purpose, based on the various types of development tools at hand. Nevertheless, the same iterative development approach that is so much emphasized in prototyping can equally be used to launch this technique successfully in your shop. We have seen that the iterative process supporting the prototyping approach helps users to learn progressively and therefore experiment with the system as it is being developed. Why not apply the very same strategy to introduce the prototyping technique in your organization? For instance, the most basic form of prototyping technique (e.g., screen painting only) can be used first on a trial basis against some selective projects. Based on the experience gained, the technique can then be refined and evolve into screen painting with editing. Once again, another cycle of small experimental projects can be initiated. Over a relatively short period of time, the technique is gradually refined, formalized, and smoothly integrated into the existing life cycle methodology, covering both throwaway and evolutionary prototyping.

If a development center function is already established, then prototyping can be introduced under the aegis of this group of professionals who are dedicated to productivity and quality improvements.[5] The development center would be the perfect vehicle to coordinate and support the prototyping pilot projects and effectively integrate this technique into the existing system development life cycle. If there is no development center group, outside consultants experienced with the prototyping approach can be used.

10.9 PROTOTYPING AND JAD-LIKE TECHNIQUES

Regardless of whether throwaway or evolutionary prototyping is used, in both instances the survey phase must be conducted before the first-cut prototype is built. Even though the preliminary analysis phase is condensed when prototyping is used in its evolutionary form, this phase must still be conducted.

JAD-like techniques can prove to be very useful to speed up the preliminary analysis process while still retaining a structured, but flexible, approach.[6] Since JAD-like techniques are extremely user-oriented, they often are successfully integrated with prototyping. Both techniques are very dynamic; they also emphasize the need to bridge the communication gap among the users themselves and between the users and the systems people. They stimulate meaningful dialogues among all project participants and offer numerous opportunities for each player to collaborate as an active team member.

The JAD approach can be advantageously adapted to meet the specific needs of a prototyping project when developing a small system. Table 10.4 describes a suggested strategy based on a variation of the JAD theme. It is customized mainly for evolutionary prototyping, but it can also be advantageously used for throwaway prototyping. The process blends the prototyping technique along with the group dynamics approach associated with JAD. The success of the whole experiment is based on several factors:

- The availability of a skilled JAD leader
- A thorough preparation before the JAD session
- The careful selection of the right participants
- A strong commitment from an executive sponsor

10.10 PROTOTYPING AND DATA MODELING

More often than not, the prototyping exercise concentrates the efforts of the development team on modeling the external characteristics of the system. During the process of defining these highly visible components of the application, the basic data requirements of the system usually become evident. If the prototyping tools

[5]For more information on the development center concept, see Chap. 11.
[6]For more information on JAD-like techniques, see Appendix C.

TABLE 10.4 PROTOTYPING WITH A JAD-LIKE TECHNIQUE

1.0   General Project Orientation and Definition

1.1   Determine purpose of the project.
1.2   Determine scope, objectives, constraints, and assumptions.
1.3   Select project user participants with executive sponsor and related management.

2.0   Conduct System Requirements Workshop

2.1   Kick off session with executive sponsor.
2.2   Review project purpose, scope, objectives, constraints, and assumptions.
2.3   Identify business functions and report needs.
2.4   Identify business data entities.
2.5   Construct initial data model.
2.6   Construct initial process model.

3.0   Conduct External Design Workshop 1

3.1   Develop high-level menu of transactions and corresponding dialogues.
3.2   Prototype screens for each specific online transaction.
3.3   Prototype reports.

4.0   Conduct External Design Workshop 2

4.1   Extend prototype with full-blown functionality.
4.2   Validate and test prototype.
4.3   Optimize prototype based on functional issues.

5.0   Implement Prototype

5.1   Document prototype.
5.2   Conduct formal implementation phase.
5.3   Transfer system into production.

---

are powerful enough to simulate the user interactions with the databases, it is not necessary to design the real databases at the time the prototype is built. However, the users must be made well aware of a potential risk. There is still an important part of the system that needs to be developed and that often remains unseen by the users: the internal design of the system.

But because one of the objectives of the prototyping process is to ensure that all the data items necessary to support the system functions get captured, the intricacies of designing the internal features are delayed until the design phase. Once the prototype has finally evolved into a substantially complete system (at this stage, the data captured in the prototype may be accurate to within 70 to 80 percent of the content of the production version), the detailed process of constructing the real physical database structures is then initiated. Depending on the flexibility of the database management system used in the production environment, it is quite possible that the actual physical database structures are not capable of efficiently supporting all the database access identified during the prototyping effort. In some instances, it might be necessary to revisit the screens and report mock-ups that were developed and modify some of them accordingly. For this reason, the users should always be made aware, before prototyping starts, of the likelihood of such an event and not be surprised if actually it turns out to be the case. No matter what, the prototype project should never be rushed before issues like these are properly addressed with the users. The expectations of the users must be properly managed by the development team.

If several subject databases are already in place, then prototyping the application should only be easier and more efficient. The availability of the database structures and the appropriate application data should make the prototyping effort very effective. The prototype should be constructed faster, which in turn should lead to exercising the prototype earlier than what would normally be expected for prototyping a system from scratch. Figure 10.5 illustrates this situation. As the number of corporate subject databases increases, the number of applications that are prototyped around these integrated databases should also increase quite substantially.

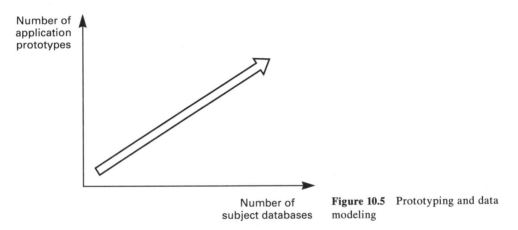

Number of application prototypes

Number of subject databases

Figure 10.5   Prototyping and data modeling

10.11 GENERAL-PURPOSE FACILITIES

Since the core of prototyping is to demonstrate and exercise the prototype with the users, adequate physical facilities should be provided for the review sessions. These facilities can range from a simple general-purpose project workroom furnished with some basic audiovisual equipment to a dedicated presentation room containing sophisticated, state-of-the-art equipment. Following is a list of facilities that could be provided for such a room:

- Terminals to exercise the prototype
- Flip charts
- Whiteboards
- Overhead projectors
- Local printers

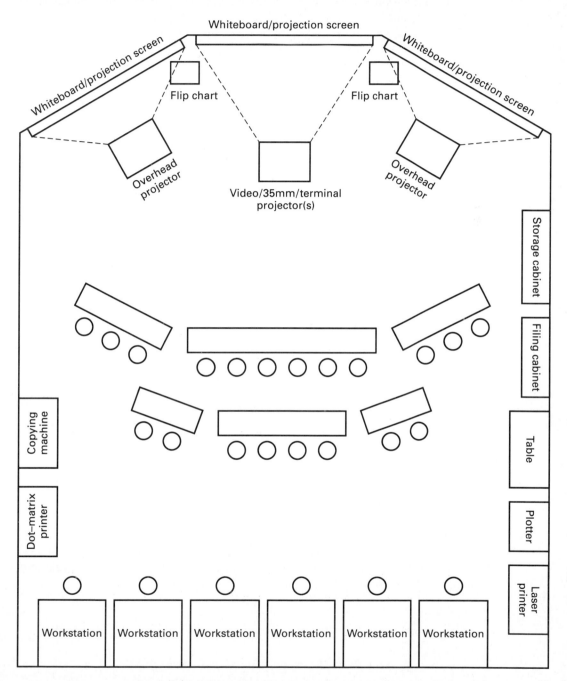

Figure 10.6 Floor plan of a multipurpose training and presentation room

- Large screen projectors that can be hooked up to a terminal for demonstration to a large audience
- Photocopier machine (nearby)

Figure 10.6 outlines the plan of a multipurpose room that could be used not only for prototyping demonstrations to the users but also for JAD-like sessions, training, and general-purpose meetings.

10.12 PROTOTYPER SKILLS

What is the profile of an ideal prototyper? Because prototyping focuses primarily on user involvement, the prototyper should undoubtedly possess very good communication skills. The individual should also be proficient in developing online systems. This is mandatory if the organization wants to improve the quality of the system's functional design. Thus, the prototyper should be familiar with the basic principles of effective but user-friendly human/machine interfaces. The prototyper should also be reasonably familiar with those logical data modeling techniques that lead to flexible and stable database designs. Obviously, he or she should be very proficient with the tools used to develop the prototypes.

The ideal prototyper is more a generalist than an expert in specialized software development fields, as long as he or she can get all the needed support from data administrators, database administrators, and so forth. The prototyping process is fast-paced and very dynamic. The system prototyper constantly deals with an environment that is uncertain but yet she or he must remain flexible and efficient. For these reasons, not all software professionals are suited to be prototypers. A critical success factor is that the professionals with the prerequisite skills obtain formal and comprehensive training on prototyping.

10.13 REFERENCES

BOAR, BERNARD H. 1984. *Application Prototyping: A Requirements Definition Strategy for the 80's.* New York: John Wiley.

CONNELL, J. L., and L. SHAFER, 1988. *Structured Rapid Prototyping,* Yourdon Press Computing Series. Englewood Cliffs, N.J.: Prentice Hall.

GANE, CHRIS. 1989. *Rapid System Development.* Englewood Cliffs, N.J.: Prentice Hall.

MARTIN, J., 1990. *Information Engineering, Book III: Design and Construction.* Englewood Cliffs, N.J.: Prentice Hall.

11

Development Center

11.1 INTRODUCTION

The development of business applications in most large enterprises traditionally has been plagued with myriad problems, such as those identified in Table 11.1. A seasoned system veteran will readily agree that the list of items in Table 11.1 is far from exhaustive. It is also very likely that most companies are, to varying degrees and at different periods of time, suffering from these problems. Moreover, on top of these so-called traditional problems inherent in the software engineering discipline, new technological breakthroughs in the industry during the last decade are seriously shaking the cage, so to speak. Table 11.2 identifies some of them.

Today, very few professionals will argue that the problems in Table 11.1 are not real issues. Even fewer will ignore the emergence of new technologies and sys-

TABLE 11.1 MIS CONCERNS

Growing application backlog of at least three years of user requests
High maintenance costs associated with old systems
Nonresponsive service to user requests
Lack of visibility of long-term strategic system plans
User dissatisfaction toward the MIS organization
Slow development of quality software systems

TABLE 11.2 TECHNOLOGICAL BREAKTHROUGHS

New Hardware/Software Technology	New Development Techniques
Electronic data interchange (EDI)	Joint requirements and design techniques
New CASE tools	Prototyping
Powerful personal computer workstations	Object-oriented analysis, design, and programming
Expert systems	Time box development techniques
Computer-aided design and computer-aided manufacturing systems (CAD/CAM)	End-user systems development
Fourth-generation languages	
Nonprocedural programming languages	
Software reengineering and reverse engineering tools	
Code generators	

tem development approaches like those in Table 11.2. One of the challenges of the decade will be to aggressively attack the old problems while at the same time smoothly harness the new technologies.

In order to meet this unique challenge, the traditional system development organization should constantly explore new ways of increasing its own productivity. It is true that improving productivity goes far beyond mere automation of the system development and maintenance process. After all, various professional tasks, such as meetings, consultations, presentations, effective communications with users, and so forth, are all areas where improvements can definitely be made without the absolute need to automate the entire process. However, the integration of new tools and techniques aiming at mechanizing the system development and maintenance factory still remains a good starting point.

Unfortunately, the rate of transfer of any new technology (read tools and techniques) within a large enterprise is often dramatically slow. According to studies done by Jones [1986], the business of transferring technology seems to be significantly slower than expected. Jones provides an example where, for a target population of approximately 1,000 professionals, the following statistics demonstrate how much time it would take to introduce that technology to the entire group:

Number of Years	Percentage of Population Reached
1	15
3	50
5	90

Reproduced by permission from Capers Jones, *Programming Productivity* (New York: McGraw-Hill, Inc., ©1986), p.227.

Jones also adds that trying to reach the entire population is almost impossible because it would have to be assumed that there would be no staff attrition during that period of time. This is very unlikely in the data processing business.

In a real-life situation, the introduction of a Cobol application generator in a medium-sized company with a target population of approximately 75 professionals took nearly three years. And even then, only 40 percent of the population had been thoroughly exposed to the tool.

Many reasons are suggested to explain why the transfer of new technology is often so agonizingly slow. The next paragraphs discuss seven such reasons.

1. Creatures of habits. Once people become accustomed to a given way of doing things, they have a natural tendency to resist new approaches unless they are pressured to do so. This is best illustrated by a simple real-life example. A few years ago a user took one year to master successfully the use of a popular database software tool operating on a personal computer. When, later on, a new software tool, far more powerful and easier to use than the previous one was proposed to him for a trial period, he replied almost horrified that it took him so long to learn the first tool that he had no intention of approaching the new software even with a ten-foot pole. In that aspect, systems people are no different than the users, and it is understandable because it is human nature to feel comfortable with things already known. However, if this behavior is not properly controlled, it can degenerate into a serious attitude problem where people stay anchored in the past and systematically refuse to grow and learn new approaches.

2. Insufficient time to learn the new techniques. There is indeed a large increase in the number of sophisticated application systems that must be developed to satisfy user needs, often with limited resources and time. This naturally creates constant pressure on systems people to deliver as many direct hours as possible to the users. The net result is less time to learn about the new tools and techniques. In some companies, it is getting so bad that the staff has no time for formal training at all.

3. Competing techniques. Many new techniques emerge one year after another. In some instances, they compete against each other. It is not uncommon to be faced with many techniques that in fact are quite similar but use slightly different terminologies. It is not much of a problem to opt for one as opposed to another. Rather, the problem arises when each has its own fan club. If not properly managed, the selection process for the acquisition of new tools and techniques can turn out to be not as straightforward as it should be, even though sound selection criteria were used in the process. Everybody gets involved; every analyst has his or her say. In some companies, it gets so bad that it looks like a zoo, with the only difference being that the zoo is run by the wild animals in the cages.

4. Not-invented-here syndrome. Some systems organizations are still in their infancy despite 20 years or more of existence. They are still haunted by the not-invented-here syndrome. Some individuals or worse, "organized" groups of individuals, have the bad habit of categorically rejecting everything new that has the misfortune of not being invented by them or their company.

5. Built-in obsolescence syndrome. Year after year, new products emerge. Each product comes up with some enhancements to provide a better way of doing things when compared to other similar products. The attitude problem surfaces when the decision to bring in a new tool is delayed until next year because something better will most likely come along. A year later, the same decision is delayed for the same reason. The same scenario happens with methods. Why bother learning structured analysis when next year something new will replace it?

6. Fear of technology. In many instances, people have been "burned" with new technology. Many candid souls bought new software tools based on bogus productivity claims. Worse, some of them were committing to foolish promises such as instantaneous productivity gains of a thousand percent or more. Needless to say, fiascos have resulted. In reaction to these unfortunate situations, skepticism has spread (rightfully, in many instances) among the ranks of the former believers. The problems arise when people become conditioned to resist anything new and start to view changes as a process that only turns the organization upside down with no real benefit. This becomes a critical issue if the people who fear the new technology or change are those who have the power to enhance the software factory process.

7. Environmental compatibility. Many of the productivity tools introduced within the system development organization work best when they are primarily used to develop brand-new systems. However, their introduction in the maintenance world takes a longer time because they might not readily be fully compatible with the existing maintenance environment.

This long introduction brings us to the main topic of this chapter: the development center. This concept has emerged as an attempt to address some of the concerns about the transfer of new technology.

11.2 THE DEVELOPMENT CENTER CONCEPT

Everybody is familiar with the old saying, "The shoemaker makes shoes for everyone except his own family, so his children go barefooted." Sadly, nothing can apply more truthfully to the traditional application development process. It is so true that several system development departments have fallen far behind many other groups within their own organization in the automation of their own internal activities. In the rush to automate the various user departments, there has been little time to apply in a consistent manner the same process within their own department.

As a result, many companies are starting to view the application development process no differently than any other standard business function. They recognize that the development process must be managed like any other business function within the company. The application development process can be normalized and automated like any other one. From there, the concept of a group of individuals assembled under the banner of the development center and made up of system development experts was developed originally by IBM. Development center people are dedicated to improving the productivity and quality of the system development and maintenance function.

Figure 11.1 shows the three major building blocks centered around the development center concept. These three key elements must be combined to create the optimal environment for the improvement of the overall application development process. The following sections discuss these three blocks in turn and describe the primary role of the development center support staff.

Dedicated hardware.   In order to improve their productivity, system development professionals must be provided with a technical environment suitable to developing software applications in the most efficient manner. In fact, providing the developers with adequate hardware equipment is an essential prerequisite for the automation of system development activities. On the other hand, it is also necessary to provide enough computer resources to enable system development staff to use the equipment put in their hands.

Two key parts that stand out from the hardware block are terminals and service levels. Studies have shown that a one-to-one developer-to-terminal ratio is the optimal way to achieve system access to the computer resources. Adequate and consistent computer service levels are also needed to improve productivity. As the job of systems professionals becomes more and more supported by interactive automated tool facilities, it becomes crucial to ensure they get a quick online response time, as well as a good, consistent batch turnaround time, when developing or enhancing software applications.

Interactive development tools.   There is a plethora of interactive software tools that can help the software professional to develop quality applications faster. Some of them specifically address project management activities, such as project estimating, monitoring, and resource control; and, some of them are geared toward providing support at the back end of the system development process, such as application code generators, design aids, interactive testing, and reengineering tools. Others cover the front-end system of the system development process, auto-

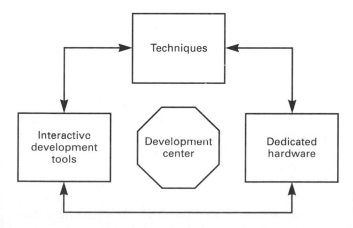

Figure 11.1 The three building blocks of the development center

mating some of the activities associated with data modeling, structured analysis and strategic planning.

The challenge consists in deciding which tools are really needed by the organization and how they can be smoothly integrated into the existing development process. This is where the development center plays an important role by establishing some consistency in the evaluation, selection, use, and support of software tools that are introduced in the development shop. Having dedicated resources to this effect, the development center concept allows a desirable shift from a standalone application-oriented approach to a more generalized process–oriented approach when the time comes to select new technologies.

Techniques.   Many development techniques have emerged during the last decade. The traditional structured methodologies covering the system development and maintenance cycle must be revisited and adapted to reflect, where applicable, these new techniques. Such methods as strategic data modeling, real-time system modeling, joint requirements planning/design, and prototyping must be considered as alternatives and/or complements to the current system development life cycle methodologies.

Once again, as the systems requested by the users become more complex and sophisticated, the developers will not be able to take the appropriate time required to evaluate these new techniques properly and even less time to integrate them successfully in their existing environment. The development center can play this important role of integrator of the new technology.

Development center support staff.   The staff is the foundation of the development center. They are a dedicated group of highly skilled professionals whose mission is to optimize the overall application development and maintenance process. They accomplish their mission by performing the following major functions:

- Identification of system development and maintenance needs
- Research and development
- Implementation of productivity tools and techniques
- Education and coaching
- Consultation and technical support
- Facilitation

They constantly search for opportunities to make improvements. In consultation with the entire development staff, they identify the real needs of the application development and maintenance groups and then either improve the existing techniques or research the market for new tools and techniques. Once the proper tools and techniques are selected, they introduce them by conducting pilot projects and by adapting them to the environment in place. They also provide training and initial support in effective use of these tools and techniques. Finally, they also monitor their use in the application field and solicit feedback from the application development and maintenance groups.

11.3 ESTABLISHING A DEVELOPMENT CENTER FUNCTION

11.3.1 Gaining Support

Before any attempts to establish the development center function, commitment from management must be gained. This is essential, and it can never be emphasized enough. Top-level management must be committed to improving the software engineering process not only in words but also by taking concrete actions. Management must provide some direction by setting up concrete objectives and be willing to provide the proper resources and environment necessary to foster productivity and quality deliverables in the software factory.

11.3.2 Development Center Charter

Careful considerations should go into creating a charter for the development center. Among other things, this strategic plan should clearly address the following topics:

- Development center mission statement
- Major objectives of the development center department
- Functions to be performed
- Services to be provided
- Identification of the clientele targeted by the development center
- Description of the proposed marketing strategy
- Proposed staffing approach
- Identification of the required hardware/software facilities
- Job descriptions for the development center staff

Other miscellaneous topics of an administrative nature (e.g., a chargeback mechanism, if any) could also be addressed in this document.

Above all, it is very important to highlight in the charter all the functions and services that will be initially provided by the development center. It might also be just as critical to identify explicitly what will not be supported. This will minimize the risk of seeing the developers misunderstand the purpose of the development center. It should not be viewed as a panacea for all the problems in the systems development and maintenance arena. People should understand that the development center cannot do everything for everyone.

11.3.3 Organizational Placement

The development center group should be established within the MIS organization as a single department but separated from the other application development groups. Ideally, the manager of the development center should report to the same level as the manager of systems development (see Fig. 11.2).

Even if initially the department is composed only of two or three people, it still would be desirable to set it up as a separate entity. Such a structure would pre-

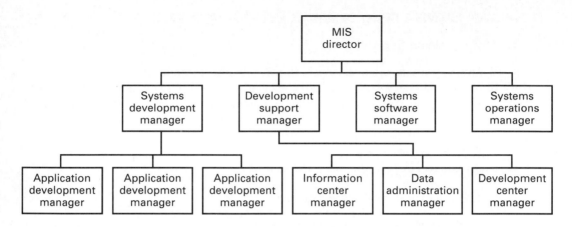

Figure 11.2 Organizational placement of the development center function

vent the development center staff from being used for the unique benefit of only one or two application groups. It should also prevent the staff from doing work outside the scope of their mission—a very tempting situation if they reported directly to the systems development manager. The development center staff should constantly concentrate on improving systems development productivity and effectiveness. This is a full-time, not a part-time, job. Allowing the development center function to be staffed with full-time personnel also projects a strong image of management commitment toward the other departments in MIS. However, a strong partnership should be established between the development center and its key customers, the various application development and maintenance groups they service. In addition, the development center staff should deal with other departments, such as systems software and systems operations, on behalf of the development groups. This structure will ease peer negotiations concerning service level agreements for the developers with other MIS groups.

11.4 STAFFING THE DEVELOPMENT CENTER

11.4.1 How Many Staff Members?

How many people should be on the development center staff? There is no single answer to this question, but ideally the start-up operations should be done with two or three people. Other people can be added as the number of products and services provided by the development center department increases. The size of the staff will depend on various factors:

- Size of the system development and maintenance organization
- Responsibilities of the development center

- Tools, techniques, and services provided
- Productivity gains generated by the development center staff itself

As a rule of thumb, a ratio of approximately 20 developers to one staff member is recommended.[1] It is clear that the cost of the development center staff must be offset by the productivity gains generated in the system development groups. The greater the productivity gains, the easier it will be to increase the development center staff.

11.4.2 What Are the Qualifications?

The skills and expertise of the development center staff will likely make or break the development center function. Selecting the right people to implement and sustain the center is certainly a critical success factor. The quality of the staff is far more important than its number.

The major functions normally performed by a typical development center are shown in Fig. 11.3. (Note that initially these functions might be combined. As the development center expands, these functions will split and new ones likely will be added.)

To fulfill these functions, the development center staff should have the following characteristics:

[1]As the development center concept matures within the organization, it might become necessary to maintain the number of personnel within that group to a workable level.

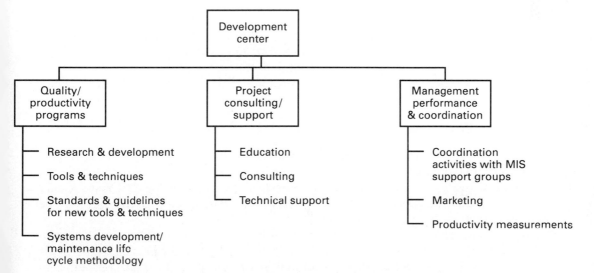

Figure 11.3   Development center functions

- Strong interpersonal skills
- Extensive experience with application development and maintenance
- Strong technical expertise
- Good oral and written communication skills
- Innovation
- Peer recognition

Additional qualities are:

- Creativity
- Patience
- Analytical mind
- Enthusiasm
- Self-starter
- Tact and diplomacy
- Hard worker
- Motivator

Note that these skills might not be found in a single individual but rather in the staff as a whole.

A good place to look for development center staff is in the systems development department itself, as the personnel required there are also experienced and highly skilled data processing professionals. The assumption is that benefits lost by not using these people in individual projects will be more than recovered by their leverage in the entire systems development organization through the development center. Because good people are always busy, it might be difficult to staff the function only with senior people selected within the shop. If this is the case, it may be advisable to consider a mix of people from within as well as from outside.

Getting good people is one thing, but motivating and retaining them is another. Therefore, career path options within and through the development center should exist.

11.4.3 What about Education?

Education is an important issue. A considerable amount of money is spent on productivity tools and techniques. Thus people should be trained to use them correctly and efficiently. There is no point in introducing new technologies if management views training costs as an additional burden. The training needs of the staff must be identified for each tool introduced.

The training can be performed either by the development center staff or professional trainers. Quality training is a serious business and demands special skills and effort in preparing adequate training materials. It is also time-consuming to train a large number of developers. Whenever feasible, it would be advisable to let experts train the developers. Keep in mind that poor quality training can hurt more than it can help.

11.5 GETTING STARTED

Once the development center has been established, one of the first tasks is to look for productivity and quality improvements projects for systems development. To get started, conduct a survey to identify the various tools and techniques that are used by systems development people, evaluate their effectiveness, and see if there is a need for improvement. After all, there might be many tools about which the developers are not even aware. Some tools might not be used properly simply because the developers do not know where to start or how to make better use of them. The survey should also cover new requirements that might have emerged over time. No matter what, the requirements for new tools and techniques must be tied to a business need. Based on the results of the study, projects can be started by seeking to optimize the methods, procedures, and tools already in place, as well as additional projects to cover any new requirements.

A portfolio of productivity and quality improvement projects can be assembled. The candidate projects should be prioritized based on the specific needs of each system organization and the expected benefits. Not surprisingly, it is likely that the developers and their managers might disagree somewhat on priorities. This is understandable because priorities can be perceived differently depending on where one sits in the hierarchical level. Perceptions tend to be slightly different. Management might be tempted by long-term projects, whereas workers might show a preference for the short-term types. For instance, management might be keen on setting up a productivity measurement program, and workers are looking at testing and debugging products. Nevertheless, once the proper course of action has been identified, pilot projects should be initiated and coordinated by the development center staff. The pilot project team members must be cooperative and willing to participate in the pilot effort.

The pilot project process should follow the following general guidelines:

- Complete a thorough evaluation of specific system needs.
- Present recommendations for enhancing existing tools/techniques or acquiring new tools or methods.
- Identify selection criteria for new tools or methods.
- Research market for candidate products.
- Choose product.
- Conduct pilot project.
- Evaluate results.

- Develop and recommend standards and guidelines.
- Prepare education, implementation, and support plan for full-scale implementation.
- Introduce product at large and conduct training.
- Provide ongoing technical support.
- Monitor use of product and seek feedback from the practitioners.

When new tools and methods are introduced within the MIS organization, it is important to pilot them not only to prove their effectiveness but also to enable the organization to identify and work out any problems encountered before the tool or method is offered at large to everybody. Standards, procedures, and user guides for new products should also be developed in advance, thus minimizing the resistance to their use by systems professionals. It also enables the development center staff to increase their practical knowledge of the tools and progressively develop their expertise.

Various strategies can be used to improve the development process. Some companies start by automating the front end of the life cycle, introducing tools for modeling the functions of a system and its data. Others take the opposite approach. They start by automating the back end of the development life cycle, introducing tools such as Cobol application generators or reengineering software facilities. Both approaches are valid because there is no specific single entry point for this type of effort. In fact, many starting points exist at all of the various stages of the system development life cycle. An organization will start at different points depending on its specific needs and the budget allocated to this effort.

The development center staff should be careful not to put all its eggs in the same basket. They should work on a mixture of long-term and short-term projects. However, if they start working only on projects that are long-term, they might have difficulty proving their value to the rest of the organization because the expected benefits will materialize only at a much later stage. In some instances, it is preferable to start small, concentrating on a few projects that offer a good return in a relatively short period of time. As the staff gains recognition, they then can concentrate on larger projects. Additional products and services should then be gradually introduced and supported by the development center.

11.6 REPERTORY OF PRODUCTIVITY PROJECTS

This section describes general projects that can be addressed by the development center. The entire system life cycle process is covered, including maintenance. For clarity, the projects have been grouped into four categories: physical environment, service level, project management, and system development and maintenance life cycle.

11.6.1 Physical Environment

The physical environment projects foster the creation of a productive work environment. They can be summarized as follows:

Terminal. This project attempts to justify the need for a one-to-one developer and terminal ratio. The justification for adding terminals must be based on the benefits associated with their use. The types of terminals required must also be identified. Many companies are now migrating to terminals with graphical capabilities. They also often opt for terminals that can display 132 characters versus 80. More and more software tools are now providing facilities to view formerly printed reports on a screen rather than on a piece of paper. Doing so allows the recipient to look at a report and from there decide to print the entire report or only specific sections. A terminal with a screen that can display 132 columns then becomes quite handy.

Office layout. This project involves determining and providing the optimal space, furniture equipment, and office arrangements suitable to foster a productive environment for the developers.

Technical library. This project involves determining the need for providing enough technical and reference manuals to systems developers and maintainers for quick reference purposes. Should a set of essential manuals such as the Cobol reference guide be distributed to each programmer? What manuals are essential? Should these technical manuals be centralized in a particular area? If so, is it easily accessible to all the software professionals?

Personal computer workstation. This project is intended to investigate the use of personal computers and local area networks as vehicles to improve the development process by offloading the mainframe environment. This would result in less variable response and turnaround time. It would also eliminate downtime. Efficient ways of transferring data back and forth from the mainframe would also be scrutinized. Mainframe-compatible software that can operate also on a PC platform would provide the developers with a well-controlled and highly responsive environment for developing applications.

11.6.2 Service Level

The development center should negotiate, on behalf of system development, the required quality of computer services that foster an optimal software development and maintenance environment. The following items may be controlled by service level agreements for both development and maintenance mainframe environments:

- Reliability of the computer resource
- Availability of the computer resource
- Accessibility to the computer resource
- Online response time for test environment
- Batch turnaround time for test environment

- Terminal ratio by developers
- Disk storage capacity for test environment
- Technical support and guidance
- Timely delivery of output listings

The following activities should be performed when negotiating acceptable service level agreements:

- Identify the quality computer services required.
- Determine the levels of computer service needed for optimum efficiency. (Keep in mind that they must be realistic.)
- Cost-justify the computer resources required to consistently produce target computer service levels.
- Establish formal service level agreements using measurable terms.
- Implement a formal mechanism to monitor, forecast, and renegotiate computer service levels.

Several types of support services other than the computer-related service levels can also be negotiated on behalf of the system developers. These include:

- Timely approval by the data administration group of the application data elements that will be loaded in the corporate data dictionary
- Timely creation of the database program specification blocks (PSB) by the database design group
- Timely approval by management of the system development phase end reports
- Timely assistance of the software group to help resolve unusual technical problems
- Extended hours of operation for the test environment

11.6.3 Project Management

Projects in this category are intended to investigate powerful interactive tools and facilities that can improve the quality of the project management process. Items of interest are

- Project planning, control, and change management tools and techniques
- Project estimating tools and techniques
- Cost-benefit analysis tools and techniques
- Productivity measurement tools and techniques
- Software configuration tools and techniques

11.6.4 System Development and Maintenance Life Cycle

Projects in this category explore alternatives to the traditional system development and maintenance life cycle methodology. Adapting the system development and maintenance life cycle to various types and sizes of projects can be investigated. New complementary methods to the existing structured techniques such as joint application requirements and design (JAR/JAD), rapid prototyping, timebox development, object-oriented analysis and design, reusable software engineering techniques, and the like should also be fully investigated. Finally, the maintenance process should be revisited to identify new opportunities for improvement.

11.7 PROMOTING THE DEVELOPMENT CENTER

The development center must maintain communication channels with different MIS groups. At least three broad channels of communications should be carefully investigated. One channel deals with the systems development community, as the development center staff needs constantly to stay in touch with their key customers. This communication process can be done through a variety of approaches, as the following discussion illustrates.

Online broadcast messages. Special bulletins can be broadcasted online via the computer network facility.

Presentations/Awareness Sessions. Formal presentations and awareness sessions can be offered to launch the development center concept and present the proposed plan of action. Later, they can be used to introduce major projects, publicize the success stories, and communicate results of the pilot projects. Other IS departments may also be invited to give presentations to the systems development organization, and the development center can coordinate these sessions.

Training Sessions. Training sessions are required to introduce the new tools and techniques in an effective manner. They can also be set up for teaching the use of existing tools and techniques that are not utilized as effectively as they should be.

Development Center Bulletins. A printed bulletin can be distributed on a regular basis to communicate information of interest (i.e., special reports, pilot projects findings) to systems development staff.

Surveys. Surveys can be used to identify the needs of systems people. They can also be used to determine employee job satisfaction. They provide a means for two-way communications since their results are invariably published.

Special Steering Committee. Productivity issues should always remain a going concern not only for the development center but also for the entire MIS organization. The practitioners must have their voice in the changes or suggestions that are being proposed to improve their productivity or the quality of their environment. Ideas should come not only from the development center but from everywhere in the MIS organization. A committee made up of system representatives should be established to provide the opportunity for participation. The mission of the committee is to air any problems or opportunity improvements that systems development may need to address in order to improve its working environment.

Product User Groups. Small user groups can be established to exchange ideas and practical experiences resulting from the use of the new tools and techniques supported by the development center.

User Guides. When new tools or techniques are introduced, customized user guides should be developed and distributed to the practitioners. These guides describe the internal standards and procedures that must be observed when using the new tools and techniques.

A second channel of communication should be maintained with various MIS support groups that operate outside the systems development organization. The development center should represent the systems development group's interests in internal service matters that affect the development and maintenance environments. Among these are negotiations of service level agreements with other MIS support groups and even the end users themselves. The third communication channel is in relation to the external world. Participation in specialized seminars is strongly desirable in order to stay abreast of the ever-evolving technology.

11.8 EVOLUTION OF THE DEVELOPMENT CENTER

Improving the productivity of an organization is a never-ending task. The development center will, over time, evolve in various directions. For the first two or three years, the department should work at consolidating its organizational structure. As mentioned, the staff can start with the evaluation, selection, and acquisition of the most appropriate hardware and software facilities that are required to support the automation of the development process.

If the staff does not increase over time and remains at a low level, it might be difficult to leverage the effort of improving the development process with the help of the development center concept. Efforts must be made to grow steadily until a reasonable number of personnel is staffing the development center. This is done by justifying the increase in staff with corresponding increases in productivity. Every year the size of the staff should be evaluated based on the productivity gains achieved so far and also as per an agreed long-range plan. Management should be made aware that large projects might take a long time and necessitate many resources. The benefits expected will not appear overnight. Yet projects of that nature will still be necessary to improve the overall software development process in the long run.

Increase in staff should be well planned and not occur all at once. It should be increased gradually with a reasonable number of people. After all, a company would not hire an outside consultant if there were no project to work on. The same applies to staffing the development center. Furthermore, the nature of the projects will dictate the skills that are needed in this department.

Another important issue is the rate at which the department can afford to introduce new tools and techniques within the organization. The development center staff is working on a full-time basis to improve the development process. At the same time, the developers must work on satisfying the users' needs. They can always attend a course, but the real effort will only begin when they start using the new tools in real-life projects. For this reason, not too many sophisticated tools or techniques should be introduced at once. Chances are that the developers will not be able to assimilate them all at once because they still have to devote most of their time to developing the software systems that are needed by the users.

Compare this situation to the marketing technique used in the record industry. If a record company has two guaranteed number-one hits, it might decide not to release both albums at the same time. Rather, it introduces one album on the market, and after a calculated period of time, it releases the second one. This strategy ensures maximum profits for both records. A similar approach should apply for the sophisticated tools and techniques that are introduced in the systems development organization.

As strange as it may seem, it is easier to create a development center than to maintain it later on. However, as long as the development center delivers services of direct value to the systems development organization, there should be no problem in justifying its existence. Unfortunately, if this is not the case, then this department runs the risk of being dismantled quite rapidly. During lean times, and there will be some, management will look only at the cost of supporting the development center function against the benefits generated in return.

A final point to consider is the number of tools and techniques that can be supported by this group. As the number increases, the time required to support them will increase proportionately. However, if the development center staff continues to support forever all the tools they introduce, this will soon take all of their time. To avoid such a situation, a first line of technical support advisers should be set up eventually among the ranks of the development organization. The advisers should be selected within the ranks of those skilled developers who have successfully mastered the use of the new tools. The development center staff would then play a role of second-line support, saving them valuable time to perform other useful tasks.

11.9 REFERENCES

CHARETTE, ROBERT N. 1986. *Software Engineering Environments.* New York: McGraw-Hill.

IBM. 1982. *The Economic Value of Rapid Response Time,* GE20-0752-0 (11-82).

———. 1983. *The Development Center: Executive Overview,* GE20-0699-2.

JONES, CAPERS. 1986. *Programming Productivity.* New York: McGraw-Hill.

LAMBERT, G. N. 1984. "A Comparative Study of System Response Time on Programmer Development Productivity," *IBM Systems Journal,* 23, 1.

THADHANI, A. J. 1984. "Factors Affecting Programmer Productivity during Application Development," *IBM Systems Journal,* 23, 1.

12

CASE Technology

12.1 INTRODUCTION

Much has been written about computer-aided software engineering technology. The acronym CASE is now a widely accepted buzzword in the software industry. For years, it was known that although structured development techniques were successfully applied to the development of complex software systems, their use still remained somehow restricted because they were very labor intensive. During the last decade the advent of CASE has brought a brand-new perspective to the software engineering scene. CASE technology promises a new era in the automation of the system development and maintenance life cycle processes through savings in both time and money. Although the expected benefits have not been fully realized, the *intelligent* use of CASE tools can definitely help an organization cut down development time while still delivering quality systems.

The word "intelligent" is emphasized because when the technology is used the wrong way, the advantages of CASE are easily offset by the problems generated. Hence, before describing CASE technology itself, we must first deal with some fallacies surrounding the CASE concept.

Fallacy 1.

CASE is the long awaited panacea that will solve all the productivity and quality problems that exist in the software industry.

For obvious reasons, marketers of new software/hardware technologies are experts at introducing these new tools or techniques as *the* solution to all problems. Strangely enough, there are always people who are naive enough to believe everything that is said in clever advertising campaigns. Not so long ago, fourth-generation languages were hailed as the answer to the growing backlog of user requests for systems development. Then came prototyping, followed by the object-oriented techniques and artificial intelligence, to name only a few. If all these tools and techniques had lived up to their marketing promises, most of the people working in the data processing field today would be doing development work instead of maintenance—and obviously, this is not the case. One of the main problems stems from the fact that many people still regard CASE as a magical solution rather than just a tool. Through some painful experiences, companies have learned the hard way the difference between speed and progress. Even though CASE tools tend to automate some of the tasks aimed at strategic systems planning, structured systems development, and maintenance, they do not replace these techniques. They are just tools, no more and no less. Behind the tools are the people using them, and CASE will not suddenly change unskilled people into outstanding software developers.

Fallacy 2.

A formal system development methodology is no longer necessary with CASE technology.

On the contrary, to remain effective, CASE tools must be used more than ever in conjunction with a methodology. We have just said that CASE tools help to support the various development techniques that are integrated into a methodology. Those who acquire CASE tools with the secret hope of transforming overnight their undisciplined and unstructured environment into an organized and efficient software factory without the assistance of a methodology are going to be very disappointed. The only result will be an automated mess. Besides, years of experience in the field have taught us that we can automate effectively only those functional areas that are already procedurally well organized and standardized. In that aspect and whether we like it or not, the MIS organization is no different than the other business units it has automated over the last 30 years. If the software development environment currently operates in a chaotic modus operandi, the introduction of CASE technology will not solve the problems. For one thing, as the introduction of CASE tools increases in breadth and depth in an MIS organization, it will only intensify the need to streamline, standardize, and stabilize the underlying activities and procedures that are being automated. A successful CASE environment needs the discipline provided by a stable software engineering methodology that is actively supported by a set of sound standards and procedures.

Fallacy 3.

CASE technology aims primarily at supporting the development of new software applications.

CASE aims at automating the entire system development life cycle, starting from strategic systems planning at one end of the spectrum to maintenance at the other end. Hence, it can surely help to support existing applications. In fact, two of the most rapidly growing segments of the CASE industry deal with application reengineering and reverse engineering. With these tools, maintenance people can streamline existing applications, making them easier to maintain in the long run.

12.2 A PANOPLY OF FUNCTIONAL TOOLSETS

CASE technology addresses the automation of the complete spectrum of the software development process. The pyramid in Fig. 12.1 illustrates the high-level inter-relations that exist between MIS activities and those of the business enterprise.

Typically, the operations of the enterprise can be grouped into three general levels of activity: strategic, tactical, and operational. The strategic level, at the top

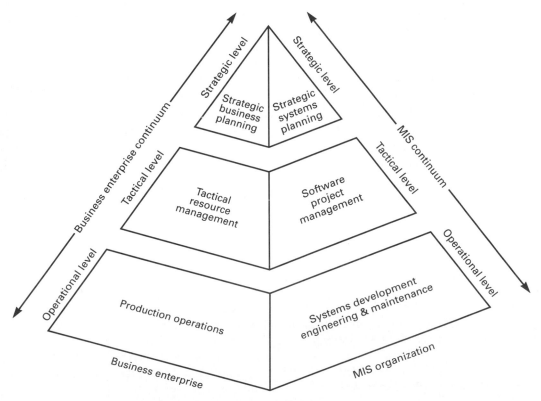

Figure 12.1   The business enterprise/MIS pyramid

of the pyramid, is where the corporate system plans are closely tied up with the plans of the business enterprise. The middle, tactical, level is primarily associated with resource management. It is here where the MIS project activities that are aimed at managing the system life cycle process are performed. Additional support functions, such as standard system administration and system quality assurance, are also accomplished at the middle level. The operational level is at the bottom. On the user side, this level represents the shop-floor level where the basic operations of the company are performed on a daily basis. On the system side, it coincides with the various software engineering stages where systems are built and maintained into the production environment.

There is a multitude of CASE toolsets on the market that seek to automate the functions performed at all three levels of the MIS organization. Some try to provide a completely integrated software engineering solution; others address a specific level of the pyramid or even a specific function inside that level. Figure 12.2 identifies the different functional toolsets that are necessary to support the automation of the software development and maintenance process in its entirety.[1]

The *strategic planning* toolset supports a strategic system plan developed in accordance with the plans of the business enterprise itself. Some of the deliverables that are most frequently developed with the assistance of this type of toolset are

- Diagrams depicting the high-level business functions and processes of the enterprise (business enterprise process model)
- High-level entity-relationship diagrams depicting the major data entities of the enterprise and their relationships (business enterprise data model)
- Organization chart diagrams depicting how the business units of the enterprise are structured
- Various association matrices used to map the high-level business functions of the enterprise against various objects such as the current user functional areas, corporate data entities, and existing systems and subject data bases
- A high-level technology architecture road map documenting the various corporate strategies that must be put in place to support the tactical deployment of new technologies such as communication networks, distributed systems, local networks of personal workstations, decentralized computers, and electronic data interchange facilities
- The critical business success factors that are required to sustain or sharpen the competitive edge currently achieved by the organization in the market place
- A narrative description of all the planning deliverables (stored in an automated central repository)

---

[1]Although this is not shown in the figure, each individual toolset should be equipped with a reusable component analyzer. This facility can be utilized by the software developers or maintainers for searching various software components of previous systems that can be reused in the development of new systems (e.g., strategic planning/analysis/design specifications or structured code).

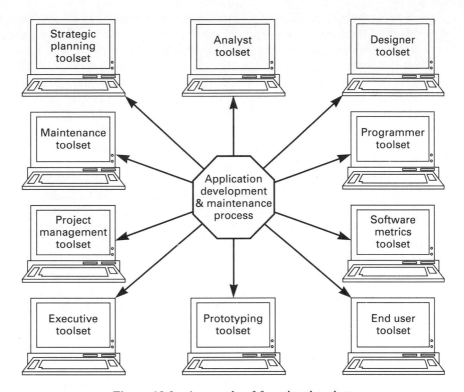

Figure 12.2   A panoply of functional toolsets

The *analyst* toolset supports the creation of graphics-oriented models to portray a proposed application system solution. In the methodology presented in this book, this stage covers the survey, preliminary analysis, and detailed analysis phases. Some of the deliverables that are generally produced with this toolset are

- Data flow diagrams (logical and physical)
- Entity-relationship diagrams
- Normalized logical data models
- Association matrices used to map the business functions with the application data entities or normalized records
- Various diagrams used to describe the detailed logic embedded in the primitive data flow processes such as decision trees, decision tables, structured English specifications, and action diagrams
- Screens and report layouts
- Diagrams showing the general control flow connecting various screens of a system
- A description of all the analysis deliverables (stored in an automated and intelligent central repository)

For real-time systems modeling, the analyst toolset also supports the creation of control flows and control processes.[2]

The *designer* toolset supports the automation of the system design process. Some of the deliverables produced with the assistance of this toolset are

- Structure charts
- Pseudo-code
- Screen and report layouts
- Program database accesses
- Database design record layouts
- System and program flowcharts
- Database schemas
- Action diagrams

For real-time systems design, the designer toolset also supports the following deliverables: state-transition diagrams, state-event matrices, and process-activation tables.

The *programmer* toolset typically supports the automation of the software programming and testing activities. Some of the deliverables that are produced with the assistance of this toolset are

- Test data generation automatically derived from the functional specifications
- Automatic code generation produced with application code generators or fourth-generation languages
- Code-tested interactively with software debugging tools
- Automatic generation of JCL

The *maintenance* toolset supports the software maintenance process. It enables the software/maintenance engineers to keep the production systems well structured, easy to maintain, efficient, and well documented. Some of the automated tools included in this important toolset are

- Source and object code version controllers
- Production JCL analyzer
- Program performance analyzer/optimizer
- Code restructuring facilities
- Reverse engineering facilities
- System documentation maintenance
- Data manipulator facilities to create test data, extract selected data from production files downloaded to test files, archive test data, and the like

[2]Two of the most widely used techniques for real-time systems development are based on the Ward/Mellor or Hartley/Pirbhai method. For more information on these two methods, refer to the bibliographies at the end of Chaps. 2 and 3.

- General-purpose data comparison facility to compare various files and identify discrepancies
- Program complexity analyzer and program understanding tools
- Regression testing facilities
- Change impact analyzer

The *project* management toolset assists project leaders to plan, monitor, control, and manage the activities of the development team during the project. The automated facilities provided include

- Cost-benefit assessment tool
- Project estimating/staff resourcing tool
- Planning/scheduling tool with graphical capabilities to create such work plans as CPM charts, GANTT charts, and work breakdown structures
- Reporting facility to generate phase end management reports
- Project activity tracking and configuration documentation management
- Graphics generator
- Specification requirements/change management tracking facility
- Tool to manage interactively systems development and maintenance standards and procedures

The *executive* toolset is a relatively new breed of automated tools specifically designed to support the high-level activities of the corporation's executives. This workbench provides senior management with immediate access to all the information required to make strategic decisions. Some of the facilities provided include

- Automated reporting of key indicators used to monitor the actual progress made by the various units of the enterprise
- Highly visual displays of sharp graphics indicating various business trends based on historical data and new projections
- Special "zooming" features allowing the executive to quickly display detailed information from the summary levels
- What-if simulation scenarios

The *prototyping* toolset supports the generic activities associated with special facilitated application specification techniques such as prototyping and joint application planning and design (i.e., JAD-like techniques). Some of the automated facilities provided by this category of tools include

- Report, form, and screen painting editor.
- Evolutionary prototyping generator.

- Documentation tool that allows for quick recording of system requirements and specifications in various formats, such as structured English, decision tree, decision table, or action diagrams for JAD-like sessions. The product also includes various graphic toolkits for data flow diagramming and data modeling activities.

The *end-user* toolset supports the user computing environment, either on a mainframe or a micro platform. It has the following facilities:

- Fourth-generation language coupled with an easy-to-use database management system
- User-friendly query language
- Report generator tool
- Graphics generator tool

The *software metrics* toolset is used to collect and monitor the progress made by the MIS organization in terms of software systems productivity and quality improvements. It provides the following automated facilities:

- Function-point gatherer/analyzer
- Cost-of-quality tracking and reporting system
- Productivity tracking and reporting system
- Historical productivity/quality data bank

Each toolset can become the object of a specialized software engineering workstation. With such an approach, the automation of the system life cycle can be built up gradually with the acquisition of specific workstations that address an organization's most immediate needs. Subsequent CASE toolsets can then be added as the enterprise's automating needs evolve over time. The toolsets we have just scanned can either play a sonata or be fully integrated into a complete orchestra. Figure 12.3 shows the targeted platform—strategic, tactical, or operational level— at which each functional toolset operates.

If a company wants to introduce CASE technology through the front door of the development cycle, then the tools identified in the upper-level category of CASE tools should be looked at. If it is desired to improve the maintenance environment first and then introduce CASE tools through the back door, the lower-level category of CASE tools should be considered. Between these two extremes of the life cycle spectrum, the middle level is populated with an abundance of CASE tools aimed at automating the analysis, design, and programming activities of the software engineering process. Until a unique toolset provides an integrated solution that comprehensively covers the entire range of functional facilities, an organization must devise the best strategy possible to assemble an optimal set of tools that

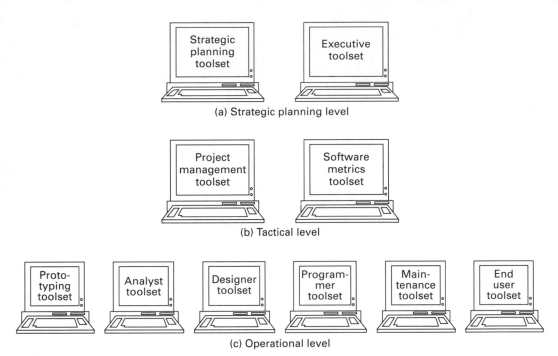

Figure 12.3   The three major toolset platform levels

work well together with a minimum of redundancy across the various layers of MIS activities.

12.3 THE INTEGRATION OF CASE TOOLS

Figure 12.4 is a holistic view of an ideal, integrated CASE architecture, covering primarily the development stages of the software life cycle. For simplicity, the maintenance cycle is not illustrated. Unlike Fig. 12.3, this diagram stresses the importance of an active, centralized dictionary-driven facility to control and integrate the peripheral CASE tools. All the information pertaining to the various deliverables that are created during the development cycle are stored in a central repository that is often called the central encyclopedia. This information is used, reused, and shared by all the peripheral tools. Another important feature is the customization module. This tool facilitates the adaptation of the CASE toolset to the development and maintenance standards already in place. The overall CASE architecture must be flexible enough to accommodate the methodology and project management standards and practices currently used by the organization instead of forcing the organization to comply to some arbitrary restrictions imposed by the product itself. Ideally, the CASE toolset should adapt to the enterprise's needs, not the reverse.

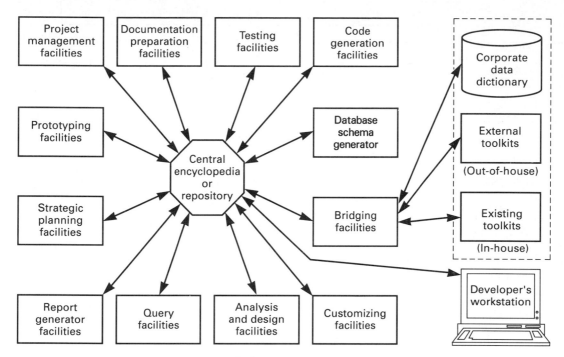

Figure 12.4   A holistic view of an integrated CASE architecture

In as much as it is very unlikely that a single CASE toolset will ever satisfy all the needs of an entire system life cycle, a module that offers various bridging facilities with the external world is desirable. Such a facility links the CASE environment with tools currently offered by various software vendors, with tools developed in-house and which work very well in your environment, and with tools that eventually will be introduced in the marketplace.

12.4 ARCHITECTURAL PERSPECTIVE

There are CASE systems that work uniquely in a microcomputer environment. There are CASE systems that operate only in a mainframe environment. And there are CASE systems that are compatible with both the micro and mainframe environments. It is quite probable that many of the largest and most complex software applications will be developed with an integrated CASE architecture that operates in a combined micro-mainframe environment. Figure 12.5 highlights some of the major components inherent in such a hybrid architecture, that successfully take advantage of the best of both worlds.

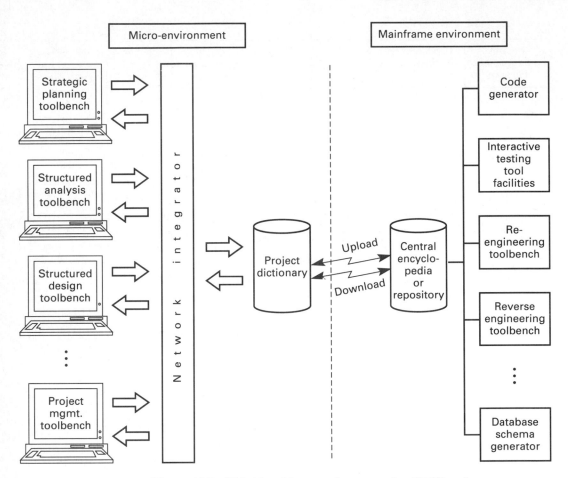

Figure 12.5   Hybrid architecture for supporting CASE tools

The PC-based workstation environment is tightly coupled with the mainframe environment. The transfer of information between these environments is rapid and fully automated. The mainframe environment offers all the power necessary to code and test very large application systems rapidly. The storage capacity offered by the mainframe environment is virtually without limits. The central encyclopedia resides in the mainframe architecture and therefore can adequately support the large and complex corporate systems of the enterprise. Several tools that reside in the mainframe environment are directly linked to the central encyclopedia. On the opposite side, the intelligent PC workstations offer user-friendly interfaces, such as pop-up windows, high-resolution color graphics, and mouse-driven facilities. Subsets of the process and data models can be shared by several software developers simultaneously. Once the work is completed at the site of a particular micro-based workstation, the updated models are uploaded to the mainframe central encyclopedia and automatically reconciled with the information residing in this repository.

12.5 INTRODUCING CASE INTO THE ORGANIZATION

There is more to CASE technology than simply installing a few automated software tool facilities. Hence, what is the best possible strategy to introduce successfully CASE technology into an organization? What critical steps should be followed to ensure a smooth implementation? Figure 12.6 presents a simple guide consisting of six important steps aimed at building a sound implementation strategy specifically tailored to your company's unique needs.

12.5.1 Make an Assessment of Your Corporate MIS Environment

Take a hard look at the existing software factory environment. The main objective is to make an honest assessment of the strong and weak points of the current software engineering standards and practices and the hardware/software/networking configuration in place. This assessment should cover both the MIS technical and management areas because improving the overall software engineering process means resolving much more than only the technological issues. It also includes addressing management, people, environment, methods, and standards issues.[3]

Listed below are some of the items that should be carefully examined:

Management

- Corporate MIS structure supporting the software engineering process:
  - Centralization versus decentralization of MIS functions
  - The interfaces among the various MIS departments
  - The roles and responsibilities of each MIS department
- Types of project management methods and practices that are currently being used in the MIS organization:
  - System quality assurance procedures
  - Change control procedures
  - Project management procedures, standards and guidelines
  - Data administration procedures
- Roles, responsibilities, and level of participation of the users in the software engineering process

[3]To conduct a very comprehensive, and in-depth audit of the current status of the software engineering process in your organization, see Pressman, [1988].

---

1. Make an assessment of your corporate MIS environment
2. Develop a meaningful set of requirements
3. Develop a transition plan tailored to the specific needs of the organization
4. Become familiar with CASE technology
5. Formulate selection criteria for the acquisition of specific CASE tools
6. Implement CASE technology

Figure 12.6   Six basic steps to implement CASE technology

- Type of training provided to the software engineering staff and level of effectiveness achieved
- Types of metrics used to measure important software productivity/quality trends
- Existence of formal service level agreements for systems development and maintenance
- Type of training provided to the users involved in system development and level of effectiveness achieved

Technical

- Existence of a comprehensive software engineering methodology, its level of penetration within the MIS organization and its effectiveness
- Types of software tools and software engineering methods currently in use in the MIS organization:
  - Their strengths and weaknesses
  - The extent and level of consistency to which they are used by the staff while planning, developing, or maintaining software systems

By the end of this assessment, you should have developed an objective, realistic picture of where the MIS organization stands in relation to software engineering.

12.5.2. Develop a Meaningful Set of Requirements

Given that the assessment study undertaken in step 1 provided some valuable insight on the status of the software engineering standards and practices, the real needs of the MIS organization should be clearly described and prioritized in detail at this point. Some of the questions that might need further investigation include

- What are the various areas in the MIS organization that present the greatest potential for productivity and quality improvements in the short- or long-term horizon?
- What are the most urgent needs that should be addressed first?

These questions can be satisfactorily answered only by each distinct organization itself, as the status of their software engineering practices is probably unique to each. For instance, if the MIS organization has already invested millions and millions of dollars in the development of Cobol programs, it might be preferable to acquire a Cobol application generator rather than a sophisticated tool that generates everything else except Cobol statements. On the other hand, if the company wants to enforce data flow diagram standards that are strictly based on the Yourdon/ DeMarco data flow diagram symbology, then there is no use in acquiring an automated analyst toolset that supports only the Gane and Sarson data flow diagram modeling conventions.

In addition, the requirements should also be evaluated in light of the hardware configuration platform that is favored by the organization. Is the organization planning to develop and maintain its software systems on a micro, mini, or mainframe development platform? On several platforms? As mentioned earlier, a stable platform of development and maintenance methods, practices and standards should be put in place before an attempt is made to automate the software development and maintenance process. This important platform is provided under the form of a standardized but yet flexible methodology.

Understanding this critical requirement will facilitate the introduction of CASE technology into your environment. After all, there is a world of difference between introducing a standalone CASE tool that automates an individual activity within a specific development phase of the software life cycle and gradually implementing a totally integrated and comprehensive CASE workbench that covers both the development and maintenance environments. The methodology should drive the requirements process for the orderly acquisition of CASE toolsets.

12.5.3. Develop a Transition Plan Tailored to the Specific Needs of the Organization

Once the true requirements have been specified, a sound plan of action should provide a detailed statement of direction describing how the organization intends to satisfy its stated needs and priorities. Instead of projecting quantum leaps that are impossible to achieve, the transition plan should reflect a realistic and feasible measure of improvement that is gradually attainable within a reasonable time frame. The scope of the transition plan might be constrained by several factors, including

- Current state of the technology used by the organization
- Budget allocated to the overall process
- Actual commitment of management
- Proposed implementation time frame

Therefore, it is important to identify, right at the beginning, all the constraints that are likely to affect the proposed plan of action.

Because the transition plan must also remain in balance with other existing MIS plans, current project development deadlines, and other commitments of this nature, a phased implementation approach should be wisely orchestrated to acquire new CASE tools/techniques. A proper equilibrium must be exercised when improving the current software engineering infrastructure while at the same time introducing new CASE tools in the MIS organization. In this way short-term solutions can be successfully applied against more long-term productivity/quality objectives. With such a strategy, progress is easier to measure. The feedback loop remains open for eventual changes in the initial transition plan based on the experience that is gradually gained by the staff through various pilot projects. Several improvements can also take place before deciding to move on to the next phase of automation. As many say, there is nothing wrong in planning big as long as you start small. Above all, the transition plan must be tailored to your own specific needs. Try to avoid all the hype associated with CASE technology.

Another crucial aspect of the migration plan to CASE is the need for stability. For most companies, the keyword should be evolution rather than revolution. Obviously, if you have the means, time, and people to do it, you might want to tackle the automation of the three MIS levels of activity (see Fig. 12.1) in a single step. However, it might be far less risky to automate one level at a time, in several consecutive stages. There are, obviously, many shades between these two scenarios. Once again, the strategy chosen must take into consideration the capacity of your organization to absorb changes and adjust accordingly to the new situation. For most organizations, it is not unreasonable to come up with a plan that encompasses a three- to five-year time horizon.

12.5.4 Become Familiar with CASE Technology

It is important to distinguish between experimental technology and proven technology. The best way to become familiar with CASE technology is to attend specialized seminars or symposiums where numerous vendors demonstrate their products. Attendance at formal courses entirely dedicated to CASE technology is definitively a viable approach. Most importantly, the selection of CASE tools should never be based solely on the claims of the vendors. However, the vendors can always be asked why they think their product is better than those offered by their competitors. Another way to measure the validity of the vendor claims is to contact the organizations that have already acquired their products and interrogate them on what is their own experience in the use of these tools.

12.5.5. Formulate Selection Criteria for the Acquisition of Specific CASE Tools

Eventually, things will boil down to the formulation of sound selection criteria for the acquisition of various CASE tools and facilities. The high-level guiding principles that should be kept in mind when selecting CASE tools include

- Acquiring CASE tools that are compatible with the existing software and hardware environment
- Acquiring CASE tools that support the software engineering methodology and standards prescribed by the organization
- Acquiring CASE tools that truly address the needs and priorities of the organization

No matter what, the choice should meet as closely as possible the organization's needs and be compatible with the mental climate and corporate culture that prevails in the MIS corporate environment.[4]

12.5.6. Implement CASE Technology

The most crucial step consists in implementing the new CASE technology. The following factors constitute the most important characteristics that will likely influence the success of this very important stage.[5]

Besides complex technical issues, the human dimension should be considered when attempting to introduce CASE tools in an organization. CASE technology will introduce new roles and responsibilities in both the MIS and user communities along with new working patterns. Handling the concerns of the staff about the major issues surrounding CASE technology should be an integral part of managing the transition process.

Formal guidelines should be developed to help people use new CASE tools in the most productive manner possible. Hence, at the end of any pilot project, each CASE tool should be customized to reflect the software development and maintenance standards and procedures in place. The preparation of a comprehensive user guide is one of the best vehicles for meeting this requirement.

Introduction of CASE technology into an organization frequently fails because of two major reasons: The staff is not properly trained on the concepts that must be well understood for the efficient use of a sound software engineering methodology. And the staff is not properly trained for using CASE tools themselves. Hence, sufficient training funds and resources should be allowed so that each individual using CASE technology can be properly trained. This assumes that adequate training time will also be made available for each employee.

The software developers' skills required to use CASE tools should not be overlooked by management. Hence, the strong and weak points of each category of people who will use CASE technology should be identified so that appropriate and sound education plans can be recommended in advance.

As noted, several categories of people in the MIS organization will be affected by the implementation of CASE technology. To ease its acceptance among the ranks of the MIS management team, as well as among the developers themselves, "marketing" presentations should be offered to explain the major concepts and issues surrounding CASE technology. But this is not enough. The targeted end user

---

[4]To facilitate the elaboration of selection criteria, Appendix B provides a special checklist in the form of questions and answers. This information should be useful when selecting various types of CASE tools. Some of the selection criteria for application packages that are covered in Appendix A can also be used as a complementary checklist.

[5]A detailed discussion of what could be the best implementation strategy for introducing the various CASE technologies into an organization is beyond the scope of this book. For a very comprehensive coverage of this topic, see Pressman [1988].

of CASE technology should definitely become an integral component of the software engineering automation process. In this particular situation, it just happens that the end users are the software developers or maintainers themselves. Consequently, some representatives of the MIS user community should actively participate in CASE tools projects from the very beginning. This will ensure that the practitioner's point of view is also taken into consideration when it is time to select the appropriate CASE tools.

The best way to introduce CASE technology into the organization is to conduct selective pilot projects. The ideal vehicle to manage the overall technology transfer program is the development center (see Chap. 11). However, it might also require the active participation of other groups, such as the data/database administration and quality assurance departments. Once the initial pilot projects are successfully completed, full-scale implementation plans should be finalized and carefully executed to incrementally deploy CASE technology throughout the entire MIS organization.

If CASE tools are not introduced by the development center, then the creation of a coordinator function becomes necessary to control and manage the implementation of such tools: the CASE tool administrator. Some of the responsibilities of this person might include

- Tailoring CASE tool(s) to meet the specific needs of the organization
- Setting proper standards and procedures for using CASE tools and maintain and evolve them over time
- Implementing new releases
- Providing consulting services

The administrator could also be the one to whom personnel can turn when they have questions or suggestions to improve CASE tools. If the person performing this function also has other duties, chances are that the introduction of CASE tools will turn out to be a fiasco. The CASE administrator function is a full-time job. The transition to CASE tool technology can be a tricky business. If the organization does not have any past experience with these types of tools or with a given software engineering methodology, it might become imperative to seek the services of a consulting group of CASE experts who can provide all the consulting, training, and coaching required during the pilot projects.

The acquisition of CASE tools can be fairly expensive. Hence, it might be necessary to justify their purchase by figuring out the expected payback. The organization should expect direct and indirect costs. Direct costs might include

- CASE product acquisition (hardware, software, and networking facilities)
- Consulting fees if external consultants are used to introduce CASE into the organization
- Training the staff on using CASE tools

- Training the staff on using the software engineering methodology
- Customization of CASE tools to meet the standards and procedures in place
- Ongoing costs for acquiring and installing new releases of software

Indirect costs might include

- Training costs for staff to learn the use of CASE tools on their own, after formal training sessions
- The time it takes for the MIS organization to adjust to the new technology, from a cultural viewpoint

The productivity gains expected from using CASE technology should warrant the cost acquisition investments. However, the payback might not necessarily happen overnight. In some instances, the CASE start-up costs might not level off for the first two to three years. This point can be best explained by the fact that initially productivity might not increase until the learning curves and cultural transition elements implied in automating the software engineering process get resolved. However, soft savings can happen immediately when improved quality deliverables are produced with CASE tools. Later, during the maintenance phase, these soft savings will translate into concrete savings. The software systems will be cheaper to maintain because they are better constructed.

12.6 REFERENCES

IBM, 1989. *Systems Application Architecture: AD/Cycle Concepts.* San Jose, Ca.: IBM, GC26-4531-0.

McClure, C. 1989. *CASE Is Software Automation.* Englewood Cliffs, N.J.: Prentice Hall.

Merlyn, V., and G. Boone, 1989. "CASE Tools: Sorting Out the Tangle of Tool Types," *Computer World,* March 27.

Pressman, R. 1988. *Making Software Engineering Happen: A Guide for Instituting the Technology.* Englewood Cliffs, N.J.: Prentice Hall.

13

Software Quality

13.1 WHAT IS SOFTWARE QUALITY?

The word *quality* very often signifies different things to different people in the context of a software system. For instance, how would someone determine if a software system is indeed a high-quality product? How would someone measure software quality? By generic terms, such as poor, acceptable, good, or perfect? Without a doubt, a better definition of software quality would be appropriate. If software quality is defined as conformance to requirements, some progress would have been made, as we should be able to determine if a software product is of high quality simply by verifying its conformance to the original system requirements.

In this chapter, however, the expression *software quality* is interpreted in a much broader context. It not only means "conformance to requirements" but is extended to embrace a much broader definition: "fitness for customer use," as suggested in a document developed by the American Society for Quality Control [1977]. One of the merits of this definition lies in the fact that quality issues are no longer arbitrarily restricted to the software product itself. Quality, then, encompasses the complete system package being created, including its supportive elements, such as system documentation, staff training, and even the postinstallation support processes—in other words, all those items that meet the expectations of our customers, whoever they are, in addition to the software product itself. Thus, quality implies pleasing the customer, not just meeting the requirements.

With this definition in mind, we talk not only about the quality of a product and its supportive elements but also about the quality of the software engineering process leading to the final product. In the software industry, the quality process encompasses all the development activities that are deemed necessary to plan and build a software system strategically, as well as all the tasks required for its maintenance.

13.2 THE MULTIPLE DIMENSIONS OF SOFTWARE QUALITY

The identification of several high-level quality factors that can be used by an organization to judge the quality of a software system was pioneered by several groups of software professionals. The study conducted by McCall and colleagues [1977] on the various dimensions of software quality identified 11 major software quality factors. A definition for each factor is provided in Table 13.1. Each of the 11 software quality factors was subsequently associated with at least two or more software quality attributes. The primary purpose of a software quality attribute was to reinforce the definition of a specific software quality factor. A total of 23 software quality attributes were identified (see Table 13.2).

Figure 13.1 illustrates how the 11 software quality factors relate to the 23 quality software attributes. Finally, Table 13.3 provides a concise definition for each of the 23 attributes.

Although other pertinent definitions of software quality have been published, such as that in Boehm et al. [1978], the terminology defined in the McCall study will be used throughout the rest of this chapter.

13.3 ESTABLISHING A FRAMEWORK FOR DEVELOPING QUALITY SOFTWARE GUIDELINES

Figure 13.2 illustrates a simple framework that can be used by software developers to define some of the nonfunctional requirements of a software system with the software quality factors and attributes that are described in Sec. 13.2. Despite the fact that the users might not explicitly request these desirable quality characteristics for their system, it is the responsibility of the developers to ensure that the system conforms to these criteria, where applicable.

Basically, the process is done by performing three steps:

Step 1.   The first step consists in selecting the software quality factors that are important for the application under development. Once this is done, the software quality factors should be ranked by order of importance, in conjunction with the users.

Step 2.   The second step is relatively simple. For each software quality factor that was retained in step 1, those software quality at-

TABLE 13.1 SOFTWARE QUALITY FACTORS AND THEIR DEFINITIONS

CORRECTNESS	Extent to which a program satisfies its specifications and fulfills the users' objectives.
RELIABILITY	Extent to which a program can be expected to perform its intended function with required precision on a consistent basis.
EFFICIENCY	The amount of computing resources and code required by a program to perform a function.
INTEGRITY	Extent to which access to software or data by unauthorized persons can be controlled.
USABILITY	Customer effort required to learn, operate, prepare input, and interpret output of a program.
MAINTAINABILITY	Effort required to locate and fix an error in an operational program.
TESTABILITY	Effort required to test a program to ensure it performs its intended function.
FLEXIBILITY	Effort required to modify an operational program.
PORTABILITY	Effort required to transfer a program from one hardware configuration and/or software system environment to another.
REUSABILITY	Extent to which a program can be used in other applications related to the packaging and scope of the functions that programs perform.
INTEROPERABILITY	Effort required to couple one system with another.

Source: McCall et al. 1977.

tributes that are pertinent to the system at hand are also carefully selected by the development team and the users.

Step 3.   In step 3, each software quality attribute is in turn used to help formulate in measurable terms software system specifications that will lead to future system testability scenarios.

TABLE 13.2 SOFTWARE QUALITY ATTRIBUTES

1. Access audit	13. Generality
2. Access control	14. Instrumentation
3. Accuracy	15. Machine independence
4. Completeness	16. Modularity
5. Communications commonality	17. Operability
6. Conciseness	18. Self-descriptiveness
7. Communications	19. Simplicity
8. Consistency	20. Software system independence
9. Data commonality	21. Storage efficiency
10. Error tolerance	22. Traceability
11. Execution efficiency	23. Training
12. Expandability	

Source: McCall et al. 1977.

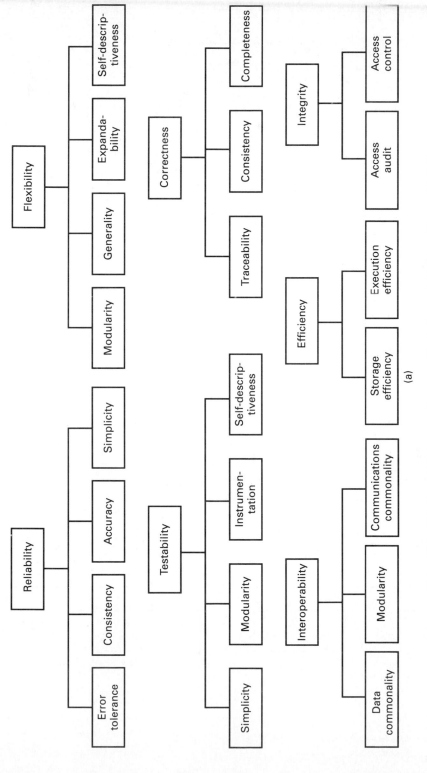

Figure 13.1 Relationship between software quality factors and attributes (*Source:* McCall et al. 1977)

(a)

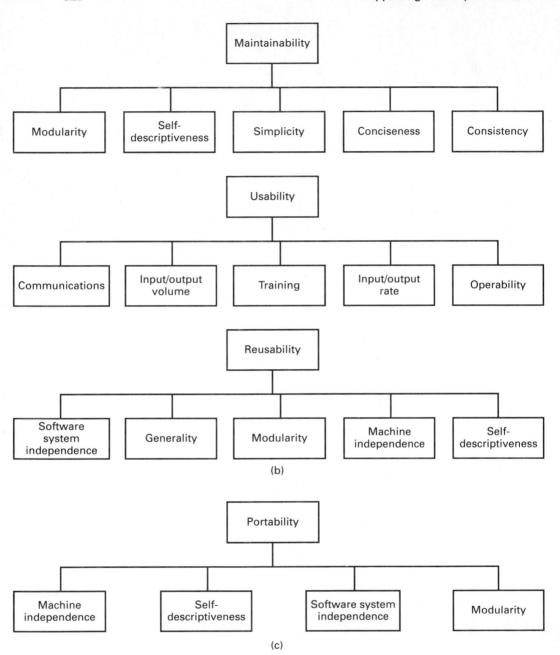

Figure 13.1 Continued

TABLE 13.3 DEFINITIONS OF SOFTWARE QUALITY ATTRIBUTES

Software Attribute	*Definition*
TRACEABILITY	Those attributes of the software that provide a link from the requirements to the implementation with respect to the specific development and operational environment.
COMPLETENESS	Those attributes of the software that provide full implementation of the functions required.
CONSISTENCY	Those attributes of the software that provide uniform design and implementation techniques and notation.
ACCURACY	Those attributes of the software that provide the required precision in calculations and outputs.
ERROR TOLERANCE	Those attributes of the software that provide continuity of operation under abnormal conditions.
SIMPLICITY	Those attributes of the software that provide implementation of functions in the most understandable manner (usually avoidance of practices that increase complexity).
MODULARITY	Those attributes of the software that provide a structure of highly independent modules.
GENERALITY	Those attributes of the software that provide breadth to the functions performed.
EXPANDABILITY	Those attributes of the software that provide for expansion of data storage requirements or computational functions.
INSTRUMENTATION	Those attributes of the software that provide for the measurement of usage or identification of errors.
SELF-DESCRIPTIVENESS	Those attributes of the software that provide explanation of the implementation of a function.
EXECUTION EFFICIENCY	Those attributes of the software that provide for minimum processing time.
STORAGE EFFICIENCY	Those attributes of the software that provide for minimum storage requirements during operation.
ACCESS CONTROL	Those attributes of the software that provide for control of the access of software and data.
ACCESS AUDIT	Those attributes of the software that provide for an audit of the access of software and data.
OPERABILITY	Those attributes of the software that determine operation and procedures concerned with the operation of the software.
TRAINING	Those attributes of the software that provide transition from current operation or initial familiarization.
COMMUNICATIVENESS	Those attributes of the software that provide useful inputs and outputs that can be assimilated.

TABLE 13.3 CONTINUED

Software Attribute	Definition
SOFTWARE SYSTEM INDEPENDENCE	Those attributes of the software that determine its dependence on the software environment (operating systems, utilities, input/output routines, etc.).
MACHINE INDEPENDENCE	Those attributes of the software that determine its dependence on the hardware system.
COMMUNICATIONS COMMONALITY	Those attributes of the software that provide the use of standard protocols and interface routines.
DATA COMMONALITY	Those attributes of the software that provide use of standard data representations.
CONCISENESS	Those attributes of the software that provide for implementation of a function with a minimum amount of code.

Source: McCall et al. 1977.

Let us assume, for example, that the software quality factor reliability is crucial for the software system at hand. Figure 13.3 shows all the software quality attributes that are normally associated with this particular factor.

Let's also assume that the software quality attribute error tolerance is particularly important for the proposed system. Hence, the software developers should not only attempt to document this software requirement with narrative statements, but they should also try to develop some meaningful quantitative measures that can apply to it. They could state, for example, that a data entry system should not produce more than one error per 2,000 transactions processed. If another software quality factor such as efficiency is also important and if the software quality attribute execution efficiency is crucial for the new application, then a statement such as "the system should be able to process 10,000 online transactions per hour, 23 hours a

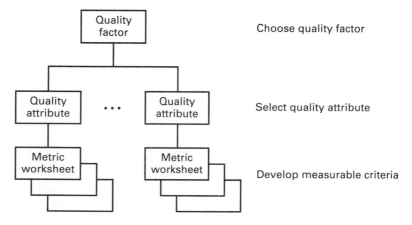

Figure 13.2 Software quality metrics

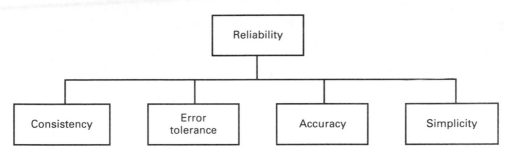

Figure 13.3   Software quality attributes associated with the reliability factor

day, with an average response time of three seconds per individual transaction" should be explicitly made. Furthermore, an additional statement should be included to the effect that the system should be able to handle input beyond the average range of transactions expected for that system, for instance, "the system should be able to process 10,000 online transactions per hour, with occasional peaks of 15,000 transactions."

Having said this, some additional observations on the software quality factors and their attributes are in order. Unmistakably, it might be impractical or even unrealistic to attempt to use all 11 software quality factors and their 23 attributes for a particular system. Consequently, the project team should concentrate effort on the few dimensions of software quality that are directly of prime importance for the system being developed. The development team should always keep in mind that it is perfectly okay for a system to score high on one software quality factor and low on another. In practice, very few systems would rank high on all 11 quality factors. Those that did would probably have some very high price tags. Besides, some existing technological restrictions may compel additional constraints that somehow might limit the ability of the developers to integrate some of the system quality dimensions into the system. Despite these potential restrictions, and depending on the context in which a specific software system is built, many of the software quality attributes can still be advantageously used to help derive measurable software quality specifications.

It is also true that each specific software system often has at least one distinctive feature that makes it different from the others. For this reason, the essential characteristics that make a system unique often dictate which software quality factors are relevant for that particular system. For example, for software systems that affect human lives, such as those using nuclear therapy to treat cancer, testability, correctness, reliability, and usability are software quality factors that are of the utmost importance. In a large banking environment, where thousands of online transactions must be processed rapidly every day, efficiency, integrity, and auditability are essential. For a system that must operate under severe atmospheric conditions, like a satellite, robustness is crucial. For a system that eventually will run on different hardware platforms, portability becomes a major criterion.

Another important point to be remembered about software quality factors is that it is possible to have conflicts between some of them. In practice, they do not always go hand-in-hand. For instance, it is usually essential that a real-time system be extremely fast and precise. Hence, one of the trade-offs to ensure precision would be to forego flexibility. A robot can perform a specific repetitive task rapidly and with precision but can be fairly limited in its ability to perform several other different tasks as well. Thus, an improvement in one particular dimension may come only at the expense of another. The reverse is also true: Some software quality factors naturally support and reinforce each other. Figure 13.4 depicts how the software quality factors interact, showing those that are mutually reinforcing and those that are not.

The software quality metrics that are developed with the practical approach described in this section should apply not only to the software system itself but also to the complete product package, including system and user documentation, training, technical support, and the like. Keeping this objective in mind, a software organization could review the list of software quality factors shown in Table 13.1 and customize or supplement the list with its own quality factors based on its unique requirements.

An example that comes to mind when thinking about the maintenance world is serviceability. Once the system has been developed, it must be maintained. The

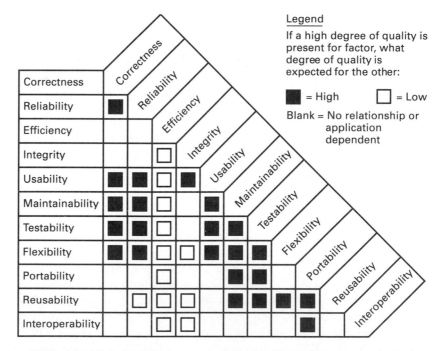

Figure 13.4 Relationships between software quality factors (*Source:* McCall et al. 1977)

users are not concerned only about the development of the system but also about the quality of the support service provided throughout the lifetime of that system. This point is important if one considers that the average life span of a large software system can easily average 5 to 15 years.

Although software quality can be enhanced during the maintenance cycle with the use of some powerful software reengineering tools, it is far more economical to engineer software quality as the system is developed. In this respect, even though we assume that quality is built into the product, the software professionals are still confronted with a formidable challenge: how to sustain software quality while evolving the system throughout its life span. Therefore, a new software quality factor such as serviceability could be introduced within the MIS organization. Several quality attributes could be associated with this quality factor such as responsiveness, timeliness, technical competence, or courtesy.

Although some of these attributes might be subject to personal interpretation, such as the level of courtesy the maintenance analyst shows toward users, others can be defined objectively and in a way that directly leads to measurability. For example, responsiveness could be defined as the mean time it takes to fix a system defect and bring the system back to its normal operational mode. Technical competence could be reflected by the capacity of the maintenance analysts to resolve system problems right the first time. Technical competence could then be evaluated based on the incidence of multiple attempts to correct a particular problem. How often do the changes done by the maintenance analysts fail to correct the system problem permanently? Does the change create other problems elsewhere? Timeliness could be defined as the level of regularity and consistency with which preventive maintenance is performed.

Software organizations differ widely in their strategy to improve the quality of their products and services. Keeping this in mind, another practical way to improve software quality and maintainability would be to provide the software professionals with a set of software quality checklists. These quality guidelines are handy for verifying the presence or absence of quality factors and attributes in the system being developed. They could also be used to define the expectations of the organization in terms of software quality, guiding the software professionals in their quest for quality and driving the entire development and maintenance process. The definitions provided in these quality checklists would emphasize not only the positive indicators that reinforce the quality attributes of a software system but the negative indicators as well. In other words, the checklists would publicly declare what the quality factors/attributes are or are not for a given organization. Better, the organization could even provide specific examples if need be. Figure 13.5 provides a very simple checklist describing the software attribute expandability in terms of concrete positive and negative quality indicators.

Creating software quality standards and guidelines for a system's entire life cycle requires an investment of time and money. Nevertheless, the return on investment might pay off with the first system developed along these quality guidelines. Even though it would only create a quality awareness among the development and

SOFTWARE ATTRIBUTE: EXPANDABILITY　　　　　　　　　　　　　　　　*NO YES*

DEFINITION:　The extent to which the software system can be adapted to:

1. Expand the existing application files/databases
2. Add new application files/databases
3. Add new functions
4. Enhance existing functions

POSITIVE CRITERIA

1. Is the system developed with structured design techniques that reinforce the concept of modularization (e.g., one entry point/one exit point per module, each module ideally supports a single function)?
2. What is the degree of cohesiveness and coupling of each module?
3. Is the system parameter-driven? Are the highly volatile fields maintained in tables that can be modified easily by the users themselves?
4. Are relational or object-oriented data structures used, where possible? Are the data structures simply designed?
5. Does the system documentation clearly identify the known system constraints and physical limitations of the current system design and how they can be altered, where feasible?
6. Are filler spaces inserted at the end of the physical data records to allow future expansion of sequential files?
7. Are error message formats and program function keys standardized across the system?
8. Are the system modules reusable?
9. Are the data structures normalized at least to the third normal form?

NEGATIVE CRITERIA

1. Are the highly volatile fields directly embedded into the application source code itself?
2. Was the system designed informally with no structured design technique and quality evaluation criteria?
3. Are the application file structures rigid? Is the use of flexible database structures nonexistent?
4. Are the system modules performing several functions not logically related to one another?
5. Was the application source code developed with complex programming constructs other than sequence, condition, and looping statements?
6. Are the various peculiarities related to the software system at hand (e.g., physical system/database limitations) not documented at all?

Figure 13.5　Software quality checklist for the attribute expandability

maintenance groups, there would still be an increased probability of improving the quality of the software systems. In this context, the peer pressure that would be exercised in such an environment is not negligible. The software developers would know what is expected of them in terms of software quality standards. In this respect, they would also keep in mind that their coworkers know too.

When an organization opts for the simple checklist approach, the acquisition of a book such as that by Weinberg and Freedman [1982], describing how to conduct effective reviews, is an excellent starting point.[1] At the end of their book, the authors provide a set of checklist items for each category of software deliverables that should be reviewed during the development of a system:

- Functional requirements
- Design
- Code
- Documentation
- Test plan
- Tool and package
- Training materials and plans
- Procedures and standards
- Operation and maintenance

The checklists could then be tailored to meet the specific needs of a particular organization, as it is preferable to build on existing and widely accepted industry quality guidelines rather than to start from scratch.

13.4 FORMAL DEFINITION OF A HIGH-QUALITY SOFTWARE SYSTEM

We have finally come to the end of our efforts to define the intrinsic characteristics of a high-quality software system. Ideally, the system should

- Conform to a set of clearly stated and traceable functional requirements
- Conform to a set of measurable and traceable system quality factors and attributes that are mutually agreed upon by the user (customer) and the system developer (supplier)
- Remain cost-effective during both the development and operational stages
- Be delivered on time and within budget
- Prove to be fit for use and easily adaptable and maintainable over its useful lifetime

13.5 INTRODUCTION TO THE COST-OF-QUALITY PHILOSOPHY

In a newspaper article written by Poulain [1988], it was pointed out that approximately $15 billion is lost every year by industry at large because of nonconformance to specifications in the manufacture of products. This astronomical

---

[1]Several professional organizations offer sound software development and maintenance quality standards and guidelines. An example is the Computer Society of the Institute of Electrical and Electronics Engineers.

amount encompasses the extra costs associated with all the defaults, rejects, reworks, and delays that are incurred during the entire life cycle of a product, starting from its original conception to the after-sale support services provided by the various manufacturing organizations once the product is finally released to the consumer.

Interestingly enough, it was also mentioned that 92 percent of these losses are directly related to the organizational system. The remaining 8 percent is caused by the workers themselves. The fact remains, however that, regardless of who is responsible for this situation (the system itself or the people in the system), gigantic amounts of money are lost year after year simply because of nonconformance to the stated requirements. Unfortunately, the software industry is no different, in this regard.

In the past, the industry was primarily concerned with the identification and rejection of completed products before offering them to the consumer. The quality checking process was done after the fact. The concept of quality at that time was a purely defensive one. Today, emphasis is being placed more and more on the validity and integrity of the process that leads to the product itself. At various stages of the software development process, the intermediate products are more frequently scrutinized to identify possible nonconformance to requirements during the earlier stages of the product life cycle. This irreversible trend is easily understandable if one looks at the costs incurred by the software industry when the time comes to fix the defects in the product.

To illustrate this point, consider another point discussed in the same newspaper article. The industrial sector chosen for the sake of argument was the electronics field. The story goes like this: If, when assembling a television set for the first time, a tiny plastic component is found faulty and is immediately replaced by the workers, it will only cost 30¢ to do so. If, to replace this part, we wait until the end of the first assembly process, the cost will be 10 times the original one, or $3. Waiting until the television set is entirely assembled to correct the problem costs $30—100 times the initial cost of 30¢! If the faulty part is not detected before the TV set finally reaches the consumer market, a potential loss of $500 might be incurred if an unhappy customer returns the set and decides to buy another from a competitor. Similar order of magnitude figures apply to the software sector. Boehm [1987] contends that identifying and repairing a software defect once the system is put in production can cost more than 100 times the original cost of fixing the problem during the analysis stage.

Thus, it becomes obvious that investing in some form of prevention while engineering a software system can positively contribute to the improvement of quality and at the same time help to reduce failure costs. It is also true that it will always cost less to build a product right the first time. After all, the defects that are prevented in the first place need not be reworked—not to mention the increased likelihood of meeting the delivery dates. All this can easily translate into tangible productivity gains. In fact, the American Society for Quality Control once stated that the return on investment for adequately managing the cost of conformance to

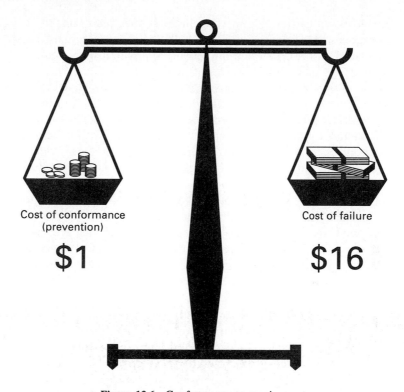

Figure 13.6   Conformance to requirements

requirements has a ratio approximately of 16 to 1. Thus, for every dollar invested in prevention, $16 are avoided in failure costs. Figure 13.6 illustrates this important point.

13.6 THE COST OF QUALITY: A DEFINITION

The cost-of-quality concept can be defined as a measure of the time and money an organization spends to achieve quality by ensuring its products and services meet the customer's requirements and are fitted for their intended use. Looking at it from a different angle, it can also be defined as a measure of the losses incurred by an organization by producing low-quality products or by offering poor quality services. Closer to the software industry, the cost of quality can be defined as the number of dollars spent to ensure that software systems do indeed conform to the customer's requirements and are fit for use. It also represents the additional number of dollars spent to correct system defects that are caused by the inability of the software developers to meet the user's requirements right the first time.

In fact, when a software system is developed, two major categories of costs can be identified: development costs and costs of quality. *Development costs* are incurred when gathering and consolidating user requirements to design, code, and implement the system. Costs of developing the system must be incurred no matter how much effort is invested into ensuring it will also be a quality product. They are the costs of doing business.[2]

Costs of quality are those incurred to ensure that the software systems are indeed developed not only in accordance with the original user functional requirements but also in accordance with built-in software quality characteristics. For instance, the costs incurred by the MIS organization for implementing new methodologies, fixing software defects, or testing a software system are all valid examples of various costs of quality. After all, nothing prevents someone from building a software system without the help of a methodology. In theory, too, a software system could also be delivered to the users with no testing at all.

Figure 13.7 identifies the four distinctive categories of costs that are associated with the cost-of-quality concept. The categories are divided into two major groups: costs of conformance and costs of nonconformance to the requirements. The costs of conformance (prevention and appraisal) are to ensure that a software product conforms to its original specifications and is fit for its intended use.

Prevention.   Prevention costs are incurred in an effort to prevent defects from happening when developing or maintaining software systems. They also include the costs that are incurred to ensure that the job is done right the first time. For instance, the cost of developing an in-house system development methodology can be considered a prevention cost. The money spent in developing and enforcing software quality standards is another example. The portion of the MIS budget dedicated to sustain a quality assurance function is also a good example of a prevention cost. Training is also a cost of conformance. The software practitioners must be properly trained to develop high-quality systems.

Appraisal.   Appraisal costs are incurred in an effort to identify defects in the systems developed or maintained by the MIS organization. They are mainly associated with measuring, evaluating, reviewing, or auditing intermediate or

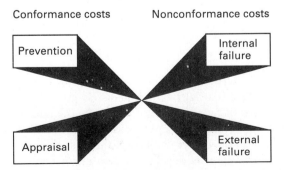

Conformance costs   Nonconformance costs

Prevention

Internal failure

Appraisal

External failure

Figure 13.7   The four categories of cost of quality

[2]The same principle applies to the maintenance process.

finished products to ensure they conform to previously documented quality standards, as well as the original users' requirements. They are considered "after-the-fact" activities as opposed to prevention activities because they measure the degree of conformance of the product only after it is completed. For instance, the costs associated with testing a system are considered appraisal costs.

The costs of nonconformance (internal and external failures) are to correct the problems detected in a software system when failures to conform to the user requirements occur.

Internal failure.   Internal failure costs are incurred in an effort to correct the defects inadvertently included in a software system. In this nonconformance category are the costs of debugging a system, correcting a program, and so on. Normally, it is relatively easy to measure these costs, as tangible time and money must be spent by the MIS staff to correct the software defects. It is important to point out that internal failure costs are detected during the development stage, once the product has been developed, but before the system is delivered to the users.

External failure.   External failure costs are very similar to internal failure costs. They constitute all the costs incurred to correct defects once the software system has been delivered to the users.

Tables 13.4, 13.5, 13.6, and 13.7 provide some examples of various cost elements that can be directly associated with the four cost-of-quality categories. These lists of cost elements are not exhaustive; they can be augmented and/or tailored to meet the specific needs of an organization.

A word of caution: In some instances, it is not always easy to determine if a given cost is indeed a cost of quality or simply a cost of doing business. For instance, should preventive maintenance be considered a preventive cost-of-quality item or just a cost of doing business? Some organizations will arbitrarily decide that it is a preventive cost, and others will argue that it is just another cost of doing business. Both positions are acceptable. What is really important is not to debate where such a cost should be reported but rather to report it in the same category all the time.

The sources of the cost-of-quality elements are not shown on the charts, for simplicity. However, for each cost element identified in a cost-of-quality program, its related cost source should be clearly defined. Most of the time, the cost sources relate to various spending items, such as salary budgets (i.e., the time spent by the staff while performing some specific cost-of-quality activities), computer processing costs, and the like.

TABLE 13.4 PREVENTION CATEGORY

Cost Element	Description
Software engineering methodologies/techniques	Associated with the development or acquisition of structured methods and techniques aimed at improving the development and maintenance of quality software systems.
Productivity tools evaluation and selection	Associated with the development or acquisition of productivity tools aimed at supporting the automation of the entire software life cycle.
IS standards, quality checklists and guidelines	Associated with the planning, development, implementation, and revision of prescribed standards. These are applied by the software professionals when they develop and maintain software systems.
Formal education/training	Associated with the development, renting, or acquisition of courses aimed at training the software professionals. It also includes the costs incurred by people who participate in various events, such as internal/external presentations, attendance at professional seminars and conferences, and so on.
Quality assurance	Associated with sustaining a quality assurance function within the MIS organization.
Quality improvement program	Associated with the planning, implementation, operation, and maintenance of a formal quality program aimed at improving systems quality and reducing the nonconformance quality costs.
Preventive maintenance (hardware/software)	Associated with monitoring the systems in production to anticipate and prevent problems.
Reusable code program	Associated with putting a program in place aimed at developing and supporting the concept of software reusability.
Backing up software programs and files	Associated with periodically saving a copy of the software programs and files used in the test and production environments.
Personnel reviews	Associated with performing periodic personnel assessment reviews to prevent misunderstanding of mutual expectations between the manager and the employees.
Applicant screening and selection	Associated with the careful screening of potential candidates to ensure the selection of quality software performers.
Job descriptions for MIS employees	Associated with the preparation of comprehensive job descriptions for each major function performed in the MIS organization. Provide a clear statement of what the personnel are expected to do and of skills required.

TABLE 13.5 APPRAISAL CATEGORY

Cost Element	Description
Reviews/inspections/ walkthrough/desk checking	Associated with conducting formal/informal inspections, reviews, and walkthroughs of the system deliverables to evaluate the conformance to requirements. These processes should be put in place to detect defects as early as possible during the system development life cycle.
Internal testing	Associated with the planning, development, and execution of activities aimed at identifying as many errors or defects as possible before implementing a system in the production environment. It does not include debugging of programs.
Auditing reviews	Associated with conducting activities aimed at ensuring that the prescribed IS standards and procedures are being applied correctly by the software developers.
Quality control reviews	Associated with activities aimed at ensuring that the system adheres to preestablished functional and quality-oriented standards and procedures.
Prototype validation	Associated with the validation of a system prototype.

13.7 THE COST OF DEVELOPING SOFTWARE SYSTEMS VERSUS THE COST OF QUALITY

Based on everything that has been said about the cost of quality, we can intuitively derive the following conclusions:

All the money spent in MIS for prevention and appraisal costs should be perceived as a sound investment. They are major contributors that help considerably to reduce expensive failure costs. Remember that developing a system right the first time does indeed pay off. Just think of the 16-to-1 saving ratio we discussed previously between failure and prevention costs. In other words, the benefit of conformance costs is the avoidance of nonconformance costs. Thus the software developers should instill in themselves an attitude of prevention rather than strictly appraisal. The errors we do not make in the first place do not need expensive corrections later on. This is not to say that appraisal costs should be totally eliminated though. Zero defects is a nice goal, but in practice it is very difficult if not impossible to attain. However, it must still remain the ultimate target for software developers.

All the money we spend in internal and external failure costs should be perceived as a bad investment. Why? Because they contribute to the reduction of the enterprise's profit margins. Failure costs can be further divided into direct and indirect costs. Direct failure costs are often associated with those famous words preceded with the prefix "re": revise, rework, reject, redesign, restructure, recode, retest.... Indirect failure costs are usually harder to quantify but nonetheless can turn out to be very harmful to the organization over time. If not properly taken

TABLE 13.6   INTERNAL FAILURE CATEGORY

Cost Element	Description
Total system rejection	Associated with the losses incurred by the organization due to the inability of the system to meet user requirements.
Rework activities	Associated with all the activities that are incurred to fix system defects in order to meet user requirements. This can include such various tasks as reanalyze, redesign, recode, and retest some components of a system.
Downgrading	Associated with the difference in money between the regular selling price and the reduced price at which the system must be sold to the customer because the system does not live up to the original specifications.[3]
Lawsuits/penalty for late delivery	Incurred due to the imposition of lawsuits because the system cannot be delivered to the customer within the established time frames. It might also consist of penalty fees that must be paid to the customer because of the late delivery of a software product.
Loss of programs and files	Incurred by the loss of programs and files in the development environment.
Job restart/recovery (in development mode)	Associated with the losses of productivity incurred by the development team and by the unavailability of the computer. They also represent the costs associated with the losses incurred by various jobs that must be resubmitted for successful completion (before production).
Debugging	Incurred by the activities necessary to locate the cause of a software problem or defect.

[3]An example of downgrading costs is found in the textiles industry. Have you ever bought a set of bed sheets offered at a lower price because of minor defects? Maybe a software package must be sold at a reduced price because of some minor defects that "do not drastically alter" its overall functionality.

care of, they can result in loss of customer confidence, loss of reputation, loss of business, and even loss of jobs. The ultimate impact is the radical elimination of the company from the marketplace. Because of the severe effects associated with external failure costs (direct or indirect), emphasis is often given to the reduction of internal failure costs in an attempt to improve customer satisfaction.

In conclusion, it becomes apparent that the MIS organization should take appropriate actions to improve software quality gradually while reducing the costs of nonconformance where deemed necessary. Does your organization score very low in the appraisal/prevention categories but very high in the internal/external failure categories? If yes, then short-term and long-term plans should be prepared with the objective in favor of prevention costs.

TABLE 13.7   EXTERNAL FAILURE CATEGORY

Cost Element	Description
Total rejection of the production system	Associated with the financial losses incurred by the organization because the system must be removed from production because of severe nonconformance to requirements.
Corrective maintenance	Associated with the losses incurred by the activities that are needed to fix software production problems. It includes such tasks as reanalyze, redesign, recode, retest, redocument, and reimplement some portions of the system.
Customer complaints and dissatisfaction	Associated with the expenses incurred for taking the time to properly address valid user complaints about the system.
Production job restart/recovery	Associated with the losses incurred when production jobs abend and must be restarted for successful completion. It also includes the loss of productivity caused to the users because they cannot use the system during downtime.
Debugging	Incurred by the activities required to locate the cause of a software problem or defect in the production environment.
Hardware/software/networking equipment and facilities downtime	Incurred by the organization when the hardware/software/networking equipment and facilities have failed for a given period of time.

13.8 A COST-OF-QUALITY PROGRAM FOR MIS

If developing quality software systems in the most cost-effective manner has always been a major objective of the organization, then it should be easier to justify the added value of a cost-of-quality program to management. On the other hand, if the organization ignores the basic principles of quality that drive the development of better software systems, then the road map to a successful quality improvement program might be a bit more difficult to follow.

In any case, the benefits associated with such a program are numerous. The following is a short list of some of the most obvious advantages that such a program can provide to an organization.

1. The definition of the cost-of-quality elements that are important to the organization provides a sound platform to set up software quality goals that are measurable and attainable in both the short- and long-term horizons.

2. Specific problem areas or opportunities that could lead to software quality improvements might be highlighted by such a program and prioritized accordingly. As a result, effective corrective action could then be initiated in a

timely fashion. Permanent solutions that will work could then be put in place in a progressive manner.

3. A cost-of-quality program creates a general awareness of quality issues and focuses people's attention on the need to improve software quality. It also emphasizes the importance of reducing expensive costs such as costs of nonconformance generated by internal and external failures.

4. It provides a feedback mechanism that helps the troops gauge the effectiveness of a productivity/quality improvement program. If no measure of the existing level of productivity/quality exists, it might be more difficult to assess objectively if the organization is really improving or moving forward or backward from its current position.

Several important questions might arise: How much effort should be spent on such a program? How formal should it be? How far should the MIS organization go in its crusade for quality? There is no simple answer to any of these questions. Some companies invest substantial amounts of money in a massive company-wide cost-of-quality program, especially in large manufacturing industries. Others do not. Once again, common sense should prevail. Each organization is different from another. In a large organization, where huge software development projects are regularly launched, it is likely that the software development process itself increases in complexity just by the sheer number of intervening people. Many specialized groups get involved, in addition to the normal system development team, such as the database group, the telecommunication/network group, the software group, and so on. As the number of interfaces increases, the success of the project relies heavily on effective communication among these various groups.

In such an environment, and because of the added complexities caused by the size of the organization, it might become critical to formalize and optimize the development and maintenance process and concentrate on the prevention of problems. A formal cost-of-quality program can prove to be quite useful in such a situation to analyze the potential causes of failure (nonconformance costs) and provide a permanent solution (prevention costs).

For smaller organizations, however, a less formal program can still be used. If it is not possible to do so, then at least an exposure to the basic concepts of a cost-of-quality program would be beneficial for everyone in the organization. It would help to stimulate people to strive constantly for quality results.

Everyone at least should become familiar with the meaning of common terms: prevention, appraisal, internal and external failure costs. After all, it would probably not hurt too much to ask some naive questions about the actual status of your own organization: Do we spend too much money on correcting defects and not enough on prevention? Do we have a methodology to help us do things right the first time? Do we properly train our people? And so on. When we look at the dramatic expenses that are normally attributed to the costs of nonconformance versus the costs of conformance, an organization cannot afford not to worry about quality conformance. In today's competitive world, the organization should seek all opportunities for permanently reducing its internal and external failure costs.

13.9 REPORTING QUALITY COSTS

The content of a cost-of-quality report may vary significantly from one organization to another. It should always be tailored to satisfy the specific needs of the enterprise. Figures 13.8 and 13.9 show a simplified cost-of-quality report for an MIS organization.[4] The report is divided into two basic sections. Section 1 shows a detailed breakdown of the various cost elements that are regrouped under a single cost-of-quality category: prevention, appraisal, internal and external failures. Section 2 summarizes the total expenditures associated with the four cost-of-quality categories. An interesting exercise for the MIS organization would be to compare the grand total cost-of-quality figure against the grand total cost of developing systems, which is the cost of doing business.

We have assumed that the primary objective of the MIS department is to develop systems, but it also provides other types of services to the users. This is particularly true for software consulting firms. The report could therefore reflect these specific situations as well.

Before setting up a cost-of-quality reporting system, an organization should answer the following questions:

- Which MIS areas should we cover in the first place?
- What are the quality cost items we want to report?
- Are these the right items to measure?
- Are they really relevant to our organization?
- Which ones should be selected?
- How many should we start with?
- How should we report them?
- Can we define them explicitly to avoid confusion with other departments within the same organization?
- Who should receive these reports?
- Who should be responsible to produce them?

[4]Many techniques can be advantageously used to report the quality costs: trend analysis, Pareto analysis, and so on. However, it is beyond the scope of this book to detail these techniques. For the reader who would like more information on this subject, consult the two excellent booklets published by the American Society for Quality Control [1971, 1977]. Although these guides were originally developed for industries other than data processing, the sample reports illustrated in these booklets can easily be adapted to the specific needs of the MIS organization. If the organization does not have the in-house expertise necessary to launch a cost-of-quality program, an alternative would be to hire outside consultants who already have successfully implemented such programs in various organizations.

	MIS COST-OF-QUALITY EXPENDITURE REPORT (DETAILED)					
	Cost Element	January	February	...	December	Yearly Total
PREVENTION	1. System development methodologies/techniques 2. Productivity tools 3. IS standards, quality checklists and guidelines 4. Education and training 5. Quality assurance 6. Quality improvement program 7. Preventive maintenance 8. Reusable code program ⋮ Prevention total	——	——	——	——	——
APPRAISAL	1. Reviews, inspection, walkthroughs, desk checking 2. Internal testing 3. Auditing 4. Quality control ⋮ Appraisal total	——	——	——	——	——
INTERNAL FAILURE	1. Total system rejection 2. Rework activities 3. Downgrading 4. Lawsuits, penalty for late delivery 5. Job restart/recovery (development mode) 6. Debugging ⋮ Internal failure total	——	——	——	——	——
EXTERNAL FAILURE	1. Total rejection of the system (in production) 2. Corrective maintenance 3. Customer complaints handling 4. Job restart/recovery (in production) 5. Debugging ⋮ External failure total	——	——	——	——	——

Figure 13.8 Detailed cost-of-quality report

MIS Cost-Of-Quality Expenditure Report
(Summary)

	Cost Of Quality Category	January	February	. . .	December	Yearly Total	TOTAL %
Costs of Conformance	Prevention						
	Appraisal						
Costs of Nonconformance	Internal Failure						
	External Failure						
	Grand Total						100%

Figure 13.9 Summarized cost-of-quality report

- How should we collect the cost-of-quality input data?
- What are the major sources for collecting the cost-of-quality input data?
- How much money do we want to spend on this?
- What percentage of the total development costs should be allocated to this effort?

Keeping these questions in mind, it is recommended to start with reporting only a very few cost elements (one to three) for each of the four cost-of-quality categories. Furthermore, it is preferable to stick to the same cost elements for at least six months to a year. As practical experience is gradually gained in dealing with a cost-of-quality program, annual revisions can be made and the cost-of-quality reports can be adjusted and augmented where need be. The measurement base will be as good as the amount of consistency in reporting the cost-of-quality items.

Various graphics, such as those shown in Figs. 13.10 and 13.11, can be used to report the quality costs. They visually portray the yearly trends of the various cost-of-quality categories. Some organizations will initiate a formal cost-of-quality program with the active support of their accounting departments, since reporting these costs is perceived by many as a regular function of an accounting department.

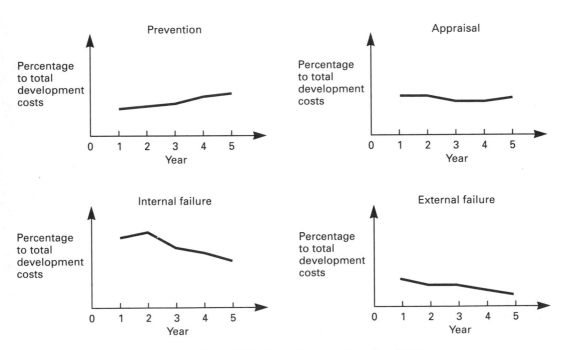

Figure 13.10   Reporting cost-of-quality figures

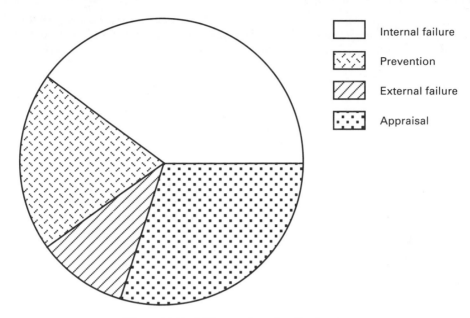

Figure 13.11   MIS cost-of-quality distribution

13.10 A GENERIC QUALITY IMPROVEMENT SYSTEM

Problems will not disappear overnight simply because a cost-of-quality program has been set up or software development quality checklists have been included in the information systems standards manuals. A formal quality improvement system should be put in place to permanently address various quality issues.

But before we describe in generic terms the basic components of a typical productivity/quality improvement system, some questions on quality improvement issues need to be answered:

Q: Where should we start to improve quality?

A: You can start anywhere you want, as long as you *do* something about it. Having said this, it is preferable to start at the beginning—that is, get the support of your management. Once again, the support must be real; you will need far more than lip service. Tangible action must be taken, such as the elaboration of a detailed plan of action that is backed up by adequate financial and staffing resources. Above all, both practical and realistic short- and long-term objectives should be set up by management. Any formal education program should also be initiated to familiarize your people with the basic concepts of quality software.

Q: Should we start concentrating our efforts on reducing the costs of nonconformance?

A: This sounds right, since external and internal failure costs should be avoided as much as possible. Let's remember that these costs are normally the most expensive ones. However, we must also increase our investments in the prevention category because the ultimate goal is to eliminate the costs associated with the "re" words (redesign, recode, retest, etc.). Appraisal costs remain equally important because they are used to detect defects before the software system is finally shipped to the most important category of people in the business world: our clients.

Q: Why should we bother with software quality issues? We have no real competitors. Our users are not allowed to go outside our MIS department to contract the services of software consulting firms.

A: Let's keep in mind that there are many forms of competition in the marketplace for the same customer base. Even when the MIS function is internal to the organization, there is still some form of competition exercised through the corporate budgeting process. In reality, the MIS organization must compete against other departments within the same company for scarce dollars. MIS must do so for the purpose of expanding its own market share within the company. In addition, if MIS does not constantly deliver quality software systems, chances are that the same business units that inherit these faulty systems will not be too excited to see the MIS budget expand, unless out of desperate necessity. They might be tempted to suggest to their executives the elimination of the entire MIS department and the use of contractors that can be more efficient and less costly in the long run. Remember, also, that the need to stay cost-effective in supporting the rest of the organization might become a question of survival for the entire company, no matter what.

Q: Surely there are some commercial programs that specifically address the generic quality improvement process. Could we look at these?

A: Yes. There are many quality improvement programs available in the marketplace. You can use them as is or customize them to satisfy your own needs. As an alternative, a simple and practical quality management system can easily be developed in-house. Most importantly, a quality improvement system should not be seen as an end in itself. Some organizations spend more time on organizing a complex internal structure aimed at managing the quality program itself versus simply trying to improve the way software systems are developed and maintained. In such a situation, the quality program itself might simply crumble under the weight of all the bureaucracy built around it. This should not become the case for your organization. We must not lose sight that such a program should never become more important than the people it serves.

We are now ready to take a look at a generic yet typical quality improvement system and its major components.

The primary objective of an MIS quality improvement system is to decrease the costs of developing and maintaining quality software systems. It is one of the major vehicles through which improvements can be made in the MIS organization. The system largely contributes an environment conducive to the delivery of quality software systems and services that not only conform to user requirements the first time but are also built to meet user needs.

As shown in Fig. 13.12, the quality improvement system is composed of three major subsystems.

Search for improvements.   The objective of this subsystem is to provide all employees in MIS with a universal mechanism that would allow them to actively participate in improving the quality of the system development and maintenance cycles currently in place. The idea is to change the attitude of the people from a reactive mode to a more proactive mode. To achieve this goal, each software professional should be provided with an environment that encourages the identification of problems that limit her or his ability to do a good job. The same principle equally applies to identifying opportunities to improve further the process of developing quality software systems by preventing problems. It is the responsibility of management to install a procedure that would enable each employee to communicate these problems and opportunities. To this effect, Fig. 13.13 provides an example of a form that can be used to record the identification of problems/opportunities submitted by the staff throughout the entire MIS organization.

Unlike a conventional suggestion system, the search for an improvement process does not require the inclusion of proposed solutions. Someone can identify a problem without having to offer a solution. That way, all can contribute to the search process and consequently influence the way they do their job.

Management should be aware that one of the best ways to destroy the search process is to withhold formal recognition of the efforts made by the contributors. Also, employees should be formally encouraged and rewarded for the submission of suggestions for quality/productivity improvements. Both managers and staff should be mature enough to accept with grace the possibility that the ideas suggested can sometimes turn out to be impractical or unworkable in the current context of things.

Analysis and prioritization.   Once a specific problem/opportunity has been officially recorded, a brief investigation should be conducted to understand the real nature of that problem. Assuming it is feasible and cost-effective to solve it, then a corrective action can be undertaken. Nonetheless, not all opportunities are necessarily exploited at once. The problems and opportunities that are highlighted by the search for improvements process should be measured (cost-benefit) and prioritized in light of certain factors. These would include their importance relative to one an-

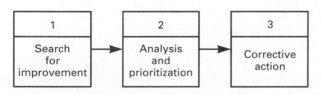

Figure 13.12   The major components of a quality improvement system

SEARCH FOR IMPROVEMENTS	Submitted by: _____ Telephone: _____	Department: _____	Date Submitted: _____ YYYY MM DD	SFI

PROBLEM/OPPORTUNITY DESCRIPTION

PROPOSED SOLUTION

BENEFITS

SFI#:	Page ___ of ___	Assigned to:	NOTE: Use back side if more space is required

Figure 13.13   Sample form to identify problems/opportunities

other and the efforts required to solve them permanently versus the anticipated benefits. Thus, the problems should be serious enough to justify the allocation of time and money necessary to hit upon a working solution and then implement it in a permanent manner. It does not mean that all decisions must invariably be based on a price tag. On the contrary, decisions can also be made based on value, but only once the calculated risk of solving the problem is worth the effort.

Corrective action.   Identifying problems and recording them will not make them go away. First, practical solutions to fix problems permanently should be formally suggested and only then can a corrective action plan be carefully put in place. Sometimes, the elaboration of a permanent solution calls for the participation of other departments either inside or outside the MIS organization. The user community at large might also be called upon to cooperate to implement the proposed solution. This is where the management commitment to a quality improvement program throughout the entire organization becomes crucial. This commitment is required at the top, middle, and working staff levels. With such a corporate-wide commitment, you will be able to emphasize the need for cross-functional problem solving.

In fact, all the various system departments in the MIS organization itself should view themselves as direct participants that get involved with their share of the work during the various stages of the system development "production" line. They should ask themselves who their suppliers are and who their customers are. In some instances, they can be customers themselves. What is their role? What services do they provide? How well do they interact with other groups? What can they do to improve quality inside their own group? What about outside their group? Can they help to prevent defects? An analogy can be made with the tiny, precision-engineered wheels that are assembled in an old watch, as shown in Fig. 13.14. Each of them has a purpose, a mission in life; and if one does not work properly or does not fit well into the ensemble, the watch does not accurately indicate the right time, or worse, completely stops.

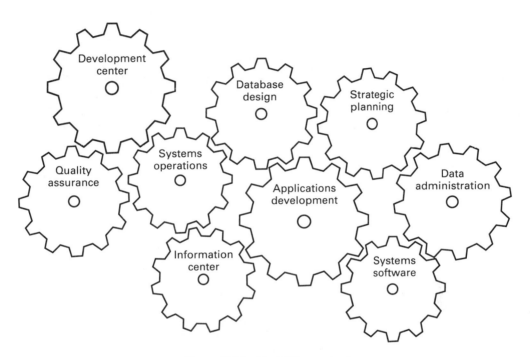

Figure 13.14   The MIS gearwheels

13.11 THE NEED FOR A NEW MIS QUALITY/PRODUCTIVITY CULTURE

Improving productivity and quality of the software organization often necessitates the investment of substantial amounts of money. Yet the return on this investment is often a long-term commitment even though the payoffs are definitely worth the expense. Several industry experts contend that most MIS organizations could realize quality/productivity gains of 2 to 1 in approximately three to four years and as much as 6 to 1 in an interval ranging between five and eight years. The secret recipe to achieve improvements of this order of magnitude is a well-thought-out quality/productivity long-range plan and a sustained effort to implement it incrementally. The effort must be well coordinated and integrated across the various "factions" of the

MIS department and user community. The productivity improvement figures advanced cannot be achieved with a piecemeal approach. Nor can the program be efficiently operated with few sporadic attacks on the problems, as when they suddenly appear at the horizon.

Even though there are no easy and instant solutions to these complex issues, most organizations should attempt to establish some kind of software productivity/quality program or culture. But as we just said, one should not expect an immediate return on the investment, especially in the prevention category. To ensure the success of such a program, the organization should also establish a clear corporate quality policy statement for all its employees and define a charter aimed at producing quality software. After all, if there are no tangible quality guidelines to follow and observe, how can each worker do quality work? In such an environment, people are basically left to their own judgment as to what applying quality really means when they perform their daily tasks. Very often, they do not know why quality should be important to them as individuals, or how to achieve quality.

The most successful productivity/quality program is one that addresses not only the technical system development/maintenance life cycle issues but equally the managerial and human aspects of the job too. The "system" itself, combined with poor management practices, is too often significantly contributing to the rapid escalation of the software costs in an enterprise.

The personnel dimension is probably the most important source of opportunity for productivity/quality improvements. Staffing the MIS organization with quality individuals who are also genuinely people-oriented is of paramount importance. This is true not only for technicians but even more so for managers. Enterprises that experience high productivity/quality gains are more often than not managed by people with optimal management skills and capabilities and who treat their staff as human beings.

To succeed in increasing the level of quality/productivity of software factories, there is no doubt that the development process must be rationalized and automated. There is also no doubt that we must use practical software engineering methodologies that are quality-oriented. But above all, we must learn to override our egos. The software factory concept is not only a technical but also a managerial issue. We must stop to consider the system development process as an art where individualism has achieved the status of a cult. Software development is like football. It is a team sport. The large and complex systems that are developed today need teamwork. There is nothing wrong with fulfilling personal ambitions. But as a corollary, management and staff should keep in mind that above all they must help the organization to achieve the more global goal of prosperity for all.

Finally, cultural anthropology has taught us that a culture is nothing more than a learned behavior. It is not transmitted by genetic inheritance but is taught and shared among various individuals. Considering the importance that the concept of quality has on the future of the software industries, it is hoped that the companies that invest good money into building an enterprise-wide quality culture do succeed in creating in the minds of their people a natural desire to develop quality products and to provide quality services. This should become so imprinted in our working habits that it should literally progress toward being second nature to all of us. The search for quality is a never-ending process.

13.12 REFERENCES

American Society for Quality Control. 1971. *Quality Costs: What and How,* 2nd ed. Milwaukee, Wis.

_____. 1977. *Guide for Reducing Quality Costs.* Milwaukee, Wis.

BERTERFIELD, D. H. 1986. *Quality Control,* 2nd ed. Englewood Cliffs, N.J.: Prentice Hall.

BOEHM, B. 1987. "Industrial Software Metrics Top 10 List," *IEEE Software,* September.

_____, et al. 1978. *Characteristics of Software Quality.* Amsterdam: North-Holland.

BOWEN, T. P., et al. 1985. "Specification of Software Quality Attributes," 1-3, RADC-TR-85-37, Air Force Systems Command, Griffiss Air Force Base, NY 13441-5700.

CASWELL, D. L., and R. B. GRADY. 1987. *Software Metrics: Establishing a Company-Wide Program.* Englewood Cliffs, N.J.: Prentice Hall.

CROSBY, P. B. 1980. *Quality is Free.* New York: New American Library.

DUNN, R., 1990. *Software Quality: Concepts and Plans,* Englewood Cliffs, N.J.: Prentice Hall.

DUNN, R., and R. ULLMAN. 1982. *Quality Assurance for Computer Software.* New York: McGraw-Hill.

EVANS, M.W., and J. J. MARCINIAK. 1986. *Software Quality Assurance and Management.* New York: John Wiley.

IEEE, 1987. *Software Engineering Standards.* SH 11098. New York: IEEE.

_____. 1983. *IEEE Standard Glossary of Software Engineering Terminology.* IEEE Std. 729–1983. New York: The Institute of Electrical and Electronics Engineers, Inc.

JURAN, J. M., and F. M. GRYNA. 1980. *Quality Planning and Analysis.* New York: McGraw-Hill.

KUME, H. 1985. "Business Management and Quality Cost: The Japanese View," *Quality Progress,* May.

MCCALL, J. A., et al. 1977. "Factors in Software Quality," 1–3, RADC-TR-77-369, Rome Air Development Center, Griffiss Air Force Base, NY 13441-5700, November.

POULAIN, J., 1988. *Les patrons, principaux responsables des pertes par suite de la non-qualité,* La Presse, Montréal, Canada, 1988/10/22.

SCHULMEYER, G. G., 1990. *Zero Defect Software.* New York: McGraw-Hill.

WEINBERG, G. M., and D. P. FREEDMAN. 1982. *Handbook of Walkthroughs, Inspections and Technical Reviews,* 3rd ed. Boston: Little, Brown.

14

Installing a Methodology

14.1 INTRODUCTION

Installing a new methodology in an organization can be a risky business if it is not handled properly. Some people have compared this complex technology transfer process to the delicate heart transplant surgery. First, a heart that is compatible with the receiver's organism must be found. Then it must be very carefully transplanted into a new environment. Despite a technically successful operation, the organism can sometimes massively reject the new heart.

One of the most popular software engineering methodologies in France is called *merise,* a derivative of the word *merisier,* which means "wild cherry tree." In their book describing this methodology, Colletti et al. [1984] claim that a wild cherry tree can only produce beautiful fruits if it has been previously grafted on a cherry tree branch. Similarly, they contend that a methodology will only produce the most effective results if the graft on the organization has succeeded completely.

Figure 14.1 presents the taxonomy of a comprehensive software engineering methodology. The standards supporting the methodology are divided into three major segments: management standards, technical standards, and miscellaneous standards aimed at supporting the software engineering process and its technological environment.

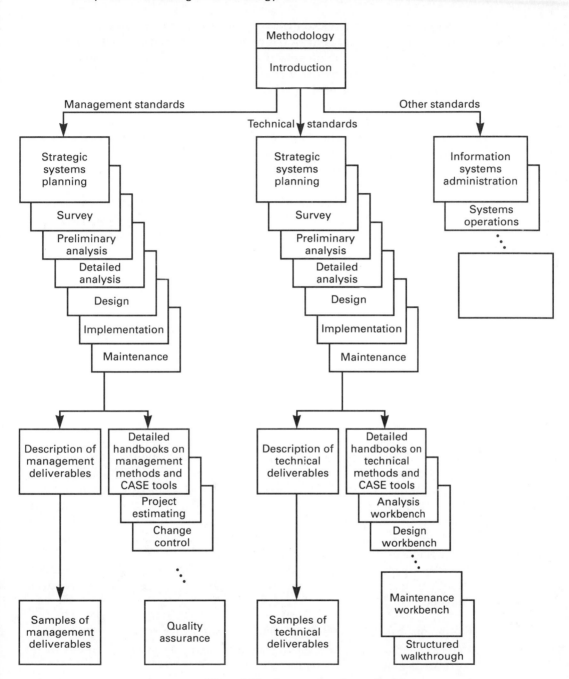

Figure 14.1   A comprehensive methodology

Management standards describe the procedures that are prescribed to formally organize, execute, and control the planning, development, and maintenance of the software systems of the organization. Technical standards describe the procedures that are prescribed by the methodology to technically plan, develop, and maintain the software systems of the organization.

The management/technical methods handbooks provide a description of the various software engineering/management disciplines and conventions that are used to build the software systems of the corporation, including structured analysis, structured design, project estimating, and the like. The management/technical CASE tools handbooks provide a set of practical guidelines that help practitioners to use the companion CASE tools of the methodology in the most productive manner possible and in accordance with the development and maintenance standards in place.

The remaining sections of this chapter present some of the most critical success factors to be taken into consideration when introducing a new methodology or enhancing the one currently being used.

14.2 TANGIBLE MANAGEMENT COMMITMENT AND SUPPORT

The management team, at all levels of the MIS organization, should be fully committed to the implementation of the methodology across all MIS departments. This is important because, to remain truly effective, the methodology cannot be used only by a few isolated business application groups. The active participation of all MIS support groups, such as the strategic planning, data administration, database design, telecommunications, and other related data processing departments is essential for ensuring the success of the methodology.

Furthermore, the introduction of a new methodology can eventually lead to a reorganization of the traditional MIS organization more along the functional lines of the newly proposed life cycle approach. Such a strategic transition, because it often implies some radical cultural and organizational changes that can seriously affect the way software people and users do business, must be endorsed and actively supported by management on a continuous basis. In other words, management must have a strong political will to alter the status quo and enforce a discipline approach to software engineering.

A strong business case should be built to highlight the benefits of a standard methodology to management. Among other things, some of the most positive arguments include

- Optimized use of the MIS development/maintenance staff
- Improved communications among the MIS and user groups involved in the software engineering of a quality system
- Elaboration and refinement of the software requirements of a large system in successive development phases that are easier to control and manage

- Standardization across the organization of the system life cycle methodology and adherence to its prescribed tools, techniques, and standards
- Improvement of the project estimation, planning, and change control processes because of the discipline imposed in the development and maintenance areas
- The adoption of a methodology provides a logical framework for gradually instituting an integrated CASE environment in the workplace

The business case should also be supplemented by a detailed transition plan that provides an incremental road map for implementing the new or revised software engineering methodology.[1]

14.3 TRAINING

Training should be planned carefully in advance for various categories of personnel:

New IS employees. The newly hired staff will need to be trained on the specific tools, techniques, and standard development practices advocated by the organization.

Current IS employees. The existing employees might need to extend their knowledge of the structured techniques or the methodology itself and familiarize themselves with CASE technology.

IS management. The different levels of supervision in the MIS organization should be educated on the important concepts of the methodology such as the need to hold regular reviews, the separation of the logical and physical characteristics of the system, and so on. They must focus their attention on the system life cycle process itself rather than on implementing various pieces of software automating tools in an ad hoc manner.

Users. Finally, the last, but certainly not the least, category to be trained are the users, who will play a major role in the life cycle projects. It is paramount that they understand the generic approach by which their systems will be developed and the active role they are expected to play during this critical process.

Remember, also, that the training process should be viewed as an ongoing task that constantly evolves with the introduction of new tools and techniques.

For most organizations, effective training is a major issue that should be seen as one of the most costly elements of the entire technology transition process. Implementing a methodology along with its policies, procedures, and standards and educating or reeducating the software practitioners on its proper use might cost more to an organization than acquiring its supportive CASE tools. Nevertheless, training

---

[1]A detailed discussion on implementing a software engineering methodology is beyond the scope of this book. For more information on this subject, see Pressman [1988]. Furthermore, the roles and responsibilities normally prescribed for the various MIS and user departments involved in planning a project, building the system, and controlling and reviewing the technical deliverables have been omitted in this book intentionally. Each organization should undertake this task in a way that reflects their current infrastructure.

in the new (or even old methodology) is a necessary process that unfortunately might temporarily slow down the introduction of CASE technology in an organization. On the other hand, it is still essential for ensuring further progress in the software engineering area.

14.4 MARKETING

The software engineering life cycle must be publicized so that the staff will be aware of its importance and relative value to the organization. Several options can be selected:

- Formal presentations
- Technical bulletins
- Support of knowledgeable outside consultants that bring with them their software engineering expertise and practical experience
- Guest speakers from organizations that have succeeded in implementing their methodology and its companion CASE tools

The expectations of MIS and user executives must be managed properly by the team in charge of the technology transfer process. The payoffs in productivity and quality associated with instituting a standard methodology across the organization should be perceived as a long-term investment. The expected benefits might not all materialize suddenly within the first months of usage.

Excellence in engineering, then evolving high-quality software systems cannot be achieved overnight. The one-minute methodology concept has little value in the context of establishing sound and durable software engineering methods and practices.

14.5 MAKING THE METHODOLOGY ACCESSIBLE

Ideally, the methodology should be put on the desk of every person involved in the development and maintenance of a software system. If the current technology supports online display of text combined with graphics, then putting the methodology online will greatly facilitate its accessibility and complement the more traditional printed information systems standards manuals. At the same time, it will also be easier to modify it and propagate enhancements more rapidly. Expert systems can also be used to automate the methodology itself and provide guidance in the proper use of its prescribed technical activities through the entire software engineering process.

14.6 OFFICIAL METHODOLOGY CUSTODIAN

A group of professionals or at least one individual who is dedicated on a full-time basis to this task should have the prime responsibility for installing the methodology and improving it over time. This task is a full-time job. If a development center group exists in the organization, then it should be officially mandated to gradually transfer the methodology into general practice across the MIS organization.[2] An official mechanism should be put in place for improving the methodology where it demonstrates ambiguities or weaknesses and to keep pace with technologies, techniques, and life cycle procedures that will emerge in the future.

A methodology is like a living creature. As new and promising paradigms are introduced in the data processing industry, they must be assessed and then smoothly integrated within the existing methodology in an evolutionary manner. This continuous process is often referred to as the software engineering tuning concept.

14.7 PILOT PROJECTS

Selective pilot projects should be used to allow the staff to gradually experiment with the new methodology and its supportive technological environment. The methodology can then be readjusted, if need be, to better match the unique needs of the organization. It must also be adapted to the different categories of projects at hand. The development center group or experienced outside consultants should help the development team in the proper use of the proposed methods, techniques, and tools. These people should be seen as the official agents of change responsible for introducing and supporting the methodology, while keeping the practitioners on course.

14.8 SYSTEM QUALITY ASSURANCE PROCEDURES

A mechanism should be put in place to ensure the proper adherence to the software system life cycle. This can be done by establishing a formal system quality assurance function that can play a proactive role in supporting the methodology and its standards or simply enforcing formal reviews of the technical products being developed during a project.

14.9 REFERENCES

BOULDIN, B., 1989. *Agents of Change: Managing the Introduction of Automated Tools,* Yourdon Press Computing Series. Englewood Cliffs, N.J.: Prentice-Hall.

COLLETTI, RENÉ, ARNOLD ROCHFELD, and HUBERT TARDIEU, 1984. *La Méthode Merise Principes et Outils.* Paris: Les Editions d'Organisation.

PRESSMAN, R. S. 1988. *Making Software Engineering Happen: A Guide for Instituting the Technology.* Englewood Cliffs, N.J.: Prentice Hall.

[2]For more information on the development center concept, see Chap. 11.

A

Package Evaluation Checklist

Following are questions that can be used in the development of selection criteria when investigating the acquisition of an application package.[1]

A.1 VENDOR PROFILE AND STABILITY

1. How long has the vendor been in business?
2. Will the vendor still be in business five to ten years from now?
3. What is the vendor's financial status? Annual revenues? Annual sales?
4. How many employees does the vendor have?
5. How many employees provide direct support to the existing package?
6. How many employees are involved in research and development activities?
7. How many copies of the package have been sold so far?

---

[1]In addition to this checklist, the development team might want to consider the use of software metric tools to evaluate the architecture of the packages. For example, they can evaluate the complexity of the package source code (i.e., number of unique logic paths), its structuredness, the existence of dead code, and so on.

8. Does the vendor provide a wide range of application packages? Are they compatible with one another? Are they supported by an integrated data architecture?

A.2 VENDOR SUPPORT

1. What is the frequency for the delivery of a new release?
2. What kind of support does the vendor provide?
3. Does the vendor offer a hot-line service? If yes, which days is it available and how many hours per day?
4. How knowledgeable are the people providing technical support?
5. Where is the nearest vendor location? Are there technical representatives or only marketing representatives at this site? How many?
6. What is the level of quality of the support provided by the vendor's staff?
7. On average, how long does it take for the technical staff to respond to a user problem?
8. Would the vendor be willing to support an in-house benchmark?
9. Is the vendor responsive to the demands of a user group?

A.3 VENDOR REFERENCES

1. Is the vendor willing to provide references on current users?
2. Can these users be contacted?
3. If yes
   (a) How long have they been using the package?
   (b) Are they satisfied with the vendor's ongoing support?
   (c) Does the package work as expected?
   (d) Are there unanticipated operational limitations?
   (e) How long did it take to install the package?
   (f) Can you visit the user sites where the package has been installed?
   (g) What is the average learning curve experienced by the staff?
   (h) Was the package customized to meet the specific requirements of the organization?

A.4 VENDOR EDUCATION SERVICES

1. What type of training does the vendor provide? At which level? For which audience?
2. Which courses are offered? At what cost? How often? Where? What is the duration, in days, of each course?

3. Are there courses specifically developed for users? Are they for beginners, intermediate, or advanced people?

4. Are there courses specifically developed for technical people? Are they for beginners, intermediate, or advanced people?

5. How many people can be trained if in-house courses are offered?

6. Are the courses evolving with the new releases of the package?

7. How well do the teachers know the package? How well do they communicate their knowledge?

8. Does the package provide a test environment for training purposes?

9. Is computer-based training available?

10. What type of training material is provided to the students?

A.5 HARDWARE/SOFTWARE/NETWORKING CHARACTERISTICS

1. On which type of hardware does the package run? Which model? Which release?

2. Can the package run in both a microcomputer and mainframe environment? Which releases?

3. On which type of operating systems does the package run? Which releases? Is the software transportable across hardware?

4. Is the package available in source language form? In which programming language was the package developed? Can the source code be placed in escrow?

5. Is the package compatible with the current networking facilities?

6. What type of file structures does the package support?

7. Is the database design structure of the package compatible with the organization's data administration standards? What about the naming convention aspect?

8. The package comprises how many programs?

9. Are the programs modularized? Were the programs developed with the use of structured coding techniques?

10. What are the package backup and recovery features?

11. Can the package be modified easily? Is it expandable?

12. Can the package be maintained easily? How many people are required to support the package in-house?

13. What are the security features offered by the package? At which level?

14. What are the package limitations in terms of number of files or tables, file size, throughput, volume of transactions processed, response time, batch job turnaround, record size?

15. What are the computer region size requirements to run the package?
16. Does the package include such facilities as query and report generators?
17. Does the package support ad hoc inquiries? One-shot reports?
18. How much CPU and I/O resources does the package consume?
19. Does the package offer fourth-generation language facilities?
20. Does the package offer micro to mainframe connections?
21. Can the application package embrace new technologies, such as bar coding or computer-assisted design and manufacturing, with minimal disruption?
22. How many users can the package support simultaneously?
23. What types of physical CRTs and printers does the package support?

A.6 ERGONOMICAL CRITERIA

1. Are the functions of the package easy to use?
2. Is there an online help facility to explain the system prompts? Can it be customized by the users themselves?
3. Are the error messages easy for a user to understand?
4. Does the package support more than one language?
5. Is the package menu-driven?
6. Does the package support the use of a mouse?
7. Does the package have multiwindowing capabilities?
8. Does the package support color screens?
9. What features of the package can be customized or maintained by the users themselves, without any programming changes?
10. Can the various package validation and lookup tables be updated and maintained by the users?
11. Are the standard reports easily modifiable by the users with no programming expertise?
12. Do the users need to input the same data more than once on different screens?
13. Are the functions menu-driven? Command-driven? Menu- and command-driven?
14. If a field is updated in one table, will the package automatically update other related fields in the same table? In other tables?
15. Does the package offer mass updating capabilities?
16. Can the screen layout be customized by the users themselves?
17. Are the screen layouts consistent across modules?

A.7 VENDOR DOCUMENTATION

1. Is the documentation available online?
2. What type of documentation is available? Under which format?
3. Is the documentation complete? Up to date? Well organized?
4. Are there tables of reference and indexes?
5. Is there a glossary for technical or business terms?
6. Are the following elements provided in the standard documentation:
   (a) Program documentation
   (b) Program listings
   (c) Files/records layouts
   (d) Description of database structures
   (e) Data element descriptions
   (f) User manuals
   (g) Technical manuals
   (h) JCL listings
   (i) Backup/recovery procedures
   (j) Source programs
   (k) Screens/report layouts
   (l) Installation guide
   (m) Training/tutorial guides
7. What are the costs of new user manuals? New technical manuals?
8. Who will maintain and update the documentation?

A.8 INSTALLATION SUPPORT

1. Are there special installation requirements in terms of software, hardware, communication?
2. What kind of technical support does the vendor provide when the package is installed at the user site?
3. What does the installation cost?
4. How long does it take to install the package?
5. Does the vendor provide test data during the user acceptance tests?
6. Are the installation procedures easy to understand and complete?
7. Does the vendor offer regression testing facilities and test data for installing the package of verifying the installation of new releases?
8. Does the vendor provide basic recommendations on the new business policies, working patterns, roles and responsibilities that should be enforced to take full advantage of their package?

A.9 FUNCTIONAL CHARACTERISTICS

1. What type of functions does the package provide?
2. Are the functions available online, batch, or in real-time modes?
3. What are the reporting facilities offered? Report formats?
4. What are the inquiry capabilities?
5. Can the package accommodate federal, state/provincial, and industrial regulations?
6. Can the package accommodate legal requirements?
7. Can the package support foreign currencies?
8. Can the package interface with other systems? What are the interfacing characteristics of the package?
9. Does the package support special features, such as graphical facilities or statistical facilities?
10. Can the package run on multiple mainframes?
11. Does the package provide transaction logging facilities?
12. Does the package provide auditing facilities?
13. Does the package provide security facilities? If yes, at which level?
14. Is the package parameter-driven?
15. Can the package be easily modified to satisfy new user requirements?
16. What are the performance limitations or constraints of the package?
17. Can new fields be added in the existing files or tables?
18. What are the sorting capabilities of the package?
19. What are the archiving facilities?
20. Does the package support a word processing facility?
21. Does the package support a spreadsheet facility?

A.10 CONTRACTUAL REQUIREMENTS

1. What is the total price of the package, including direct and indirect costs?
2. What is the expected delivery date?
3. What type of financial arrangements are available? What are the payment terms?
4. Are there constraints on modifications that are made to the package by the organization?
5. What is the vendor's maintenance policy?
6. What is the vendor's warranty?

7. Will future enhancements be available? At what cost?

8. Is there an additional cost to install the package on more than one user site?

9. What type of training is supplied by the vendor? At what cost?

10. What type of documentation is provided initially by the vendor? How many copies? At what cost? Can the organization make its own copies of the user and system manuals?

11. Which release of the package will be installed?

12. Is the vendor willing to modify the package to suit user needs? At what cost?

13. What type of services and support will be provided by the vendor during the installation of the package? After?

14. Does the vendor agree to penalties for late delivery?

15. What happens if the vendor goes bankrupt before, during, or after the installation? Does your company keep the source code on site if so desired? Should the source code be put in escrow? Can your company modify the source code?

16. Does the vendor propose special procedures for verifying that the material put in escrow is indeed valid, complete, and usable?

17. Are the procedures required to transform the application source code into a running system adequately covered by the vendor? Is the application source code properly documented?

B

Questionnaire for Selecting CASE Tools

This appendix presents a list of questions/answers that can be used to assist an organization in formulating a comprehensive set of selection criteria for the acquisition of a CASE tool.[1] Some of the questions are applicable to a fully integrated CASE architecture that aims at automating the entire system development life cycle (planning, analysis, design, coding, and testing). Others pertain to CASE tools that automate a specific function of the software development life cycle, such as the analysis or design process.

Q: What type of architecture is supported by the CASE product?

A: There are basically two types of architecture: proprietary and open-ended. Pros and cons are associated with both types.

The *proprietary CASE architecture* offers a complete software engineering automation solution. It is usually composed of tools that are well integrated into an environment that automates the entire development life cycle, from strategic planning to generation of code. Such an approach might provide some additional productivity gains because the various tools in such a framework are well integrated.

---

[1]Since CASE technology is in constant evolution, this book does not provide any exhaustive list of CASE software products on the market. However, a wide variety of specialized periodicals regularly present complete listings of CASE vendors with specific information about their products.

However, it is important to point out that this kind of architecture is normally driven by a formal companion methodology. In other words, the different tools composing the integrated CASE environment were engineered under the control of an automated methodology.

If you do not intend to follow the standardized software engineering methodology supported by the integrated CASE environment, the organization will not realize all the productivity gains that normally would be expected from such an architecture. Even if the management team wants the software staff to use the methodology, is the MIS staff already trained and prepared to follow all the discipline imposed by the methodology? Keep in mind that if you buy a fully integrated CASE workbench, you might have to marry its particular methodology.

The *open-ended CASE architecture* allows various complementary CASE products to work together as if they were integrated with one another. With such an approach, an organization could better position itself to take full advantage of the array of new products that will emerge on the market over the next few years.

Thus, most integrated CASE environments currently available on the market started to open their architecture by offering various types of import/export facilities to the external world. Despite this, if you opt for a totally proprietary CASE architecture, be certain that the facilities provided by the various CASE tools are well balanced and user-friendly. In addition, verify if the vendor offers a type of CASE workbench characterized by a modularized architecture. If so, you might then be able to acquire one CASE module at a time to incrementally automate the activities associated with a particular phase of the system life cycle, based on your most urgent needs.

To conclude, chances are that most organizations today feel the necessity to integrate CASE into their respective software development and maintenance environments in conjunction with their current methodologies, standards, procedures, and tools. Few of them are prepared to discard their existing environment and completely start from scratch with a brand-new one. The organizations want to protect their investment into existing skills, techniques, and tools while gradually evolving toward new software engineering paradigms.

Q: Are there standards regulating CASE technology?

A: Despite the fact that the CASE industry is still relatively young, the trend is toward the establishment of standards that will help "regulate" this industry. However, because the CASE industry and standardization are still in their infancy, it is premature to predict exactly when and what type of standards will emerge in terms of CASE tool interfaces and connectivity. However, once standardization is reached, significant progress will be made at a much faster pace. The CASE industry will boom even further since MIS users and vendors should be able to develop or retrofit their own products to agree with the standards put forth in the software industry. Until then, the lack of interfacing standards among the different CASE products tends to limit the wide acceptance of CASE technology by the average MIS organization.

Q: Can the CASE tool allow sharing of information among several software analysts during the development of a system? If so, what are the control features to manage such a shared environment?

A: This situation is not so important if only one analyst does the entire system development work from beginning to end. Conversely, in a real-life environment, several analysts might have to work simultaneously on the same project deliverables. When this is the case, the facility to share information suddenly becomes critical. In such a context, the CASE tool should be able to manage efficiently the interfacing activities that occur between the various analysts working on the same project and sharing the same information.

Some CASE products truly achieve data sharing simultaneously via a controlled access to a common database dictionary. Others do so through periodic updates of the central repository or with various check-in/check-out mechanisms.

Q: Does the CASE tool properly support multiple versions of the same project deliverables?

A: The system development process is inherently highly interactive. Consequently, the CASE tool should be able to support simultaneously more than one release version of the same data and process models that are developed during the project.

Q: Are the various CASE tools harmoniously integrated under the control of an active data dictionary feature?

A: An active dictionary facility (sometimes referred to as central repository, repository manager, or central encyclopedia) provides greater integration capabilities for sharing information across the various families of tools used. This facility is essential for large and complex software projects. A relational database management system offers much flexibility to support the various data dictionary features of the CASE platform. However, the current trend points toward object-oriented database management systems to manage the complexities associated with a fully integrated CASE environment.

Another area to investigate is the ability of the active central repository facility to import/export files automatically from and to the corporate data dictionary. During the past years, several companies have recognized the need for a strong data administration function better to control or eliminate the proliferation of incompatible data across the organization, and consequently they have begun storing information about their existing systems in a centralized corporate data dictionary.[2] If this is the case for your organization,

---

[2]Even though they might use various development tools on different computer platforms that to an extent, already offer some isolated and standalone data dictionary capabilities (such as several fourth-generation language environments), several organizations still use a corporate data dictionary where essential information about the various corporate systems of the enterprise are centrally stored.

then the selected CASE product ideally should provide an automated interface with your corporate dictionary to minimize the proliferation of redundant data. For instance, assume that a company has acquired a PC-
based computer-aided data flow diagramming tool. Let's also assume that the
PC-based tool comes with an automated feature that allows the developer to
populate its standalone dictionary with the description of the components
shown on the data flow diagrams as these are being drawn. To eliminate the
need to manually reenter the same data definitions in the corporate dictionary, an automated interface should directly upload this information from
the micro-based tool up to the mainframe-based corporate dictionary and
vice-versa.

Q: Does the tool support a unique set of planning/analysis/design drawing
symbols?

A: Some tools support a single development technique (whether it is part of a
proprietary methodology or not), while others can support several popular and
widely used analysis and design diagramming techniques (Yourdon/DeMarco,
Gane and Sarson, *merise,* Michael Jackson, Warnier-Orr, Ward/Mellor, or
Hatley/Pirbhai real-time modeling approach). If a very large organization uses
more than one technique, then such a factor might become an important criterion for selecting a tool that supports more than one diagramming technique.

Q: Does the tool provide real-time extensions to the more traditional structured
analysis techniques?

A: Some tools offer real-time modeling facilities via an extension to their standard product. It becomes an additional option that can be acquired when
needed. Yet it might operate in a standalone environment. Others have integrated this feature directly into their existing CASE architecture, allowing
software engineers to work simultaneously on process models, data models,
and real-time system models using a unique interface, with several comprehensive cross-checking facilities.

Q: Does the CASE tool come in with extensive checking facilities that are built
into its architecture? What kinds of automated checking facilities are provided by the CASE product to help validate separately the process, data, and
real-time models that are constructed during a single development phase?
What kinds of automated facilities are provided for cross-checking the various levels of system models that are constructed during the different phases of
the development life cycle? Is the tool capable of automatically cross-checking
the integrity and consistency of common elements used in the process, data,
and real-time models that are developed during the same development phase?

A: Sophisticated rule-based consistency-checking features should be provided to
validate all the models that are developed during a single phase, as well as
across the different phases, of the life cycle. From the analysis phase to the
design phase, the models are progressively transformed from a purely logical
structure to a more physical type of structure. Still, all the components that

are shown on the logical models should somehow appear on the models that are subsequently developed during the design phase. Some of the automated error checking facilities to look for are

- Duplicate components
- Horizontal/vertical balancing of data flow diagrams
- Incomplete or missing data dictionary entries
- Naming conventions inconsistencies
- Graphic syntax and standard rules enforcement
- Data normalization validation
- State-transition diagrams editing and validation
- Data items coming into a data store but not going out

Q: Can the CASE product be customized to the specific needs of your organization?

A: Each organization has an environment that is relatively unique to its own business. In principle, the CASE workbench should be compatible with both the hardware environment and software development and maintenance methodology in place. Moreover, it should be flexible enough to be easily customized to meet the organization's specific needs of today and be able to evolve in those of tomorrow.

Q: Does the CASE tool offer word processing facilities?

A: Some CASE tools offer built-in word processing facilities that also support the integration of graphics with text on the screen and in print. If the software organization is using a mixed micro and mainframe type of environment, then it would be nice if the word processor used in one environment is indeed compatible with the other environment. The CASE product should also offer an interface capability to the most popular standard word processing systems in use today. Some products also offer interfaces with a variety of electronic or desktop publishing systems. The resulting system documentation is of high quality and helps reduce documentation-related maintenance costs in the long run.

Q: Does the CASE product support a single hardware configuration platform?

A: To support adequately the development environment of several large and modern organizations, the application that will be generated with the CASE toolsets should in some instances be capable of running either on a micro or mainframe computer. There might also be a need to acquire a CASE tool that can be used to develop an application that can operate in two different hardware platforms, such as in an IBM environment and a Digital environment, for example.

Q: Can the CASE product generate first-cut physical database design layouts that are derived from the functional design specifications?

A: Today there are tools that will automatically normalize and transform the logical data model into a first-cut physical database structure diagram (hierarchical, network, or relational). Although an equivalent facility might not yet exist for the process model, it would be nice if the CASE tool could derive from the data flow processes an initial set of first-cut structured charts.

Q: How user-friendly is the CASE product?

A: Most PC-based planning, analysis, and design CASE tools offer extensive high-resolution graphical facilities with full windowing and mouse-driven capabilities. Are these functions user-friendly? Are the mouse movements also supplemented with function key commands? Is there an in-context online help facility? Can the diagrams or their related documentation be easily modified? Are the error messages easy to understand? Is there a facility for querying the central repository or corporate data dictionary? Does the integrated CASE architecture provide a consistent user interface from one tool to another? From one development platform to another?

Q: Can the tool automatically draw a first-cut data flow diagram based on a parametized list of input data?

A: The best way to illustrate this concept is through an example: When a logical data model is constructed, the analyst would not have to draw the first-cut entity-relationship model but would only need to provide the tool with a parameter list of the entities to draw, along with their relationships. The tool would then be smart enough to draw a first sketch of the proposed data model. In other words, not only would these tools provide powerful and easy-to-use interactive diagramming facilities, but they would also provide an automated diagramming facility based on parameter-driven input data. Such a feature would provide a more productive environment since the drawing process, even if it is automated, is sometimes quite time consuming.

Q: Does the CASE tool offer windowing capabilities?

A: It would be advantageous to select CASE tools that offer multiple windowing capabilities. For example, while the analyst is drawing data flow diagrams, he or she can use a portion of the screen to describe and document simultaneously the various data flow diagram components as they are being developed.

Q: What is the acquisition cost of the CASE product?

A: Basically, there are two major costs to consider: acquisition costs and maintenance costs. How much will it cost you to acquire the license for the product? How much will it cost you to obtain the new releases? In any case, a cost-benefit analysis should be conducted to identify the bottom-line acquisition costs and payback information necessary to make a purchase decision.

Q: What are the documentation, training, and support facilities offered by the CASE vendor?

A: The ability for the vendor to provide quality technical support and education should be evaluated and taken into consideration. Is a hot-line provided? Does the vendor adequately support the installation of its product in your environment? Is the supporting documentation complete, easy to understand, and well organized? Is the documentation available online and also in a printed format? How much time is required before the MIS staff can become relatively proficient with the CASE tool in order to use it productively? Are there courses offered by the vendor to train your people? How often are the courses offered? Are the courses given in-house and/or at the vendor site? Is the vendor properly equipped to train your staff? Does the vendor have several categories of training courses that focus on educating different levels of MIS staff, such as programmers, analysts, designers, project leaders, managers, and even executives?

Q: What is the future direction proposed by the vendor for the CASE product?

A: The vendor should not only be evaluated based on the current features offered by its product but also on its ability to improve and evolve its product in the long run. CASE technology is still in its infancy. Many vendors will enhance their product and complement them with new facilities providing upward compatibility with their existing tools. Does the vendor have a stated plan of action to expand the functionality of its product with official target delivery dates? How much money is the vendor investing each year in research and development? Is the vendor financially stable? Is the vendor still going to be in the marketplace three years from now? Will its product become functionally or technologically obsolete? Despite this, a good CASE tool should not be rejected solely because it does not yet offer all the capabilities you are looking for.

Q: Is there a user group?

A: Can you join a product user group to share information with other organizations using the same product? Can you participate in a user group session before you acquire the CASE tool? Is the vendor receptive to the recommendations made by the user group to improve the product? Does the vendor offer a library of user-developed functions at no charge?

Q: Does the CASE product offer flexible reporting facilities?

A: Many CASE tool environments offer powerful interactive diagramming facilities to create several technical deliverables, such as data flow diagrams, entity-relationship diagrams, and others. However, it goes without saying that hard-copy documents are also needed. For instance, a printed document is very useful when conducting a structured walkthrough with several users. What are the reporting facilities provided by the CASE tool, and how flexible are they? The information displayed on a screen might be formatted and presented quite differently in a printed document. For instance, how well do the printed reports provide cross-referenced information tying together the data flow diagrams and the description of their various components? Can the reports be customized to your own specific needs? If yes, how easy is it to do? Can various fonts of different sizes and shapes be used when formatting the reports with different titles and headings? Can the information be uploaded and printed on a mainframe printer?

Q: Does the CASE product support the concept of reusability?

A: Ideally, the CASE product should provide a user-friendly facility to import/ export portions of the analysis/design specifications documents that are reusable for the development of other systems. The same rule should also apply for reusable code.

Q: Does the CASE tool provide auditability features?

A: Some CASE tools will allow the tracking of the last change made to an entity or data flow diagram or a data dictionary entry by user, date, and time.

Q: What type of housekeeping functions are provided by the CASE vendor to manage the CASE environment?

A: An integrated CASE environment will necessitate a comprehensive set of housekeeping facilities for controlling and managing the information contained in it. What does the vendor propose in this area?

C

JAD-Like Techniques

C.1 THE KEY PLAYERS IN A JAD-LIKE PROCESS

Before describing the generic process supported by the various JAD-like techniques, it is necessary to identify the key players involved in a JAD-like process and to define what their respective roles and responsibilities should be.

Executive sponsor. The executive sponsor is a senior manager coming from the ranks of the user organization and who is strongly committed to the JAD-like process. His role is to sponsor the entire process from beginning to end. He is the individual who provides a strong statement of direction as to what the major goals and objectives of the project should be. He also sets clear expectations for the outcome of the JAD process. The executive sponsor often kicks off the session by making a brief opening speech. Although he might not actively participate in the detailed sessions, he might be called upon to help resolve some critical management issues. He might also assist in selecting the key participants on the user side.

Functional managers and end users. These individuals are the business subject matter experts who participate in the detailed JAD-like session(s). They are the people who need the system. The right players should be carefully selected based on their knowledge of the business area under study. Selecting the appropriate participants will ensure the success of the session. Consequently, they must be chosen not solely on the basis of their ability to describe the current business practices better than anyone else but also in a way that warrants that all the required decision-making parties are present during the structured group dynamics sessions.

Information systems representatives. These are the few systems people who are invited to participate in the JAD-like sessions. They bring with them their technical knowledge of the existing business application, from a system's point of view. Typically, the suggested ratio of system participants to user participants is 1 to 4. This ratio is prescribed to maintain a strong business perspective during the sessions. The system requirements are elaborated through the users' eyes.

JAD-like session leader. The session leader is at the heart of the JAD-like process. Her role is to conduct preparatory interviews before the actual JAD-like sessions with the business executive sponsor and the key functional managers to define the ultimate scope of the JAD-like process. During the various interviews, she gathers as much material as possible to prepare in advance the JAD-like session. Before conducting the interviews, the session leader has already familiarized herself with the organization by reviewing questionnaires that were filled out by the users and aimed at defining the overall application context. She will also conduct the JAD-like session(s), ensuring they progress as smoothly and as effectively as possible.

Scribe(s). The role of the scribes is very important. They must officially record all the information proven to be pertinent to the system being studied. They also transcribe the action items that cover the miscellaneous issues raised during the session but that can be resolved at a later date. In large sessions, two scribes can be elected. One scribe, from the ranks of the MIS organization, documents the description of all the system components. The other scribe, usually a member of the user organization, keeps an account of the business issues raised by the users during the group dynamics session. Automated tools are used to capture the requirements and to display the screens, reports, or process and data models created during the JAD-like sessions back to the users for comments.

C.2 GENERIC DESCRIPTION OF THE JAD-LIKE PROCESS

The traditional joint application design (JAD) process, as originally supported by IBM, is composed of four elementary steps:

- Initial orientation
- Familiarization with the business area under study and its related application system
- Preparation of the workshop material
- Conducting the workshop

Following is a brief description of the activities performed in each step.

Initial orientation. This step consists in firming up the overall project direction by documenting the following items:

- Purpose of the project
- Project scope and functional areas involved
- Objectives that must be achieved by the end of the workshop
- Business and technical assumptions affecting the project
- Objectives of the workshop
- Critical success factors

The JAD leader gathers all this information by working with the executive sponsor, the functional managers, and the systems managers concerned with this project, before the workshop. Typically, the key participants in the workshop are carefully selected during this initial orientation process. The information gathered at this stage will serve as guidelines throughout the duration of the workshop and provide direction to the JAD team. The major objectives of the JAD session are usually prioritized by order of importance at this stage.

As a rule of thumb, this planning effort requires approximately three or four days of intensive work for an experienced JAD leader.

Familiarization with the business area/application.   This step consists of analyzing current business procedures and identifying the general work flow of documents in the workplace. All the business tasks that are performed with these documents are categorized into various groups and properly recorded. Typically, each business task is documented in the following manner:

- Purpose of the task
- Input data
- Output data
- Description of the processing done
- Problems/opportunities

The information gathered during this step will help the JAD leader to understand better the nature of the application, its related functional area(s), and any potential area of conflicts. This information gathering process will enhance the leader's ability to lead the group discussions during the workshop and to identify those issues that are outside the scope of the workshop and should be assigned to someone for resolution later on. This step lasts approximately two or three days.

Preparation of the workshop material.   During this step, a system analyst (it can also be the JAD leader) usually constructs an elementary model of the system. The analyst uses as a starting point the list of business tasks that were identified during the previous step. Depending on the nature of the project, this basic model might consist of roughly sketched screens and reports that will be reviewed during the design workshop. The purpose of developing this first-cut model of the system is not to design a perfect solution in the first instance. Rather, it will be used as the main vehicle to stimulate ideas and discussions from the JAD participants during the workshop. Since the entire JAD process is fast-paced, such a preliminary design will minimize the risk of going on a tangent during the workshop and wasting valuable time. It also improves the quality of the functional design, assuming it is done by an experienced analyst.

The draft model will be constantly refined during the meeting through successive iterations. Business tasks may be added, deleted, or modified as the team progresses through the analysis of the business and systems requirements. Various overhead foils and slides are also prepared during this stage to describe the information gathered so far. These will be used later on during the workshop to focus the attention of the participants on various issues related to the system to be designed. Sometimes, the prepared material is sent to the JAD session participants ahead of time. The JAD agenda is customized to the needs of the project at hand.

Conducting the workshops.   Once all the previous preparatory steps are completed to the satisfaction of all parties, the workshop itself is then initiated. Normally, the workshop lasts three to five days. Early during the first day, the executive sponsor opens the session, explaining the purpose of the project and describing the commitment of all the participants, starting with management's backing. Then a brief review of the general information pertaining to the scope, objectives, and assumptions of the project follows. Once the JAD leader has presented the basic framework within which the team participants will operate, the leader starts to review the detailed material that was consolidated prior to the meeting. For this purpose, a structured approach is used, allowing the progressive design of the system. As the discussions advance through the daily sessions, the user requirements are carefully translated by the scribe into screens and report layouts with the help of a CASE tool. These are then quickly projected on a large screen, allowing fast revisions of the work done thus far.

C.3 VARIOUS USES OF JAD-LIKE TECHNIQUES

Although there might be some slight variations from the scenario we have just described, the JAD-like approach can be advantageously adapted to various situations.[1] For example, it can be used to

- Prototype the screens and report layouts of the system
- Build a first-cut conceptual process model
- Build a first-cut conceptual data model

[1]Some of the group dynamics techniques that support the JAD-like concept include joint application planning and/or design (IBM 1986), consensus (Boeing Computer Services), wisdom (Western Institute of Software Engineering), the method (Performance Resources), fast (MG Rush Systems), and joint application design (Jatec Designer systems). Most of the consulting firms providing such techniques also offer a variety of courses aimed at preparing future JAD session leaders to become successful facilitators as well as how to implement the concept within an organization.

- Determine the problems that the new system should solve
- Gather the user needs and justification for a new system

In these situations, a CASE workbench is frequently utilized to depict graphically the data and process specifications for a system (data flow diagrams, entity-relationship diagrams, screens and report layouts).

Some companies have adapted the JAD-like concept to their own particular needs and have successfully used the concepts of this popular group dynamics approach for various purposes, such as

- Planning the technical activities for a large project
- Discussing the project scope and objectives
- Estimating the number of hours required to develop a large and complex system

It is important to point out that most JAD-like techniques work best for small and medium-sized projects requiring between 800 and 3,200 hours of effort. For a complex and large system, a more rigorous approach might be necessary. However, multiple JAD-like sessions might still be used to accelerate the definition of the system requirements, as explained in the next section.

C.4 THE LIFE CYCLE APPROACH AND JAD-LIKE TECHNIQUES

Figure C.1 pinpoints some potential areas where the use of JAD-like techniques can contribute positively to the success of a variety of projects. JAD-like techniques may be customized to meet the requirements of the survey phase. Basically,

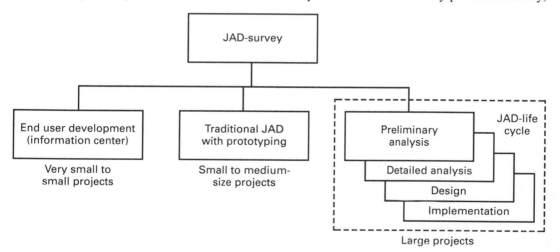

Figure C.1 The methodology integrated with the JAD-like techniques.

JAD-like techniques can then serve as a dynamic way to gather all the information necessary to create the technical deliverables coming out of the survey phase.

After the JAD survey phase, the development team is in a better position to assess the size of the proposed project. At that time, a direction for the next project phase can be proposed to the users, depending on how large the project is. Several scenarios can be considered:

Very small to small projects. If the project is fairly simple, it can be quickly developed by the users themselves with fourth- and fifth-generation development tools and the assistance from the information center department, if necessary.

Small to medium-sized projects. A traditional JAD-like technique can be used to accelerate the analysis of the user requirements and to design the external components of the proposed system. However, the documentation produced by the JAD-like process should still be compatible with the development standards and technical deliverables prescribed by the methodology. This rule should apply even though some deliverables might have been combined together or simply eliminated to fit the needs of a relatively simple project.

Large projects. The JAD-like approach should be specifically tailored to meet the standards set during the preliminary analysis, detailed analysis, and design phases. Multiple JAD-like sessions might be required within each specific development phase with a high degree of coordination among them and across the different phases.

C.5 REFERENCES

August, J. H., 1991. *Joint Application Design: The Group Session Approach to System Design,* Yourdon Press Computing Series. Englewood Cliffs, N.J.: Prentice-Hall.

Boeing Computer Services, Professional Services Group, 919 Southwest Grady Way, Renton, WA 98055.

IBM. 1986. *JAD Workshop Book.*

Jatec Designer Systems, Ltd., 461 Lakeshore Road West, Oakville, L6K 1G4, Ontario.

Kerr, J. D., 1989. "Systems Design: Users in the Host Seat," *Computer World,* February 27.

MG Rush Systems, Box 848, Newton, NJ 07860.

Performance Resources, Inc., 5 Skyline Place, 5111 Leesburg Pike, Falls Church, VA.

Rush, G., 1985. "A Fast Way to Define System Requirements," *Computer World,* October 7.

Western Institute of Software Engineering (WYSE), 1407 116 Avenue N.E., Bellview, WA 98007.

Afterword

The author would appreciate receiving readers' comments, suggestions for improvements, corrections, or criticisms regarding the format and content of this book.

In the eventuality of a second edition, the information provided by the numerous practitioners around the world who are committed to software quality will help to improve and evolve the software engineering methodology proposed in this book.

Please forward your input directly to:

Roger Fournier
2673 Victoria Street
Longueuil, Quebec, Canada
J4L 2L5

Index

A

Access audit, 321
Access control, 321
Accessibility requirements. *See*
    Performance requirements
Accuracy, 321
Acronym, system life cycle phase, 2–3
Action diagrams, 102, 153
Adaptive maintenance, 214
Ad hoc queries, 137–41, 149–50
Agents of change, 353
Ambiguities, 235–36
American Society for Quality Control,
    316, 337
Analyst toolset, 302–3
Application code generators, 156, 193, 273
Application program:
    coding of, 192–95
    desk checking of, 197
    documentation, 195
    performance tuning, 196

Appraisal costs, 330–31
    list of, 333
Architectural system design standards,
    146–48
Archiving requirements, 136, 180–81
Artificial intelligence, 10
Auditability requirements. *See* Control
    requirements
Audit trail, 133, 243
Automated tools, 10, 125
Automation boundary, 68–71
Autotest, 241
Availability requirements. *See*
    Performance requirements

B

Bachman/DA, 230
Backlog, 281
Backup/recovery requirements. *See*
    Control requirements